Bringing Technology and Innovation into the Boardroom

Bringing Technology and Innovation into the Boardroom

Strategy, Innovation and Competences for Business Value

European Institute for Technology and
Innovation Management

First published 2004 by
PALGRAVE MACMILLAN
Houndmills, Basingstoke, Hampshire RG21 6XS and
175 Fifth Avenue, New York, N.Y. 10010
Companies and representatives throughout the world

PALGRAVE MACMILLAN is the global academic imprint of the Palgrave Macmillan division of St. Martin's Press, LLC and of Palgrave Macmillan Ltd. Macmillan® is a registered trademark in the United States, United Kingdom and other countries. Palgrave is a registered trademark in the European Union and other countries.

ISBN 0–333–99459–0
ISBN 978–0–333–99459–7

This book is printed on paper suitable for recycling and made from fully managed and sustained forest sources.

A catalogue record for this book is available from the British Library.

Library of Congress Cataloging-in-Publication Data
Bringing technology and innovation into the boardroom: strategy, innovation, and competences for business value / Thomas Durand . . . [et al.].
    p. cm.
    Includes bibliographical references and index.
    ISBN 0–333–99459–0 (cloth)
    1. Technological innovations – European Union countries – Management.
2. Strategic planning – European Union countries. 3. Industrial management – European Union countries. 4. Organizational effectiveness. I. Durand, Thomas.
HD45.B685 2003
658.4´012—dc21   2003054754

10   9   8   7
13   12   11   10   09   08

Printed and bound in Great Britain by
Antony Rowe Ltd, Chippenham and Eastbourne

Contents

Acknowledgements

This book has been created by the combined efforts of all EITIM members. However, we should particularly like to thank David Probert and Noordin Shehabuddeen at the Centre for Technology Management in the University of Cambridge for coordinating this effort, editing the contributions and bringing the vision to reality.

The editors, contributors and publishers acknowledge the following for permission to reproduce copyright material: *Revue Française de Gestion*, Cachan, France; Elsevier Ltd, Oxford, UK; *Communication & Strategie*, Montpellier, France; John Wiley & Sons Ltd., Chichester, UK; Research Studies Press, Baldock, UK.

Every effort has been made to contact all copyright-holders, but if any have been inadvertently omitted the publishers will be pleased to make the necessary arrangement at the earliest opportunity.

Foreword

Innovation and technology help shape a better world. They contribute to serving the needs of citizens and consumers, creating jobs in the economy, while helping preserve the environment in line with a strategy of sustainable development.

In this sense, technology and innovation are essential to the competitiveness of European firms. Recently, however, Europe has lagged behind other major world economies in the race to innovate – that is to both create and *exploit* the opportunities that arise from technological progress, scientific development and the flow of new ideas. This is not simply a matter of R&D, nor is it just a matter of financial resources to be poured into the European system of innovation. It is also a matter of awareness in companies at top management level, adequate organization within and between firms and other institutions, management practices and an understanding of the right market opportunities.

This is a major challenge for all of us.

The European Commission has the role to promote initiatives which contribute to facing this challenge. The aim of our policy is to reinforce the actions of the Member States, leveraging the transnational dimension to bring a global scope to firms while helping them develop and grow in their specific local contexts. We work at the three levels of awareness raising, inter-organizational networking, and dissemination of good management practices. More specifically, the initiatives of the Commission deal with the creation of networks involving the main actors of the innovation system, support to incubators and start-up firms, transnational learning and dissemination of good practices, support via financial instruments to help fund innovative projects, and more generally the overall promotion of a culture of innovation.

In this context, this book is a unique contribution from a group of seven European professors working on technology and innovation management in seven leading scientific and engineering universities in Europe (Cambridge, Centrale Paris, Chalmers, Eindhoven, ETH Zurich, Hambourg-Harburg and UC Dublin). They share the same interest in the theme of innovation and technology management. They joined forces and set up an academic network in their field of work.

This book comes as a call which they direct to all of us. They express concerns about the adequacy of boardroom decision-making in addressing innovation-related issues. Their call comes at a time when the role and activities of corporate governance are under serious scrutiny. They rightly advocate bringing technology and innovation into the boardroom. They claim that its absence is not unavoidable – the means exist to provide the board with the necessary support. They explain and discuss how.

In this sense, this book brings a unique contribution. This 'wake-up call' is most welcome. As they put it: 'it is technology and innovation time'. I am glad to see a group of pan-European academics investing time and energy in this important area, adopting a European perspective on business, revisiting and complementing the contributions which have traditionally come from North American business schools.

I encourage top-managers to review the various issues raised and the recommendations formulated in this volume. They will benefit from the four parts of the book: Part I setting the stage ('Meeting the challenge of technology and innovation') while each of the subsequent three parts raises a different set of issues around a key dimension ('Strategy: using technology, and innovation strategically'; 'Competence: building up and exploiting technology assets'; (and 'Innovation: fostering and managing the innovation process'). I also found it very useful to scan through the set of questions which concludes each part. These help show how the content of the book may be applied in a specific firm.

I am grateful to this group of professors for having taken the initiative of making their thinking and ideas available. Their insight into the issues of technology and innovation management is very useful and I hope they will soon provide us with more ideas.

ERKKI LIIKANEN
European Commissioner for Enterprise and Information Society

Introduction

What is the challenge?

Have you heard about technology management? Maybe yes, but probably not very much. Does it matter? We believe it's vital. Why? Technology aspects are as essential to management in contemporary business as
economics. They should not need a special label, and might be assumed
to be given as equal attention as other business aspects. Unfortunately,
however, this is currently not the case. We even venture to say that more
often than not important technology aspects are neglected in general
management. For example, how many CEOs can say which technology is vital to the future of their company? Managers are challenged
constantly on their economic performance, but who challenges their
technology management?

We believe this is a key role for the Board.

The European challenge

Europe is waking up to the challenge of technology. We see the EU commitment to spend 3 per cent of GDP on R&D, but who is thinking about
how to spend? Who is thinking about the technology management? Does
the Board have the means to manage this spend? Should a percentage of
the R&D be spent on improving technology management?

This is the area in which this book aims to make a contribution. It
brings together the latest practice, research findings and thinking, presented in a way that addresses top management requirements. The goal
is to secure the economic future of the firm, in the context of a sustainable industry and society. Using the ideas and methods in this book, the
Board can assess and improve its own ability to deal with the challenge
of technology and innovation.

The key issues in technology management and innovation

In raising these issues for top management attention, there are a number
of perspectives which need to be addressed, and which give structure
to this book. The overriding concern is one of economic return – how
can investments in the development and application of technology be
assessed?

The perspectives which contribute to this assessment are not only that of the engineer or technologist. Success depends on a synthesis of views from experts in marketing, finance, operations, and many other disciplines. The ideas and methods presented in this book provide the means to do this, and will enable senior management to address these issues for the economic benefit of both their company and the wider community.

How well does your business meet this challenge?

10 key questions the Board should ask itself

	Yes	No	Don't know
1. Are our senior managers convinced of the key importance of technology and innovation in creating value and improving economic performance?	☐	☐	☐
2. Do we have the mechanisms in place to enable these issues to be tackled at board level?	☐	☐	☐
3. Can we link our core technologies and competences to market opportunities?	☐	☐	☐
4. Do we know who owns our innovation process and how it works?	☐	☐	☐
5. Do we have processes and tools to support technology strategy and planning throughout the business?	☐	☐	☐
6. Are we actively managing our technology portfolio?	☐	☐	☐
7. Are we exploiting the value of our technological assets through a well formulated IP (intellectual property) strategy that links to our business strategy?	☐	☐	☐
8. Are we making best use of alliances to acquire new technology?	☐	☐	☐
9. Is our innovation process supported by appropriate tools and adaptable to different market needs?	☐	☐	☐
10. Have we established a 'culture of innovation'?	☐	☐	☐

Structure and content of the book

The book is presented in four parts – each dealing with a particular set of key issues. Taken together, the parts provide a comprehensive approach

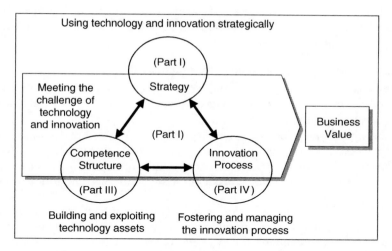

Figure I.1 EITIM model – bringing technology and innovation into the boardroom

to addressing technology management within the firm. As Figure I.1 shows, the chapters within each part are written by experts in particular aspects of these issues, thus providing a range of perspectives. Each part concludes with the 10 key diagnostic questions that the Board should ask concerning the way these issues are dealt with in their business.

Part I   Meeting the challenge of technology and innovation

Meeting challenges requires new ways of thinking to motivate action and implement change. This part provides frameworks for new thinking, plus the practical means to convert these ideas into action. Key links that underpin market success and economic performance are identified.

The importance of recognizing the challenge presented by technology and innovation at board level is explored in a European context. Comparisons are made with other parts of the world and the urgent need for companies to address this challenge is explained. A variety of historical, theoretical and practical perspectives on the issues is discussed with recommendations for actions at all levels of the firm. The analysis and understanding of technology itself is a fundamental requirement, together with the ability to track the progress of technological change over time. By incorporating technology management practices and processes into the activities of the company, the board can ensure that relevant information is available when decisions need to be made.

This may be taken further. The whole organization of the business can be considered in terms of enabling the effective management of technology and innovation.

Part II   Strategy: using technology and innovation strategically

The role of technology and innovation in achieving sustainable business success is of such significance that both should be considered as an integral part of the business strategy.

Companies may adopt a variety of strategic approaches to dealing with these issues, depending on the resources available and the competitive context. However, in all cases structured ways of developing a business strategy that includes a full consideration of technology and innovation are required.

This part provides many examples of how a company can develop a strategy that fits its own unique circumstances. A key challenge is to balance the development of new technological capabilities (for example through R&D), with leveraging those that already exist. Different strategic postures are described which address this challenge, in the context of current and emerging markets.

Part III   Competence: building up and exploiting technology assets

This part focuses on technology itself – the core asset that is to be exploited in a whole range of ways. In order to ensure a comprehensive approach to exploitation, technology should be viewed from several perspectives – for example, strategic, financial and commercial.

The commercial view considers technology as something that needs to link to market opportunity in order to generate value for the firm. However it also has value in its own right, and can be marketed and traded to create additional value for the company. The financial view is concerned with assigning value to technology, and the intellectual property that it represents. This opens a whole new field of strategic management dealing with the exploitation and protection of intellectual property.

R&D management has traditionally been concerned with the choice of R&D projects and the management of science and engineering resources, but increasingly these horizons are widening to consider other means of developing and acquiring technology. Strategic alliances, partnerships and other forms of collaboration are now very important ways for firms to access new technology. New business models are required to ensure that the value generated is shared by the collaborating parties and that intellectual property is adequately protected.

Part IV   Innovation: fostering and managing the innovation process

While technology is a key enabler of economic growth, it is the innovation process that brings new developments to the market. Thus no consideration of technology and innovation management would be complete without a close look at how the innovation process works.

In this part the key importance of the innovation process is explored from several perspectives. A particular difficulty experienced by many mature organisations is a decline in innovative ability. Dealing with this problem requires a full understanding of the competences of the company, and how they may have evolved to support operational efficiency rather than innovation.

There are many models of the innovation process. These can provide a better understanding of how the process works in a particular company, and help to identify any weaknesses in the process. An area of special interest is the 'fuzzy front end' – the stage in the process where ideas are generated and from which creative new possibilities emerge. It is a real challenge to support this valuable part of the innovation process with tools and techniques to enhance creativity and at the same time make sure the best ideas come through to realisation.

Other key aspects of a healthy innovation process are an ability to assess and deal with risk, an awareness of the impact of cultural differences on innovation, and balancing radical and incremental innovation. Even radical innovation, the most challenging innovation of all, can be supported by the structure and techniques described here.

Taking action

We don't know how your answers look, but we expect there will be areas for action and follow-up. We believe that this book will help you focus on the right actions.

The authors

The book has been produced by the European Institute for Technology and Innovation Management (EITIM). This is a collaboration between leading European universities, focused on technology and innovation management from a science and engineering perspective. The principal collaborators in this project are:

- Thomas Durand, Ecole Centrale Paris, France
- Ove Granstrand, Chalmers University of Technology, Sweden
- Cornelius Herstatt, Technical University Hamburg-Harburg, Germany

- Arie Nagel, Eindhoven University of Technology, The Netherlands
- David Probert, Cambridge University, UK
- Breffni Tomlin, University College Dublin, Ireland
- Hugo Tschirky, Swiss Federal Institute of Technology, Zurich

Notes on the Contributors

Volume editors

Thomas Durand is Professor of Business Strategy at Ecole Centrale Paris where he heads the 'Strategy and Technology' research unit and the 'Technology and Management' master program (www.ecp.fr). He works in the field of strategic management and the management of technology and innovation. He has published extensively in the field over the last twenty years. Thomas Durand is President of CM International, a management consulting firm based in Paris (www.cm-intl.com). Past-president of AIMS (association internationale de management stratégique), he is a board member of Euram (European Academy of Management) and chairs the interest group 'Knowledge and Innovation' at the SMS (Strategic Management Society).

Ove Granstrand was educated at Chalmers University of Technology, University of Gothenburg, Sweden and Stanford University with graduate degrees in mathematics, economics and engineering and a Ph.D. degree in industrial management and economics. His work experience includes teaching, research and consultancy in various eastern and western countries. He serves as Professor in Industrial Management and Economics at Chalmers University and Chairman for Center for Intellectual Property Studies. His research interest concerns economics and management of technology and innovation. In particular, he has studied innovation, corporate strategy and diversification in multi-technology corporations in Europe, Japan and the USA, as well as various issues related to R&D, intellectual property and intellectual capital more generally. He has authored and edited several books and articles on these topics, a recent one being *The Economics and Management of Intellectual Property. Towards Intellectual Capitalism* (Edward Elgar, 2000).

Cornelius Herstatt is Director of the Institute for Technology and Innovation Management at the Technical University of Hamburg-Harburg, Germany. He received his MBA and Ph.D. degree at the University of Zurich, Switzerland. He has 7 years of industry experience and 7 years experience in management consulting.

Arie Nagel is a part-time associate professor of Strategy and Technology Management and a management consultant. Published in Long Range Planning, *International Journal of Technology Management*, a book on Technology Management (1994, in Dutch), president of ISPIM (http://www.ispim.org) 1993–1997. Participated in the EC-smart-project on Strategic Alliances (http://www.smarte-urope.org), associate partner of S3i (http://www.s3inter.net). Member of the International Advisory Board of the Journal of Enterprising Culture, Singapore.

David Probert is Head of the Centre for Technology Management, and a senior lecturer at the University of Cambridge. He had an industrial career with Marks & Spencer, and Philips for 18 years before returning to Cambridge in 1991. His experience covers a wide range of industrial engineering and management disciplines in the UK and overseas. David is author of a book *Developing a Make or Buy Strategy for Manufacturing Business*, published by the Institute of Electrical Engineers, and is co-author of *Technology Management Assessment Procedure* and *Make-or-Buy: A Practical Guide to Industrial Sourcing Decisions*, published by the Institute for Manufacturing.

Hugo Tschirky is chair of the Group of Technology and Innovation at ETH-Center for Enterprise Science in Zürich, Switzerland. Former CEO of Carl Zeiss Ltd. and Cerberus Ltd., Sabbaticals in Tokyo (1992) and MIT Sloan School (2000).

Contributors

Jeff Butler is an editor of the *R&D Management* journal and a research fellow in PREST. He is interested in 'the future of R&D management', processes to promote design and creativity, action learning and 'innovation and sustainable development'. PREST is a department within the Institute of Innovation Research at the University of Manchester and is a member of the Manchester Federal School of Business and Management.

Geert Duysters is the Professor of Organization Science and Scientific Director at ECIS (Eindhoven Centre for Innovation Studies). Geert Duysters has published in leading academic journals such as *Organization Science, Journal of International Business Studies, Organization Studies, Journal of Management Studies, Research Policy, R&D Management, Journal of Small Business Economics* as well as in many other international refereed journals.

Jean-Philippe Escher is a research assistant at the ETH-Center for Enterprise Sciences. He completed his masters degree in Mechanical Engineering at the Swiss Federal Institute of Technology Zürich (ETHZ) in 1997. Before joining the actual science team, he worked for one year at the Lightweight Structures and Ropeway Institute of the ETHZ.

Clare Farrukh is a senior researcher at the Institute for Manufacturing, Cambridge University Engineering Department. Clare spent six years as a process engineer before joining the University in 1995. Her research activities are concerned with the development of practical tools for supporting technology management in industry.

Johannes I. M. Halman is professor in the School of Business, Public Administration and Technology at University of Twente and associate professor at the Department of Technology Management at Eindhoven University of Technology. His research interests are in the field of innovation management with a primary focus on programme and project management of innovation processes, new product platform development and high tech start ups. He specializes in the area of risk management.

Hans-Helmuth Jung worked as scientific collaborator at the Swiss Federal Institute of Technology Zurich (ETH Zurich). He wrote his dissertation about 'Technology Management Control Systems in technology-based Enterprises'. During his thesis he consulted in several multinational enterprises including ABB Ltd, BMW Group and Infineon Technologies. He is now a consultant with SIMMA Management Consultants, Switzerland.

Jimme A. Keizer is associate professor at the Department of Technology Management at Eindhoven University of Technology in The Netherlands. His main research interest is in innovation management, especially risk management. He publishes in books and journals on various topics regarding determinants of innovation efforts, knowledge constraints, risk management, learning organization and field casework.

Robert Phaal joined the Centre for Technology Management at the Institute for Manufacturing in 1997, conducting applied research in the area of strategic technology management. The focus of this work has been on how to support companies to initiate technology roadmapping processes, leading to the publication of a practical guide (T-plan). Rob is also author of an on-line management tool catalogue (T-Cat), and co-author of *Technology Management Assessment Procedure*, published by the Institute of Electrical Engineers. He has a mechanical engineering background, with industrial experience in technical research, consulting and software development.

Pascal Savioz has an engineering background and finished his Ph.D. on Technology Intelligence in SMEs in 2002 at the ETH Center for Enterprise Science, Technology and Innovation Management, at ETH Zurich. Today, Pascal Savioz works as Assistant Head of Technology of a world leading curtain wall system manufacturer.

Michael Song holds the Michael L. and Myrna Darland Distinguished Chair in Entrepreneurship in the Business School at University of Washington in Seattle. He is also advisory research professor at Eindhoven University of Technology. His primary research interests include methods for assessment and valuation of new ventures and of R&D projects, strategic management of technology and innovation, and models of technology portfolio management.

Ash Vasudevan is the vice president of Strategic and Investment Initiatives of CommerceNet. In his role, he oversees all the collaborative programmes – Next Generation Internet, Supply Chains and Global Marketplaces – and venture investments, where he is principally focused on making early stage investments in Internet technologies and the business use of those technologies.

Birgit Verworn is a Ph.D. student at the Institute for Technology and Innovation Management at the Technical University of Hamburg-Harburg. She received an MSc in process engineering from the Technical University of Hanover, Germany. She has two years of industry experience as a process engineer for Procter & Gamble.

Part I

Meeting the Challenge of Technology and Innovation

Executive Summary
David Probert

The four chapters in Part I introduce the concepts of technology and innovation as meriting serious management attention. The trends in both the accelerating development of technological progress, and in the practical and academic treatment of the subject area, give witness to the major impact it now has on business management. It is not an exaggeration to assert that the successful economic performance of an enterprise is now largely dependent on the quality of its technology and innovation management.

However, the integration of these ideas into general management thinking, particularly at boardroom level, has been much neglected. This is due in part to an absence (or at least a lack of adoption) of suitable conceptual frameworks, low management awareness and unfamiliarity with the relevant practical tools and techniques. Part I goes a long way to address this deficiency, by presenting complementary perspectives on technology and innovation management, in the context of achieving a good business result.

The introductory Chapter 1 'Wake-up Call for General Management: It's Technology Time' identifies the increasingly important role of technological change in the development of industry and society. The challenge this poses for Europe in particular, in contrast with superior performance in the US and other parts of the world, is discussed in the context of the need to integrate technological considerations into top management thinking. The role and contribution of technology management in bridging this gap is explained, together with the major potential benefits for economic performance.

Chapter 2 'Bringing Technology to the Boardroom: What Does It Mean?' argues strongly for technology to be considered as a fundamental unit of analysis in management thinking, in the same way that money and time are units of analysis. The deficiency of many Western companies in taking this view is clear; however, there are many possible practical techniques that can be implemented to address this problem. A model of general management is presented which provides a structure on which to build these techniques.

Three levels of general management are proposed:

1. *policy* – which relates to policy, culture and structure, the setting of the conditions under which the firms will carry out its business;
2. *strategic* – which relates to strategy formulation and implementation, the middle- to long-term planning of how the firm will steer its course; and
3. *operational* – which relates to project processes, structures and goals, the means by which the firm executes its day-to-day business.

Example techniques are given which address each level of this model – there is truly no lack of knowledge and experience available to support firms who wish to tackle this important area in a proactive manner. The practical tools proposed to assist the technology manager are some of the most significant contributions that can be made in this field, and many other examples are also given later in the book.

Chapter 3 'The Strategic Management of Technology and Innovation' explores these ideas from a historic review of technology management, and the need to manage the evolution and lifecycle of technologies. The relevance of practical links to operations and project management is demonstrated, including such recent organizational innovations as JIT and TQM. The comparison between technology and competencies is drawn, and frameworks and techniques to integrate these ideas into strategic management are presented. A key analytical tool is the representation of technology trees – a means of depicting how individual technologies aggregate to address market needs. Ways of organizing for innovation are considered, with the associated implications for the cultural aspects of the firm. Finally, the need to look ahead and identify the technology and competence that will be required in the future is discussed, together will practical suggestions on how this can be done.

Chapter 4 'Structuring a Systematic Approach to Technology Management: Processes and Framework' provides working definitions of the concepts of technology and technology management, in a way that they can be operationalized in a business. Five technology management processes are presented which relate to the practical activities of the firm, and the subject is explored in the context of the key business processes (strategy formulation, innovation and operations). The important requirement of taking an integrated view spanning both technological and commercial perspectives is emphasized. A conceptual framework is provided to assist the implementation of these ideas, and comparisons made with the technology management systems of two company examples.

Collectively, these four chapters present a comprehensive and coherent view of the issues fundamental to technology and innovation management. The importance to the economic success of technology-intensive enterprise is clear, and the means to deal with many of these issues are currently available.

The following parts of the book will also go on to elaborate the conditions under which firms compete and collaborate in this dynamic environment, while striving to generate, exploit and protect that extremely valuable intellectual property, technological knowledge.

Ten key questions for the Board

1. How is our company being affected by technological change?
2. Is technology competence adequately represented in our original decision taking management boards such as board of directors and top management group?
3. Do we have a Chief Technology Officer (CTO) as a member of the top management group?
4. Can we identify the means (processes) whereby the people in our business manage technology and cope with technological change?
5. How do we cope with the external technology information explosion? Do we have an adequately systematized procedure for external technology information scouting and its internal distribution ('technology intelligence')?
6. What are our core technologies? Is there consensus among R&D, production, marketing, finance and HR on the strategic priorities of these core technologies (i.e. in terms of technology portfolios and roadmaps)?
7. Are we aware of the innovation rate (percentage of sales from new products and services) of our company in the past and is our innovation pipeline (total of innovative products oriented R&D-projects in progress) sufficiently 'filled' to match the forecast innovation rate?

8. Are we prepared concretely and ambitiously to aim for breakthrough innovations?
9. To what extent are we prepared to master the increasing necessity to acquire and sell technologies (intellectual property) professionally?
10. Do we have a picture of how technological and commercial perspectives are integrated in our key business processes?

1
Wake-up Call for General Management: It's Technology Time

Hugo Tschirky

Overview

Coping with technological change affects not only R&D and production but also the entire enterprise. Nevertheless, a comparison of general management theory and the practice of solving a technology management related problem, at present, reveals a critical gap between management theory and technological reality. Therefore, on one hand, closing this 'technology gap' in general management literature has become a research issue of considerable concern. On the other, analysing Europe's weak innovation performance, creating technology and innovation awareness in enterprise management at all management levels appears to be equally important. Chapter 2 'Bringing Technology to the Boardroom: What Does It Mean?' addresses this necessity.

Technology is altering the global landscape

Accelerated technological change has become a fact and will continue to challenge industrial and societal development into the next century. The fact that all areas of life and the economy are increasingly affected by technology is undisputed. Nearly everyday, without really noticing it, we benefit from innovations which not long ago were inconceivable. For example, by merely touching a keyboard in Zurich it has become quite possible, via satellite, to steer a computer in Tokyo that transmits English translations of Japanese texts back to Zurich. Groupware and communication networks such as the Internet, facilitate real time availability of knowledge and thereby reshape business processes fundamentally. With the help of stereo-lithography, CAD data can transform a work specimen into a prototype within hours. Thanks to consistent process management, the production time for locomotives has been reduced from months to weeks at ABB. Banks have more than doubled their internal productivity by means of optical character reading. The Sojourner rover, on 4 July 1997, made a perfect landing on Mars and sent high resolution pictures to the earth from a distance of 55 million km (Figure 1.1). This reflects extraordinary achievements in mechatronics and telecommunications, clearly influencing our everyday technology.

Gene technology and the recently available complete information of the human genome harbours a potential for incalculable changes in biological and pharmaceutical research and production. Endoscopy allows complex medical operations to be performed without surgery. On 30 July 2001, the implantation of an artificial silicon retinal chip into the eyes of three people blinded by retinal disease was announced (Figure 1.2).

Finally, nanotechnology (Figure 1.3) is opening the door to innovations such as tera-bit memories, which will revolutionize industry in the 21st century. The use of tera-bit memories will allow the storage of entire classical music of all time on one CD. Or all-carbon nanotube, which promises applications ranging from new structural materials that are stronger and lighter to electronic components for new supercomputers to drug delivery systems.

Figure 1.1   Pathfinder mission: The Sojourner rover (left) conducting experiments and taking pictures from the Mars, i.e. from the 'little Matterhorn' (right)

Source: (Picture left) Mars Pathfinder, NSSDC. (Picture right) 'little Matterhorn' processed by Dr Timothy Parker, Jet Propulsion Laboratory.

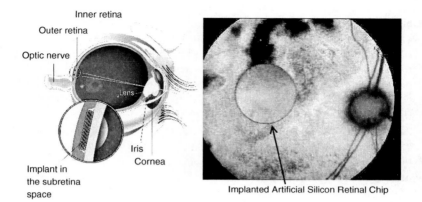

Figure 1.2 Artificial silicon retinal chip implanted into the eyes of three people blinded by retinal desease

Source: Operations conducted on 25 and 26 July, 2001 under Dr Alan Chow of Optobionics Corp. at Central DuPage Hospital in Winfield, Illinois, and at Chicago's Rush-Presbyterian-St. Luke's Medical Center (www.obtobionics.com). According to *Newsweek* of 19 May 2003 (p. 63–4), the artificial impant that replaces the retina has been implanted in 10 patients.

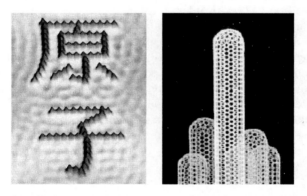

Figure 1.3 Nanotechnology allows the identification and location of single atoms; nanotubes will be the basis for new materials, new electronic component and advanced drug delivery systems

Source: (Picture left) IBM Research, STM Gallery (www.ibm.com). (Picture right) University of Cambridge, Nanoscale Science Laboratory (www-g.eng.cam.ac.uk/nano).

Typical company problems and open questions facing technological change

On 31 July 1998, Siemens announced the closure of its 16-megabyte chip works in British North Tyneside. This closure, on the grounds of falling prices in the chip market, affected around 1,100 employees. It also affected Siemens' yearly accounts for 1998 by around 1 billion DM. The factory had only been opened in May 1997; up to its closure Siemens had invested some 1.7 billion DM in plant and operation. The closure took place during the start-up phase (*Neue Zürcher Zeitung*, 1 September 1998). On 5 September the same year, Siemens announced that it was making its semiconductor business independent and listing it on the stock exchange (*Financial Times*, 5 November 1998). Matsushita, one of the largest Japanese electronics manufacturers, similarly announced on 9 September the closure of its 4-megabyte chip production plant in Pyallup, Washington, earlier planned for December. Similar restructuring measures had been announced the previous week by Fujitsu and Hitachi (*Financial Times*, 10 September 1998). *What management instruments might have lowered the risks of such investments? What other possibilities might have been explored by these firms, in view of their responsibility for the social effects of employee dismissal?*

The European Laboratory for Particle Physics (CERN) was forced, for budget reasons, to make cuts (*NZZ*, 5 July 1998). While in 1980, 3,800 people were employed there, today the number is 2,800, and in the year 2005 it will be 2,000. In order to fulfil the current demand for technologies in spite of this restructuring, industry has been called in to cooperate in development projects under an initiative entitled 'Call for Technology'. According to this cooperative model, CERN will provide its accumulated technological and scientific expertise, while its industrial partners deliver specific development know-how, and personnel and material resources. Already, several firms of various sizes have made use of this opportunity for technology transfer. In many cases, a major attraction of the arrangement is the possibility of obtaining new technological expertise and using it to launch new products on the traditional market. A typical example is the firm Lemo SA in Ecublens, which specializes in electronic plugs. For CERN, Lemo has for some time been developing a miniaturized plug for co-axial cables. A world standard has emerged from this development, and today the company has a product range of over 40 models, not only used in particle physics but also in telecommunications and medical electronics (*NZZ*, 5 July 1998). *What were the main so-called Make-or-Buy decision-making factors for CERN and Lemo SA? What structures and rules-of-the-game in communication can be decisive for successful technology transfer? Which competences need to be built up for large or small firms to become competitive in new, future technology markets as well as in traditional ones?*

Early in 1997, the consultants Deloitte Touche Tohmatsu International conducted a study among the 1,000 leading companies in Germany,

France, Great Britain and the Netherlands. The aim was to determine which decision-making factors were considered by top management as most important for the next century. The effects of technological change were accorded the greatest significance; in second place came the introduction of a single currency neck and neck with the recruiting of qualified staff (Deloitte Touch Tohmatsu International, 1997). *Is the company equipped with management infrastructure to cope with this challenge?*

The questions presented above reflect typical challenges which are increasingly becoming facets of companies' everyday realities. They raise the question as to whether existing management approaches are sufficiently adapted for dealing with today's technology driven-business reality.

Are we prepared? The European paradox

In 1995, the European Commission presented a report entitled *Green Paper on Innovation* (EC, 1995). Its main message focuses on the challenges of innovation for Europe, against a background of globalization and rapid technological change. In the Commission's opinion, Europe's research and industrial base is suffering from a paradoxical series of weaknesses, the greatest being the comparatively limited capacity to convert scientific breakthroughs and technological achievements into industrial and commercial successes. Anlaysis reveals that, compared to the scientific performance of its principal competitors, the European Union is excellent, but over the last fifteen years its technological and commercial performance in high-technology sectors such as electronics and information technology has deteriorated. Among the factors explaining the American and Japanese successes, emphasis is placed on: a generally higher R&D effort measured by the percentage of total R&D expenditure as a share of GDP (Europe: 2%, US: 2.7%, Japan: 2.8%), a larger proportion of engineers and scientists in the active population, closer university/industry collaborations, cultural tradition favourable to risk taking and to entrepreneurial spirit and a strong social acceptance of innovation (US), a culture favourable to the application of technologies and the ongoing improvement and reduced lead times for firms' creation and limited red tape.

Based on this evaluation, numerous suggestions for improving Europe's unfavourable situation are made and thirteen routes of actions are presented. Among them is a strong recommendation to foster and develop technology and innovation management, since these disciplines of management '. . . are not yet adequately used in the European Union'.

Did this serious 'warning' have a significant impact?

Not really. Surprisingly, six years later a study covering exactly the same subject but originating from an entirely different source came out: in 2000, the Union of Industrial and Employer's Confederations of Europe (UNICE, 2000) published the Benchmarking Report under the title *Stimulating Creativity and Innovation in Europe*. This time the comparison focused primarily on the USA. The UNICE evaluation culminates in the following assessment: 'Although there are many European success stories, taken overall, companies based in Europe have failed to match the performance of innovative companies based in the USA'. Again, almost identical reasons are mentioned in order to explain the situation. Interestingly, as an additional negative factor, education level is stressed: 'European education systems are less successful than those in many other countries in equipping its citizens with key skills, in area such as mathematics, science, technology, ICT (Information and Communications Technologies) and management.'

Finally, UNICE published a further benchmarking report *The reNewed Economy – Business for a Dynamic Europe*, in March 2001. Again it insistently suggested that 'if Europe is to catch up with the USA, governments must provide companies and individuals with stronger incentives to innovate, and to adopt and adapt innovations made by others. Entrepreneurs must be better rewarded for risk-taking. Employees must be more motivated to update their knowledge and skills continually' (UNICE, 2001).

Is there a lesson learned? Obviously the sequence of such repetitive evaluations over a long period of time does not shed a bright light on Europe's learning curve. It seems that institutional messages alone are not strong enough to initiate major changes. Moreover, Europe's situation does not seem to contradict Peccei, the former founding member of the Club of Rome (Peccei, 1979). Reflecting the human innovative behaviour over time, he came to the conclusion that mankind primarily follows the pattern 'learning after shock'. This may have been a workable attitude in the past. However, since today's mankind is in the position to self-initiate fatal shocks, following this principle has certainly become questionable.

Therefore, the preferred vision for the new century would more likely be 'learning before shock', which means an anticipatory attitude towards change. Building up such a capability is primarily up to individuals, particularly individuals with influence on others in management. In this sense it is the main purpose of this publication to provide a basis for responsible management representatives to self-initiate innovative management improvements in coping with technological change.

The technology management paradox

Early significant impulses for today's technology management concept came from the USA, at a time of threatening progress from Japanese technology. A report edited in 1987 by the US National Research Council recognizes that 'to an ever-increasing extent, advanced technologies are a pervasive and crucial factor in the success of private corporations, the effectiveness of many government operations, and the well-being of national economies'. Credit is also given to some, at that time, practicing strategies of technology management 'to devote more resources to research and devlopment (R&D) than less.' However it is added, that 'guidelines for allocating those resources among projects are vague, schedules are necessarily imprecise, and results can be unpredictable'. And 'as technology changes, the tools of management will also need to change, but the process of determining what those new tools should be is in its infancy'. Faced with this unsatisfactory situation, it is concluded that a lasting improvement in a situation assessed as threatening could only be made by building up effective technology management as 'the key to America's competitive future' – in research, teaching and management practice. In this context 'technology management' can be perceived as follows: '*Management of Technology links engineering, science, and management disciplines to plan, develop, and implement technological capabilites to shape and accomplish the strategic and operational objectives of an organization*' (see Figure 1.4).

The following are identified as key elements of technology management in practice:

- identification and evaluation of technological options;
- management of R&D itself, including project feasibility;

Figure 1.4   Technology Management: 'the missing link'

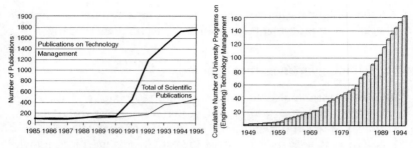

Figure 1.5 Development of technology management publications (a) and university programmes on technology management (b)
Source: (a) Kocaoglu, 1996: 1; (b) Pfund, 1997: 2

- integration of technology into the company's overall operations;
- implementation of new technologies in a product and/or process; and
- obsolescence and replacement.

Since 1987, there has indeed been a significant growth in the popularity of, e.g., literature on technology management (see Figure 1.5, left). Correspondingly, the number technology management programmes offered by universities worldwide has increased rapidly (see Figure 1.5, right).

This development is positive since it mirrors the well justified concern of academia to actively enhance the competence needed for coping with technological change. *However – and this is the above mentioned astonishing paradox – the general management literature is curiously silent on issues of technology and innovation management.* Typically, reference to the significance of technology is restricted to its non-binding inclusion in the list of factors influencing the enterprise. Whereas the enterprise functions such as marketing, finance and sometimes legal and economic aspects are traditionally well represented in concepts of general management, equally useful managerial references on best practices of acquisition, development and deployment of technology are not provided. Here are some typical examples.

In the comprehensive publication *Introduction to General Business Economics Theory* by Wöhe in 2000, the task of business economics theory is concerned with 'the explanation of real interrelationships and courses of events (cause-effect relationships)' (Wöhe and Döring, 2000: 19). Despite this emphasis on 'real interrelationships', *the problem presented by technological change is dealt with (in the section on* 'Instruments of Marketing Policy') *in just two sentences*[1] *concerning the task of research and development.*

More concrete statements concerning general management tasks are found in Kotter (1982), but here central aspects, such as those of technological change and its sociotechnical implications for every type of enterprise, are not addressed. Similar gaps are found in Mintzberg (1989), a work which presents the management task with vivid illustrations of cases from practice.

A similar picture is presented in the *Handbook of Management* edited by Crainer (1995), with contributions from over eighty authors. The actual technology sensitivity of companies is granted only a marginal position. The theme of 'technology' is reduced to aspects of information technology, and the treatment of research and development is limited to confirming the growing consciousness that R&D tasks should be actively included as part of company activities.

The discussion of such examples could be continued almost endlessly, referring to publications by authors such as Ulrich (1970), Busse von Colbe and Lassmann (1991), Kogut and Zander (1992), Rühli (1996) and Eisenführ (1998). Even the extensive and often visionary works of Drucker – often referred to as being the dean of management – have to be mentioned in this context. They present numerous facts of company management and its interaction with society in a plausible and highly practice-related way. However, the chosen level of investigation and conceptual depth places Drucker's work rather as a basic complement to methodology-oriented textbooks on companies and their management. The latest publication *The Essential Drucker* (2001) is a further example.

Facing the technology gap: what's next?

A juxtaposition of current enterprise and enterprise management concepts with company problems, as illustrated above, reflects a noticeable gap between the pereceived picture of company reality and what actually goes on. *No substantial impetus towards the practical solution of company problems is found in any of the approaches and theories discussed.*

One reason for this critical gap between management theory and technology reality may be that theories in business administration have their roots in the mercantile education which *per se* has been focused in the past on non-technological issues. This may also explain why various technology universities/institutions, because of their technology culture and competence, began only lately to engage in research and teaching in the area of technology management.

The existence of this gap has, firstly, generated the attitude on the part of upper-echelon management that technology is an issue for lower-level management; and led to the (directly linked) lower attention accorded to both the opportunities and the perils of technology deployment, despite the risk that these may be embedded in initial upper management and administrative decisions. Secondly, it is uncertain whether, or how, isolated aspect-wise management statements may feasibly apply to the process of management decision-making. Thirdly, education taught with current literature on general management is giving students a distorted and unrealistic picture of current corporate reality. And finally, the above mentioned uncomplete content of publications on general management certainly does not lower the widespread ivory tower prejudice against academia.

Facing this paradoxical discrepancy is inferring a basically new understanding of technology's enterpreneurial role. It's implications are of such consequences that referring to a paradigm shift is justified. This means in essence that at first the metaphor of technology management being the missing link between engineering and science and general management has to be revised. Rather than being a missing link and thus an activity 'outside' general management, technology management ought to be considered as being an integrated part 'inside' general management. This thought is visualized in Figure 1.6.

What does this paradigm shift imply? It implies that all activities directed towards technology related issues are not isolated and merely function-focused activities, but rather elementary parts of management activities on all levels of company management. This includes in particular, a strong technology competence in the upper level of management, represented by the top management group and the board of directors. This is in essence the core of the guiding thought 'Bringing Technology and Innovation into the Boardroom' which will be illustrated in greater depth in the following sections.

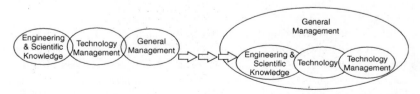

Figure 1.6 Technology and its management being integrated parts of general management

Note

1. 'Every supplier must try via the best possible achievements in internal research and development to remain at the forefront of technological progress.' Wöhe with Döring (2000: 527): 'Product development in the technical sense: prototype, taste sample.'

References

Busse von Colbe, W. and G. Lassmann (1991), Betriebswirtschaftstheorie, Band 1. Grundlagen, Produktions- und Kostentheorie. 5. Auflage, Berlin: Springer.
Crainer, S. (Hrsg.) (1995), *Handbook of Management*, London: Pitman Publishing.
Deloitte Touch Tohmatsu International (1997), *The Next Millenium: the Challenges for Business*, Opinion Research Business.
Drucker, P.F. (2001), *The Essential Drucker*, New York: HarperCollins Publishers.
Eisenführ, F. (1998), Einführung in die Betriebswirtschaftslehre. 2. Auflage. Stuttgart: Schäffer-Poeschel.
European Commission (1995), *Green Paper on Innovation*, Document drawn up on the basis of COM(95) 688 final, Brussels.
Kocaoglu, D. (1996), *Development of University Programs in Engineering and Technology Management*, Portland, Personal Communication.
Kogut, B. and U. Zander (1992), 'Knowledge of the Firm, Combinative Capabilities, and the Replication of Technology', *Organization Science*, 3, 4, pp. 383–397.
Kotter, J.P. (1982), *The General Manager*, New York: The Free Press.
Mintzberg, H. (1989), *Mintzberg on Management*, New York: The Free Press.
Peccei, A. (1979), *No Limits to Learning: Bridging the Human Gap*, Oxford: Pergamon Press.
Pfund, C. (1997), *Entwicklung der Publikationen über Technologie-Management*, Interne BWI-Studie, Zürich: BWI
Rühli, E. (1996), Unternehmensführung und Unternehmenspolitik. Band 1, 3. Auflage, Bern: Haupt
Tschirky, H. (1991), 'Technology Management: An Integrating Function of General Management', in D.F. Kocaoglu and K. Niwa (eds), *Technology Management – The New International Language*, proceedings of the Portland International Conference on Management of Engineering and Technology, Portland, Oregon, USA 27–31, October 1991.
Tschirky, H. (1996), 'Bringing Technology into Management: The Call of Reality – Going Beyond Industrial Management at the ETH', in D.F. Kocaoglu and T.R. Anderson (eds), *Innovation in Technology Management – The Key to Global Leadership*, Proceedings of the Portland International Conference on Management of Engineering and Technology, Portland, Oregon, USA 27–31, July 1997.
Tschirky, H. (1998a), 'Lücke zwischen Management-Theorie und Technologie-Realität', in H. Tschirky and St. Koruna (Hrsg.), *Technologie-Management – Idee und Praxis*, Zürich: Verlag Industrielle Organisation.
Tschirky, H. (1998b), 'Konzept und Aufgaben des Integrierten Technologie-Managements', in H. Tschirky and St. Koruna (Hrsg.), *Technologie-Management*

– *Idee und Praxis*, Zürich: Verlag Industrielle Organisation.

Tschirky, H. (1999), 'Technology and Innovation Management: Leading the Way to (New) Enterprise Science', in D.F. Kocaoglu and T.R. Anderson (eds), Proceedings of the Portland International Conference on Management of Engineering and Technology, Portland, Oregon, USA 25–29, July 1999.

Ulrich, H. (1970), Die Unternehmung als produktives soziales System. 2. Auflage. Bern: Haupt.

Ulrich, H. (1984), *Management* (Hrsg.: Th., Dyllick G.J.B. Probst). Bern: Haupt.

UNICE (2000), *Stimulating Creativity and Innovation in Europe*, The UNICE Benchmarking Report 2000.

UNICE (2001), *The reNewed Economy–Business for a Dynamic Europe*, The UNICE Benchmarking Report 2001.

Wöhe, G. (1996), Einführung in die Allgemeine Betriebswirtschaftslehre. 19. Auflage. München: Vahlen.

Wöhe, G. (with U. Döring) (2000), Einführung in die Allgemeine Betriebswirtschaftslehre. 20. Auflage. München: Vahlen.

2
Bringing Technology to the Boardroom: What Does It Mean?
Hugo Tschirky

Overview

The presence of technology in the boardroom reflects a top management process in which business decisions are taken with an awareness of the fundamental opportunities and risks associated with technological change. To comply with this responsibility, relevant questions need to be raised and answered within top management. These typically cover the quality of company policy, the availability of technology competence within top management, the nature of company culture, the inflow of relevant business (technology) information, the completeness of strategic business planning with respect to technology and innovation issues, and the implementation of management instruments which integrate the technology aspects of all major enterprise functions.

Understanding technology as an ordinary unit of general management

It is common to consider money as a basic unit of management. Cost, expenditure, assets, investments and finally bottom lines are expressed in dollars, pounds, roubles and now in euros. Time is another such unit. Working and operation times are measured in hours, project completion times are planned in months and sometimes strategic planning horizons are depicted in years. Technologies are *de facto* similarly manageable entities. Technology constitutes specific knowledge, abilities, methods and equipment, facilitating deployment of scientific and engineering knowledge. In order to remain competitive, companies are mastering a countable number of technologies with four purposes: they enable researchers and engineers to develop new products and services, they

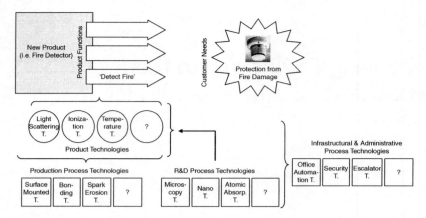

Figure 2.1   Product and process technologies constituting product creation (example: development of fire detection sensor device)

Source: Tschirky, in Tschirky and Koruna: 228

allow products to perform specific functions, they serve manufacturing to produce products and, finally, they enable companies to operate their administrative processes and infrastructure. *Product technologies* on the one hand deploy scientific or engineering principles, e.g. from optics, electronics, nuclear physics, aerodynamics, etc. dealing with a specific effect and determine how an effect occurs. This effect allows the fulfilment of a specific product function, e.g. 'detect fire' which – from the point of view of the market – is oriented towards expected customer needs, e.g. 'protection from fire damage', as outlined in Figure 2.1. Product technologies that can fulfill this product function are, for example, light scattering, ionization or temperature technologies.

R&D faces the challenging task of making a reasoned choice between various technologies – both current and to be developed – representing variables in order to realize product functions.

Process technologies on the other hand deploy the *effects* of an existing product technology. R&D process technologies are used for performing R&D activities and may include technologies such as microscopy, nano and atomic absorption technology. Typical production process technologies include casting, milling, galvanizing, soldering and surface mounted technology (SMT). They also consist of logistics and quality assurance technologies. Administrative process technologies usually comprise office automation technologies and, finally, infrastructural process technologies typically may comprise security, elevator, escalator and air conditioning technologies.

The above refers to an understanding of technology in the *limited domain* of product and market. As technological change permeates many social and economic domains, a further-reaching, *holistic* understanding of technology must also be developed. This extends beyond the domain of product and market and encompasses higher concepts of technology progress, quality of life and the social efficacy of technology.

How does technology management relate to general management?

With the vision that technology management should be part of general management, an immediate question comes up: what is an appropriate framework of general management to constitute a meaningful shell for technology management issues? When attempting to answer this question, it becomes obvious that the number of available frameworks is limited. Among them, the concepts of 'potential and process approach to the enterprise' and 'integrated management' appear to be best suited to the purposes:

With respect to concepts of *enterprise management* it is widely accepted that considering tasks on the *strategic* and subsequently on the *operational level* is indispensable to general management. For the management of the technology enterprise, however, a restriction to these two levels is not satisfactory since factors beyond strategy play an important role. Primary among these are company policy, company culture and original enterprise structures. This deficiency is taken into account in so-called 'integrated management' concepts (Ulrich, 1984; Bleicher, 1991), in which the strategic and operational levels are grouped under a higher *policy level* of management[1] (Figure 2.2).

Figure 2.2   Three levels constituting general management
Source: Ulrich, 1984: 329

First, on the *policy* level, primary decisions must be made according to the long-term goals of the enterprise. This requires the development of a consistent *company policy*. At the same time an awareness of the culture permeating the company is essential. Company culture includes the values held collectively by its employees, which is expressed, for example, in how employees identify with company goals and in the company's behaviour towards the environment, and manifest themselves in the company's ability to change and innovate. On the normative level it is not only the *making* of long-term decisions which is vital for the company's future. Just as essential is *who makes these decisions*. This question involves the upper decision-making structures of the company. The far-reaching nature of technology decisions requires that technology expertise be applied to the decision-making process from the outset. The guiding principle for the normative level is the *principle of meaningfulness*.

On the *strategic level* it is essential that company policy be transposed into comprehensible strategies. Strategies lay emphasis on the selection of those technologies necessary for the development and production of present and future products and services. In particular, decisions are made as to whether these technologies will be developed in-house or in conjunction with other firms, or whether they will be purchased completely from other companies. Relevant trends in strategic technology management indicate that strategic alliances, process management and innovative and innovation-boosting structures are taking on increasing significance, as is technology scanning and monitoring, i.e. the comprehensive and systematic collection and accumulation of information concerning existing and developing technologies. This 'early warning function' is often referred to as *technology intelligence*, which is part of an overall business intelligence system. A further focus involves concepts of socio-technical systems design which postulate the quality of work-oriented deployment of technology *and* work. On the strategic level the *principle of efficacy* – meaning 'doing the right things' – is prime.

Finally, on the *operational level* of management, responsibility is taken for transforming strategies into practice in the context of short-term goals. Operational management expresses itself, for example, in concrete R&D projects in which the necessary personnel, financial and instrumental resources are deployed according to a plan. Here the pointer is 'doing things right', implying accordingly the *principle of efficiency*.

According to this view, technology management can be conceived as an integrated function of general management which is focused on the design, direction and development of the technology and innovation potential and directed towards the policy, strategic and operational objectives of an enterprise.

This concept of technology and innovation management will be exemplified now in detail.

Technology and innovation management as an integrated part of general management: practical examples

Example 1: expressing technology and innovation values in visions, policies and mission statements (policy level)

The longest-term decisions taken by company management are expressed in documents like *company vision, company policy* and *mission statements*. As a rule, these kinds of statements are generalized but nevertheless aim at verbalizing the company's uniqueness. The content usually covers long-term objectives, main areas of activities, geographical dimensions of businesses, major resources and competencies, innovative ambitions, the desired relationship with customers, attitude towards societal and ecological expectations, the role and development of human capital and the values which determine communication and collaboration.

For companies relying on technology it is necessary to stress this dependence within such normative statements, because they represent strong signals inside and outside the company. In particular, in times of increasingly flattened hierarchies, such signals are gaining importance as guiding ties around decentralized responsibilities and competencies.

The following examples in Figure 2.3 illustrate normative statements which mirror the technology dependence of companies.

Compaq's Vision

Inspiration Technology
As an industry we talk a lot about speeds and feeds, and that's fine. Performance matters. But the real power of technology is not the machine; it's in the inspiration. The web was not a product of technology. It was one part technology and three part inspiration. The decoding of the human genome was less a technological achievement than a human inspired achievement, enabled by technology. At Compaq we look at it this way: People enabled by great technology can achieve great things.

Michael Capellas CEO, Compaq

President's Message

We are used to seeing technological development as a help to improve our standards of living.
Today, we are increasingly alert to their impact as to sustainability, efficient use of energy and environmental protection – for all our tomorrows.
We in ABB – as leaders in several key industrial areas – are at the very center of these challenges.
With our leadership role comes the responsibility to secure real and practical innovations.
Every year we invest a significant amount of our resources in research and development(R&D) in order to ensure that we remain a leader in our industry.
Our aim: to sustain growth and profitability through meaningful innovation.
That is the thought behind our ABB group slogan 'Ingenuity at Work'.

Göran Lindal
President and Chief Executive Officer, ABB

Figure 2.3　Examples of normative statements of technology-based companies

Example 2: taking into account the vital link between technology and innovation strategy and company culture (policy level)

The uniqueness of each enterprise is primarily defined by its *organizational culture*. Understanding the organizational culture is an indispensable prerequisite for successful leadership of an enterprise under rapidly changing environmental conditions. Only cultural characteristics can ultimately explain why a new strategy has been implemented satisfactorily or not. In other words: working on a new strategy must aim at reaching a 'cultural fit', i.e. correspondence has to exist between the behavioural pattern under which a strategy can be implemented effectively and the given culture determining current enterprise behaviour. Achieving such a cultural fit can mean intentionally changing the organizational culture as a proactive alternative to adapting a strategy to a given culture. This has been the case, for example, at ABB after the merger between BBC and ASEA (Figure 2.4).

After the merger on 5th January 1988, ABB was challenged by enormous managerial problems. These included the organizational integration of companies in more than 50 countries, the creation of 3500 profit centres, the execution of programmes to increase productivity, to realize numerous strategic alliances, and to maintain a high level of innovation capability despite cost reductions. The main challenge consisted

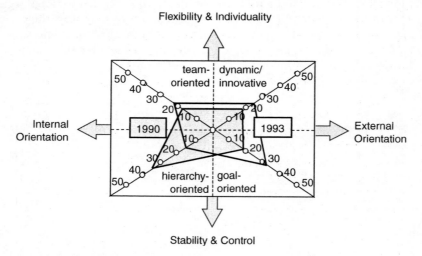

Figure 2.4 Examples of normative statements of technology-based companies
Source: Meyer, 1994: 47

of implementing the new decentralization strategy 'think global-act local'. These fundamental changes were accompanied by investigations to determine the extent to which the company culture is responding to these changes. To this end a concept of company culture was developed as shown in Figure 2.4. Two main dimensions of cultural orientation were identified, which are internal orientation vs. external orientation and stability/control vs. flexibility/individuality. The results of the study are interesting: whereas in 1990 the company culture had a focus on internal orientation and stability/control, a distinct shift towards external orientation and flexibility/individuality could be observed in 1993.

Example 3: equipping top management decision bodies with technology competence (policy level)

As a consequence of technology change and its inherent – often existential – opportunity and risk potential, a well-balanced representation of technological and non-technological competences to make business decisions is required. In this context, the composition of the board of directors and the top management group is of primary importance. For example, this criterion is key to corporate governance at Intel (Figure 2.5, *left*).

A frequently chosen solution is to nominate a Chief Technology Officer (CTO) as a member of the top management group. According to a study completed by Roberts from MIT in 1999, this solution is realized in 95 per cent of Japanese companies, the corresponding figures for Europe and the US are 32 per cent and 8 per cent respectively (Figure 2.5, *right*).

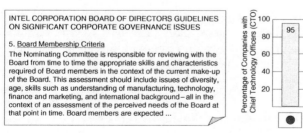

Figure 2.5 Competence structure of boards of directors and top management groups

Source: (*right*) Roberts, 1999: 5

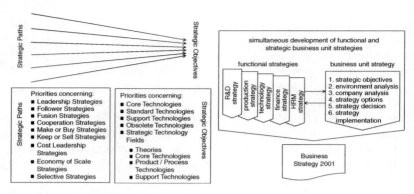

Figure 2.6   Content of technology strategies as a result of simultaneous development of functional and strategic business unit strategies

Source: Tschirky, in Tschirky and Koruna: 295

Example 4: keeping the scope of technology strategic options wide open (strategic level)

Let's first ask the question: what are technology strategies? The answer often refers to leader or follower strategies. This may be correct but the useful content of strategies goes much further. In general, strategies are mid-term decisions on business activities and allocated or to be built-up resources. It can be useful to differentiate strategic statements from statements on 'what will be reached?' (goal statements) and 'how shall we reach the goals?' (path statements). This idea is expressed in Figure 2.6, *left*.

In terms of technology strategies this means that on the one side 'goal statements' focus, for example, on decisions on core technologies, base technologies, support technologies and obsolete technologies. Often, decisions are taken on the level of strategic technology fields, which represent a grouping of structured technological knowledge around selected core technologies. On the other hand, 'path statements' reflect decisions taken on being a leader or a follower in reaching the goals and on pursuing cooperation strategies, make or buy strategies or other selected strategies.

Example 5: developing integrated technology strategies (strategic level)

The development of technology strategies is not an isolated activity but rather ought to occur within a joint and simultaneous collaboration

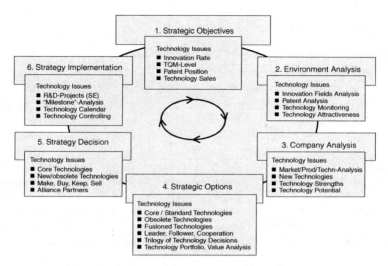

Figure 2.7   Integration of technology issues into strategic business planning
Source: Tschirky, in Tschirky and Koruna: 295

between those responsible for functional and strategic business unit strategies (Figure 2.6, *right*).

The pattern of such a collaboration could, for example, consist of a stepwise and iterative integration of technology issues into the typical steps of strategic planning, such as setting strategic objectives, analysing the environment, analysing the company, elaborating strategic options, taking strategic decisions, implementing the strategy (Figure 2.7). This means, for example, when setting strategic business goals such as market shares and ROE-goals, matching strategic technology objectives such as innovation rate, quantitative quality goals (i.e. six sigma) and patent position are simultaneously set.

In other words, pursuing such a procedure means closing 'technology gaps' which are often observed in strategic business planning. These gaps are typically informational and are apparent in the following areas: technology objectives (see above), technology forecasting and assessment; technology networks relating technology and business units or relating product technologies to process technologies; market–product–technology analysis; defining technology potential; identifying the strategic technology position portfolio; specifying strategic technologies and, correspondingly technology strategies; defining technology projects consisting of R&D projects to develop product and process technologies; and, finally, the technology calendar, which represents a schedule for technology introduction.

Example 6: analysing carefully the current and prospective innovation rate (strategic level)

To be innovative is undisputedly a well-justified recommendation for all business activities. Being innovative, however, is a quality which still characterizes a limited number of companies. Among them, 3M is certainly a good example. In the annual report for the year 2000, the new president W. James McNerney Jr proudly reports that $5.6 billion or nearly 35 per cent of total sales has been generated from products introduced during the past four years, with over $1.5 billion of sales coming from products introduced in 2000. A closer look at the company's management practice makes it easy to explain this impressive achievement, since above all, taking every measure to keep the company culture open and creative is obviously an outstanding leadership competence.

Becoming innovative may start with the analysis of the innovation rate, a recording of the amount of annual sales from new products. To this end, first, criteria for 'new products' has to be established, which in the case of 3M, means market introduction over the past four years. Further steps focus on analysing the innovation rate for the past few years and comparing the values with estimated values from competitors. Then, a decision has to be taken on how the innovation rate ought to develop in the years ahead. As a rule, it would be most unrealistic to assume that the long-range innovation rate will not rise. Whatever assumption is made, the natural question has to be how well the company is prepared to meet the prospective innovation requirements. It is, in other words, the question on the appropriate content of the often cited 'pipe line'. The first answer to this question can be obtained relatively easily from the following analysis (see Figure 2.8): First, using a suitable matrix, all ongoing R&D-projects are listed according to their starting and completion times. Then for all the projects, individually planned prospective sales contributions are 'translated' into percentage values equaling 'new product sales on sale' NPOS. Next, the NPOS values are calculated vertically for each year. Comparing these yearly values with the planned innovation rate allows a first estimate of how well the future innovation target will be met.

In the fictitious case, in Figure 2.8, the company is facing a considerable innovation gap over the next few years, quantifiable in terms of percentage of sales. In this case the next steps are evident. They will have to focus on additional 'innovation contributors', which may include

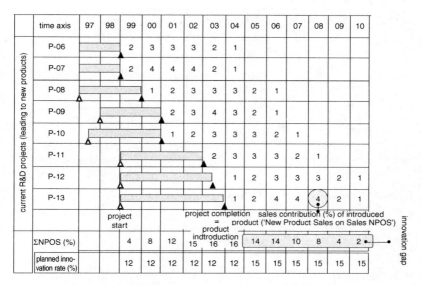

time axis	97	98	99	00	01	02	03	04	05	06	07	08	09	10
P-06			2	3	3	3	2	1						
P-07			2	4	4	4	2	1						
P-08				1	2	3	3	3	2	1				
P-09					2	3	4	3	2	1				
P-10				1	2	3	3	3	2	1				
P-11							2	3	3	3	2	1		
P-12								1	2	3	3	3	2	1
P-13								1	2	4	4	4	2	1
ΣNPOS (%)			4	8	12	15	16	16	14	14	10	8	4	2
planned innovation rate (%)			12	12	12	12	12	12	15	15	15	15	15	15

current R&D projects (leading to new products)

project start — project completion = product indtroduction — sales contribution (%) of introduced product ('New Product Sales on Sales NPOS')

innovation gap

Figure 2.8   Analysis of the past and prospective innovation rate
Source: Tschirky, in Tschirky and Koruna: 342

increased buying-in of components and technologies, increasing market attractiveness of products in development, extending life cycle of existing products, setting-up research collaborations or planning additional R&D projects aimed at attractive new products.

Example 7: optimizing technology knowledge resources: trilogy of technology decisions (strategic level)

Strategic technology planning as part of business strategy planning implies making three fundamentally different but mutually complementing decisions: The *first decision* ('Which technologies?') originates from an extensive analysis of current and future products. In particular, key technologies that determine the product performance, and the process technologies required for product production and infrastructure. This analysis is based on so-called technology intelligence activities, which include cross-industry search of current technology, technology forecasting and technology assessment. Based on this analysis, a decision has to be made as to which of the available and yet-to-be developed technologies are required for the continuous development of the enterprise. The *second decision* ('Make or buy?') is concerned with the question as to whether the required technologies are to be made available through

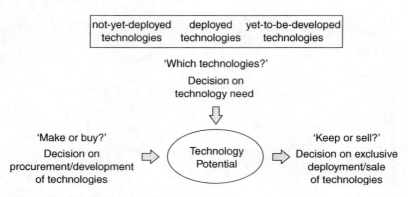

Figure 2.9   Trilogy of strategic technology decisions
Source: Brodbeck *et al.*, 1995: 108

acquisition, collaboration with other companies or through in-house development. The *third decision* ('Keep or sell?') deals with whether available technologies are to be applied exclusively for company purposes or can – or even must – be made available to other companies.

These three decisions are tightly interdependent, and together, represent the 'trilogy of strategic technology decisions' (Figure 2.9).

Having this trilogy in mind and working on the three decisions quasi-simultaneously offers various advantages. Above all, it allows productive use of information since all three decisions rely on mostly identical information concerning technology performance, technology application, technology forecasting, technology assessment, technology users and technology providers. Then, an increased coherence of the three answers is to be expected, which certainly contributes to the quality of strategic technology planning. Finally, the trilogy concept leads to innovative structural solution. It consists of combining the buy and sell activities of technologies within an organizational element which can be called 'Technology Intelligence Centre'. Its basic role is to improve the trilogy of strategic decisions, for example, with the establishment and operation of a company specific technology early warning system, with the actual execution of buy and sell negotiations of technologies and, finally, with the elaboration of proposals for technology strategy decisions. This concept, is in sharp contrast to classical company organization, where the procurement department and the marketing units are usually widely separated entities.

Figure 2.10 Prospective two-level market activities to be mastered by technology-based companies

Source: Tschirky, in Tschirky and Koruna: 302

This so-called functional integration might manifest itself in practice as a central unit bringing together – partly temporarily and partly permanently – representatives from R&D, production, marketing and finance and carrying joint responsibility for periodic elaboration of strategic technology decisions.

Working on the trilogy concept leads to the hypothesis that, in the future, technology-intensive companies will need to position themselves in two quite different market domains: the traditional supplier–consumer market and the technology supplier–technology user market (Figure 2.10). This visionary concept of technology marketing has to be investigated further, under the assumption that its systematic implementation will contribute considerably to successful technology management.

Example 8: overviewing technology strategic positions completely (strategic level)

One instrument of technology management in particular has been seen to gain relatively wide acceptance early on: the strategic technology position portfolio (Figure 2.11, *left*).

It is a matrix tool that provides an easily interpreted and communicated overview of current and future technology positions. Its popularity is attributable to the fact that thinking in terms of portfolios is fundamental to strategic business planning, where strategic product and business positions are to be dealt with.

This portfolio rates and positions all major technologies according to their 'technology attractiveness' with respect to their innovation and market potential, and their corresponding 'technology strength', i.e. the resources currently available within the company.

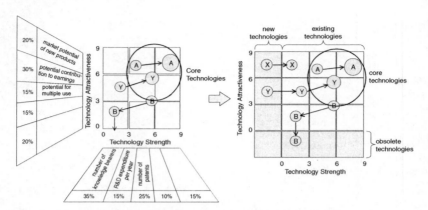

Figure 2.11 From the traditional to the dynamic technology portfolio
Source: Tschirky, in Tschirky and Koruna: 315

This rating can be carried out in several ways. One, a theoretical approach, consists of making extensive assessments of the numerous factors which determine the two dimensions of the portfolio, such as market potential of new products, potential contribution to earnings and potential for multiple use (for technology attractiveness) and number of knowledge bearers, R&D expenditure and number of patents (for technology strength). Another, practice-oriented but nevertheless useful, consists of independently inviting experts from inside and possibly from outside the company to express their opinions on the attractiveness and competitive strength of various technologies. This procedure leads relatively quickly to the data required to draft the portfolio. This second approach has been successfully implemented recently by several Swiss companies from the mechanical, electrical and even the pharmaceutical industry.

Once the portfolio has been developed, its strategic evaluation can take place. This focuses on setting priorities as to the promotion or reduction of technology development resources or even the phasing-out of aging technologies. The latter decision usually follows intensive internal discussions. In particular, consensus has to be reached on core technologies. They constitute strategic knowledge assets of companies and are usually developed in-house with high priority (see Example 10).

The main merit of the technology portfolio lies in its high degree of condensation of strategic information and at the same in its ease in communicating strategic decisions. In addition, a successfully finalized technology portfolio reflects completion of a constructive collaboration between experts from R&D, production and marketing, which is a valuable goal on its own.

Despite the undisputed popularity of technology portfolios, they are still lacking essential strategic information. In its traditional form, the portfolio visualizes the positions of technologies which are currently being used by the enterprise and therefore their corresponding technology strength can be identified. It does not represent however, technologies which are attractive despite the lack of company resources. This information is significant, because the future promotion of new technologies will require company resources, in addition to that needed for the promotion of existing technologies. In order to include this information in the technology portfolio, the use of 'dynamic technology portfolio' (Figure 2.11, *right*) is recommended instead; in addition to the traditional portfolio, it is extended by the column 'new technologies' and at the same time by the line 'obsolete technologies'. This allows the inclusion of information about technologies that had once been part of the company's technology activities. Overall, this expands the time horizon of the portfolio.

Example 9: core technologies as strategic backbone of technology and innovation management (strategic level)

In recent years, the notion of 'core competencies' has become a widely accepted concept in general management. More precisely, it is a strategic concept which aims at explaining a company's competitive strength. Earlier competitive positions were related to available resources, such as capital, human resources and logistics potential. In contrast to company resources which can be obtained or 'bought', core competencies describe capabilities that result from organizational learning over years. They are therefore more inherent, more genuine to the company and certainly less 'purchasable' than resources. A typical core competence of Sony for example is miniaturization. Honda's distinct core competence is mastering 'high revolution engines', which started in the early days when Honda produced high revolution scooters and mowing machines. This core competence enabled Honda to enter the Formula-1 competition successfully, at an amazingly early stage compared to its competitors.

Core technologies fall into the category of core competences. These are usually key technologies that give the company its unique competitive advantages. As mentioned, core technologies are preferably original technologies developed with priority funds within the company. Whereas companies depending on their size have to master hundreds or up to

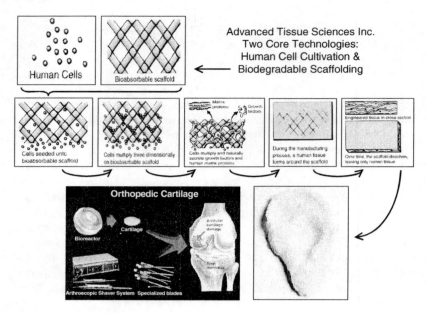

Figure 2.12   Example core technologies
Source: Advanced Tissue Sciences Inc., Personal Communication, 2000

thousands of technologies, the number of core technologies is limited and may amount to a small proportion of all technologies. The ionization technology, described earlier, has been a core technology for Cerberus, a leading fire security company for over twenty years.

A final example refers to Advanced Tissue Sciences Inc. This company is renowned for its capability to produce human tissues. In essence, this capability is based on mastering two core technologies (Figure 2.12): cultivating human cells and building biodegradable scaffoldings. By combining these two core technologies the company is in the position to manufacture two-and three-dimensional tissues. The first batch of products, artificial skin in various configurations, is on sale. The next batch of products will consist of orthopaedic cartilages and ears.

Core technologies play a central role in strategic technology planning. Often they constitute the core of so-called strategic technology fields (STF), which as a structure can be used to reduce the complexity of the large number of technologies that usually need to be handled. STF's are the counterpart to Strategic Business Areas (SBA) which assemble knowledge on specific markets and their relevant customer needs/benefits, product functions, products and services.

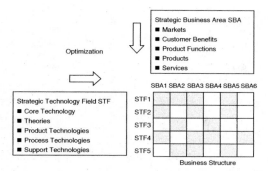

Figure 2.13 Optimizing core technology penetration in the strategic business areas (SBA)

Source: Tschirky, 1996: 80

Within STFs, in addition to core technologies, relevant theories, product, process and support technologies are grouped, which as a whole represent a strategic entity suitable for setting strategic priorities. Optimizing the technology potential, for example, means reducing the number of STFs to an economically and strategically justifiable minimum. At the same time, penetration of STFs throughout the SBA is aimed for (Figure 2.13).

Example 10: visualizing core technology forecasting effectively using technology roadmaps (strategic level)

Technology roadmaps are widely used strategic technology and business management tools which depict comprehensively the predicted development of essential technologies over time. They result from extensive research on available information on technology intelligence combined with concise company internal evaluation of technological in-house development. The following examples may illustrate this technique by illustrating the development of wafer and stepper technology predicted by Canon (Figure 2.14).

Example 11: relating the value of technology strategies directly to the company's value (strategic level)

A further strong link between technology issues and the general management perspective consists of evaluating technology strategies in such a way that allows for directly relating the value of technology strategies to the company's value. In the past, so-called investment and pay-back calculations have been applied in order to financially justify technology

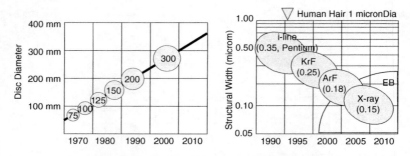

Figure 2.14   Technology roadmaps visualizing the predicted development of wafer (*left*) and stepper (*right*) technology

Source: Canon, 2001

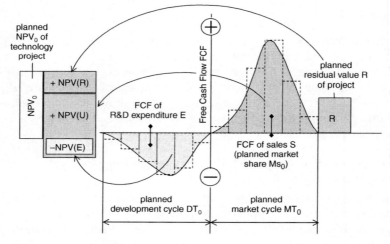

Figure 2.15   Establishing of the Net Present Values (NPVs) R&D projects

Source: Tschirky, in Tschirky and Koruna: 348

strategies or single R&D projects. The decision to approve or reject project proposals was usually based on minimal rates of return (i.e. 15 per cent) or maximum pay-back periods (i.e. 3 years). Using the discounted free cash flow analysis, according to Rappaport (1986), it is possible to establish strategy and project values in terms of Net Present Values (NPVs) (Figure 2.15), which represent numerical values referring to increases or decreases of the total company value. It is evident that, through this procedure, the interest of top management in technology strategies and R&D projects is much higher than in financial project data which only express a 'local view' from the R&D department.

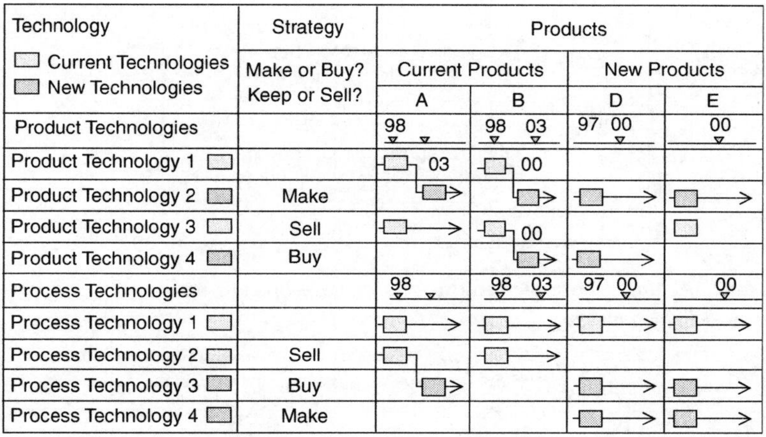

Technology	Strategy	Products			
☐ Current Technologies ▨ New Technologies	Make or Buy? Keep or Sell?	Current Products		New Products	
		A	B	D	E
Product Technologies		98 ▽ ▽	98 03 ▽ ▽	97 00 ▽	00 ▽
Product Technology 1 ☐		▭⌐ 03	⌐▭ 00		
Product Technology 2 ▨	Make	⌐▤⊳	⌐▤⊳	▤—▷	▤⟶
Product Technology 3 ☐	Sell	▭⟶	⌐▭ 00		☐
Product Technology 4 ▨	Buy		⌐▤⊳	▤—▷	
Process Technologies		98 ▽	98 03 ▽	97 00 ▽	00 ▽
Process Technology 1 ☐		▭⟶	▭⟶	▭⟶	▭⟶
Process Technology 2 ☐	Sell	▭⌐	▭⟶		
Process Technology 3 ▨	Buy	⌐▤⊳		▤⟶	▤⟶
Process Technology 4 ▨	Make			▤⟶	▤⟶

Figure 2.16   Technology calendar
Source: Tschirky, in Tschirky and Koruna: 320

Example 12: technology calendar: documenting interdisciplinary consensus (strategic level)

This technology management tool has a high integrative value. It provides an overview of all product and process technologies with respect to their timely introduction in existing and new products and in the production process respectively (Figure 2.16). The elaboration of the technology calendar requires a high degree of interdisciplinary collaboration since it summarizes plans from marketing, R&D, production and financial points of view. Therefore in addition to being a useful management tool it represents a documented evidence of above average level of internal communication quality.

Example 13: gaining time to market using simultaneous engineering (operational level)

Given the accelerated pace of technological change, the main focus of R&D management has shifted from keeping project costs under control to timely introduction of new products. According to an often cited investigation by Siemens (Figure 2.17), a project cost overrun by 50 per cent causes reduced earnings in the order of 5 per cent. However, if a five-year project is exceeded by only six months, the earnings are reduced by 30 per cent.

Project completion time can be reduced by what is commonly known as 'Simultaneous Engineering' (SE) (Figure 2.18, *left*).

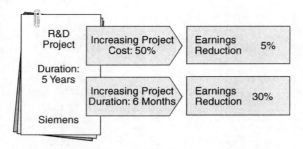

Figure 2.17   Project completion time: its leverage on earnings
Source: Tschirky, 1996: 95

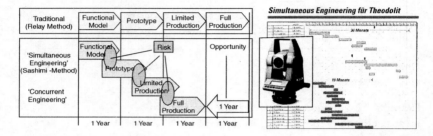

Figure 2.18   Project management by way of simultaneous engineering: case from practice (Development of Leica theodolite)
Source: Tschirky, 1996: 101

This project management concept converts the traditional procedure of completing the individual phases of product development (functional model, prototype, limited production, full production) in series to a procedure in which the phases are partly overlapping. This means on the one side to take risks, since essential project information may be uncertain during times of overlaps. On the other, however, valuable project time can be gained to the benefit of shortened R&D cycles and accelerated market entry. 'Concurrent Engineering' is often used as a synonym to SE.

In practical cases time reductions of 30 per cent and more are not unrealistic. In the Leica case, a theodolite has been developed using simultaneous engineering, resulting in a shorter project time from 30 months to 19 months (Figure 2.18, *right*).

Example 14: being aware of intracultural barriers and ways to overcome them (operational level)

Recently, one of the major players in the pharmaceutical industry expressed concern about the faltering collaboration between its R&D and

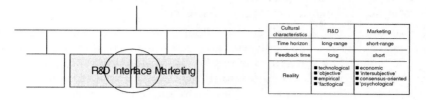

Cultural characteristics	R&D	Marketing
Time horizon	long-range	short-range
Feedback time	long	short
Reality	■ technological ■ 'objective' ■ empirical ■ 'factlogical'	■ economic ■ 'intersubjective' ■ consensus-oriented ■ 'psychological'

Figure 2.19   The intracultural barrier between R&D and marketing
Source: Wiebecke *et al.*, 1987: 5

marketing departments. Typical in this situation, was for example, the presence of prejudices between members of the two departments: marketing would consider R&D to be 'narrow-minded, too specialized, not aware of "real-word"-problems, too slow, and not cost conscious'. And R&D were of the opinion that marketing was 'impatient, incapable of understanding technical problems, exclusively interested in short-term problems, unreliable with respect to confidential R&D-information'.

Further investigations focused on the 'interface' between marketing and R&D (Figure 2.19, *right*) and came to the conclusion that this situation was not the result of any 'bad will' of the people concerned but rather the natural consequence of the fact that cultural determinants of the two groups were fundamentally different (Figure 2.19, *right*).

Therefore, subsequent research concentrated on the question of how to overcome such internal cultural barriers. The answer was threefold:

- building procedural bridges: joint planning of all aspects of R&D-programmes: research, technology, product and process development, joint staffing of projects, pre- and post transfers, common proposals, including product specifications, jointly established criteria for project discontinuance, common base of information;
- building structural bridges: physical proximity, 'organizational' proximity, integrators, process management, specialized transfer groups, internal multidisciplinary venture groups, simultaneous (concurrent) engineering project work; and
- building human bridges: people movement, both upstream and downstream (most effective of all bridging approaches), improve: formal information and meetings, promote: informal contacts, rotation programmes, 'liaison' personnel, joint problem solving sessions, common training, create: interface awareness and atmosphere of mutual trust.

Example 15: 'Gatekeepers': usually anonymous carriers of informal communication (operational level)

One of the rare full-scale investigations in technology management, which got an extraordinarily wide acceptance, concerns the 'gatekeeper' phenomenon. It was carried out by Tom Allen from MIT in the 1980's and reveal a valuable insight into the dynamics of knowledge transfer in R&D organizations (Allen, 1986). Main findings emphasize the dominance of communication and the key role which relatively few people play as carriers of communication processes.

Typical result of the investigations states that the frequency of internal and external communications is a determining factor for project success (Figure 2.20).

Not surprisingly, the contributions from the individual researchers and engineers to this frequency are unevenly distributed. In typical communication networks of R&D organizations which visualize the communication intensity during a given time period (i.e. one month) usually a small number of people attract attention as being 'communication nodes' of the network (Figure 2.21, *left*). At first these people were called 'communication stars'. Since detailed analysis of their daily activities showed that in addition to being preferred discussion partners within the company they also were perceptibly above average in fostering external communication and literature study (Figure 2.21, *right*).

Based on these findings the 'communication stars' were baptized 'gatekeepers' since these people obviously functioned as gates for channeling external information and its internal distribution (Figure 2.22). In other words: information flow and thus knowledge transfer into companies occur at the first stage, mainly through the gatekeepers, who in the second stage are also responsible for the dissemination of the incoming knowledge.

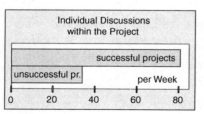 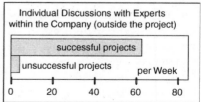

Figure 2.20   Internal and external communications of successful and unsuccessful R&D projects

Source: Allen, 1986: 112, 114

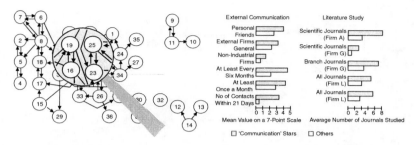

Figure 2.21 'Communication stars' (gatekeepers) within communication networks of R&D structures

Source: Allen, 1986: 146, 147

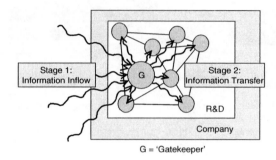

Figure 2.22 Dominant role of gatekeepers in the two-stage process of information in-flow

Source: Allen, 1986: 162

The answer to the question 'who are the gatekeepers?' revealed that they had above average competence in their professional field, they were members of lower management and their service in the company was neither the shortest nor the longest compared to their colleagues. And most surprisingly: the gatekeepers were unknown to the company management as carriers of roles crucial to the company's survival.

Sometimes when discussing the gatekeeper phenomenon in management seminars it is suggested to introduce something like a 'gatekeeper management' in order obtain maximum results from the communication networks. This may not be a good idea. This is because informal communication processes, which constitute the underlying theme of the gatekeeper phenomenon, are not tightly manageable but need to be effectively supported, for example through generously supporting business travel and attending conferences.

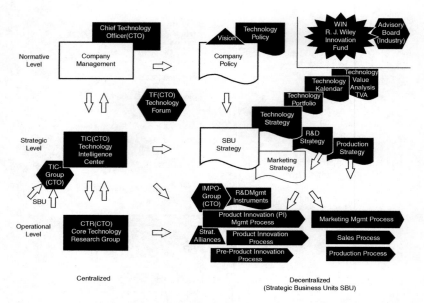

Figure 2.23   Elements of technology and innovation management of the Human Tissues Corporation Inc. (HTC)

Source: Tschirky, in Tschirky and Koruna: 370

A model case of technology and innovation management

The following case example (Figure 2.23) of the Human Tissues Corporation Inc. (HTC) demonstrates the structures and tools of technology management which were chosen in order to build up a strong competitive market position.

The technology management of HTC contains a few centralized and a larger number of decentralized elements associated with the normative, strategic and operational level of management. The *first element* is the CTO-function established at the top management level. The *second element* is the vision 'Technology for Quality of Life', which had been developed to express dominating values as a long-term orientation ('polar star'-function) of the enterprise. The *third element* is a technology policy, which had been elaborated in conjunction with an analysis of the enterprise culture in order to reach agreement between the long-term technology goals and the basic enterprise behaviour. The analysis led to measures aimed at increasing the flexibility and external orientation of the enterprise.

The *fourth element* is the Technology Intelligence Center (TIC) reporting to the CTO. It represents the technology information pool of the enterprise. Its tasks comprise:

- the worldwide collection of technology-sensitive information;
- the establishment of relations to relevant technology users and suppliers inside and outside the medical branch;
- the preparation of make-or-buy and keep-or-sell decisions; and
- the strategic evaluation of key and pacemaker technologies and negotiations on technology collaboration of any sort including the legal work.

TIC is also in a position to perform patent analyses and to handle patent application procedures. In collaboration with the SBUs, the technology portfolio's are brought up-to-date periodically and support is provided to the SBUs for elaborating the technology calendars, which determine the sequence of introducing new and/or obsolete technologies. The TIC-tasks are handled by three people including one patent lawyer. The *fifth element* is the interdisciplinary TIC-Group consisting of SBU representatives from R&D, marketing and production and the manager of the Core Technology Research Group (CTR). This group meets bimonthly under the guidance of the CTO. Main agenda items are news from technology intelligence, ongoing and future alliances, patent situation and licensing businesses.

The *sixth element* consists of the Core Technology Research Group also reporting to the CTO. It is focused on the evaluation and development of strategically significant technologies. It has close relations with universities and institutes of technology such as Caltech, Stanford and MIT. The *seventh element* represents the technology strategy which constitutes an integrated part of the SBU business strategies. Main planning instruments include technology portfolios, technology calendars and technology value analysis (TVA) which allows – as mentioned above – a way of relating the business value of a technology project to the enterprise value based on the free cash flow methodology by Rappaport. From the technology policy, SBU-specific R&D and production strategies are derived. The *eighth element* reflects the process orientation and consists of three operational SBU processes, the product and process innovation (PPI) process, the pre-product and process innovation process and the production process. The PPI process is focused on known technologies in order to keep the risk associated with development time low. The same is true for the production process, which is coupled with the sales process. New product and process technologies are evaluated within the pre-PPI process. This task is closely related to CTR. The *ninth element* represents two management processes. The PPI management process takes responsibility for the PPI and pre-PPI processes. This assignment is based on a close collaboration with TIC. The marketing management process is in charge of the sales and production processes.

The *tenth element* is the innovation management process owner group (IMPO). It brings together those responsible for the PPI management processes and enhances the exchange of experience, the coordination technology alliances and the development of suitable R&D management instruments (such as target costing, project management tools, etc.). The TIC and IMPO groups meet 3–4 times yearly in order to discuss basic questions of technology competitiveness. The *eleventh element* is the technology forum (TF). Under the leadership of the CTO, it takes place twice a year and is addressed primarily to the non-technical management, those responsible for HTC. The main topics presented include the current technology situation of HTC, the progress of strategic technology projects and technology alliances, aimed at promoting the technology understanding across functional boundaries. The *twelfth element* finally is the R.J. Wiley Innovation Fund (WIN). It had been established, by the enterprise founder, to increase the chances of acceptance of attractive innovation projects. This way, within HTC, two entirely separate routes exist to apply for innovation project funds, namely the ordinary procedure within the SBUs and the extraordinary path leading directly to WIN. The evaluation of WIN proposals is done by an external committee consisting of representatives from industry and academia.

Does actively practising technology management pay off?

As always, when attempting to relate business success to specific variables such as strategy, company culture, leadership or even entire management concepts, it is inherently difficult to come to unequivocal conclusions. A research study carried out at the Swiss Federal Institute of Technology on the 'technology management intensity' of 60 SMEs belonging to different industries of varying technology levels, identified a group of obviously innovative and financially successful enterprises which are practising technology management proactively on all management levels, and another group of non-innovative and unsuccessful firms in which technology issues are at best marginally integrated into processes of general management (Kohler, 1994).

In addition, an individual in-depth study of such renowned technology enterprises as ABB, Siemens, 3M, Canon, NEC, Hewlett Packard,

Honda, Hilti, Novartis, Monsanto, Roche and others revealed a high level of awareness of technology and innovation management issues in many forms. Of particular interest is the fact that these companies do not take a singular but rather an integrated approach to managing technology. They simultaneously manage on the normative level in terms of explicit technology policy and innovative organizational culture, on the strategic level in terms of a clear focus on core technologies and at the same time on a high intensity of strategic technology alliances, and finally on the operational level in terms of up-to-date management instruments such as target-costing, concurrent engineering project management, process management and the promotion of informal communication.

No crystal ball is required to predict a significantly increasing need for management awareness of technology and its management, as we face the unprecedented challenges of the next millennium. There are 'good' and 'bad' ways to go about this, using the frameworks outlined above as well as others that follow in subsequent chapters.

Note

1. In the original literature (Ulrich, 1984; Bleicher, 1991) this top level management is referred to in German 'normativ'. A literal translation into English would lead to 'normative'. Since this translation may lead to confusion, the term 'policy level' is used instead.

Bibliography

Advanced Tissue Sciences Inc. (2000), Personal Communication.

Allen, T. (1986), *Managing the Flow of Technology: Technology Transfer and the Dissemination of Technological Information Within the R&D Organization*, third printing, Cambridge: The MIT Press.

Biedermann, M., H. Tschirky, B. Birkenmeier, and H. Brodbeck (1998), 'Value Engineering Management und Handshake Analysis', in Tschirky, H. and Koruna, St. (Hrsg.), *Technologie-Management – Idee und Praxis*, Zürich: Verlag Industrielle Organisation.

Bleicher, K. (1991), *Konzept Integriertes Management*, Frankfurt: Campus.

Brodbeck, H., Birkenmeier, B. and Tschirky, H. (1995), *Neue Entscheidungsstrukturen des Integrierten Technologie-Managements*, Die Unternehmung, 49, 2, pp. 107–23, Bern.

Canon (2001), 'Strategic Technologies', Personal communication.

Katz, R. and Allen, T. (1985), 'Investigating the Not Invented Here (NIH) Syndrome: A Look at the Performance, Tenure & Communications Patterns of 50 R&D Project Groups', *R&D Management*, 12, pp. 7–19.

Kohler, O. (1994), 'Technologiemanagement in schweizerischen kleinen und mittelgrossen Unternehmen (KMU)', ETH-Diss Nr. 10477.

Kuark, J.K. (1988), 'Der Informationsaustausch zwischen Operateuren in einer Fertigungsanlage', *Nachdiplomarbeit Mechatronics*, Zurich: Institut für Arbeitspsychologie der ETH Zurich.

Meyer, A. (1994), 'Dynamische Anpassung an eine sich wandelnde Wirtschaftswelt', *Io Management Zeitschrift* 63 (1994), Zurich.

Pfund, C. (1997), *Entwicklung der Publikationen über Technologie-Management*, Interne BWI-Studie, Zürich: BWI.

Porter, M. (1985), *Competitive Advantage – Creating and Systaining Superior Performance*, New York : The Free Press.

Rappaport, A. (1986), *Creating Shareholder Value – The New Standard for Business Performance*, New York: The Free Press.

Riedl, J.E. (1990), *Projekt-Controlling in Forschung und Entwicklung*, Berlin: Springer.

Roberts, E.B. (1999), *Global Benchmarking of Strategic Management of Technology*, MIT Cambridge: The Press.

Smith, P.G. and D.G. Reinertsen (1991), *Developing Products in Half the Time*, New York: Van Nostrand Reinhold.

Tschirky, H. (1991), 'Technology Management: An Integrating Function of General Management', in D.F. Kocaoglu and K. Niwa (eds), *Technology Management – The New International Language*. Proceedings of the Portland International Conference on Management of Engineering and Technology, Portland, Oregon, USA October 27–31, 1991.

Tschirky, H. (1996), Lecture Notes 'Technology and Innovation Management', Wintersemester 1996/97.

Tschirky, H. (1997), 'Bringing Technology into Management: The Call of Reality – Going Beyond Industrial Management at the ETH, in D.F. Kocaoglu and T.R. Anderson (eds), *Innovation in Technology Management – The Key to Global Leadership*. Proceedings of the Portland International Conference on Management of Engineering and Technology, Portland, Oregon, USA July 27–31, 1997.

Tschirky, H. (1998a), 'Lücke zwischen Management-Theorie und Technologie-Realität', in H. Tschirky and St. Koruna (Hrsg.), *Technologie-Management – Idee und Praxis*, Zürich: Verlag Industrielle Organisation.

Tschirky, H. (1998b): 'Konzept und Aufgaben des Integrierten Technologie-Managements', in H. Tschirky and St. Koruna (Hrsg.), *Technologie-Management – Idee und Praxis*, Zürich: Verlag Industrielle Organisation.

Tschirky, H. (1999), 'Technology and Innovation Management: Leading the Way to (New) Enterprise Science', in D.F. Kocaoglu and T.R. Anderson (eds), *Proceedings of the Portland International Conference on Management of Engineering and Technology*, Portland, Oregon, USA July 25–29, 1999.

Ulich, E., C. Baitsch and A. Alioth (1983), 'Führung und Organisation', in Schriftenreihe 'Die Orientierung', Nr. 81. Bern: Schweizerische Volksbank.

Ulich, E. (1994), *Arbeitspsychologie*, 3. Auflage. Zürich: vdf, Stuttgart: Schäffer-Poeschel.

Ulrich, H. (1984), *Management* (Hrsg., Th. Dyllick, G.J.B. Probst). Bern: Haupt.

Wiebecke. G. and H. Tschirky (1987), 'Interface zwischen Forschung & Entwicklung und Marketing', *Io Management Zeitschrift* 56, 1, pp. 23–26.

Wiebecke, G., H. Tschirky and E. Ulich (1987), 'Cultural Differences at the R&D-Marketing Interface: Explaining the Interdivisional Communication Barriers', Proceedings of the 1987 IEEE, Conference on Management and Technology (Atlanta), pp. 94–102.

3
The Strategic Management of Technology and Innovation
Thomas Durand

Overview

This chapter presents an overview of definitions of key words and concepts (techniques, technology, science, invention, innovation). It also describes what the management of technology and the management of innovation are about. The chapter reviews the literature and identifies seven streams of contributions (managing R&D; connecting science, technology and innovation; understanding the dynamics of technologies; promoting innovation; recognizing the importance of organizational innovation; managing technologies and competencies; integrating technology into strategic management). On that basis, the chapter then identifies current challenges for practioners (technology and knowledge intelligence, organizing for innovation, gaining access to technologies and competence) and presents an integrated framework to think technology and innovation strategically.

Introduction

Technology is a new issue in the field of management. Innovation and technical change have affected the business world for years and the importance of technology on firms and markets was understood long ago. However, engineering and management remained two different spheres with too few connections.

Things however have been changing in recent years. There is now a field of research and education known as the management of technology and innovation. First, we need to clarify the vocabulary and concepts.

Technology is the daughter of science and techniques. Yet, it cannot be reduced to the simple use of scientific discovery nor is it just implementation of technical empiricism.

Science relates to basic knowledge produced through research activities. Science aims at identifying, characterizing and modelling natural phenomena taking place in our environment. These can be physical, chemical, biological, medical, social, etc.

Techniques relate to know-how built empirically through human action, as concrete experience builds up, learning by doing. Techniques are made up of human skills, recipes on how to operate, practical ways of producing an artefact or conducting a routine. To a large extent, techniques are tacit (Nonaka and Takeuchi, 1995), i.e. they are not codified – or only in part – thus difficult to replicate and imitate without previous experience. Transferring technical know-how requires some form of companionship, meaning working together with experienced masters who teach by demonstration. Techniques are embedded in practice and action. This represents both a strength and a weakness. Obviously techniques are powerful precisely because they work, as they result from experimentation and accumulated experience. Conversely, techniques may be difficult to adapt and extend to new contexts and situations because no explicit, articulated knowledge of why it works is available. Empirical know-how may be costly to transfer, with uncertain results.

Technology relates to design, production and distribution of goods and services, in response to market needs. Technology is more than a technique: technology combines technical know-how with scientific knowledge to fulfil explicit socio-economic goals. In this sense, technology should to be managed, even though it includes tacit know-how which is by nature difficult, arguably impossible, to manage. Managing technology is thus no easy task.

Innovation may be defined as the making of the new. Invention is limited to expressing a new idea, a new concept, sketching a new path with no real confrontation with technical or marketing feasibility. A patent signals an invention. In contrast, innovation bridges the gap between the idea and its real implementation to serve a human need. Innovation is an idea put to work. It is change implemented, be it incremental or radical, for product design, manufacturing process or organizational, etc. An innovation requires an invention to be further developed, industrialized and commercialized.

There is a natural link between technology and innovation. Technology is improved continuously through a flow of incremental innovations which construct and shape a technological trajectory (Dosi, 1982). The trajectory exploits the potential of the technological seam or paradigm (dominant design, dominant process) until a radical innovation occurs, substituting a new dominant technology for the former dominant technology now becoming obsolete. This is what Schumpeter (1943) described as creative destruction.

With these definitions in mind, we can now clarify what we mean by the management of technology and innovation. *The management of technology includes the following:*[1]

(a) observation, identification and assessment of competing technologies to fulfil a certain market need;
(b) selection of the most relevant technologies from the feasible options to help the firm build a sustainable, possibly long lasting competitive advantage;
(c) access to the knowledge base required for the technologies selected, be it through internal development, R&D partnerships or acquisitions;
(d) management of research activities, development, feasibility studies and more generally project management;
(e) subsequent implementation and improvement of product and process technologies integrated in the firm's portfolio; and
(f) picking out former technologies, progressively or suddenly rendered obsolete by new technologies.

Basically, most if not all the issues listed above describe the extent to which the management of technology gravitates around the theme of technical change. The main challenges have less to do with technology itself but more with the shift from an old to a new technology. This is probably why the theme of innovation has been historically identified as equivalent to the management of technologies, even though not all innovations affecting firms are technological; far from it. Organizational or social innovations (what are sometimes called soft innovations) have been in fact as important, if not more important in practice.

The management of innovation thus goes beyond the limits of technologies to address the larger scope of change in general. Innovation can indeed deal with the technological side of human activities, thus with product design and manufacturing processes, but it may also deal with the organizational and social side, e.g. external interactions with suppliers, clients or partners, internal processes which became routines in the way the firm operates (Nelson and Winter, 1982).

The management of innovation thus includes:

(a) the promotion of innovation to facilitate and encourage the emergence of new ideas, both listening to proposals, regardless of where they originate from within the company or how disturbing they may appear at first, and sponsoring subsequent development projects;

(b) selection of relevant innovations for the firm, managing a portfolio of innovative opportunities which are each financially accessible with reasonable expectations for their marketing and technical feasibility;

(c) management of the resources and knowledge base of the firm required to conduct the innovation projects, including through external partnerships; and

(d) managing the social and organizational implications of innovations, including the sources of inertia and possibly the opposition which may arise when change is taking place.

As a result, the management of technology and innovation addresses issues which are at the heart of strategic management: which technologies should the firm select? Which technological change to promote against competition? How to access the necessary knowledge, especially the skills and capabilities which may be lacking? How to reinforce the innovative capability of the organization? How to and according to which criteria select innovation projects?

The management of technology and innovation thus relates to many other fields of management, including strategy with the selection of technologies and core competencies, organization with the interaction between innovation and organizational change, law with the issue of protecting innovation and thus IPR, project management as well as operations management with process innovations, e.g. all along the supply chain, in manufacturing or logistics.

The importance of this theme for management in general does not just stem from the relevance of the intrinsic dynamics of technologies and the specificities of the processes of innovation. The real challenge of technology and innovation comes from their ability to intersect with virtually all aspects of the firms. It is thus extremely important to understand better how technology, technological change, and also non-technical innovations affect companies, their competitive position and their operations. This is why the management of technology and innovation is one of the key entry points into management.

Historical perspective and literature review

The literature in the management of technology and innovation reports the development of investigations in the field. For the sake of clarity, seven clusters of contributions may be identified in the literature, each addressing a specific theme.

Managing R&D

Many still view the management of technology and innovation as concerned with the management of R&D. Along this line, many management researchers interested in technology matters have studied the contribution of R&D activities to the growth of the firms, as well as the emergence and development of new technologies and capabilities.

Research activities have specificities and should thus be managed accordingly: R&D budgets are discretionary, meaning that there is no intrinsically optimal level of expenditures for a given company in a given context. In addition, researchers need to build some form of specialization which is contradictory to the flexibility required by market change. This is also contradictory to the need for human resource mobility as careers develop in the organization. Careers for experts with a true specialization thus need to be adapted to permit relevant incentive mechanisms away from the natural career path usually leading best talents into higher management, thus losing ground in their technical expertise.

Allen (1977) analysed research centres in large organizations and the way they best operate. Although slowly losing pace in recent years, this line of research is represented by the journal *R&D Management*, now *R&D, Technology Management* as well as the society of R&D managers in large European companies (EIRMA).

Connecting science, public research, technology and innovation

A second cluster of contributions found in the literature deals with the role played by scientific activities, including public research, in the development of new technologies and innovations. This perspective clarified the nature of the complex interrelations which prevail within 'national systems of innovation', especially between public and private research activities. (Lundvall, 1988; Foray and Freeman, 1992; Nelson, 1993; Niosi, 1994; Gambardella, 1995).

Bibliometrics or scientometrics is another field of contributions which analyse the dynamics of national or international scientific communities through their main output, the publications, and the network of

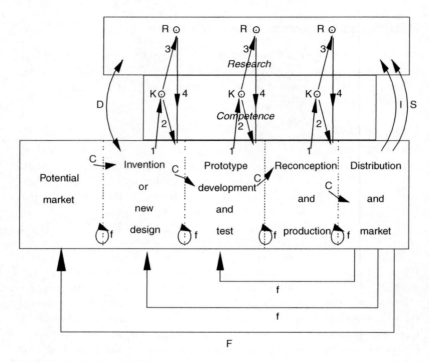

Figure 3.1 The chain link model
Source: Kline and Rosenberg, 1986

cooperations which can be identified within and across the communities by looking at co-authoring (Okubo, 1997). The issue of technology transfer and the 'valorization' of public research are other dimensions of the same theme (Gonard and Durand, 1994).

A major contribution in this context is the 'chain-link' model from Kline and Rosenberg (1986). The model shown in Figure 3.1 clarifies the distinct role of the two components put together under the label R&D. Internal research builds a pool of competencies which may be called upon to solve problems encountered at any stage of the innovation process, not just at the invention stage. (The innovation process is the organizational process which transforms an idea into an innovation.) In contrast, development contributes directly to the innovation process, when the initial idea is elaborated further, when a prototype is designed and when the product design and production process are subsequently optimized. The model also stresses the importance of feed back

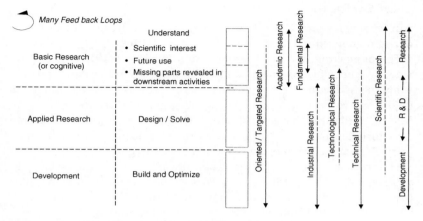

Figure 3.2 Categories of research and their specific objectives
Source: Adapted from the work of Michel Rapin

loops all along the innovation process. Along similar lines, Figure 3.2 presents and clarifies various terms often used to qualify all or part of R&D activities.

Another perspective on these matters comes from the sociology of research and innovation which calls upon the methodological tools of sociology (Akrich *et al.*, 1988a,b) or anthropology (Latour, 1996) to analyse research activities in labs as interactions among participants in scientific or innovative projects. This approach showed that technology should not primarily be viewed as emerging from the dynamics of science and techniques but rather stems from the coalition of players taking part in the networks around innovations, including their three main poles: science, technology and markets (Callon, 1991). The role of users, clients and suppliers had already been extensively pointed out (von Hippel, 1988). This should also be the case for the various partners of the firms, who directly or indirectly contribute to the innovation projects (Midler, 1993).

A central idea emerged from these various models: the process of innovation is non linear, with many iterations and interactions, feed back loops. In addition, research activities cannot be seen as the primary source nor the main contributor to technological development in firms but more as a key support function which permits the establishment and reinforcement of a technical knowledge base within organizations.

Understanding the dynamics of technologies

A number of research contributions describe the mechanisms of diffusion of technological innovations in firms and industries.

The pioneering work of Abernathy and Utterback (1975, 1978) provided a framework to understand technological change based on the study of the history of several industrial sectors. Dosi (1982) offered a theoretical reconstruction to clarify the concept of technological trajectory, similar to what Nelson and Winter (1982) described as natural trajectories. Clark (1985) suggested a process of exploration, in a triple hierarchy, for technical options and market concepts.

The concrete description of radical innovations was made by Cooper and Schendel (1976), followed by Foster (1986) who extensively illustrated the S curve model while Durand and Gonard (1986), Durand and Stymne (1991) and Durand (1992) constructed technology trees.

The key elements of the corresponding models may be summarized as follows:

- In a given market, a generic need has been, historically, fulfilled by a certain technology, which over the years, became dominant. A dominant technology is the technology which has been widely accepted and adopted as state of the art by the players in the industry. Competing technological options have been considered but have not been adopted because they were too expensive, too futuristic or not sufficiently robust. As the dominant technology matured, the market was segmented into an array of specific needs, some of which were fulfilled by specific sub-technologies. In any case, the dominant technology remained the reference on the market place as no other technology at this point in time was in a position to better fulfil the market needs. All in all, this is a slow process of maturation.

- Progressively, among the many other options considered to cover the same generic needs, one or two emerge as the natural challengers, with the potential of bringing superior performance, new functionalities, significantly reduced costs or a combination of the three. This new technology is usually brought about by new entrants who use specific market niches as a Trojan horse. The new technology is focused on specific needs, which so far were improperly covered by the current dominant technology. This new technology is not necessarily the best technology available at this point in time. But the industrialization and commercialization of this new technology will help build an experience base, which in turn, will make it increasingly attractive compared to other options, as it will reach superior functional performance and/or much lower costs than competing technologies. This effect will reinforce itself over time, thus leading to a 'lock-in' situation. A new trajectory appears to explore the new paradigm.

- In the market niche where it was first introduced, the new technology is rapidly improved and soon starts cannibalizing other market segments through iterations, trial and errors thus leading to cumulative improvements. At some point in time, followers enter the market with me-too offerings to benefit from part of the expected growth potential, thus accelerating the learning process of technology adaptation, improvement and diffusion.

- The new technology progressively extends to larger and larger parts of the market and literally cannibalizes the market shares of the now 'former dominant' technology. The substitution process is both explosive and irreversible. Leaders on the previous dominant technology now have the choice of either keeping to improve an obsolete technology or to being late in adopting the new dominant technology, accepting the new rules of the game and in particular the newly required set of competencies.

- In the meantime, market re-segmentation takes place once again, market and industry borders become blurred, and new applications and new segments emerge. An entire new process of maturation is at work, awaiting for the next episode of de-maturation, when a radical innovation will strike again, as this is the life of technologies.

Figure 3.3 (Durand, 1992) represents graphically some aspects of this model, which is in line with the so called evolutionary perspective in industrial organization and relies upon the concepts of organizational learning and routinization. This in turn also relates to the resource based view of the firm and its corrolary, the emerging theory of competence in management (more on this in 'Managing technologies and competencies', below).

Promoting innovation

Since the 1970s and even more so since the 1980s, technical change and, more generally, innovation have been viewed as a source of disruption and shake out in industries, thus making it possible to use them, when they occur, as a way to enter established markets and build competitive advantage while former leaders are struggling through the change.

Porter (1985) points out that technology is important as it affect competitive game, modifying industry structure as well as the rul

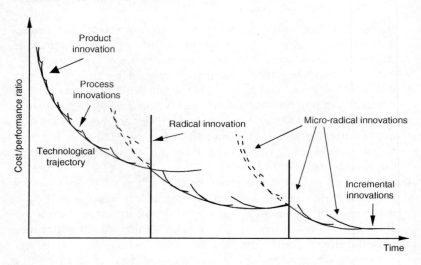

Figure 3.3   Evolution of competing technologies for a generic market need
Source: Durand, 1992: 372

game. Technology, as it evolves, may challenge or even destroy established market positions and create opportunities for new entrants. In this very Schumpeterian perspective, technology is in fact the primary force capable of significantly modifying market shares. This was the case in the multimedia sector, which transformed the computer industry, consumer electronics, publishing and the TV business. Technological change can operate as an effective competitive weapon for those who can use it.

Burns and Stalker (1961) were among the first to suggest that the way the organization is structured and operates may strongly affect its capacity to innovate. Roberts and Frohman (1972), Maidique (1980), Doz *et al.* (1985), Burgelman and Sayles (1987), Roberts (1987), Van de Ven (1989), Dougherty (1992), Bellon (1994), Utterback (1994) and ᴺ and O'Reilly (1997) have in their own ways analysed forms of ᵔs which are more adapted to innovation than others. The ᵐ Burgelman and Sayles (1987) on intrapreneurship is ᵊning. They show how the large firm may tend to kill ᵔar to disturb the normal everyday operations of ᵗ is possible to protect both those who bring ᵔ and to provide them with support (from

Not surprisingly this literature and the corresponding interest for start-ups prompted a surge of new business creation in Europe, with much attention paid to funding, including through venture capital and public support for innovation, including from the European Union.

Recognizing the importance of organizational innovations: (JIT, TQM, concurrent engineering, etc.)

The management of technology is directly related to operations and project management. Manufacturing includes process technologies and a large number of development projects, for product design or processes deal with improving or changing the technology. Yet, the management of technology and innovation literature addressed the issues of manufacturing, operations and project management mostly through the study of organizational innovations.

If one tries to recapitulate over a twenty or thirty year period the crucial innovations which most affected industries such as electronics or automotives, clearly organizational innovations stand out as the sources of major revolutions. Just-in-Time or the use of total quality principles have significantly transformed the way a firm operates. Skinner (1978), Hayes and Wheelwright (1984), Teboul (1990), de Meyer (1992) or Kanji and Asher (1996) all described the consequences of these new organizational approaches in the world of manufacturing and beyond.

Similarly, inter-functional project teams or concurrent engineering (also known as parallel development), helped significantly improve time to market and decrease development costs for new products (Clark and Fujimoto, 1991; Midler, 1993; Nishigushi, 1996). Along the same lines, the concept of modularity also enhances the development capabilities of organizations (Sanchez, 1996). The idea is to decompose products into modules with strictly specified interfaces, making it possible to develop each module independently of the others. Again, this is quite a significant organizational innovation.

Interestingly enough, the technology foresight report published in France in October 2000 *Key Technologies 2005* paid much attention to organizational or soft technologies.

Managing technologies and competencies

Beyond the flow of new technologies described by Allen (1977), Morin (1985) suggested looking at technology as a critical resource which needs to be systematically identified, evaluated and monitored in order to be better protected, optimized and enriched. He thus advocated a management of technological resources. In so doing, he extended an idea initially put forward by consultants at ADL who suggested building and managing a portfolio of the firm's technologies. They offered to characterize each technology as key (those which may help create a sustainable, hopefully long-lasting competitive advantage), pacing (those still under development or just being implemented, not yet assessed as potentially key) or basic (those widely diffused technologies for which trained and skilled staff, suppliers or sub-contractors are readily available). With a slightly different objective, Durand (1988) and Kandel *et al.* (1991) present tools to grasp and describe the technological base of a firm.

Conversely, some authors looked at strategies to gain access to technology. Durand (1988) built a typology of generic strategies for a firm to access technology. See Figure 3.4. The classical make or buy distinction or the central/divisional research split appears just as elements of a much larger set of options in the typology. When discussing the issue of acquiring technology from outside, Bidault (1986) shows how difficult it is to evaluate how much a technology is worth, suggesting that the so-called market for technologies does not really operate as a market, as it is highly asymmetrical, with a monopolistic position on the supply side while demand is rarely expressed formally.[2]

After Mansfield (1985), Teece (1986) analysed the appropriability regime of a new technology by the innovator or the follower (the imitator or the owner of 'complementary assets'). He pointed out to the

		Internal		External	
		Development		Acquisition	
		Internal	External	Of Technologies	Of a Firm
SPIRIT	Competitive, Centralized, Exclusive	• Centralized, internal R&D • Decentralized, internal R&D	• Subcontracting R&D (parcelled out, exclusive)	• Information gathering • Hiring specialists away from competitors • Buying the technology directly	• Take overs
	Cooperative, Spirit of Partnership, Decentralized (internal venturing)	• Internal venturing	• Cooperative subcontrating	• Swapping	• Buying shares in order to gain access to R&D programs
		Collaborating on R&D			
		Joint Ventures			

Figure 3.4 Generic strategies to gain access to technology
Source: Durand, 1988

importance of IPR (intellectual property rights) as well as the control of the necessary capabilities and resources needed to develop the innovation (he calls them the complementary assets). In a way, part of the contributions on strategic alliances and their dynamics overtime are built using the same argument (Dussauge and Garrette, 1995).

This line of thinking stems from transaction cost theory (Williamson, 1975), which after Coase, offers an answer to a basic question: why do firms exist? Organizational learning and competence are at the heart of this theoretical reconstruction. Markets should normally be enough of a mechanism to fulfil economic needs. If firms exist, if 'hierarchies' seem to win over market at least in some instances, it is precisely because they have this unique ability to build routines, knowledge base and skills. These competencies make firms more efficient than other governance mechanisms, including markets.

In this context, technology is one of the key components of competence. One should note in passing that this purely economic perspective ignores the psycho-social dimension of organizations which are obviously human-constructed as much as they are economic entities.

This competence based perspective was first introduced as the 'resource-based-view' by Wernefelt (1984) and Barney (1986), drawing from former work by Penrose (1959), before it was popularized by Prahalad and Hamel (1990) with their famous 'core competence' piece. A mass of subsequent contributions then followed, see for example Durand (2000) for a review. See also Chapter 6 in this book.

Integrating technology in strategic management

Kantrow (1980) had already advocated a better integration of technology into strategic management. Ansoff (1986), Dussauge and Ramanantsoa (1986), Ait el Adj (1989), Durand (1988), Larue de Tournemine (1991) and Broustail and Fréry (1993) all pushed in the same direction.

As mentioned earlier, technology intersects virtually all other aspects of the firm. Technological evolution can thus significantly affect organizations, disrupting strategic positions in industries. Most authors thus recommend that more attention be paid to technology in strategic processes.

A very enlightening contribution came in the form of bonsai trees. In this approach, the firm is primarily a set of technologies, which are in turn called upon to serve various markets through ad hoc products and services according to the needs. This obviously relates to the competence based perspective discussed above. Figure 3.5 summarizes this idea in the form of a technological bonsai tree, with roots fed by science to

Leveraging the core
technologies in various
sectors, for specific
products and markets

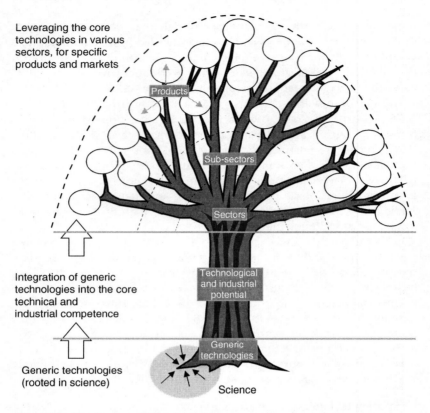

Integration of generic
technologies into the core
technical and
industrial competence

Generic technologies
(rooted in science)

Figure 3.5   The firm as a technological tree

Source: Giget Marc (1984) 'Les bonsais de L'industrie japonaise', CPE études no. 40, in *Encyclopédie de la gestion et du management*, Dalloz, Paris, p. 440

nurture the trunk symbolizing the technical and manufacturing base of the firm. Branches of the tree then bear the fruits, i.e. the products and services, leveraging the technologies for the benefits of clients and markets.

Strategically, therefore, the firm should no longer be seen as a portfolio of product segments, as suggested in the 1970s and early 1980s, but more as a base of technologies and technical competence. Durand (1992) follows the same line of thinking in the model presented in Figure 3.6: the model balances the relative importance of products and markets on one hand to that of technologies on the other hand. A balanced perspective is what is being advocated for, staying away from a techno-centred view

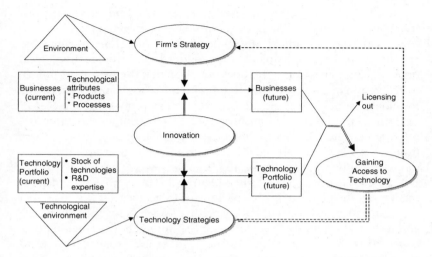

Figure 3.6 The strategic management of technology and innovation
Source: Durand, 1988

of the firm which is certainly not what this book is advocating. Technology is important but should by no means be regarded as the only, nor even the primary, resource for the firm.

All in all, this review of the literature on management of technology and innovation, with seven main clusters, illustrates how most authors tend to offer managers ways to better integrate technology and innovation into their practice.

The section below first deals with some of the typical shortcomings which may be observed in companies concerned with technology and innovation. On that basis, three recommendations for good practice formulated. This section is thus more normative in natu~ section, 'Future trends and conclusion', will conc~ drawing perspectives on potential future tr~ management of technology and i~

Challenges for practitioners ,
concrete recommendations f~

When observing how firms go abo~ tion, various shortcomings may be i~ do not pay much attention to techn~

due to a lack of awareness on the part of senior management, low interest in technical matters or, more frequently, sole managerial focus on running day-to-day operations, absorbing all attention for optimizing what already exists without taking the time to investigate other technological or organizational options. This does not mean that these firms are unable to evolve and innovate. It is just that they tend to do so only when clients formulate requests for new offerings, suppliers propose new pieces of equipment to improve or transform the process, competitors innovate, offering new products and services to the market. In other words, these firms are passive and essentially react to technological evolution and more generally innovations coming from outside.

A second cluster of firms can be identified. There, marketing departments lead the play. There may be a thrust to deal with technology in a more proactive way as well, but marketing leadership is such that R&D and technical departments are more or less limited to working on briefs issued to them by marketing. In these firms, R&D managers tend to complain about this rather limited role, explaining how difficult it is for them to convince their colleagues in the commercial functions about the potential interest of new, though still uncertain technological options. The opposite situation is also commonly found. That of firms, a third group of companies, where technical departments dominate, sometimes imposing costly, lengthy and risky development projects in search of technological sophistication while not necessarily adapted to real market needs. Broustail and Fréry (1993) have analysed at length the case of Citroën, the car company which spent in vain most of its resources venturing in risky technical developments before being taken over, first by a supplier of tyres, Michelin, and then by Peugeot. In addition, these techno-centred firms usually have a really strong technological base and have difficulties going outside to acquire technology that they may need. The 'Not Invented Here' syndrome is most often found in such companies.

These different contexts lead to a variety of frequently heard comments, each mirroring the typical difficulties encountered in the organization when it comes to managing technology and innovation. 'In our company, our marketers just ignore what we [technicians] have to offer. As a result we tend to miss opportunities'; or 'We have to work under so much pressure in operations to deliver the promised financial results that we do not have time to innovate'; or 'Our competition always moves faster'; or 'Our top management does not seem to understand the value of these new technologies. They are just not interested'; or 'In our firm, technicians are very powerful, except that they do not fit market requirements.'

Each of these situations is specific. Yet, three complementary lines of action may be useful to cope with the challenges identified. Firstly, technology requires a systematic activity of surveillance and monitoring. Secondly, it is relevant in most organizations to promote and organize innovative activities, designing ad hoc processes and influencing the organizational culture to value new ideas, innovation and innovators. Thirdly, firms may find it useful to organize access to sources of new capabilities soon to be required by expected innovations. This can be done through internal or external development, by acquisition or in partnership.

A dual task of technological and knowledge intelligence: internal and external

The starting point of any real attempt to manage technology and promote innovation is to conduct two parallel tasks, scanning for new technological development outside on one hand, and closely monitoring internal potentialities on the other hand.

It is an essential task of management to have the organization scan the environment:

- searching for scientific breakthrough and new technological options;
- assessing the associated risks and potential benefits;
- monitoring strategic moves by competitors to identify which technology they select;
- exchanging with suppliers about their own perspectives; and
- listening to clients to test new ideas, collect their suggestions and validate functional needs, given what may now become feasible due to the potential offered by new technological options, etc.

This type of technological intelligence activity is not necessarily very costly. It needs to be organized and managed properly to nurture the strategic decision process regarding technology and innovation projects for the firm. In some instances, e.g. biotechnologies, pharmaceuticals or new materials, it is important to closely monitor the most recent scientific developments, keeping an eye on what basic research labs are working on, even in universities. As publications tend to come as late signals of such activities, many companies choose to have their own researchers participate in scientific communities they want to follow, in order to be informed in real time about new findings. This often means contributing to the scientific production process, attending major conferences, etc. In other instances, sources of relevant information on trends and new ideas are mostly technical partners, engineering contractors, suppliers, competitors or clients. In most cases, the dynamics of innovation indeed follow a trajectory within the existing dominant paradigm, where existing players are best positioned to play an active role in the technology improvement process, at least for the mid term.

In a way, this technological intelligence aims at drawing maps of technological territories yet to be explored. Based on what has been learnt from past exploration and building on current dominant technologies and options identified, the aim is to help decision-makers build and share representations of technological options for the future. Visual maps of such options may be drawn as the dual technology tree shown in Figure 3.7 (Durand, 1992). This essentially represents the hierarchies of product design, production process and market concepts which Clark (1985) described.

This mode of representation starts from the generic need in the market, then organizes all technological options (past, i.e. obsolete, present and prospective) as branches in a tree. Each technology is a branch or a path in the tree where (a) design options are drawn horizontally while process options are drawn vertically; and (b) options significantly affecting the competence base of the firm are presented higher up on the tree, while minor variations around the same technological concept are drawn lower down on the tree. Such a representation helps to visualize how product designs and process technologies are interrelated. In addition this map may help track the sequence of options on which the firm and its competitors allocate their resources. Above all, this representation helps convey the message about the vulnerability of the firm, should technology radically evolve, offering a straightforward visualization of the concept of 'competence gap': how far is the current competence base of the firm from what may be needed, should the anticipated changes take place?

Hence, external technology intelligence should be complemented systematically by a close monitoring of the internal competence base. The challenge is indeed to continuously adapt the competence base of the organization to the requirements which technological evolutions impose on the firm. Therefore, to a large extent, this is a process of reaction and adaptation. Yet, the firm also needs to adopt a proactive stance to try to innovate faster than its competitors, for example, by recombining some of its resources and capabilities in new, refreshing ways, possibly calling upon external resources to fully deploy its innovations.

Monitoring the competence base of the firm relates and extends Morin's plea for a management of technological resources (1985). Technologies form only part of the capabilities of an organization.

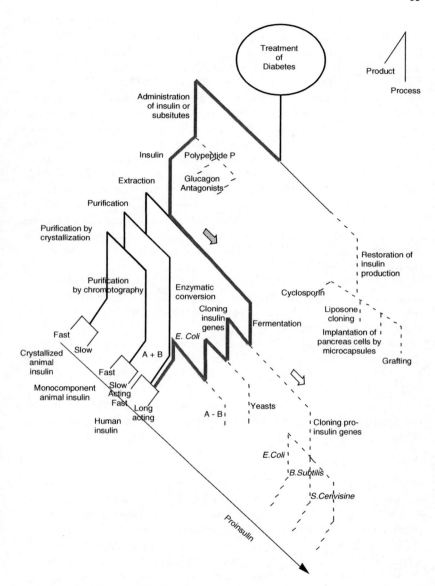

Figure 3.7 Dual technology tree
Source: Durand, 1992: 368

ompetence base of the firm is comprised of individual as well as organizational capabilities. They are partly tacit, i.e. not formally codified and thus difficult to describe and transfer. Competence may be decomposed into three dimensions, (a) knowledge, (b) practice (know-how) and (c) behaviour (know how to behave). The last two dimensions are not easy to grasp in real life, especially those dealing with organizational processes and culture. It may be worth noting that competence may be negative, meaning that they may operate as an obstacle to smooth operations or even hinder attempts to change. One may actually talk about incompetence when a firm just cannot cope with change, e.g. because of routines so deeply rooted in the organization and the culture that became part of the identity of the firm. Durand (1996) gives the example of public utilities having a monopolistic position on their home market, inherited from the past, having a hard time to adapt to the new regulations. Another example may be found in central and eastern European countries finding it difficult to adapt to market economy. This leads to the idea that the most difficult part in learning may actually be unlearning. Technological revolutions are a threat to established firms as long as change is not anticipated and seen as disruptive. On the contrary, firms that are ready to go for the change may benefit from it. For them, change is an opportunity.

The monitoring of the competence base of the organization thus means to be aware of what the firm can achieve, based on its set of competence (and incompetence) and its relations to clients, suppliers and partners.

All in all, the objective of this dual intelligence activity, internally and externally, is the first step towards a systematic strategic thinking process about technology and innovation. It is the starting point for action.

Organizing for innovation

Large organizations have a natural tendency to generate internal mechanisms that oppose innovation. A major challenge for management is thus to fight against these mechanisms which favour operations, i.e. efficiency in the current activities, at the expense of creativity, idea generation and launching innovative projects. Innovation is indeed first seen as a disruption that disturbs the operations of the existing activities. These have been designed and organized to last. Rational decision-making and operational pressures in the large organization rely on many reporting and control layers. This, quite naturally, tends to favour the amortization of the heavy investments made in the existing activities. Venturing into risky and potentially costly projects are thus not a priority.

In this sense, organization and innovation are two opposite sides of managerial concerns. Firms and, more generally, all organizations need to both operate and evolve.

Thus the wording 'organizing for innovation' may at first sound as an oxymoron. Yet, this is a major challenge for management.

A first step is to organize project management and possibly adopt concurrent engineering methodologies to save time and cost, while permitting more flexibility and adaptability in the projects.

A second step is to make sure that top management accepts the promotion of a dual set of objectives for the organization, namely efficient operations to generate the expected level of financial performance but also a capacity to evolve through innovation, thus promoting an atmosphere of openness for those who come out with new ideas, even if these are disturbing.

A third step is to engineer organizational processes which facilitate discussion and exchange of ideas across functional silos. This also requires listening to others, being curious and respectful for what they have to propose. It also means making sure that for every suggestion made, a feed back response will be issued, even if the idea is turned down. It is particularly important to explain why the idea is rejected, using a supportive mode so that proponents will feel like formulating other proposals in the future. Most failures in setting up processes to collect ideas and suggestions from individuals in organizations have been attributed to lack of explicit responses to proponents.

Promoting innovation in a firm often requires working on the prevalent organizational culture. The objective is to embed, deep in the collective identity, the value of innovators as triggers of future performance, but also trust, solidarity, enthusiasm, openness which are key ingredients of innovation. Cultural change is difficult to manage. The outcome is not necessarily in line with what was intended. Yet, in many cases, there is no other way. This is especially relevant when socio-organizational habits are so deeply rooted in the heart of the identity that any other attempt would be vain.

Organizing for innovation also means recognizing the relevance of what Mintzberg calls emerging strategies, i.e. strategies which appear along the way as trajectories unfold, outside of the strategic plan as it was designed *ex ante*. This requires calling upon the creativity and intelligence of everyone in the organization to 'invent the future of the industry' as Hamel and Prahalad (1995) suggest. The future is not written somewhere, waiting to be uncovered. A deterministic view would be misleading. The future is to be invented and constructed. It will shape up as a result of the interactions of many players, each with their own agenda and strategy. It is thus up to every single player to influence the game, using their creativity and market power.

All in all, there are many ways to go about promoting innovation, cultural change to re-open dialogue between members of the organization who lost contact and trust in each other, proactive attitudes to support new ideas, good practices in project management, etc.

Yet, one should stay away from overdoing it, as too much investment in innovation may be counterproductive. The firm needs to strike a balance between its innovative activities and the everyday performance of its operations. In other words, innovation is not an objective *per se* but a means to an end, competitiveness and performance.

Gaining access to technologies and competence

The third set of recommendations, which emerges from this analysis, has to do with accessing technologies and competence.

Technology foresight exercises show how difficult it is to predict what future technologies may look like. Future dominant technologies are not easy to identify and again there is no determinism, as history of industry clearly showed that technology usually unfolds in its own unpredictable ways. It is however possible to describe in general terms the main families of technologies that may be considered as options for tomorrow. As a corollary, it is possible to describe the types of resources and capabilities that would be needed, should a technological option disrupt competition and become dominant. Recognizing that the future is not predictable does not mean that a passive stance is acceptable. Quite the contrary in fact. A prospective attitude implies scanning for potential options for the future and anticipating the types of requirements such changes would impose on the firm. This is a 'just-in-case' attitude which is at the core of managerial action when it comes to technology and innovation.

Figure 3.7 illustrated a technology map which attempts to represent technological options identifiable at present. Behind each branch, one may try to analyse the type of competence required: (1) new pieces of equipment; (2) patents; (3) complementary assets such as distribution channels, possibly requiring to enter a partnership; and (4) new organizational process which may be difficult to design and implement, especially if part of the required know-how is tacit. As an example of this last category, total quality is much documented in the management literature. Yet it is difficult to implement in practice as this requires setting up a complex set of routines in the organization. Deciding to go for it is one thing, achieving long-term performance in stabilizing smooth operations within specified target norms is much more difficult.

There exists a wide array of ways to access technology and more generally capabilities. This was illustrated above, in Figure 3.4. The most relevant ways to gain access to technology and competence vary according to the context and need. But in any case, the challenge for the firm remains the preparedness to tap and deploy the resources and capabilities which may eventually be needed. Technology and competence may be held directly inside the firm or indirectly through external partners, which in a way, extend the capabilities of the organization. This may even lead to the so-called virtual enterprise which externalizes most of the activities, except what is regarded as essential (designing the offerings or marketing, etc.).

Durand *et al.* (1995) present a tool to systematically scan the existing competence base of the firm compared to the portfolio of competence which may be needed tomorrow, given the families of innovations which are anticipated. This is shown in Figure 3.8. They use the example of interactive digital TV to suggest the most relevant ways for each category of players to access competence and conduct a strategic analysis within and around the industry.

Anticipating and preparing for a variety of possible future outcomes (and not only to the scenario which may appear most probable at present) requires adopting the pro-active, open and flexible stance recommended by Godet (1992). This means buying 'insurance policies', that is accessing the capabilities which may be needed tomorrow, or at least being prepared to do so.

This is the third set of recommendations for action, which may be formulated to help managers take the firm towards what Ackoff (1970) called the 'desirable future'.

Future trends and conclusion

Despite the richness of what has already been learnt, the management of technology and innovation still needs to consolidate itself as a sub-field of its own in management.

The theme of technology strategies emerged in the 80s but was gradually taken over by the competence based perspective. Nevertheless, the core issues remain very similar, namely identify and access technologies and competence relevant for tomorrow, as a way to build long lasting, sustainable competitive advantages. The major challenge for future years remains the issue of operationalization of the concept of

Element of competence	Professional Equipement Manufacturers	Operators	Content Providers	TV / Terminal Manufacturers	Software Companies
R&D, Design, Industrialization • R&D expertise • R&D linkages to other functions • Technological scouting • Project management	Strong gap. New technologies	Small gap. Technology is familiar	Very strong gap. Technological revolution	Strong gap. New technologies	No or small gap. Interactive and digital technologies are familiar
Purchasing, Supply • Linkages to suppliers • New suppliers • New components / materials • Subcontracting • Specifications, quality control	Very strong. Vulnerability / Dependence to suppliers of the new technologies	Low. Basically same suppliers	Strong. New subcontractors and suppliers	Very strong. Dependence to suppliers of the new technologies	Low. Same players
Manufacturing • Plants / lines operations • Production management • Logistics • Inventories • Work design • Process control	Strong. New products	Average. New range of services offered	Strong. New format of contents / new production modes	Very strong. New products based on new technologies	Low. Same activities and processes
Marketing, Distribution, Sales • Distribution channels • After sales services • Clients relationship • Market knowledge • Information on competitors • Communication • Firm's image, brand names	Low. Same clients plus some new clients	Low. Same clients and same distribution channels	Very strong. New entrants. New customer behaviour New interaction content / "pipelines"	Low. Same clients and same distribution channels	Average. New clients but strong position with respect to them
General • Interfunctional linkages • Controlling • Human resources management • Organization • Culture	Strong. Very difficult move towards activities of providing services; possible tough.	Low. New organizational structure, routines and culture to deal with multimedia	Very strong. New organization. Ex: managing a bunch of channels instead of one channel	Strong. New technical competence required internally	Low. In line with current business
Overall Assessment	Strong gap	Low gap. Well prepared for the change	Very strong gap. Not prepared for the change. Despite what they think!	Strong gap. Should expect trouble	Low gap. Opportunity to enter the business

Figure 3.8   Operationalizing in competence gap

Source: Durand *et al.,* 1995

core competence. One may thus expect new development around this sensitive and fascinating topic.

The theme of technology and competence also relates to the issue of strategic alliances. Although strategic alliances have been studied over the last 20 years, much remains to be done to better understand the dynamics and outcome of partnerships in time, the role and importance of trust or the mechanisms at work to transfer knowledge and know-how (intentionally or not) across the organizational interfaces between partners.

The theme of the promotion of innovation should remain high in the agenda of both practitioners and managers. But there might be a shift in focus from the downstream phase (how to protect and support the development of innovative projects once ideas have been expressed in the organization) to the more upstream end (what Herstatt and Verworn describe in Chapter 16 of this book as 'the fuzzy front end of innovation'), namely the creativity part when ideas are first generated. There is plenty of work to do along this line, probably calling upon frameworks stemming from social science and typically psycho-sociology to grasp the processes of creation.

A set of topics around the economics of technical change may also experience new developments, e.g. theory of norms and standards, economics of contracts or an economic theory of knowledge, which appears to be an essential new production factor, beyond capital and labour. This last theme is probably one of the most promising, as several implications may follow. Firstly, one may expect to see the emergence of a theoretical reconstruction of the firm, thus enriching and consolidating the competence based perspective as it emerged in management theory. Secondly, this may help standard economic theories better integrate technology and science into the picture (economic theory has always had some difficulties in dealing with science, technology and technical evolution). Thirdly and finally, this type of work may help better understand how regional development takes place in territories, in the form of districts, networks or clusters emerging around a local arrangement of technologies and complementary competencies.

The underlying theme turns out to be the articulation between economics and technology. Following Gilles' work on 'technical systems' (1978), one should expect and hope for new developments in the understanding of how scientific progress and technological change contribute to growth and economic development. Science, technology, innovation and economic development are the corner stones of a conceptual construct still being erected. At the heart of this monument, the firm, the entrepreneur and the manager have each a key role to play, especially on issues related to the management of technology and innovation.

A last comment should be made at this final stage of this overview chapter. One of the major difficulties encountered in implementing the management of technology and innovation in the organization comes from its cross-sectional nature. Technologies and innovations intersect most other dimensions of the firm but have no real constituency, no formal representative who could be naturally in charge of promoting some of the good practices discussed in this book.

Obviously, R&D is often seen as the function in charge of this theme, but one should realize that this is not ideal. As previously discussed, technology and, even more so, innovation go significantly beyond R&D matters (on top, research and development are themselves of a different breed). Some large multinational groups attempted to create technology departments or innovation departments. Most of these attempts did not work. Some have argued that top management should directly deal with managing technology and innovation but this is a bit too techno-centred and unrealistic given the number of other aspects which simultaneously need to be dealt with at the top of organizations. A better way is to try to coordinate such concerns for technology and innovation in all layers of the organization, including the boardroom, helping the firm leverage technology and innovation to build competitive advantages instead of coping with changes imposed from outside.

This specific sub-field of management, called the management of technology and innovation, will not only remain important in the future but should even become more important as our societies invest more heavily in science and knowledge. A specific body of literature emerged over the years, offering the conceptual foundation for the field, making it possible to identify good practices and formulate recommendations for practitioners. In addition, new developments are expected in the field. This book already discusses some of what has been learnt. For more on these matters, stay tuned.

Notes

1. Also see the ISAEP model in Chapter 4.
2. For a detailed discussion of 'technology marketing', see Chapter 11.

References

Abernathy, W. and J. Utterback (1975), 'A Dynamic Model of Process and Product Innovation', *Omega*, 3, 6, pp. 639–56.
Abernathy, W. and J. Utterback (1978), 'Patterns of Industrial Innovation', *Technology Review*, 50.
Ackoff (1970), *Concept of Corporation-Planning*, John Wiley.
Ait el Adj (1989), 'L'entreprise face à la mutation technologique', Editions d'organisation.
Akrich M., M. Callon and B. Latour (1988a), 'A quoi tient le Succès des Innovations? L'Art de l'Intéressement', *Gérer et Comprendre*, 11, June pp. 4–17.
Akrich, M., M. Callon and B. Latour (1988b), 'A quoi tient le Succès des Inno-vations? L'Art de Choisir les bons porte-paroles', *Gérer et Comprendre*, 12, Sept. pp. 14-29.
Allen, T.J (1977), *Managing the Flow of Technology*, Cambridge: MIT Press.

Ansoff, I. (1986), 'Strategic Management of Technology', *The Journal of Business Strategy*.

Barney, J. (1986), 'Strategic Factor Markets: Expectations, Luck and Business Strategy', *Management Science*, 32.

Bellon, B. (1994), 'Innover ou disparaître', *Economica*.

Bidault, F. (1986), 'Le Prix des Techniques: des Principes à la Stratégie', thèse Université de Montpellier I.

Blondel, D. (1990), *L'innovation pour le meilleur et pour le pire*, Hatier.

Broustail, J. and Fréry, F. (1993), *Le management stratégique de l'innovation*, Dalloz.

Burgelman, R. and Sayles, L.H. (1987), *Les Intrapreneurs*, McGraw-Hill.

Burns, T. & Stalker, G.M. (1961), *The Management of Innovation*, London: Tavistock.

Callon, M. (1991), 'La Science telle qu'elle se fait: Anthologie de la sociologie des Sciences de Langue Anglaise', *La Découverte*, 91.

Callon, M., Ph. Laredo and Ph. Mustar (1995), 'La Gestion Stratégique de la Recherche et de la Technologie: l'évaluation des Programmes', *Economica*, 95.

Clark, K.B and Fujimoto (1991), *Product Development Performance*, Harvard Business School Press.

Clark, K.B. (1985), 'The Interaction of Design Hierarchies and Market concepts in Technological Evolution', *Research Policy*, 4.

Cooper, A.C. and D. Schendel (1976), *Strategic Responses to Technological Threats*, Business Horizons.

de Meyer, A. (1992), *Benchmarking Global Manufacturing: Understanding International Suppliers, Customers and Competitors*, Irwin.

Dosi, G. (1982), 'Technological paradigm and technological trajectories', *Research Policy*, 11.

Dougherty, D. (1992), 'A practice-centered model of organizational renewal through product innovation', *Strategic Management Journal*, 13, pp. 77–92.

Doz Y., R. Angelman and C.K. Prahalad (1985), 'Technological Innovation and Interdependence', *Technology in Society*, 7.

Durand, Th. (1988), 'Management pour la Technologie: de la Théorie à la Pratique', *Revue Française de Gestion*, Nov.–Dec.

Durand, Th. (1992), 'Dual Technological Trees: Assessing the Intensity and Strategic Significance of Technological Change', *Research Policy*, July.

Durand Th. (1992), 'Stratégie et Technologie', in *Encyclopédie du Management*, Paris: Vuibert.

Durand, Th. (forthcoming), 'Strategizing Innovation: Competence Analysis in Assessing Strategic Change', in A. Heene and R. Sanchez (eds), *Competence-Based Strategic Management*, John Wiley.

Durand, Th. (2000), 'L'akhimie de la compétence', *Revue Française de Gestion*, Jan.

Durand, Th. and Th. Gonard (1986), 'Stratégies technologiques: le cas de l'insuline', *Revue Française de Gestion*.

Durand, Th. and S. Guerra-Vieira (1997), 'Competence-Based Strategies When Facing Innovation. But What is Competence?', in H. Thomas and D. O'Neal (eds), *Strategic Discovery: Competing in New Arenas*, John Wiley.

Durand, Th. and B. Stymne (1991), 'Technology and Strategy in a Hi-Tech Industry: Reflections on the Past and Future of Two European Telecom Companies', in L.G. Mattsson and B. Stymne (eds), *Corporate and Industry Strategies for Europe*, Elsevier Science Publishers BV.

Durand, Th., A. Weil and L. Mortchev (1995), 'Se préparer aux défis de la TV numérique interactive', *Communications et Stratégies*, No. 19, Sept.

Dussauge, P. and B. Garrette (1995), *Les stratégies d'alliances*, les Editions d'Organisation.

Dussauge, P. and B. Ramanantsoa (1986), *Technologie et stratégie d'entreprise*, McGraw-Hill.

Foray, D. and Ch. Freeman (1992), 'Technologie et richesse des nations', *Economica*.

Freeman, Ch. (1982), *The Economics of Industrial Innovation*, Frances Pinter.

Foster, R. (1986), *Innovation: avantage à l'attaquant*, Interéditions.

Gambardella, A. (1995), *Science and Innovation: the US Pharmaceutical Industry During the 1980's*, Cambridge University Press.

Gilles, B. (1978), 'Histoire des Techniques', *Encyclopédie de la Pléiade*, Gallimard.

Godet, M. (1992), *De l'Anticipation à l'Action: Manuel de Prospective et de Stratégie*, Dunod.

Gonard, Th. and Th. Durand (1994), 'L'Efficacité des Relations Recherche Publique/Industrie: les Stratégies de la Recherche Publique', *Revue d'Economie Industrielle*, No. 69, Sept.

Hamel, G. and C.K. Prahalad (1995), *La Conquête du Futur*, Interéditions.

Hayes, R. and S. Wheelwright (1984), *Restoring Our Competitive Edge: Competing Through Manufacturing*, John Wiley.

Kandel, N., J-P. Remy, Ch. Stein and Th. Durand (1991), 'Who's Who in Technology: Identifying Technological Competence within the Firm', *RandD Management*.

Kanji, G. and M. Asher (1996), *100 Methods for Total Quality Management*, Sage Publications.

Kantrow, A. (1980), 'The Strategy Technology Connection', *Harvard Business Review*.

Kline, S.J. and N. Rosenberg (1986), *An Overview of Innovation: The Positive Sum Strategy*, R. Landay and N. Rosenberg (eds), Academy of Engineering Press, p. 275.

Larue de Tournemine, R. (1991), *Stratégie technologique et processus d'innovation*, Interéditions.

Latour, B. (1996), *La Vie de Laboratoire: la Production des Faits Scientifiques*, La Découverte.

Le Duff, R. and A. Maisseu (1991), *Management Technologique*, Sirey.

Lundvall, B.A. (1988), 'Innovation as an Interactive Process: from User-Producer Interaction to the National System of Innovation', in G. Dosi *et al.* (eds), *Technical Change and Economic Theory*, Frances Pinter.

Maidique, M. (1980), 'Entrepreneurs, Champions and Technological Innovation', *Sloan Management Review*.

Mansfield, E. (1985), 'How Rapidly Does New Industrial Technology Leak Out?' *Journal of Industrial Economics*.

Midler, Ch. (1993), *L'auto qui n'existait pas*, Interéditions.

Morin, J. (1985), *L'excellence technologique*, Publiunion.

Nelson, R. (1993), *National Innovation System: a Comparative Analysis*, Oxford University Press.

Nelson, R. and S. Winter (1982), *An Evolutionary Theory of Economic Change*, Cambridge, Mass.: Harvard University Press.

Niosi, J. (1994), *New Technology Policy and Social Innovations in the Firm*, Frances Pinter.

Nishiguchi, T. (1996) *Managing Product Development*, Oxford University Press.

Nonaka, I. and H. Takeuchi (1995), *How Japanese Companies Create the Dynamics of Innovation in The Knowledge-Creating Company*, Oxford University Press.

Okubo, Y. (1997) *Science et Technologie: le mariage japonais*, Eska.

Penrose, E. (1959), *The Theory of the Growth of the Firm*, Oxford: Blackwell.

Porter, M.E. (1985), *Competitive Advantage*, New York: The Free Press.

Prahalad, C.K. and G. Hamel (1990), 'The Core Competencies of the Corporation', *Harvard Business Review*.

Roberts, E. (1987), *Generating Technological Innovation*, Oxford University Press.

Roberts, E. and A. Frohman (1972), 'Internal Entrepreneurship: Strategy for Growth', *Business Quarterly*.

Sanchez, R. (1996), 'Strategic Product Creation: Managing New Interactions of Technology, Markets, and Organizations', *European Management Journal*, 14, 2, pp. 121–138.

Sanchez, R. (forthcoming), 'Managing Articulated Knowledge in Competence-Based Competition', in R. Sanchez, A. Heene and H. Thomas (eds), *Dynamics of Competence-Based Competition*, London: Elsevier.

Schumpter, J.A. (1943), *Capitalism, Socialism and Democracy*, New York: Harper and Row.

Skinner, W. (1978), *Manufacturing and the Corporate Strategy*, John Wiley.

Teboul, J. (1990), *La dynamique Qualité*, les Editions d'Organisation.

Teece, D.J. (1986), 'Profiting from Technological Innovations: Implications for Integration, Collaboration, Licensing and Public Policy', *Research Policy*, No. 5.

Tushman, M. and Ch. O'Reilly (1997) *Winning Through Innovation*, Harvard Business School Press.

Utterback, J. (1994), *Mastering the Dynamics of Innovation*, Harvard Business School Press.

Van de Ven, A., H.L. Angle and M.S. Poole (1989), *Research on the Management of Innovation, the Minnesota Study*, Harper and Row.

von Hippel, E. (1988), 'The Dominant Role of Users in the Scientific Instrument Innovation Process', *Research Policy*, 5.

Wernerfelt, B. (1984), 'A Resource-Based View of the Firm', *Strategic Management Journal*, 5, pp. 171–80.

Williamson, O.E. (1975), *Markets and Hierarchies: Analysis and Antitrust Implications*, New York: The Free Press.

4

Structuring a Systematic Approach to Technology Management: Processes and Framework

David Probert, Clare Farrukh and Robert Phaal

Overview

The importance of effective integration of technological considerations into business decision-making increases with the gathering pace of technological development. Companies require a technology management system with structure, processes and resources to tackle this challenging problem.

This chapter presents a set of technology management processes and a conceptual framework to assist companies to address these issues in a comprehensive manner.

The contribution these ideas can make to the improvement of technology management systems is shown with two examples drawn from practice.

Introduction: technology and technology management

As the pace and intensity of technological development increases (Abetti, 1994), so does the need for manufacturing (and other) enterprises to adopt systematic ways of incorporating these issues into business decision-making. It is no longer sufficient (if it ever was) to leave technology strategy in the hands of a few expert R&D scientists. The serious implications for corporate survival in a rapidly changing environment require the effective integration of market, financial, political and many other sources of knowledge in addition to science and engineering.

To compete successfully, companies must assess their management of technology strategy and practice, and address how they:

- recognize technological opportunities and threats and convert them into sales and profit.

- exploit existing technology by the effective translation of strategy into operational performance.
- differentiate products using cost-effective technological product and process solutions.
- identify and evaluate alternative and emerging technologies in the light of company policy and strategy and their impact on the business and society.
- reduce the risks inherent in new or unfamiliar technologies.
- harness technology that supports improvement in processes, information and other systems.
- decrease the time to market of new products through effective identification and exploitation of technologies that give competitive advantage; and
- protect and exploit intellectual property.

A comprehensive and well-founded approach to this range of issues requires a clear understanding of the technologies at the firm's disposal, and the coordinated actions of many people inside and outside the firm. These actions are carried out as part of the technology management processes that the firm operates, and together with its resources, form the technology management system.

Various definitions of technology (e.g. Steele, 1989; Whipp, 1991; Floyd, 1997) and technology management (e.g. Roussel *et al.*, 1991; Gaynor, 1996) have been proposed, but for practical application in the context of the technology management system of the firm, the following are particularly useful:

- *Technology* is broadly defined as the 'know-how' of the firm, which emphasizes the applied nature of technological knowledge. While technology is often associated with science and engineering ('hard' technology), the processes which enable its effective application are also important – for example new product and innovation processes, together with organizational structures and supporting communication/knowledge networks ('soft' aspects of technology).
- *Technology management* 'addresses the effective identification, selection, acquisition, development, exploitation and protection of technologies needed to maintain a market position and business performance in accordance with the company's objectives'.[1]

Since the mid-1980s, the subject area of technology management has grown in academic and practitioner interest as a consequence of rapid technological change. Successively, the US, Europe and Japan have instigated major programmes[2] of technology management exploration, development and collaboration between the academic and industrial communities. This expansion has drawn together many fields of academic endeavour; a striking characteristic of application in industry is the multidisciplinary nature of the activity. While on the one hand this is a reflection of the richness, diversity and relevance of the field, on the other it demonstrates a comparative conceptual weakness in terms of the lack of a common theoretical base to which all contributions may be referred.

The consequences of this conceptual weakness may initially appear to be more interesting to the academic community than to the practitioner. However, since technology management is frequently concerned with providing guidance to managers in industry, it is important that proposed problem solving approaches are in harmony rather than in conflict. There is a real risk that solutions based on very different theoretical foundations (or none at all!) could have a damaging effect on business operations if implemented simultaneously. The management of change and improvement in complex technology-based enterprise is usually carried out by means of business processes, which engage people and other resources in specific activities. It is thus necessary to have a clear view of what these processes are, and in particular how technology management processes may be executed.

A valuable aid to understanding relationships between the various issues involved in this or any other complex field, is the development of a diagrammatic framework to illustrate their linkage. Miles and Huberman (1984) define a framework as a conceptual representation of reality. A framework explains graphically, or in narrative form, the main dimensions of the subject area, i.e. the key factors or variables and the presumed relationship between them. A conceptual framework for technology management should incorporate key technology management issues, linking theory and practice. Such a framework is described below, and should also support the establishment of on-going technology management activities in a company, in the form of a technology management system.

It is important at the outset to define the purpose of this work, and hence the context of the processes and framework presented. The aim is to provide practical guidance to managers in (manufacturing) industry, to enable them to integrate technological considerations better into their decision-making. Given the complex multidimensional nature of the problem, it is helpful to take a systems-based view of the issues (Checkland, 1981). This involves understanding the boundaries,

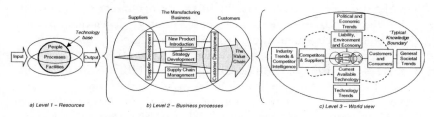

Figure 4.1   Cambridge Manufacturing Leaders Programme audit model
Source: Hillier, 2001: 2–4

elements, processes, resources and properties of the system under consideration. The meaning of these terms will be explored later in the chapter, and will provide guidance on the nature of the technology management processes and framework.

Business and technology management processes

Analysis of the key business processes of the enterprise has been found to be useful in improving business performance. It also provides a route to a better common understanding of how a business operates, and the role of the various parts of the organization. A technology management system needs to integrate well with the overall business system if it is to be effective; a model of how the business operates is a useful starting point to support this goal. A good example is the business model developed for use in the University of Cambridge's Manufacturing Leaders Programme (MLP), and which forms the basis of a company audit (Hillier, 2001). The manufacturing business is considered as the full cycle of activities from understanding markets through product and process design to operations and distribution, taking into account economic and human issues. The MLP model is built up in three stages (or levels), as shown in Figure 4.1.

- *Level 1:* a simple resource-based process view, where resources are identified as comprising people and facilities, which are combined with operational processes to transform inputs into required outputs. The technology base of the firm can be considered to be a sub-set of these resources and processes.
- *Level 2:* expansion of the model to the firm level, defining the manufacturing business, in the context of the value chain that

links suppliers to customers, highlighting a number of important business processes. These processes are strategy development, supply chain management and new product introduction, supplemented by supplier and customer development processes.

- *Level 3:* expansion of the model to include the business environment in which the firm operates: industry sectors, competitors and suppliers, currently available technology, customers and consumers, and liability, environment and economy. The broader trends that govern the evolution of this business environment are included in the model (i.e. industry trends, technology trends, general societal trends, and political and economic trends).

The key business processes are identified at level 2. They are typical of other representations and can be supplemented by many other supporting processes, for example order acquisition, materials procurement, material conversion, etc. The three top-level processes that need to be represented in a technology management framework are (Probert *et al.*, 2001):

- *Strategy formulation:* the process for developing the overall strategy of the organization, ensuring that it survives and fulfils its objectives in a changing world.
- *Innovation:* the process for ensuring a flow of new product and process ideas, supporting the continuity of the business.
- *Operations:* the process for running the business on a day-to-day basis, ensuring the supply of current products to customers.

In addition to representing these three key business processes in a technology management framework, it will be useful to separately identify the technology management processes that relate to the definition given above. The activities encompassed in this definition have been identified by means of a five-process model of technology management (Gregory, 1995), shown in Figure 4.2:

- *Identification* of technologies that are not currently part of the firm's technology base, but may be important in the future (e.g. by attending conferences, reading journals, visiting trade fairs, questioning suppliers, conducting pure research, etc.). In many organizations, technology identification is undertaken on an ad hoc basis, based on informal networks and unstructured activities. In addition to making this more systematic, the challenge is to develop appropriate systems to collate and analyse the data collected, and to disseminate it effectively throughout the organization.

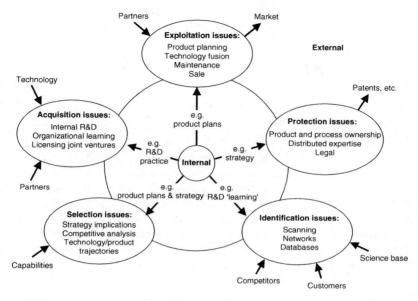

Figure 4.2 ISAEP technology management process model
Source: Gregory, 1995: 350[3]

- *Selection* of those technologies that the firm needs for its future products and technologies (e.g. by using portfolio-type methods, expert judgement, pilot studies, financial methods, etc.). This is a decision-making process, which depends on an understanding of the technology requirements of the organization, together with the characteristics of identified technologies and any constraints which may affect the selection process. Establishment of the decision criteria is a critical step.
- *Acquisition* of the technologies that have been selected (e.g. by R&D, licensing, purchase of equipment, hiring of staff, acquisition of firms, etc.). An important aspect of this process is the assimilation of the new technology into the organization, as weakness in this area can greatly reduce the value of the technology to the firm.
- *Exploitation* of the technologies that have been acquired (e.g. by incorporating into products and services, licensing, etc.). Many options exist for technology exploitation, which vary with the life cycle of the technology. For example, a very new (emerging) technology that is of critical importance to the future of the business, may require considerable support from specialists in order to make it operational.

On the other hand, a mature technology may be passed on to suppliers operating at a lower level of technical competence, and still yield valuable returns.

- *Protection* of the technological assets of the firm (e.g. by legal means such as patenting, contracts, trademarks, copyright, together with security measures, retention of key staff, etc.). Again, choice of protection method is an important step in the process.

These five processes have been used as the basis of an audit technique to assess the actual range of activities undertaken within a manufacturing business (Farrukh *et al.*, 2000; Probert *et al.*, 2000; Phaal *et al.*, 2001a), and to identify areas for improvement. One of the key findings of this work has been the need to relate these apparently straightforward processes to the day-to-day activities of individuals in the firm. In many cases, technology management activities are integrated into the more conventionally recognized business processes (strategy formulation, innovation or new product development, and operations), and it is not a trivial task to ensure that a comprehensive set of technology management processes is in place, and operating effectively at all levels of the business.

There are many other views that can be taken of the technology management activity in the firm. A frequently used representation is the technology strategy formulation process, showing how this relates to business strategy (Stacey and Ashton, 1990; Floyd, 1997), although the presentation can take many forms. See also, Chapter 5, 'Technology in Strategy and Planning' for a further review of these processes. Such models may provide a good guide to developing a technology strategy, however, they frequently do not address the ongoing technology management processes in the firm. The issues of integrating technology management into operations are just as important if good business results are to be achieved.

A comprehensive set of technology management processes will cover such activities as technology foresight and scanning, technology and R&D project selection, new product development and introduction, technology insertion and transfer. Firms give a variety of names to these activities, but the five-process model has been found to provide a generic and encompassing definition of the range of activities. However, there is a difficulty in showing how these processes link into the other key business processes of the firm; as presented they appear to 'float' in space, with no tangible connection to other representations or business models. The proposed technology management framework described below seeks to provide that linkage.

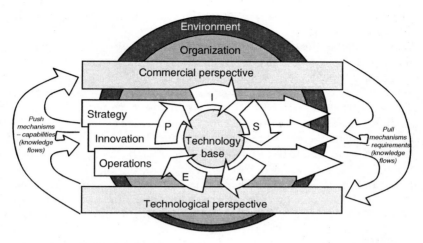

Figure 4.3 Technology management framework
Source: Phaal *et al.*, 2001b

A framework for technology management

The framework for technology management, shown in Figure 4.3 (Probert *et al.*, 2001; Phaal *et al.*, 2001b), is the result of extensive research and accumulated experience in the development of practical approaches to dealing with technology management issues. This includes the assessment of technology management processes (Farrukh *et al.*, 2000; Probert *et al.*, 2000; Phaal *et al.*, 2001a), audit of new product introduction processes (Gardiner *et al.*, 1998), decision support for make or buy issues (Probert, 1997; Canez *et al.*, 2001), and technology roadmapping (Phaal *et al.*, 2001c). It was particularly in this last area, which deals with the linkage between technology resources and business planning, that the need for, and the shape of, the framework emerged.

The overall aim of the framework is to support understanding of how technological and commercial knowledge combine to support the strategy, innovation and operational processes in the firm, in the context of both the internal and external environment. Note that this is a high-level framework that supports broad understanding of key aspects of technology management. The many particular activities and aims that are associated with technology management practice in firms (e.g. technology strategy, foresight, transfer, selection, R&D management, make vs. buy, etc.) depend on the particular context and objectives. Detailed frameworks have been developed to support decision-making and action in some of these more specific areas (for example, Canez *et al.*, 2001; Shehabuddeen, 2001).

At the heart of the framework is the technology base of the firm, which represents the technological knowledge, competences and capabilities that support the development and delivery of competitive products and services. The five technology management processes (ISAEP) operate on this technology base, in both its generation and exploitation.

These processes do not operate in isolation, and are generally not managed as separate 'core' processes. The various activities that constitute these processes tend to be distributed within other business processes (for instance, technology selection decisions are made during strategy formulation and the new product development or innovation). The framework depicts the three core business processes, strategy, innovation and operations (SIO), acting at different levels in the firm, and drawing on the activities embedded within the ISAEP processes.

The framework emphasises the dynamic nature of the knowledge flows that must occur between the commercial and technological functions in the firm, linking to the strategy, innovation and operational processes, if technology management is to be effective. An appropriate balance must be struck between market 'pull' (i.e. requirements), and technology 'push' (i.e. capabilities). Various mechanisms can support the linkage of the commercial and technical perspectives, including traditional communication channels (e.g. discussions, email, etc.), cross-functional teams/meetings, management tools, business processes, staff transfers, training, etc.

The specific technology management issues faced by firms depend on the context (both internal and external), in terms of organizational structure, systems, infrastructure, culture, and the particular business environment and challenges confronting the firm, which change over time. In this regard, contingency theory (Jackson, 2000) is very relevant.

Time is a key dimension in technology management, in terms of synchronizing technological developments and capabilities with business requirements, in the context of evolving markets, products and technology. Although time is not explicitly depicted in the framework, it is implicit in the SIO business and ISAEP technology management processes.

Practical application of framework

Critical characteristics of a good management framework include a clear definition of the system boundaries and the purpose to which it refers, together with a sound basis in both industrial practice and academic theory. A framework provides a conceptual picture of a complex system, and is balanced between representing the static aspects of the system (its structure and elements), and the dynamic nature of the system (aspects of interaction and causality).

The theoretical nature of management frameworks has been explored elsewhere (Probert *et al.*, 2000; Shehabudeen *et al.*, 2000), and the focus here is on illustrating the practical application of the key principles or themes contained within the framework:

(a) The importance of technological assets to sustained business performance.
(b) The role of technology management processes (ISAEP) to support the generation and exploitation of these technological assets.
(c) The need to link the technology management processes to the 'core' business processes of strategy, innovation and operations.
(d) The importance of communication between the commercial and technological functions in the firm, to establish an appropriate balance between market 'pull' and technology 'push'.
(e) The dependence of technology management on the internal and external context, in terms of business purpose, market environment, technology type, corporate culture, etc.
(f) The need to synchronize efforts across the company on a time basis.

Two practical examples of technology management systems that reflect these principles are described below, based on project work with collaborating companies.

Lucas Industries

The purpose of this project was to develop a common approach to technology management across the three main business divisions of Lucas – Aerospace, Automotive and Applied Technology (Probert *et al.*, 1999). This was a requirement from the senior management of the company, in particular the Chief Technology Officer. The system that was developed, as shown in Figure 4.4, focused on integrating technology considerations into the annual business planning cycle.

In terms of the principles contained within the technology management framework (Figure 4.3), the following observations are made:

(a) The technology base of the firm is shown explicitly in the model.
(b) The identification, selection, acquisition and exploitation technology management processes are highlighted in the model, showing

how they relate to the activities and methods in the Lucas model. However, the mechanisms for supporting exploitation are not shown explicitly, and protection is not shown at all.

(c) The model focuses on the integration of technological considerations into business planning (and hence strategy), with strong links to innovation in terms of product plans (PP), technology roadmaps (TRM) and R&D projects. The model can be used for supporting the management of technology for operations (i.e. manufacturing, project management, logistics, facilities management, etc.), as well as product development.

(d) The model includes both commercial and technological perspectives, with the mechanisms for supporting communication between these functions built into the process, activities and methods.

(e) The internal and external context of technology management is reflected in the particular activities and methods in the model (which were specific to Lucas), together with consideration of external markets, competitors and technologies.

(f) Time is not included explicitly in the model, but is inherent in the business planning cycle that drives the process, together with the need for forecasting future market and technology trends.

Thus, most of the principles contained in the framework are clearly embedded in the Lucas technology management system. In addition,

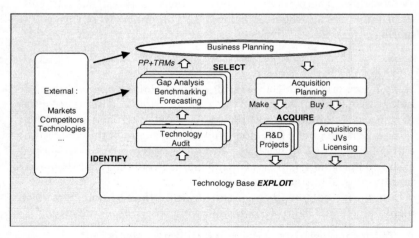

Figure 4.4   Lucas technology management system
Source: Probert *et al.*, 1999

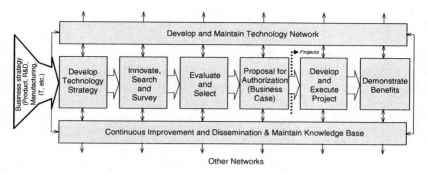

Figure 4.5   Glaxo Wellcome technology management system diagram
Source: Farrukh *et al.*, forthcoming

the framework prompts some areas that could be further developed or at least made more explicit. In practice it is not possible to show such full detail on one diagram, with the Lucas model representing a high-level view of how technology management operates in the company. Implementation of the model in practice requires more detailed procedures and guidance, which may vary to some extent in different parts of the firm, depending on the context.

Glaxo Wellcome

In 2000, prior to the merger with SmithKline Beecham, Glaxo Wellcome had already developed a corporate-wide approach to new product development, but required a supporting technology management system, which would be transparent across all business units throughout the world. The system shown in Figure 4.5 was the result of an international project team drawn from across the business, collaborating to develop a commonly accepted system. It makes a particular feature of the role of a network of technologists from around the business, and it would not be an overstatement to say that the whole system operation is dependent on this network.

In terms of the principles contained within the technology management framework (Figure 4.3), the following observations are made:

(a) The technology base is embedded within the technology network, forming part of the knowledge base of the firm.
(b) Technology management processes form an important part of the system, in terms of identification ('innovate, search and

survey'), selection ('evaluate and select'), acquisition and exploitation ('develop and execute project' and 'demonstrate benefits'). Again, the protection of technological assets is not explicitly shown in the model, although maintenance of the knowledge base implies some consideration of this.

(c) The business processes of strategy and innovation lie at the heart of the model, while the link to operations is perhaps less clear. Corporate strategy guides the development of technology strategy, which in turn guides the innovation process, and the development and execution of projects. The system is designed to support the management of manufacturing process technology, as well as product development. Manufacturing and projects can both be considered as operational aspects of the business.

(d) Communication is an important aspect of the model, which is strongly linked to the information and knowledge management systems that are required to support effective technology management, encompassing both commercial and technological perspectives.

(e) The internal context of technology management is reflected in the particular systems, activities and methods in the model (which were specific to Glaxo Wellcome). A number of the elements in the model relate to the external context, including strategy development, the 'search and survey' process, the execution projects, and the technology networks.

(f) Again, time is not included explicitly in the model, but is inherent in the business trends and cycles that drive the process.

In summary, it can be seen that the Glaxo Wellcome technology management system model incorporates most of the principles contained in the framework. However, as for the Lucas case, there are limitations as to what can be depicted on one diagram, and the detailed mechanisms for implementing the model tend to be included in other lower-level procedures and methods, which can vary to some extent, depending on the local context.

Conclusions

The technology management framework presented in this chapter aims to support understanding of how technological and commercial knowledge combine to support the strategy, innovation and operational processes in the firm, in the context of both the internal and external environment. The framework represents a conceptual model for guiding the development of effective and integrated technology management systems in industry, together with providing a bridge to the theoretical foundations that underpin good management practice.

The framework highlights a number of key principles of technology management, including:

- The role of technological resources in sustaining the competitive position of the firm.
- How the technology management processes of identification, selection, acquisition, exploitation and protection act on the technology base to ensure that this important resource is sustained appropriately.
- The need to integrate technology management considerations with other systems in the organization, and in particular the business processes of strategy, innovation and operations.
- The importance of developing effective mechanisms for bringing together the commercial and technological perspectives within the firm.
- The context-sensitive nature of technology management, where the most appropriate solution depends on the particular business aims, market environment, company size, corporate culture, etc.
- The importance of synchronizing the various commercial and technological activities needed for business success, on a time basis.

The practical application of these principles has been illustrated by means of two industrial examples of technology management systems. The high-level conceptual framework emphasizes the principles inherent in good technology management practice, but the specific application of these principles requires customisation in order to integrate technology management activities with existing company systems, processes and methods.

Notes

1. This is the definition for technology management agreed by theEuropean Institute for Technology and Innovation Management (EITIM).
2. Increasing awareness of technology management has been signalled in the US (1987) by the National Academy of Science's *'Management of Technology: The Hidden Competitive Advantage'*, in the UK by the White Paper (1993) 'Realising our potential: a strategy for science, engineering and technology', and in Japan new legislation (1999) is encouraging academics to work more closely with industry.
3. This material has been reproduced by permission of the council of the institution of Mechanical Engineers.

References

Abetti, P.A. (1994), 'Impact of technology on functional roles and strategies: illustrative cases in the USA, Japan and France, and lessons learnt', *International Journal of Technology Management*, 9(5/6/7), pp. 529–46.

Canez, L., K.W. Platts and D.R. Probert (2001), *Industrial Make or Buy Decisions*, Institute for Manufacturing, University of Cambridge.

Checkland, P.B. (1981), *Systems Thinking, Systems Practice*, Chichester: John Wiley.

Farrukh, C.J.P., R. Phaal and D.R. Probert (2000), *Technology Management Assessment Procedure – a Guide for Supporting Technology Management in Business*, London: The Institute of Electrical Engineers.

Farrukh, C.J.P., R. Phaal, D.R. Probert, P.V. Fraser, D. Tainsh and D. Hadjidakis (forthcoming), 'Developing an integrated technology management process at Glaxo Wellcome', *Research Technology Management*.

Floyd, C. (1997), *Managing Technology for Corporate Success*, Aldershot: Gower.

Gardiner, G., T. Ridgeman and C. Gilmour (1998), *Speeding New Products to Market – a Practical Workbook for Achieving More Successful New Product Development and Introduction*, Institute for Manufacturing, University of Cambridge.

Gaynor, G.H. (ed.) (1996), *Handbook of Technology Management*, New York: McGraw-Hill.

Gregory, M.J. (1995), 'Technology management – a process approach', Proceedings of the Institution of Mechanical Engineers, Part B, issue B5, pp. 347–56.

HMSO (1993), 'Realising our Potential', UK Government White Paper.

Hillier, W. (2001), *The Manufacturing Business Audit*, Manufacturing Leaders Programme, University of Cambridge.

Jackson, M.C. (2000), *Systems Approaches to Management*, New York: Kluwer Academic/Plenum Publishers.

Miles, M.B. and A.M. Huberman (1984), *Qualitative Data Analysis: an Expanded Source Book*, 2nd edn, Sage Publications, p. 18.

Phaal, R., C.J.P. Farrukh and D.R. Probert (2001a), 'Technology management process assessment: a case study', *International Journal of Operations & Production Management*, 21(8), pp. 1116–32.

Phaal, R., C.J.P. Farrukh and D.R. Probert (2001b), 'A framework for supporting the management of technological innovation', Proceedings of the Eindhoven Centre for Innovation Studies (ECIS) conference, The Future of Innovation Studies, Eindhoven, 20–23 September.

Phaal, R., C.J.P. Farrukh and D.R. Probert (2001c), *T-Plan: Fast-start Technology Roadmapping – a Practical Guide for Supporting Technology and Product Planning*, Institute for Manufacturing, University of Cambridge.

Probert, D.R. (1997), *Developing a Make or Buy Strategy for Manufacturing Business*, The Institution of Electrical Engineers, London.

Probert, D.R., C.J. Paterson, N. Robinson and M.J. Gregory (1999), 'Linking technology into business planning: theory and practice', *International Journal of Technology Management*, 18(1/2), pp. 11–30.

Probert, D.R., R. Phaal and C.J.P. Farrukh (2000), 'Development of a structured approach to assessing technology management practice', Proceedings of the Institution of Mechanical Engineers, 214, Part B, pp. 313–21.

Probert, D.R., R. Phaal and C.J.P. Farrukh (2001), 'Structuring a systematic approach to technology management: concepts and practice', Proceedings of the 10th International Conference on Management of Technology (IAMOT), 19–22nd March, Lausanne.

Roussel, P.A., K.N. Saad and T.J. Erickson (1991), *Third Generation R&D – Managing the Link to Corporate Strategy*, Boston: Harvard Business School Press.

Shehabuddeen, N. (2001), 'Developing a comprehensive technology selection framework for practical application', PhD thesis, University of Cambridge.

Shehabuddeen, N., D.R. Probert, R. Phaal and K. Platts (2000), 'Management representations and approaches: exploring issues surrounding frameworks', Working Paper, British Academy of Management (BAM 2000): Managing Across Boundaries, 13–15 September, Edinburgh.

Stacey, G.S. and Ashton, W.B. (1990), 'A structured approach to corporate technology strategy', *International Journal of Technology Management*, 5(4), pp. 389–407.

Steele, L.W. (1989), *Managing Technology – the Strategic View*, New York: McGraw-Hill.

Whipp, R. (1991), 'Managing technological changes: opportunities and pitfalls', *International Journal of Vehicle Design*, 12(5/6), pp. 469–77.

Part II

Strategy: Using Technology and Innovation Strategically

Executive Summary
Thomas Durand

Part II of the book is devoted to strategy, using technology and innovation as a competitive weapon, in search of economic performance and value creation.

If strategy is about allocating scarce resources to build sustainable competitive advantages, then technology as a key resource should be part of the strategic business planning process. Similarly, innovation as a key process should be integrated into the formulation and implementation of strategy. Tools and methodologies are available to help firms leverage technology and innovation as a way to increase their overall strategic and economic performance.

Chapter 5 shows how technology should be taken into account at each and every step of the strategic planning process. The effective integration of technological considerations into business strategy is increasingly essential in most industries. Technology strategy should not be developed independently from the business strategy. Instead, technology resources should be considered as an integral part of strategic business planning. Analytical tools useful for strategic analysis and strategy formulation are discussed, illustrating how to take technology into the thinking process, thus delivering greater economic value.

Chapter 6 adds innovation into the picture. It discusses how firms may choose to react when faced with change. In an industry, change is both an opportunity for potential new entrants and a threat for incumbents. Companies should analyse whether and to what extent the firm's competence base fits the competence required by the innovation, and how capable the firm is to influence the change. On that basis, four strategies are considered, illustrated and discussed: trigger, shape, stretch or redeploy. When facing change, in their search for economic performance, firms may choose from this set of strategies: if fitted or almost fitted to the change requirements, the firm should trigger the change or at least stretch itself to adapt to the change, including by means of alliances or acquisitions. If capable of influencing the change, the firm may have to try to shape the change according to its own interest and if this cannot be done, the firm is left with the option of diversifying away from the change, leveraging both its existing technology base and its existing market linkages to re-deploy into new activities.

Chapter 7 shows how the firm may construct its own trajectory, leveraging its competence base or building new technological capabilities to address existing or new markets. It is a matter of choosing to pivot around either technology or market linkages. The strategy of the firm may thus be viewed as a quest for an optimum trajectory through time, a sequence of building and leveraging technology capabilities and market access. The chapter shows that the most successful firms are those which best manage their technology diversification, optimizing their R&D expenses across businesses. In other words, the tricky game of business strategy is about constructing the future of the firm, combining two sets of capabilities (technology and market access, not just market) through two complementary activities (leveraging and building, not just leveraging). This is the way of designing and building a unique trajectory for the firm. This is about building new business models for economic performance.

In turn, all of this makes it necessary to survey, protect and nurture the technological base of the firm, also made possible by the conduct of R&D activities, acquiring and selling technologies or entering alliances (Part III). It also requires fostering the ability of the organization to leverage technology through innovation (Part IV).

Ten key questions for the Board

1. Is there a need in our firm or business unit to convince top managers and board members about the importance of technology and innovation in increasing economic performance and value creation?
2. How is technology included in the strategic planning process of our firm or business unit today (internal capabilities and external opportunities and threats)?
3. Is there a strategic plan for R&D? Is it discussed in a strategic context with business line managers and top decision-makers?
4. Are the linkages between technology, product and market development plans clear and communicated throughout the organization?
5. Is there a comprehensive and integrated set of frameworks, processes, tools and techniques to support technology strategy and planning?

6. Is there an owner of the innovation process?
7. Have we carefully listed all the innovations which could potentially affect our business in the next 5 (or so) years? Have we identified which innovation would be beneficial to our firm? What about the innovations which would be detrimental? Have we defined inexpensive, reasonable steps which we could take today to either promote or prevent the desirable or undesirable change?
8. Have we carefully identified and listed the core competence of our firm (business unit)? Both technological competence and market linkages? Have we run creativity sessions to try to conceive other ways of leveraging these existing competencies in totally new ways?
9. On what economic grounds do we make the trade-off between business diversification and business specialization? How do we know that we are not specializing ourselves to death?
10. How do we monitor the right time for adopting new technologies and discarding obsolete ones?

5
Technology in Strategy and Planning

Robert Phaal, Clare Farrukh and David Probert

Overview

Including technological considerations in business strategy and planning is crucial for many firms if commercial success is to be sustained, driven by the increasing pace, cost and complexity of technology development. It is important to understand how the likely advances in key technologies will impact on the firm, and to agree and communicate the most appropriate response in terms of research investment, acquisitions, intellectual property, etc. This chapter describes the key steps that must be followed for developing an integrated strategic business plan, highlighting the technological issues that must be considered and providing examples of tools and techniques that can support this.

Introduction

The development of effective business strategy is important if the activities and resources in the firm are to be aligned with its vision, mission and goals. This requires a sound understanding of the external market environment, including social, technological, economic, environmental and political trends that are likely to affect the company in the future. The opportunities and threats posed by these trends and drivers need to be assessed in terms of the internal strengths and weaknesses of the firm, so that the strategic options open to the organization can be determined and assessed. Equally important are the processes and systems in place to enable strategy implementation in the firm.

The effective integration of technological considerations into business strategy is a key aspect of business planning. Many companies are increasingly aware of the strategic importance of technology in delivering value and competitive advantage. These issues are becoming more important as the cost, complexity and rate of technology change increase, in an environment of increasing global competition.

A key premise is that a technology strategy should not be developed independently from the business strategy. Instead, technology resources should be considered an integral part of strategic business planning. This concept is illustrated in Figure 5.1, which also sets out key questions a manager must ask when developing an integrated business and technology strategy (Matthews, 1992). The technology strategy itself can then be derived from the business strategy, to aid communication and implementation of the technological aspects of the business strategy.

To answer the questions raised in Figure 5.1 in a coherent way that is of benefit to the business requires a structured business process to follow, comprising a set of clear, integrated steps. An effective strategic planning process should also consider infrastructure needed to support the business, such as information and knowledge management systems, organizational structures, together with the necessary resources, such as capital, equipment, information, knowledge and human resources. The type and scope of the process and supporting systems depend on the particular business context, in terms of the nature of the particular strategic issue under consideration, the aims of the organization, the sector in which it operates and available resources. An effective strategy development and implementation process has the potential benefits of improved business focus, reduced risk and improved effectiveness of

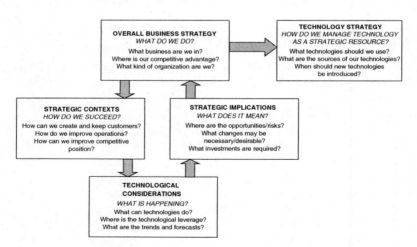

Figure 5.1 Framework for integrating technology into business strategy
Source: Matthews, 1992: 529

resource deployment (synergy and leverage), resulting in competitive advantage and enhanced financial performance.

In addition to the questions raised in Figure 5.1, the following higher-level strategic issues need to be considered (Johnson and Scholes, 1988), all of which may include technological considerations:

- *What basis?* Selection of a generic strategic approach, such as cost leadership, differentiation or focus.
- *Which direction?* Identification and selection of alternative directions, such as taking no action, withdrawal, consolidation, market penetration, product development, market development, integration or diversification.
- *How?* Identification and selection of alternative methods, such as internal development, acquisition or joint development.

Despite the obvious importance of strategy to the long-term success of business, many firms struggle to develop and implement effective strategy. Porter (1996) identifies a number of reasons why strategic thinking is weak in many companies:

- The view that trade-offs are not necessary, resulting in competition in too many areas simultaneously.
- The pursuit of operational effectiveness is seductive because it is concrete and actionable, resulting in the firm being trapped in a 'hyper-competitive' mode, with a focus on operational efficiency.
- Blurring of strategic choices. Customer focus does not mean serving *every* customer need; trade-offs and limits do not necessarily constrain growth.
- Most companies start life with clearly differentiated strategy, which slowly becomes diluted through incremental changes that lack strategic focus.

There are no universal answers to the strategic questions raised above, which depend on the particular situation that a company faces. Each organization must develop processes and systems that suit its needs. The material in this chapter provides a conceptual framework for thinking through the important issues that face companies developing an integrated business and technology strategy, and includes the following topics:

- An overview of the nature of strategy, including the issues and key questions that need to be considered.
- A generic strategy process model (Figure 5.2), together with a range of topics relating to the practical application of each step in the model.

- A selection of tools and techniques for supporting strategy development and implementation in business.

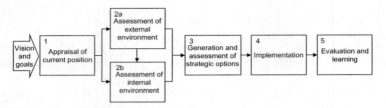

Figure 5.2　Generic strategy process

Generic strategy process model

There are many published process models for business strategy (for example, Hofer and Schendel, 1978; Johnson and Scholes, 1988; Abetti, 1991; Wheelan and Hunger, 1993; Mintzberg, 1994) and technology strategy (for example, Porter, 1985; Stacey and Ashton, 1990; Metz, 1996; Floyd, 1997). Comparison of these models shows that they all have similar characteristics and can be directly related to the generic strategy process model shown in Figure 5.2, defined below, with the main steps discussed in more detail in the following sections.

1. Appraisal of current position	Based on clearly defined vision, goals and objectives, collation and assessment (audit) of information currently available (e.g. company reports, strategy documents, budgets, programmes and projects, etc.), together with a review of the current business model, and historical strategy, activities and performance.
2a. Assessment of external environment	Collection and assessment of information relating to external factors, issues and drivers that influence the area of interest (e.g. market research, competitor benchmarking, technology trends and suppliers, etc.), to identify opportunities and threats.
2b. Assessment of internal environment	Collection and assessment of information relating to internal resources, capabilities (including core competences) and constraints, to identify strengths and weaknesses, in light of the opportunities and threats identified above.

3. Generation and assessment of strategic options	Generation of strategic options open to the organization, in terms of the opportunities, threats, strengths and weakness identified above, identification of gaps in terms of resources or performance, and assessment of the options to derive strategic plans that reflect the potential value and possible risks associated with the options.
4. Implementation	Putting the strategic plan into action, including management of the resulting systems, processes, programmes, projects, activities, etc.
5. Evaluation and learning	Review of outcomes and dissemination of results, linked to organizational learning and knowledge management practices in the firm.

It should be noted that the process described above is fairly linear and 'rational' in nature. In practice, strategic processes are often more complex and iterative, and compromises must often be made when limited available information and resources are taken into account. In addition, as described in 'Step 4: implementation of strategy' below, business strategy depends to a large extent on the historical decisions and activities that have resulted in the current business situation, together with the organizational structures and culture that influence behaviour in the firm. However, it is helpful to begin with a structured and rational view, based on systems and process thinking, while appreciating the dynamic and complex nature of the business environment.

Step 1: appraisal of current position

A sensible starting point for strategy development is an appraisal of the current position. Based on a clear understanding of the vision, mission, goals and objectives, available information needs to be collated and assessed, such as strategy documents, budgets and technical reports. Past activities should also be reviewed, to assess strategic performance and to facilitate learning.

Consideration should be given to the current business model (how does the business operate? how is competitive advantage achieved? what management systems are in place to monitor and control the business?). If strategy is to be effective in terms of sustaining business performance, it is important to understand how value is generated in the firm. Porter (1985) has proposed the concept of the 'value chain', which describes a set of value-adding activities in the firm, performed to develop, produce, market, deliver and support its products and services:

1. Primary activities: inbound logistics; operations; outbound logistics; marketing and sales; service.
2. Support activities: firm infrastructure; human resource management; technology development; procurement.

The concept of the value chain can be a useful aid in the development of strategy. It focuses attention on identification of value-adding activities within the firm, which are technologically and strategically distinct, and exposes activities that do not contribute significantly to value generation.

The activities that lie within the value chain and its supporting systems need to be organized into business and management processes, which enable their effectiveness, coordination and efficiency. Such processes include strategy, innovation, operations and logistics, resource allocation, supply chain and customer management. For technology strategy, the activities and processes for managing the technology base, and how these relate to the other business processes, are of particular importance. The five-process technology management model proposed by Gregory (1995) focuses on *identification, selection, acquisition, exploitation* and *protection* of technology (Figure 5.3), as discussed in Chapter 4.

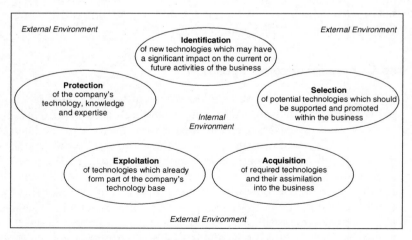

Figure 5.3   Technology management process model
Source: adapted from Gregory, 1995: 350

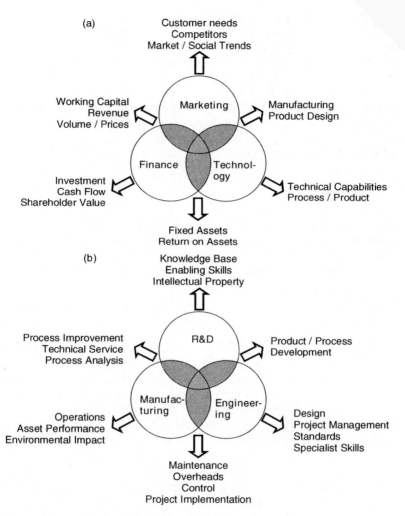

Figure 5.4 (a) Business strategy and (b) technology strategy
Source: EIRMA, 1997: 9

The effective generation and implementation of technology strategy also requires understanding how the business and management processes relate to the different functional perspectives in the firm, with marketing, finance and technology being of particular importance (see Figure 5.4). This represents a particular challenge, as it requires efforts to build and support cross-functional communication, systems and tools.

ent of external environment

opportunities and threats associated with the exter-
nment is an important part of the generic strategy
de social, technological, environmental, economic,
....rastructural trends and drivers ('STEEPI' factors), and how
these are likely to change in the future. The impact of these drivers on the
behaviour of customers, competitors and suppliers should be considered.
The nature of change, and the uncertainty of forecasts and predictions, is
considered below, together with approaches for assessing the competitive
environment.

Change and uncertainty

A key aspect of strategy relates to understanding the nature of the changing business environment, and the uncertainties associated with possible
change in the future. Johnson and Scholes (1988) have identified four
patterns of strategic change:

- continuity (no change);
- incremental (series of small changes);
- flux (no clear direction); and
- global (major change).

The strategic management issues vary depending on the type and scope
of change. Johnson and Scholes consider that strategy typically tends to
be somewhat incremental, with strategic change being a continual process of relatively small adjustments to existing strategy through activity
within the sub-systems of the organization. The strategic direction is
constrained by the 'momentum' of the organization, with incremental
change required to account for strategic 'drift', eventually reaching a
point of crisis where radical change is required.

The uncertainty of a prediction about the future, or the risk associated
with an investment, increase significantly as the time horizon extends.
The nature of the decisions, and the required decision-making process,
varies with time horizon (Figure 5.5):

- The *short-term* time horizon relates to operational decisions, such
  as the number of units to manufacture, and what materials to
  order.
- The *medium-term* time horizon relates to decisions concerning product
  and process development and innovation, such as what products to
  develop, and which markets to penetrate.

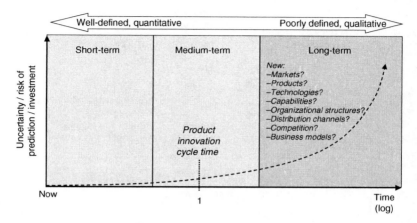

Figure 5.5 Planning framework

- The *long-term* time horizon relates to strategic decisions, such as what technologies to develop, which markets to exploit, which organizational structures and culture to foster, etc. (see Figure 5.1).

Hamel and Prahalad (1994) consider that the future is inherently unpredictable, owing to the complex, non-linear nature of the interactions between the organization and its environment (Stacey, 1996). A key requirement for ensuring that an organization can adapt to the future is by ensuring flexibility through focusing on core business competences (see 'Step 2b: assessment of internal environment' below).

Assessing the competitive environment

The 'competitive forces approach' proposed by Porter (1980) focuses on the actions a firm can take to create defensible positions against competitive forces in the industrial environment. These forces can be characterized in terms of five basic types: entry barriers, threat of substitution, bargaining powers of buyers and suppliers, and rivalry among industry incumbents (competition). These forces define the dynamic business environment in which the firm exists, and the strategic context within which technology strategy must be developed. Market intelligence is crucial, in terms of both customers and competitors, in terms of current activity, capabilities and strategic position.

Anticipating the market and technological trends of the future is an important aspect of the strategy process. The 'S-curve', shown in Figure 5.6, provides a means for understanding how technological

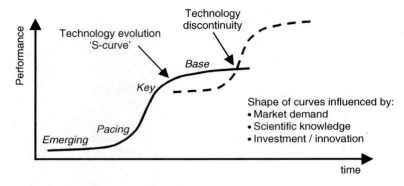

Figure 5.6   The nature of technological evolution

performance evolves over time. The shape of the S-curve depends on a number of factors, including the level of market demand and resulting rate of investment, together with the underlying principles of physics and rate of scientific discovery. Initially, the rate at which the performance of a particular technology increases is fairly slow, typically associated with early R&D in the laboratory. As a technology is proven, and incorporated into products, the level of performance increases rapidly, until the limits of the technology, defined by basic principles of science, are reached. At this point, the pressure for innovation and investment in new technologies rises, and eventually a new technology is likely to be developed as a substitute. See Chapter 3 for a more detailed account of technology change and evolution, together with Chapter 10 for an account of technology intelligence.

Technological change can be categorized in terms of the life cycle position: embryonic, growing, mature and declining, or competitive advantage: key, base, pacing and emerging (Floyd, 1997). There are many well-defined methods for modelling and forecasting technology development on this basis (see, for example, Twiss, 1992). Also of vital importance are possible technological discontinuities, or disruptive technologies, which can fundamentally change the nature of competition (Bower and Christensen, 1995).

One of the most common approaches for incorporating the high levels of uncertainty associated with future business environments into strategy development processes is the 'scenario planning' method. Ringland (1998) defines a scenario as an internally consistent view of what the future might turn out to be – not a forecast, but one possible future outcome. The general approach is to identify the key issues that are both

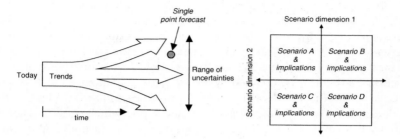

Figure 5.7 Scenario planning
Source: adapted from Ringland, 1998: 47

important and uncertain, which define a set of scenarios (see Figure 5.7). These scenarios are not intended to be accurate predictions, but rather a set of extreme possible futures, which form a useful input to the strategic planning process.

National 'Foresight' initiatives provide a source of information on long-range trends and potential futures (including technology trends and requirements) that are useful as an input to business strategy development. Many countries have initiated such programmes, including the USA, UK, Japan, Singapore, The Netherlands and others. Typically, foresight initiatives are sector-focused, and include participation from industry, government, research agencies, consultants and trade associations. Techniques that are used for supporting these initiatives include scenario planning, Delphi techniques (based on consultation and expert judgement), and technology roadmapping (see 'Step 4: implementation of strategy', below).

Step 2b: assessment of internal environment

The strengths and weaknesses of the organization need to be considered, and assessed with respect to the opportunities and threats posed by the external business environment. Technology can be considered as an important company resource and methods for identifying key technologies and their potential value is an important part of technology strategy development.

Resource-based perspective

Resource-based approaches focus on the competitive advantage obtained by efficient and effective deployment of resources that the firm controls (Wernerfelt, 1984; Grant, 1991; Penrose, 1995). Resources include both tangible and intangible types, such as facilities, land, equipment, patents, knowledge, partnerships and brand. Resource-based approaches are of particular interest in terms of technology strategy, as technology is essentially a type of resource, albeit of a complex knowledge-based kind. This type of approach has its basis in the 1960s, and emphasises that the actions of the firm are dictated by its resource capabilities as much as by market opportunities. More recently, competence-and capabilities-based approaches to firm resources have been developed, which stress that flexibility is a key strategic posture for coping with increasingly rapid and uncertain change (Hamel and Prahalad, 1994; Teece *et al.*, 1997). A key aspect of the resource-based view is that technological and competence resources can be very firm-specific and history-dependent, and are generally not readily transferable or traded. See Part III for a more detailed account of the resource-based perspective.

Technology audit

The technologies that are important to the firm, in terms of current and future revenue streams, must be identified, and their competitive impact assessed. Teece *et al.* (1997) identify the following types of assets (resources): technological, complementary, financial, reputational, structural (formal and informal), institutional, market (structure) and boundaries (which resources to maintain in the firm). Johnson and Scholes (1988) have proposed a method for analysing resources in the strategic context, shown in Figure 5.8, starting with Porter's value chain concept.

Ford and Saren (1996) propose ten key questions a technology audit should attempt to answer, relating to the technology itself, and the processes for managing technology (see Farrukh *et al.*, 2000):

1. What technologies does the company possess?
2. Where did the technologies come from?
3. What is the range of our technologies?
4. What categories do our technologies fit into?
5. How competitive are our technologies?
6. How new are our technologies?
7. What is the life-cycle position of our technologies?
8. What is our performance in acquiring technologies?
9. What is our performance in exploiting technologies?
10. What is our performance in managing technologies?

'Grid-based' tools are one of the most useful and widely applied methods for supporting technology audits, illustrated in Figure 5.9.

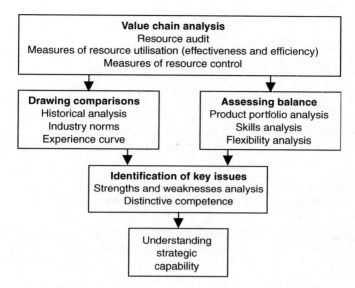

Figure 5.8 Methods of analysing resources (Johnson and Scholes, 1988: 85)

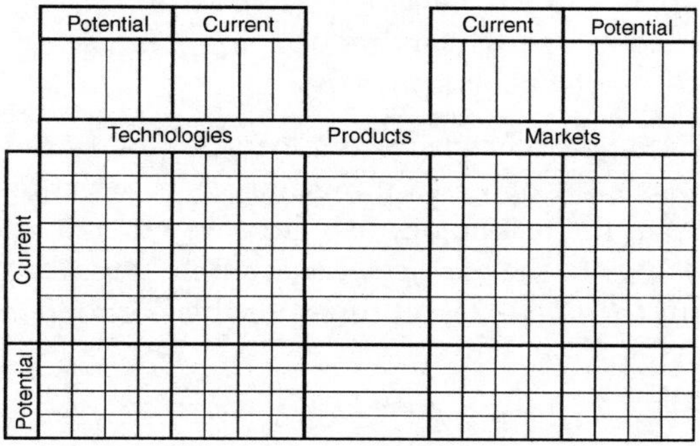

Figure 5.9 Technology–Product–Market (TPM) diagnostic
Source: Lindsay, 2000

Such methods are similar to the quality function deployment (QFD) approach, used frequently for supporting engineering design (Cohen, 1995), although generally used at a higher level. The grids can be separate (for example, to link technologies with products), or linked (such as the TPM grid in Figure 5.9, which connects technologies, products and markets). The approach is very flexible, as many different business aspects can be included, such as processes, skills, customers, systems,

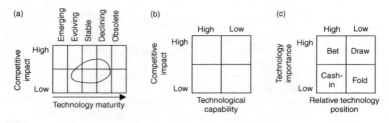

Figure 5.10   Technology portfolio methods
Sources: (a) and (b) Dussauge *et al.*, 1994: 82 (adapted), (c) Burgleman *et al.*, 1996: 5

dimensions of performance, partners, etc. In addition, the cells of the grids can be used in various ways, such as to assess impact, value, risk, effort, etc.

At the highly aggregated level, a key concept is that of the strategic technical area (STA), as proposed by Bitondo and Frohman (1981). An STA can be defined in terms of four constituent parts, which emphasizes the link between technology and the market:

1. Skills or disciplines;
2. which are applied to particular activities;
3. which are used in a particular products or/or services;
4. which address specific market needs.

Various 'matrix' approaches to technology portfolio assessment have been proposed as a way of representing and communicating the balance of technologies in the technology base, in a way that demonstrates the value of technology to the business. For example, Dussauge *et al.* (1994) and Burgleman *et al.* (1996) report three possible portfolio methods – see Figure 5.10.

Step 3: generation and assessment of strategic options

On the basis of a sound understanding and assessment of both the internal and external environments, in terms of strengths, weaknesses, opportunities and threats (a SWOT analysis – see Figure 5.11), a range of strategic options should be developed and assessed.

Strategic posture

The set of strategic options open to a firm typically includes high-, medium- and low-level types. Generally, the high-level options should be

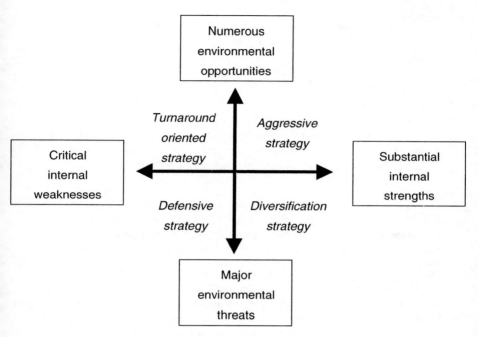

Figure 5.11   Pearce and Robinson technological SWOT analysis
Source: Cardullo, 1996: 66

considered first, and Courtney *et al.* (1997) have proposed three generic strategic postures relating to technological change.

- *Shape the future,* where investment is made in the development of technology to stay in the lead.
- *Adapt to the future,* where technological developments of leading competitors are closely followed.
- *Reserve the right to play,* where technological developments are closely monitored, and appropriate steps taken so as to enable rapid acquisition of the technology.

Porter (1985) considers that the choice of whether to be technology leader or follower is based on three interacting factors:

- *Sustainability of the technological lead,* which depends on the source of technological change, the level of competitive advantage attributed to the technological development, the relative technological skills of the firm compared to its competitors, and the rate of technological diffusion.

- *First-mover advantages,*including reputation, reservation of an attractive product or market position, switching costs associated with customers changing suppliers at a later date, unique channel access, proprietary learning curve, favourable access to scarce resources, definition of standards, institutional barriers (e.g. patents or special relationships), and early profits.
- *First-mover disadvantages,* including pioneering costs, demand uncertainty, changes in buyer needs, commitment of investments in early generations of technology, technological discontinuities, and low cost imitation.

The type of strategic posture adopted depends on the attitude towards risk that the company and its senior management adopt. Courtney *et al.* (1997) has proposed three strategic postures, highlighting the relationship between the uncertainties of predicting the future in strategy formulation processes:

- *No regrets* – decisions that yield a positive outcome for all scenarios.
- *Optimistic* – decisions that yield significant positive payback in some scenarios, and small negative payback for others.
- *Big bet* – decisions that yield large positive payback for specific scenarios, and negative payback for others.

See Chapter 2 for a more detailed account of high-level technology strategy.

Tools for assessment of strategic options

Various considerations need to be included when assessing strategic options, including markets (for example, segments, competitiveness, growth potential), financial considerations (such as revenues, profit, investment), human resources (for example, skills and recruitment) and risk (uncertainties, impact of success and failure). Matrix or portfolio tools are commonly used to link these various dimensions, to provide a framework for discussion and assessment of strategic options, with a selection identified in Figure 5.12 (see also Figure 5.10).

Various financial assessment approaches have been proposed, including direct financial measures, such as ROI and discounted cash flow analysis, together approaches such as 'real options' (Faulkner, 1996; Scarso, 1997), technology stock depreciation models (Kameoka and

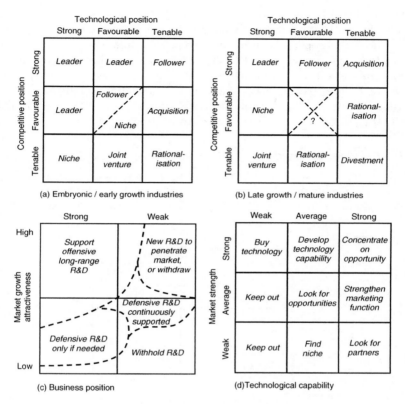

Figure 5.12 (a) and (b) A.D. Little technology strategies

Sources: Dussauge *et al.*, 1994: 100, (c) R&D strategy Bitondo and Frohman, 1981: 20, (d) Lowe, 1995: 92

Takayanagi, 1997), and shareholder value concepts (McTaggart *et al.*, 1994). However, it has proved very difficult to express the 'value' of technological investment and assets in terms of financial reward, especially for industries where the technology and product life cycles are long (e.g. aerospace and pharmaceutical industries).

Step 4: implementation of strategy

The development of strategy is only worthwhile if it results in positive change in the business. As Gregory (1995) points out 'A strategy is only of value if mechanisms for its implementation and renewal are in place'. One reason why many strategies are not effectively implemented is that the nature of implementation, scheduling and planning is fundamentally different from strategy formulation, being 'closed and convergent', whereas strategy is 'open-ended and divergent' (Mintzberg, 1994). Implementation of strategy needs to focus on both the practical steps required for communicating and managing the strategic plans, as well as an appreciation for the challenges associated with organizational change, and an understanding of how historical events and decisions have led to the current situation and culture in the organization.

The challenge of change

It is estimated that up to 90 per cent of business strategy is not effective in terms of delivering the expected business outcome (Mintzberg, 1994). While some of this can be attributed to changing business circumstances,

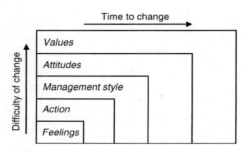

Figure 5.13   Difficulty of different aspects of change
Source: Atkinson, 1990: 47

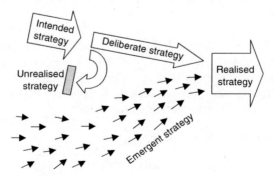

Figure 5.14   Forms of strategy
Source: Mintzberg, 1994: 24

the difficulties associated with organizational change are a major barrier – see Figure 5.13.

Mintzberg (1994) emphasises the importance of 'emergent' strategy (see Figure 5.14), which is largely ignored in formal strategic planning processes. It is important to realise that a firm's strategy is defined by its actions, rather than its intentions. Emergent strategy, which depends to a large extent on past actions and decisions, arises from resistance to organizational change, the 'momentum' built into the current business activities, the changing business environment, the uncertainty of forecasts, and the impact of non-centralized decision-making.

Understanding how a firm's technology strategy evolves over time is an important consideration for defining a strategy for the future (for example, Burgleman *et al.*, 1996), where the experience created from the implementation of past strategies creates capabilities that influence future strategy (organizational learning framework of strategy-making). The strategy-charting technique developed by Mills *et al.* (1998, 2001) emphasizes the importance of past events and activities.

Strategic planning

Mintzberg (1994) notes that the translation of strategy into implementation typically relies on converting strategic goals into quantified objectives, which can cascade down the organization. The setting of objectives is sometimes an integral part of the strategy formulation process, or may follow on from it. Johnson and Scholes (1988) identify a number of levels of strategy in the organization:

- *Corporate strategy* is concerned with the types of business in which the organization as a whole should be engaged in.
- *Competitive or business strategy* is concerned with how to compete in a particular market.
- *Operational strategies* are concerned with how the various functions in the business contribute to the strategic goals of the organization.
- *Personal strategies* are concerned with the individual career choices of staff.

Twiss and Goodridge (1989) consider that the two key components for managing technological change are the physical (or technical) system, and the organizational (or human) system. Successful change requires a due consideration of both the 'hard' analytical issues (models, analysis, process, etc.) together with the 'soft' issues associated with the management of people, organization and learning. The soft issues are often the most important determinant of successful strategic planning and implementation.

:rategic planning and implementation

ey aspects of technology strategy, planning and implementa-
...un is now to integrate and communicate technological considerations
into product and market planning processes. A particular challenge is
that strategic plans must be communicated across both hierarchical and
functional boundaries within the firm. Thus, *integration* is a key theme,
and an important objective when designing and selecting tools for supporting strategy formulation and implementation is to link effectively
with other key business processes and tools in the firm. Of particular
importance is the integration of technology and marketing functions
(Griffen and Hauser, 1994).

Apart from project management tools and approaches, two other
techniques are worth mentioning, particularly because they support
communication across both hierarchical and functional boundaries:

1. 'Cascading grids' for communicating strategic objectives and actions
   within the organization – see Figure 5.15 for an example.
2. Technology roadmaps for developing and communicating strategic
   plans, discussed in more detail below.

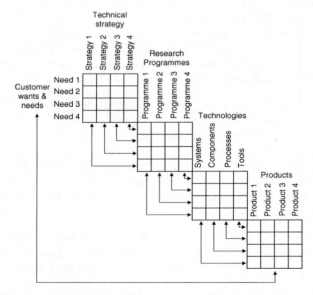

Figure 5.15   Cascading grids: Caterpillar strategy deployment grids
Source: Zadoks, 1997: 50

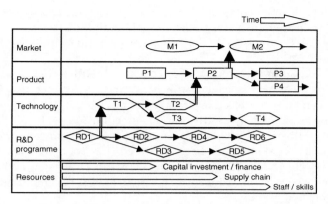

Figure 5.16   Generic technology route map structure
Source: adapted from EIRMA, 1997: 7

Technology roadmaps are widely used in industry to support strategic planning and implementation (for example, Willyard and McClees, 1987; EIRMA, 1997; Groenveld, 1997; Phaal *et al.*, 2000), and more recently to support national sectoral foresight programmes, most notably in the USA (Kostoff and Schaller, 2001). The most common type of roadmap has a structure similar to that shown in Figure 5.16 and looks somewhat like a Gantt planning chart. However, roadmaps serve a different function from that of detailed project planning and control, operating at a higher level to communicate the 'strategic logic' associated with market, product and technology plans.

Technology roadmaps serve two main potential uses:

1. Planning (how to reach an identified goal). The focus here is on market-pull, and the method is largely deterministic, convergent and customer driven.
2. Envisaging possible future outcomes (opportunities that could arise). The focus here is on technology-push, looking for potential market opportunities, and the method is largely open-ended and divergent.

Step 5: evaluation and learning

The development and implementation of strategy is vital to the long-term success of most companies. It is thus important that the outcomes of the strategy process are monitored and evaluated, to enable learning and process improvement. It is helpful to benchmark the strategy and planning process with those of other groups within the company, and external to the company. There is a considerable amount of litera-ture on general approaches to benchmarking in business (for example, Ransley, 1994), which can be applied to business and technology strategy processes.

A key question for the manager concerned with strategic planning and implementation is what performance measures are appropriate to assess the quality of the strategy, and what feedback and control mecha-nisms are appropriate to ensure that the direction and quality of strategy improves with experience. Various approaches to designing performance measurement systems have been proposed (for example, Kaplan and Norton, 1996; Neely *et al.*, 1996; Kerssens-van Drongelen and Cook, 1997), which can be used directly or adapted for use in strategy formation and implementation.

Summary and conclusions

Businesses are complex organizations that operate in complex and changing environments. Long-term success requires a combination of vision and strategy, together with the flexibility needed to take advan-tage of opportunities that present themselves. A sound understanding is needed of both the opportunities and threats posed by the external business environment, and the internal strengths and weaknesses of the organization. An appropriate balance needs to be struck between market 'pull' and technology 'push' if the technological knowledge that the firm controls is to be exploited to maximum advantage. It is important that technological issues are not considered in isolation from the commer-cial perspectives in the firm, in particular marketing and finance. Rather, the firm should be considered as an integrated set of competences and capabilities that need to be aligned with the business opportunities that it aims to exploit. Technology is a key asset for many firms, which needs to be managed if the potential value from it is to be gained.

This chapter has provided a broad introduction to technology strategy and planning, which is considered to be an integrated part of business strategy and planning. A generic strategy process has been introduced, which has provided the structure for more detailed discussion of each process step. A range of practical tools and techniques has been pre-sented which are used widely in industry to manage the complex task of integrated business strategy development and implementation.

References

Abetti, P.A. (1991), 'The impact of technology on corporate strategy and organization: illustrative vases and lessons', *International Journal of Technology Management*, Special publication on the role of technology in corporate policy, pp. 40–58.

Atkinson, P.E. (1990), *Creating Culture Change: the Key to Successful Total Quality Management*, Bedford: IFS Publications.

Bitondo, D. and A. Frohman (1981), 'Linking technological and business planning', *Research Management*, November, pp. 19–23.

Bower, J.L. and C.M. Christensen, (1995), 'Disruptive technologies: catching the wave', *Harvard Business Review*, January–February, pp. 43–53.

Burgleman, R.A., M.A. Maidique, and S.C. Wheelwright, (1996), *Strategic Management of Technology and Innovation*, 2nd edn, Chicago: Irwin.

Cardullo, M.W. (1996), *Introduction to Managing Technology*, John Wiley, New York.

Cohen, L. (1995), *Quality Function Deployment – How to Make QFD Work for You*, Addison Wesley Longman, Mass: Reading.

Courtney, H., J. Kirkland and P. Viguerie (1997), 'Strategy under uncertainty', *Harvard Business Review*, 75, 6, pp. 68–79.

Dussauge, P., S. Hart and B. Ramanantsoa (1994), *Strategic Technology Management: Integrating Product Technologies into Global Business Strategies*, Chichester: John Wiley.

EIRMA (1997), *Technology Roadmapping: Delivering Business Vision*, Paris: European Industrial Research Association.

Farrukh, C.J.P., R. Phaal and D.R. Probert (2000), *Technology Management Assessment Procedure – a Guide for Supporting Technology Management in Business*, London: The Institution of Electrical Engineers.

Faulkner, T.W. (1996), 'Applying 'options thinking' to R&D valuation', *Research Technology Management*, 39, 3, pp. 50–6.

Floyd, C. (1997), *Managing Technology for Corporate Success*, Gower, Aldershot.

Ford, D. and M. Saren (1996), *Technology Strategy for Business*, London: International Thomson Business Press.

Grant, R.M. (1991), 'The resource-based theory of competitive advantage: implications for strategy formulation', *California Management Review*, Spring, pp. 114–35.

Gregory, M.J. (1995), 'Technology management: a process approach', *Proceedings of the Institution of Mechanical Engineers*, 209, pp. 347–56.

Griffen, A. and J.R. Hauser (1994), 'Integrating R&D and marketing: a review and analysis of the literature', *Sloan School of Management Report*, No. 112–94.

Groenveld, P. (1997), 'Roadmapping integrates business and technology', *Research-Technology Management*, 40, 5, pp. 48–55.

Hamel, G. and C.K. Prahalad (1994), *Competing for the Future*, Harvard Business School Press, Boston.

Hofer, C.W. and D. Schendel (1978), *Strategy Formulation: Analytical Concepts*, St Paul: West Publishing Company.

Johnson, G. and K. Scholes (1988), *Exploring Corporate Strategy*, 2nd edn, New York: Prentice Hall.

Kameoka, A. and S. Takayanagi (1997), 'A "corporate technology stock" model – determining total R&D expenditure and effective investment pattern', *Proceedings of the Portland International Conference on Management of Engineering and Technology* (PICMET), Portland, 27–31 July.

Kaplan, R.S. and D.P. Norton (1996), 'Using the balanced scorecard as a strategic management system', *Harvard Business Review*, January–February, pp. 75–85.

Kerssens-van Drongelen, C. and A. Cook (1997), 'Design principles for the development of measurement systems for research and development processes', *R&D Management*, 27, 4, pp. 345–57.

Kostoff, R.N. and R.R. Schaller (2001), 'Science and technology roadmaps', *IEEE Transactions on Engineering Management*, 48, 2, pp. 132–43.

Lindsay, J. (2000), *The Technology Management Audit – the Tools to Measure How Effectively You Exploit the Technological Strengths and Know-how in Your Company*, Financial Times/Prentice Hall, London.

Lowe, P. (1995), *The Management of Technology: Perceptions and Opportunities*, Chapman & Hall, London.

Matthews, W.H. (1992), 'Conceptual framework for integrating technology into business strategy, *International Journal of Vehicle Design*, 13, 5/6, pp. 524–32.

McTaggart, J.M., P.W. Kontes and M.C. Mankins (1994), *The Value Imperative: Managing for Superior Shareholder Value*, The Free Press, New York.

Metz, P.D. (1996), 'Integrating technology planning with business planning', *Research Technology Management*, 39, 3, pp. 19–22.

Mills, J.F., A.D. Neely, K.W. Platts and M.J. Gregory (1998), 'Manufacturing strategy: a pictorial representation', *International Journal of Operations and Production Management*, 18, 11, 1067–85.

Mills, J.F., K.W. Platts, A.D. Neely, H. Richards and M.C.S. Bourne (2001), *Creating a Winning Business Formula*, Cambridge University Press, Cambridge.

Mintzberg, H. (1994), *The Rise and Fall of Strategic Planning*, The Free Press, New York.

Neely, A., J. Mills, M. Gregory, H. Richards, K. Platts and M. Bourne (1996), *Getting the Measure of Your Business*, Works Management, UK.

Penrose, E. (1995), *The Theory of the Growth of the Firm*, Oxford University Press, Oxford.

Phaal, R., C.J.P. Farrukh and D.R. Probert (2000), 'Fast-start technology roadmapping', *Proceedings of the 9th International Conference on Management of Technology* (IAMOT), 20–25th February, Miami.

Porter, M.E. (1980), *Competitive Strategy – Techniques for Analysing Industries and Competitors*, Macmillan, New York.

Porter, M.E. (1985), *Competitive Advantage: Creating and Sustaining Superior Performance*, The Free Press, New York.

Porter, M.E. (1996), 'What is strategy', *Harvard Business Review*, 74, 6, pp. 61–78.

Ransley, D.L. (1994), 'Do's and don'ts of R&D benchmarking', *Research Technology Management*, 37, 5, pp. 50–6.

Ringland, G. (1998), *Scenario Planning: Managing for the Future*, John Wiley, Chichester.

Scarso, E. (1997), 'Quantitative methods for the economic appraisal of a new technology: a critical review', *Proceedings of the Portland International Conference on Management of Engineering and Technology* (PICMET), Portland, 27–31 July.

Stacey, G.S. and W.B. Ashton (1990), 'A structured approach to corporate technology strategy', *International Journal of Technology Management*, 5, 4, pp. 389–407.

Stacey, R. (1996), 'Management and the science of complexity: if organizational life is nonlinear, can business strategy prevail?', *Research Technology Management*, 39, 3, pp. 8–10.

Teece, D.J., G. Pisano and A. Shuen (1997), 'Dynamic capabilities and strategic management', *Strategic Management Journal*, 18, 7, pp. 509–33.

Twiss, B.C. (1992), *Forecasting for Technologists and Engineers: a Practical Guide for Better Decisions*, Peter Peregrinus/IEE, London.

Twiss, B.C. and M. Goodridge (1989), *Managing Technology for Competitive Advantage*, Pitman Publishing, London.

Wernerfelt, B. (1984), 'A resource-based view of the firm', *Strategic Management Journal*, 5, pp. 171–80.

Wheelan, T. and J. Hunger (1993), *Strategic Management and Business Policy*, 3rd edn, Mass, Addison-Wesley, Reading.

Willyard, C.H. and C.W. McClees (1987), 'Motorola's technology roadmap process', *Research Management*, September–October, pp. 13–19.

Zadoks, A. (1997), 'Managing technology at Caterpillar', *Research Technology Management*, 40, 1, pp. 49–51.

6
Strategic Options When Facing Technological Change: Trigger or Shape, Stretch or Re-deploy?
Thomas Durand

Overview

How can a firm act when faced with change? This chapter discusses and illustrates a taxonomy of strategies for a firm confronted with business transformation triggered by technology. Since many players participating in the process of change shape the future of the business, there is room for strategy. Organizational competence is used as the central concept for considering strategic change. The idea of 'competence gap' is discussed to evaluate how fit or unfit the firm is for the new competence requirements brought about by the change. The concept of market power is then used to describe how a firm may influence the deconstruction-reconstruction process of change. On that basis, a taxonomy of strategies available to firms facing change is presented and discussed (Trigger or Shape, Stretch or Re-deploy). Examples are provided to illustrate each strategy.

Introduction

How can a firm act when faced with change? A world of innovation is a world where creative destruction is at work. Be it triggered by deregulation, technological innovation, political events, turmoil on financial markets or strategic moves from competitors, the essence of deconstruction and business transformation is change. In a sense, change is disruption, meaning threats for those existing firms well positioned in the markets, but change also represents opportunities for challengers, new entrants or existing firms not so well positioned in the market.

The issue of anticipating the result of the deconstruction–reconstruction process associated with change is therefore important. Yet, determinism would be a misleading perspective on change: the future of the business is still to be invented and constructed. The future rules of the competitive game are not pre-printed somewhere, waiting to be discovered. They will result from the competitive battles that take place during the deconstructing–reconstructing process. This means that the firms involved will contribute to shaping the new rules. There is room for managerial action. There is room for strategy.

The strategic impact of innovation and change on the competitive dynamics in Industry has been much documented in the management research literature. Classical distinctions have been suggested, e.g. technological (product/process) vs. organizational innovations, or incremental vs. radical categories, thus characterizing the nature or the intensity of change. Examples of radical innovations affecting industries have been discussed, e.g. Cooper and Schendel (1976) or Durand (1992). Yet, more is needed to specify what strategic options are available to a firm faced with significant business transformation in its industry.

This chapter is aimed at identifying and describing a taxonomy of strategies for a firm confronted with the issue of change.

Organizational competence is being challenged, disrupted or conversely reinforced by change. Change relates to both reinforcement and destruction of, at least a part of, the progress made along a natural trajectory, Nelson and Winter (1982). Dosi (1982) also adopts an evolutionary perspective, suggesting that a trajectory exhibits some cumulative features while a paradigmatic change means a shift in trajectory.

This actually relates directly to the description of seams or trajectories illustrated in Figure 3.3 of this book.

Incremental innovation improves and thus reinforces the firm's routines, capabilities and competence along what Durand (1992) called a 'seam'. Radical innovation disrupts and breaks the routines and the organizational capabilities, requiring a more or less radically new set of competence. Schumpeter's 'creative destruction' is therefore complemented by some form of 'improved continuation', what Tushman and Anderson (1986) identified as the 'order breaking/order creating' duality.

Thus, we propose to discuss change by adopting the resource-based view of the firm and its corollary, the competence perspective of the organization.

The resource-based view and the competence-based perspective

The resource-based theory of the firm arose after Penrose's (1959) work, later developed by Rumelt (1984), Wernerfelt (1984), Barney (1986a,b), Collis (1991), Amit and Schoemaker (1993), Grant (1996) and several other contributors. This perspective very rightly pointed out that the firm's performance is not just the result of the external environment in the competitive game (Porter's five forces, the external positioning, etc.) the firm's performance also varies according to the way resources are tapped and leveraged by the organization to satisfy clients' needs in the market place.

Interestingly enough, the resource-based view of the firm did not really raise any interest among practitioners until Prahalad and Hamel (1990) published their core competence piece, as Wernerfelt (1995) suggests. In Prahalad and Hamel's terminology, to be 'core', the competencies have to meet three criteria, namely (1) offer real benefits to customers, (2) be difficult to imitate and (3) provide access to a variety of markets. The heart of the matter has precisely to do with the uniqueness of the various re-combinations of core competencies which the firm may achieve, to design, manufacture and distribute products and services to the customers in the market place. A higher level resource bundling process is thus at work to create an offer which may be attractive to and valued by the clients, Segal-Horn and McGee (1997). This clearly stresses that a unique combination of core competencies can indeed generate a truly competitive advantage, constructing new forms of business. In addition, Prahalad and Hamel suggested re-thinking strategy in terms of competence rather than organizational SBU's. This has far reaching implications: the firm is primarily its competence base, not just a set of business units.

In turn, the resource-based view led to a knowledge-based perspective (Conner and Prahalad, 1996; Kogut and Zander, 1992). At the same time, an attempt was made to build a theory of competence-based strategy. The term competence is meant here to enlarge the concept of resource while building on the resource-based perspective.

The Prahalad and Hamel (1990) core competencies lead to Hamel and Heene (1994) and Sanchez *et al.* (1996) as well as to the Sanchez and Heene (1997) volumes.

As Durand (1998) puts it: 'In medieval times, alchemists were seeking to turn base metals into gold. Today managers and firms seek to turn resources and assets into profit. A new form of alchemy is needed in the organization. Let's call it competence.'

Therefore, by referring to competence, not only do we mean all forms of available assets, capabilities and knowledge, know-how and skills, technologies and equipment in the organization, as most of the existing literature would suggest, but primarily the coordinated deployment of the above assets and capabilities. Obviously part of the competence base may in turn lead to competence rigidity when facing radical change.

Bridging the 'competence gap' or influencing the change?

Hence, a key element of the strategic thinking process when facing potential change has to do with the competence base of the organization. The former business context of an industry, now under deconstruction, had imposed a set of strategic requirements onto the existing firms, pushing them over time to build competence that addresses these requirements. The new emerging business context, now under construction, is already requiring new resources, capabilities and competence, rendering obsolete part of the firms' portfolio of competence while conversely reinforcing and entrenching part of the firms' competence. In that sense, competence is a central concept for considering strategic change.

A first element of strategy when facing change thus emerges from the competence perspective. Depending whether it is fit, at least partially, to the new competence requirements or largely unfit, the firm may intend to *stretch* itself to bridge the 'competence gap'. Alternatively, it may choose to escape and diversify away from the change, i.e. to *re-deploy*, pivoting around its competence base to develop new activities. Should the change be minor or even incremental, then chances are that the portfolio of competence of the existing firm will be not too far from what is needed. Should the change be radical, then the question of the fit becomes extremely important. Therefore, stretch and re-deploy are the first two strategic options.

But one more dimension can be added to the analysis. The firm may be in a position to strongly influence the process of change, or it may be condemned to react to exogenous moves and events. (As an example, a large and powerful firm may be in a position to impose a standard or a technology which may not be the best available option. A new promising patent may be bought and buried to kill what the large powerful player may view as a threat, etc.) In other words, is the firm a real player of the game of deconstruction–reconstruction, or is it facing change as if it essentially came from the outside? In the first instance, the firm may *shape* or even *trigger* the change, thus constructing the future of the business, what Prahalad and Hamel called 'inventing the future of your industry'. In contrast, in the second instance, the firm has a low or marginal ability to influence the process of change and is thus put

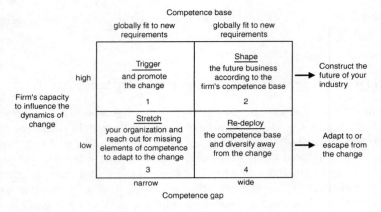

Figure 6.1 Strategic options when facing change

on a responsive mode: adapt to or escape from the change. Stretch and re-deploy are the only two available options left.

This actually leads to a two-dimensional model of strategic behaviour when facing change, as illustrated in Figure 6.1.

Strategic options when faced with change

When the firm has both a significant influence on the dynamics of change and a good fit to the corresponding competence requirements, quadrant 1, it may advantageously promote and even *trigger* the change as a way to disturb competitors and build a defendable, long-lasting market position. This is the typical strategy of innovators and first movers, who attempt to destabilize existing market leaders. This may be called path creation.

Salomon is a remarkable example of an innovator in the sports industry, who chose to trigger change in the markets it had entered historically (skis, roller skates, golf with Taylor Made, bikes with Mavic, hiking shoes). Initially in ski equipment, the firm adopted a strategy of intense R&D to develop in related markets, entering with radically new products with superior performance. First, they systematically targeted professional racers and national teams in order to enter the upper end of the market and thereby establish a superior brand name through advertising with world leaders. Progressively, they extended their initial core business to other sporting equipment, introducing very innovative technologies in all new segments, one after the other. On several occasions, in the recent past, when the performance of a newly developed product was not significantly superior to competition, Salomon invariably chose not to release the new offerings. Salomon's strategy is thus to displace competition by triggering changes which are difficult and time consuming for competitors to imitate or adapt. Obviously, triggering new rules of the game is relevant when your organization is more prepared than others to play with the new rules.

In quadrant 2, the firm has some potentially significant influence on the dynamics of change, while being rather poorly fit in terms of competence base: it may then try to use its influential power to make the change process drift away from competence requirements too far off the firm's reach. Instead, it may push towards a path closer to its core capabilities and further away from its competitors'. Through a proactive strategy, the firm thus tries to *shape* and construct the business for its own benefit.

The bottled water leaders, Nestlé and Danone, struggled to influence the legislation in most countries to protect their mineral water brands from direct competition from local bottlers. Through active lobbying based on scientific published work and medical clinical testing which they fund, these leading players do actively shape their industry. Indeed, the business of bottled water was essentially a market for expensive, high end water coming from unique locations across the world. Nature was kind enough to filter the water through mountains, providing mineral water with unique properties for human health. This meant costly manufacturing and logistics, shipping ponderous products the world over. Yet, in recent years, new competition arose, offering bottled water at much lower prices. That water is no longer naturally filtered for several years in the mountains but comes from wells dug into the ground near cities where consumers live. Costs of logistics are thus minimized, making it possible to sell cheap bottled water though with lower quality. Obviously this change did not correspond to what large multinational players in the industry expected. Therefore, they reacted by trying to reinforce the image of 'true' mineral water and its benefits on health, lobbying for regulations that preserve their own high end offerings. They also acquired key local players in emergent markets in order to control the evolution of the business. Powerful players react to unexpected and undesirable change by shaping the dynamics of their industry for their benefit.

These first two types of situations are described at length by Prahalad and Hamel (1994). However not all firms can have a direct influence in reshaping their industry. Quite the opposite, actually. Most of them have only a marginal effect on the future of the competitive game prevailing in their market. This does not mean that they are left with no strategic options when faced with changes triggered and shaped by their environment. There is a future even for companies lacking the power to reshape their industry.

Although with no or little influential power on the dynamics of their industry, the firm may be in relatively good fit with the competence requirements of the new competitive game, quadrant 3. The 'competence gap' is bridgeable. The firm may thus *stretch* to reach out for these newly needed competence. Strategies to get access to these missing capabilities through competence building, alliances or acquisition may thus be followed.

An illustration of such strategies can be found in the case of telecom operators looking for existing infrastructures in target countries where they want to expand (now possible due to deregulation). Some operators, therefore, enter partnerships with electric utilities or railways to benefit from their existing cable infrastructure. These operators have most of the relevant competence to operate in these new countries, except for the market linkages, which they plan to develop progressively through aggressive pricing and intense marketing, and the missing infrastructure which they try to obtain through partners, thus stretching their organization to reach out. To benefit from the change, firms may do their best to reach out for the newly required competence, stretching their organization.

Finally, if it is both unfit for the new conditions and incapable of opposing or influencing the change, quadrant 4, the firm would have a hard time stretching and bridging the competence gap. The firm may thus escape from the turmoil of the change by *re-deploying* its competence base to *diversify* from what used to be its business.

A good illustration of this can be found in the case of TV magazines confronted with TV menus and scanning systems announcing programmes and presenting previews directly on the TV set, thus helping viewers select their programmes from hundreds of channels. The previously very profitable TV magazines have little choice but to abandon their traditional programme sections and convert to more classical magazines. Indeed there is little hope for them to learn the competence required to supply the TV navigation systems that enable channel and programme selection via the remote control. The competence gap is too wide. They know how to deal with the content but lack the software capabilities and the understanding of the hardware. Journalists would have a hard time turning into software developers. Technology revolution as radical as the one currently affecting the TV broadcasting industry leaves little option for existing firms but to re-deploy away.

All in all, this analysis clearly illustrates how competition actually starts long before new offerings are put to the markets. Competing firms, i.e. existing players as well as potential new entrants, fight for new ideas and new business models. They struggle to tap the necessary resources, build and leverage competence. By the time the new offerings appear on the market, a significant part of the competitive game has already taken place.

This leads to a rather simple, though difficult to implement, set of recommendations for top management in industries where change may affect the dynamics of competition. The starting point is obviously for the firm to have a good understanding of its competence or knowledge base. Identifying potential changes at the horizon (organizing company watch as well as fostering internal innovative activities) and then assessing the competence gap for each anticipated change (strategic analysis) are then important managerial tasks to put the firm in a position to evaluate relevant strategic options. The worst choice would be to ignore outside technological threats. This is what Ken Olsen, the founder of Digital Equipment, did when he directed his company to ignore the PC revolution. This is also what some telecoms operators did when they deliberately chose to ignore the wave of the Internet. Then, there is no other choice left but to run behind the train.

References

Amit, R. and P.J. Schoemaker (1993), 'Strategic Assets and Organizational Rent', *Strategic Management Journal*, no. 1, pp. 33–46.

Barney, J.B. (1986a), 'Strategic Factor Markets: Expectations, Luck and Business Strategy', *Management Science*, 32, pp. 1231–41.

Barney, J.B. (1986b), 'Organizational Culture: Can it be a Source of Sustained Competitive Advantage?', *Academy of Management Review*, vol. 11.

Bettis, A.R. and C.K. Prahalad (1995), 'The Dominant Logic: Retrospective and Extension', *Strategic Management Journal*, 16, pp. 5–14.

Collis, J. (1991), 'A Resource-Based Analysis of Global Competition: the Case of the Bearing Industry', *Strategic Management Journal*, 12, pp. 49–68.

Conner, K.C and C.K. Prahalad (1996), 'A Resource-Based Theory of the Firm: Knowledge Versus Opportunism', *Organization Science*, 7, 5, September–October.

Cooper, A.C and Schendel D. (1976), 'Strategic Responses to Technological Threats', *Business Horizons*, 19, 61–9.

Dosi, G. (1982), 'Technological paradigm and technological trajectories', *Research Policy*, No. 11.

Dosi G., D. Teece and S. Winter (1991), 'Toward a Theory of Corporate Coherence', in *Technology and the Enterprise in a Historical Perspective*, edited by Dosi G., R. Gianetti and P.A. Toninelli, Oxford University Press.

Durand, Th. (1992), 'Dual Technological Tress: Assessing the Intensity and Strategic Significance of Technological Change', *Research Policy*.

Durand, Th. (1998), 'The Alchemy of Competence', in C.K. Prahalad, G. Hamel, D. O'Neil and H. Thomas (eds), *Strategic Flexibility: Managing in a Turbulent Environment*, John Wiley.

Durand, Th. (1997), 'Strategizing Innovation: Competence Analysis in Assessing Strategic Change', in A. Heene and R. Sanchez (eds), *Competence-Based Strategic Management*, John Wiley.

Durand, Th. and S. Guerra-Vieira (1997), 'Competence-Based Strategies When Facing Innovation. But What is Competence?', in H. Thomas, D. O'Neal and R. Alvarado (eds), *Strategic Discovery : Competing in New Arenas*, John Wiley.

Grant, R.M. (1996), 'Prospering in Dynamically-competitive Environments: Organizational Capability as Knowledge Integration', *Organization Science*, 7, 4, July–August.

Hamel, G. and A. Heene (eds) (1994), *Competence-Based Competition*, John Wiley.

Kogut, B. and U. Zander (1992), 'Knowledge of the firm, combinative capabilities and the replication of technology', *Organization Science*, 3, 3, pp. 383–97.

Leonard-Barton, D. (1992), 'Core Capabilities and Core Rigidities: a Paradox in Managing New Product Development', *Strategic Management Journal*, 13.

McGrath, R.G., I.C. McMillan and S. Venkatarama (1995), 'Defining and Developing Competence: a Strategic Process Paradigm', *Strategic Management Journal*, 16.

Nelson, R. and S. Winter (1982) *An evolutionary Theory of Economic Change*, Cambridge, Mass:, Harvard University Press.

Penrose, E. (1959), *The Theory of the Growth of the Firm*, Blackwell.

Porter, M.E. (1980), *Competitive Strategy: Techniques for Analyzing Industries and Competitors*, The Free Press.

Porter, M.E. (1991), 'Towards a Dynamic Theory of Strategy', *Strategic Management Journal*, 12.

Prahalad, C.K. and G. Hamel (1990), 'The Core Competence of the Corporation', *Harvard Business Review*, pp. 79–91.

Prahalad, C.K. and G. Hamel (1994), *Competing for the Future*, Harvard Business School Press.

Rumelt, R.P. (1984), 'Towards a Strategic Theory of the Firm', in R. Lamb (ed), *Competitive Strategic Management*, Prentice-Hall, pp. 556–70.

Rumelt, R.P. (1995), 'Inertia and Transformation', in C.A. Montgomery (ed), *Resource-Based and Evolutionary Theories of the Firm*, Kluwer Academic Publishers.

Sanchez, R. and A. Heene (1997), 'A Systems View of the Firm in Competence-Based Competition', in R. Sanchez, A. Heene and H. Thomas (eds), *Dynamics of Competence-Based Competition*, Elsevier.

Sanchez, R., A. Heene and H. Thomas (1996), 'Towards the Theory and Practice of Competence-Based Competition', in R. Sanchez, A. Heene and H. Thomas (eds), *Dynamics of Competence-Based Competition*, Elsevier.

Segal-Horn, S. and J. McGee (1997), 'Global Competences in Service Multinationals', in H. Thomas, D. O'Neal and R. Alvarado (eds), *Strategic Discovery : Competing in New Arenas*, John Wiley.

Tushman, M.L. and P. Anderson (1986), 'Technological discontinuties and organizational environments', *Administrative Science Quarterly*, 31, pp. 439–465.

Wernerfelt, B. (1984), 'A Resource-Based View of the Firm', *Strategic Management Journal*, 5, pp. 171–80.

Wernerfelt, B. (1995), 'The Resource-Based View of the Firm: Ten Years After', *Strategic Management Journal*, 16.

7
Multi-Technology Management: The Economics and Management of Technology Diversification*

Ove Granstrand

Overview

Recent research in large corporations in the world has shown that technology diversification has important economic and managerial implications with a major potential for growth. While there are many contributions in the literature on business or product diversification of firms, only very recently have there been some attempts to understand the patterns of technology diversification and their implications on various strategic dimensions of corporate development, such as internationalization, business diversification, strategic alliances, external technology acquisition, organizational structure and economic performance. This chapter provides an account of some of the recent research with analysis of data and case studies of the phenomenon of diversification into multi-product/multi-technology firms and its theoretical underpinnings in terms of economies of scale, scope, speed and space. The chapter also addresses the managerial capabilities needed to develop a multi-technology management approach for reaping the dynamic economies of diversification arising from converging technologies. This type of economies at the same time challenges the conventional wisdom of the economies of specialization, emphasizing focus on core business and core technologies, 'back to basics', 'stick to your knitting', etc.

Introduction

How proper is the diversification fashion?

Fashions and fads plague management thinking, and to some lesser extent – hopefully – management practice. It is in fact a significant challenge to members of corporate boards and top management to avoid being overly fascinated by fashions and fads. These may very well build on some sound ideas but are then typically oversold by a host of preachers among fame-driven scholars, money-driven consultants and stock-traders, and novelty-driven managers (often at a higher level!) and media, all jockeying for advantages. Diversification, and its converse specialization, is one particular example of a strategic issue being heavily subjected to fashionable thinking. An average corporation's list of product offerings has been lengthened and shortened like a woman's skirt over the years, at least in the Western industrialized world. In the 1960s and 1970s, US-style conglomerate diversification came into vogue, based on ideas of attaining attractive growth and risk dispersion through applying various management skills across a portfolio of businesses, acquired or home-grown, related or unrelated, financed externally or internally via a corporate capital market. For this strategy, it was perfectly proper to use the by now fairly well-known divisionalized organization structure, pioneered by General Motors and Du Pont in the 1920s, as well as recent advantages in management accounting. As it gradually became clear that the promises held out were not materializing and conglomerate profits soured under over-taxed management, 'survival of the fattest' became an issue and the fashion pendulum started to swing to the other extreme. In the 1980s and 1990s, specialization became fashionable (in the West), dressed in words like 'back to basics', 'stick to the knitting', 'focus on core business', 'be lean and mean', 'slim the organization', downsizing, outsourcing, demerging, etc. Stock prices came increasingly to reinforce this management fashion (and discounting conglomerates) as the financial markets and ownership concerns developed and occupied an increasingly large share of minds of corporate boards and top management.

However, as is well known, stock prices at times do not reflect the real economy very well, so how have the conglomerates and the specialized companies fared economically over the years? In other words, what has been the relation between degree of diversification (or specialization) and economic performance over the years? As a rule, the US-inspired type of conglomerates of the 1960s and 1970s did not perform very well (ITT, Philips, Siemens, etc.), with General Electric as a still (as of 2002) outstanding exception confirming the rule. On the other hand, many Japanese companies diversified successfully in the 1980s (Canon, Hitachi, Toshiba, etc.).

Specialization in the 1980s and 1990s improved economic performance in many cases of Western companies, which influenced by fashionable management thinking had become overdiversified in one way or another (too many unrelated products and/or markets). In other cases, specialization or too little diversification jeopardized the company's long-run economic performance, making it too vulnerable to downturns in business cycles or special markets or patent positions, possibly leading to an M&A restructuring (as for Astra-Zeneca in pharmaceuticals). Also many Japanese companies had become overdiversified, mostly as a result of previous diversification successes, and were pressured to dediversify in the Japanese economic crisis of the 1990s (Gemba and Kodama, 2001).

Thus, business histories offer many lessons but do not show a clear, overall picture. In fact, economic research has not found any significant connection between diversification (or specialization) and economic performance in terms of profitability (see especially Ravenscraft and Scherer, 1987 and Montgomery, 1994).

However, diversification is a mixed bag of various strategies, including conglomerate diversification into more or less unrelated businesses as well as diversification into businesses that are highly related product- or market-wise in terms of shared resources or other synergies. Moreover, the benefits (economies) associated with shared resources and synergies do not end up automatically on the P/L account but have to be reaped through active management. But what kind of guidelines are there for company boards and management to judge what is the proper type and amount of diversification?

Purpose and outline

The purpose of this chapter is to answer this question by penetrating a particular type of diversification related to technology and presenting some guidelines for how to manage this type of diversification successfully. In so doing we need to distinguish between product diversification, commonly understood as extending the range of products (outputs) of a company, and technology diversification, i.e. extending the range of technologies (inputs) a company uses together with other resources for its output products. As will be seen below, recent research has shown that technology diversification has a strong, positive impact on growth of sales, but likely also on growth of expenditures on R&D and technology acquisition, in turn giving management an incentive to utilize the company's technologies for diversifying into new product businesses, i.e. to undertake a technology-related product diversification. The chapter will first briefly illustrate the processes of product diversification as well as technology diversification, then present and explain some results from studies of company diversification strategies and their economic performance. Finally, the chapter will focus on a number of management skills or capabilities needed to successfully manage technology-related diversification processes.

Literature

A quick account of literature on diversification in general, mostly then focusing on product and market diversification, mostly in a US context, would include classic studies of large corporations such as Ansoff (1957), Penrose (1980 [1959]), Chandler (1962, 1990), Gort (1962) and Rumelt (1974).

More recent studies, still in a US context, are Ravenscraft and Scherer (1987), Scott (1993) and Markides (1995). Literature surveys are given by Ramanujam and Varadarajan (1989), Montgomery (1994) and also in management handbooks such as Hitt *et al.* (2001). Essentially, the literature so far gives a mixed verdict regarding the virtues of product diversification in terms of economic performance, apart from pointing out the average underperformance of unrelated conglomerate diversification.

Literature on technology diversification is of more recent origin and in fact has more of a non-US orientation. Kodama (1986) studied technology diversification at industry level in Japan, Pavitt *et al.* (1989) at company level in the UK, Granstrand (1982) and Granstrand and Sjölander (1990) at company level in Sweden, followed up by Oskarsson (1993), Patel and Pavitt (1994) and Granstrand (1994) and Granstrand *et al.* (1992, 1997) for samples of large corporations in Europe, Japan and the US. Essentially, this literature has pointed out the prevalence and nature of technology diversification and its association with economic growth and diversification in general. The literature on this topic has thus grown considerably and is surveyed and elaborated in Cantwell *et al.* (2003).

Empirical findings

Cases of corporate and technology diversification

Diversification occurs at various levels in industry. A number of not very well defined levels can be discerned, e.g. levels corresponding to different sector levels (e.g. manufacturing, vehicles, cars), product area (e.g. passenger car), product line (e.g. station wagon) and product variant or model (e.g. blue, 2003, turbo).[1] At corporate level, Figure 7.1 illustrates some types of diversification in the evolution of a particular firm. The company Alfa-Laval has a long, diversified history of which Figure 7.1

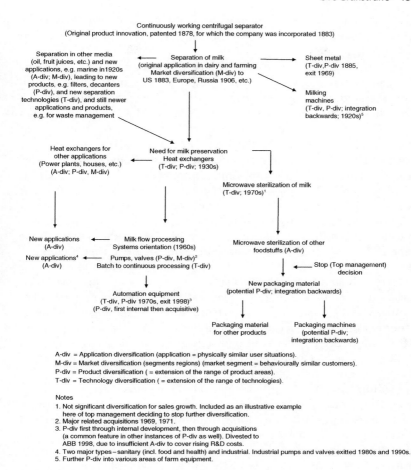

Figure 7.1 Diversification tree – case of Alfa-Laval AB (as of 2000)

can give only a very incomplete picture. For example, the company was acquired by the packaging group Tetra Pak in 1991, then divested in 1998, although without its liquid food processing business area, which had become integrated into Tetra Pak after the acquisition, while other areas had not. The technologies, originating around centrifugal separation of milk, involving mechanical engineering related to metal forming, material science and precision engineering, then evolved (diversified) over the years, revolving largely around processing of mostly liquid (rather than air or material) flows, i.e. flow processing, for which a portfolio of fairly general-purpose products was developed (separators, heat exchangers, pumps, valves, etc.).

Market pull development of new technologies and then technology leveraging (technology push) into new applications, often involving initiatives and ideas from users, then leading into new but related product areas, has been a general driving force. Most of the successful product diversifications have been technology-related in this way rather than market-related. (Cases of the latter have occurred when customers have asked to be supplied with other complementary products in their flow process. In order to ensure sufficient economies of scale and scope, diversification policies have been implemented saying that at least X per cent of the value of an order should relate to core products as defined in technology terms.) However, diversifications have often had many relations and it is difficult to classify them as being related only in a single dimension. The diversification tree in Figure 7.1 is rather a complex diversification network. The four main types of diversification that can be discerned are the two traditionally recognized ones – product diversification into different product areas (P-div), leading to a multi-product company (MPC), and market diversification (M-div), including internationalization as a special case, leading to a multinational company (MNC) – and then two newly recognized ones: technology diversification (T-div), leading to a multi-technology company (MTC), and application diversification (A-div), leading to a range of applications for technologies within a product area. More types could of course be identified and labelled, e.g. business diversification (including services as well as products) and resource diversification (including knowledge in general and technology in particular).

Application diversification is not generally recognized in the literature as a diversification type, but is generally recognized as an important phenomenon. Business histories provide ample cases of companies with new technologies and products finding and developing a range of applications over time, often in unexpected ways with unexpected successes, sometimes even overshadowing the original application. Examples are mobile phones migrating from car phones to pocket phones – or an old drug finding new medical indications as with betablockers, originally developed and used for heart rhythm disorders, then migrating also into the treatment of hypertension.

Interaction between these types of diversification processes over time provides a significant impetus to the dynamics in corporate evolution. For example, new technologies are developed or acquired (T-div) for a new product (P-div) in a specific application, as a kind of market-pull process. Then technologies thus acquired can be adapted to new applications (A-div) and/or further developed for new products (P-div), possibly requiring still more new technologies (T-div). At the same time new markets (in terms of new market segments and market regions rather than applications) are entered (M-div), bringing the company into contact with new customer groups with new requirements and ideas, leading to new products, technologies and applications and so forth. However, in cases of resource constraints, different types of diversification may become adversary when competing for the same resources. For example, it has proven to be very risky to perform product diversification concurrently with market diversification (internationalization in particular), critical resources then being managerial competence and attention.

In a study of diversification processes in eight large, European MNCs[2] (Granstrand, 1982) it was found that:

1. Raw-material-based companies were historically early product diversifiers, incentivized thereto mainly by physical by-products in raw material processing, while late internationalizers. Product-innovation-based companies were early and fast internationalizers while being product-specialized, with product diversification growing (sometimes accidental rather than strategic, often with external impulses) in the postwar boom of the 1950s and 1960s, mainly through acquisitions, producing some failures (due to lack of competence, management and market demand), leading to dediversification on average in the 1970s. The two world wars had on average spurred both growth and diversification (e.g. through import substitution).

2. The continuity and path-dependence were high in the evolution of the companies, and more so at higher levels of diversification (sector, product area) where corresponding product life cycles are then longer. Shifts in core business or dominant business had occurred, but all companies (with century-long histories on average) had stayed in their original sector and most of them in their original product area. Diversification had thus been rooted in most cases, and in general related in some way to existing resources and technologies, spurred by combinatorial opportunities in generic technologies and generic products (as with materials, chemicals and universal machine elements such as electric motors, lamps, bearings and separators), spurred also by systems orientation in industrial marketing – hampered, however, by top management's unwillingness to integrate forward and thereby start competing with powerful industrial customers. For companies with

generic (general-purpose) products, typically universal machine elements, the degree of diversification into various product areas was low while product differentiation within a product area was high, sometimes clearly uneconomically high (as when SKF's different foreign subsidiaries had developed extensive ranges of bearing variants to serve all types of their domestic customers). Leading, invention-based engineering companies such as Alfa-Laval, Philips and SKF thus ran the risk of overspecializing in a product area and overdiversifying within that area.

3. Product diversification strategies had been mixed, changing and controversial, while internationalization strategies had been steadily embraced by top management.

4. Diversification through acquisitions was a preferred mode, except in R&D-intensive companies. Using R&D for product diversification had indeed occurred before the Second World War but gained momentum in the postwar era, during which corporate R&D also grew, internationalized and diversified. In general there was a close, although lagged, connection between growth, diversification and internationalization at company and R&D level – i.e. R&D grew, diversified (technologically) and internationalized eventually as the company did in terms of sales in various product areas and foreign markets.

5. Additions to, as well as shifts in, the dominant core technology of almost all corporations were found, e.g. generation shifts from carbide engineers to polymer technologists at KemaNobel (later merging into Akzo-Nobel); a series of generation shifts in electrical engineering from vacuum tubes to transistors to integrated circuits to microcomputers at Philips; chemistry, biology, electronics and systems engineering being integrated in mechanical engineering at Alfa-Laval; material scientists being promoted at SKF; metallurgists and chemists being added to the 'the mining people' at Boliden; biologists and mechanical engineers being promoted at Iggesund (pulp and paper); a transition from chemistry to biology taking place at Astra; and mechanical engineers being supplemented by various other types of engineers (electrical, chemical, engineering physics, etc.) at Volvo. These changes in the portfolio of technological competencies depended on external technological developments and internal conditions, such as the rise of advocates or resistance among management and technologists. Both companies and products thereby became technologically diversified, although not necessarily technologically advanced, i.e. companies and products became multi-technological ('mul-tech') rather than 'hi-tech'. In connection with technology

diversification the need for new technologies grew, leading to growth of both in-house R&D and external technology acquisition through various means, in turn making in-house R&D a means also for accessing and absorbing external R&D.

6. Four different types of technology diversification were discerned. Firstly, there was a diversification of competencies pertaining to the core technologies of a corporation, for instance, the differentiation of polymer technology or tribology. This was a kind of 'ordinary' specialization within a technology of decisive importance to the corporation. Secondly, there was a diversification pertaining to adjacent technologies. These adjacent technologies could concern supporting technologies such as automation technology in production, surface chemistry for lubrication in a part of a product, or materials technology. Corporate R&D often diversified into adjacent technologies through an initial stage of perception of product problems followed by attempts to solve them by extending internal knowledge, often amateurishly, or acquiring external R&D services. Thirdly, there was substitution among different technologies, such as the transition from chemistry to biology in pharmaceutical research. Fourthly, a new technology was 'picked up' for exploration because of its potential benefit to the corporation, e.g. because it could create entirely new businesses (e.g. KemaNobel acquired polymer technology and Astra went into antibiotics). Often these new technologies were science-related, emerging, and possibly generic, technologies, for which the implementation in products and/or processes was not yet clear. Entry into these could proceed through internal exploratory work (e.g. Ericsson experimenting with computers in the 1950s and 1960s) and/or external acquisition of personnel, licenses, projects or companies. Of these four types – (1) differentiation of and specialization within a core technology, (2) expansion into adjacent technologies, (3) substitution of technologies and (4) involvement in new and so far unrelated technologies – the first three are product-related, while the fourth is not (for the time being, at least). Thus, most but not all types of technology diversification could be said to be related to products (and their production processes) already existing in the companies.

7. The diversification into a new technology for new kinds of businesses was quite often evolutionary, with a progression over adjacent or substituting technologies. For example, the need to preserve milk led Alfa-Laval into heating and cooling, in turn leading to heat exchangers, microwaves, the preservation of other types of food and finally to a new packaging technology. Alfa-Laval then decided not to go

into packaging (see Figure 7.1). The concept of evolutionary chains is too simplified, though; rather, technologies advance along some lines, may rest until combined with some other technologies, and may then advance a bit further.

Finally, any typology of diversification of technology and R&D is vague, since conceptions of a technology are diffuse and changing. Confluences and combinations occur. Strictly speaking, technology diversification should be considered to decrease if a combination of two technologies gains coherence and recognition. For example, many corporations started to encounter different environmental problems in the 1970s and developed countermeasures in the form of corrective technologies. New competences had to be acquired, and perceptions of which technologies were adjacent and relevant changed rapidly. Thus the kind of technology diversification triggered by environmentalism is hard to classify. It may not even be considered a diversification at all after environmental technology became recognized as a specific technology. Thus, when assessing type and degree of diversification, changes in the underlying typology create classification and measurement problems.

Survey of diversification strategies for growth

Oskarsson (1993) explored whether there were certain corporate diversification sequences that were associated with high sales growth. Observations of 57 large multinationals worldwide were classified according to sequences of diversification and specialization of technologies, products and markets. Four main patterns of strategic behaviour were identified:

A. Fourteen companies[3] followed a diversification sequence of, first, increased technology diversification (T-div), followed by product diversification (P-div) and market diversification (M-div) in this or reverse order. These companies were called 'aggressive diversifiers'.
B. Nineteen companies[4] followed a sequence of, first, increased technology diversification, then either product specialization or market diversification, or its reverse with market diversification followed by product specialization. These companies were called 'stick to the knitting' companies.
C. Five companies[5] followed a strategy sequence of increased technology diversification followed by product diversification concurrent with market specialization. These companies were called 'market specializers'.
D. Eight companies[6] specialized both product-wise and market-wise and sometimes even technology-wise. These were called 'defenders'.

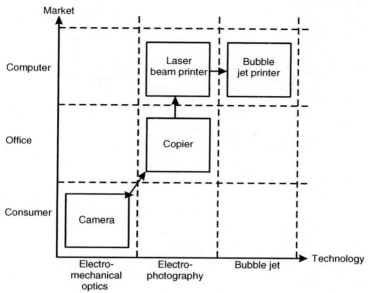

Figure 7.2 Canon's diversification trajectory
Source: Yamaji, 1994

Eleven companies had selected four other strategic sequences, all of them either growing slowly or declining. They underwent neither rapid increase nor decrease in diversification.

The 'aggressive diversifiers' had significantly higher sales growth (in 1980–90) and expanded their technology base, product base and market base significantly more.

Canon was the company with the fastest growth of all the 57 companies between 1980 and 1990. Canon also followed an 'aggressive diversifier' strategy; see Figure 7.2. The Canon case also illustrates three different types of diversification: firstly, concurrent (and indeed risky as it was) diversification (into copiers); secondly, technology-related business (product, market) diversification into laser beam printers, exploiting the competence in electro-photography; and thirdly, business-related technology diversification into bubble jet printers, exploiting the competence and position in the printer industry.

A qualitative model of diversification in general is given in Figure 7.3. Oskarsson (1993) tested a simplified and modified (due to lack of data on feedbacks) version of this model for 1980–90 with results shown in Figure 7.4.

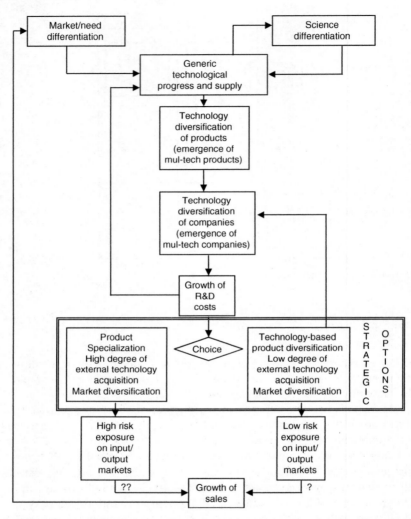

Figure 7.3 A strategic choice for technology management in 'mul-tech' companies

Source: Granstrand *et al.*, 1992: 128

Technology diversification at firm level was thus an increasing and prevailing phenomenon in all three major industrialized regions, Europe, Japan and US. This finding has also been corroborated by Patel and Pavitt (1994).

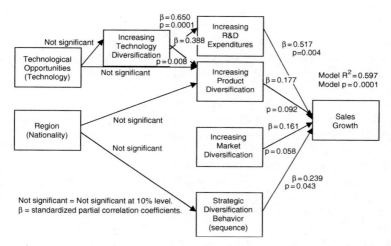

Figure 7.4 A test of a model for growth and diversification ($N = 55$)
Source: Oskarsson, 1993: 31

Moreover, technology diversification was a fundamental causal variable behind corporate growth. This was also true when controlled for product diversification and acquisitions.[7] Technology diversification was also leading to growth of R&D expenditures, in turn leading to both increased demand for and increased supply of technology for external sourcing.

These findings were not readily explainable in terms of received theories of the firm. Without going into detail about the pros and cons in using received theories to describe, explain and predict the behavior of technology-based firms, taking idiosyncrasies of technology as a special type of knowledge into account, one can note that technology diversification does not feature at all in received theories. Moreover, most theories do not explicate the dynamics and heterogeneity of technology, and many restrict their focus to process technology. (For an elaboration on these theoretical issues, see Granstrand, 1998.)

Economics of diversification dynamics

Technology diversification as an empirical phenomenon with its causes and consequences has only recently gained attention among researchers.[8] The key role apparently played by this variable in corporate evolution, as described above, is a new finding for which any explanation at this stage must be tentative. Tentative modelling, as presented above, emphasizes progress in S&T together with differentiation of both S&T fields and market needs. In fact, it may be argued that technological opportunities are generated in a fundamentally important and inexhaustible way through the combination and recombination of various technologies, new as well as old. Such a process of combinations and recombinations could be considered to lie at the heart of the invention and innovation processes, in which technologists, managers and markets filter out technically and economically infeasible combinations.

In the process of taking advantage of technological opportunities, technology diversification at the corporate level may lead to four different but complementary types of economies of diversification: economies of scale, scope, speed and space (the four S's behind diversification). Firstly, there are static as well as dynamic economies of scale. Static economies of scale accrue to the extent that the same, or close to the same, technologies can be used in several different products with minor adaptation costs. Since exploiting knowledge in various applications is typically characterized by small and decreasing marginal cost for each additional application, while the fixed cost of acquiring the knowledge is substantial, static economies of scale are significant when a technology has a wide applicability to many different product areas in a corporation (which is the case for generic technologies by definition). Moreover, as is well known, knowledge is not consumed or worn out when applied. On the contrary, knowledge is typically improved through learning processes when applied several times, which also allows for dynamic economies of scale in technology-related product diversification or technology-related application diversification.

Secondly, different technologies have a potential to cross-fertilize other technologies, yielding new inventions, new functionalities and increased product and/or process performances when combined. This cross-fertilization yields economies of scope, but not primarily the kind of cost-related economies of scope in production that arise from shared inputs, and thus are special cases of economies of scale. This second type of economies of scope of technology diversification depends on the specific technologies which can be combined or integrated. Such economies of scope also vary over time, depending upon the different intra-technology advancements over time. Thirdly, combining technologies usually requires some technology transfer, and (under certain conditions) intra-firm technology transfer is faster and more effective than inter-firm, giving rise to early mover advantages in a multi-technology corporation (MTC). These advantages, related to speed and timing, can be labelled economies of speed. Fourthly, many regions in the world are multi-technological, i.e. they are technologically diversified, e.g. the Silicon Valley area or the Tokyo area – regions that also mostly have diversified eminent universities. These regions generate a stream of technological and business opportunities, which are localized and poorly codified, at least initially. An MTC is then better positioned to take advantage of these opportunities through building close external linkages in different areas. These economies, related to location, agglomeration and geographical coverage in general, can be labelled economies of space.

According to the empirical findings above, technology diversification leads not only to sales growth but also, however, to growth of R&D expenditures. Tentatively, the reason is that a larger number of technologies is involved, which means that a larger amount of coordination and integration work is needed, apart from the cost of acquiring each new technology, as difficulties arise in connection with conducting multi-disciplinary R&D. These difficulties are widely reported and typically involve conflicts between professional subcultures in science and technology, NIH-effects and other innovation barriers (see below and, for more detailed accounts, Granstrand, 1982). Thus, in order to reap net benefits from technology diversification leading to growth of both sales and R&D expenditures, the integrative skills of both technologists and managers become decisive.

There are two contrary but complementary types of diversification having a strong economic potential – diversification into new technologies, mostly related to existing products, and diversification into new technology-related products. The first type, P-related T-diversification, corresponds to a shift in the technology base or portfolio of the company, while the latter, T-related P-diversification, corresponds to a shift in the product (business) portfolio. These two shifts could in principle take place independent of each other, still being economical; but when they combine over time as shown in Figure 7.5, economic benefits can be strongly enhanced. In fact, it could be argued that a crucial dynamic factor in corporate evolution is the interdependence or interaction over time between *business-related resource diversification* and *resource-related business diversification*.

The economies of scale, scope, speed and space associated with resource-related product diversification change over time and must be continually assessed and monitored, also relative to other companies. For example, diversification into a new product P_2 (e.g. light trucks)

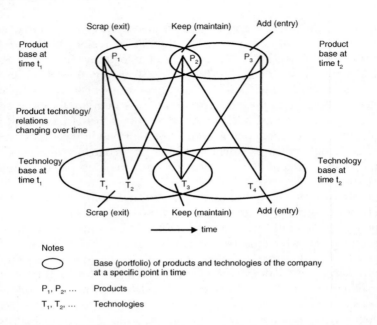

Figure 7.5 Evolution of a company in terms of changes in its product and technology bases

might initially share a lot of resources, including technologies, with an existing product P_1 (e.g. passenger cars), but over time the resource sharing may very well decrease as the new product gradually needs more specialized resources, for example in production. Such resource divergence (with diverging technologies as a special case) may perhaps lead to the point where divestment of some technology or product has to be considered, due to losses of scale and scope advantages relative to other suppliers. Sometimes, a reaction against resource divergence comes too late, leading to overdiversification.

The opposite may also occur. Two initially fairly unrelated products, e.g. computers and telecom equipment in the 1950s, may over time 'come closer' in their resource requirements, e.g. through sharing new technologies (e.g. integrated circuits) or serving similar new customer segments.[9] Another example would be heavy trucks becoming more similar over time in resource requirements to construction machinery, while distancing themselves from passenger cars. Construction machinery then corresponds to P_3 in Figure 7.5, sharing technologies T_3 and

T_4 with P_2 (trucks) while sharing only T_3 with P_1 (passenger cars). This kind of resource convergence (with converging technologies as a special case) may then at some point justify diversification one way or the other, through mergers, acquisitions, alliances or organic growth, depending upon the resource position and resource acquisition costs relative to other companies. The resource positions and acquisition costs for different companies are typically asymmetric and uncertain, which makes the direction of diversification important but difficult to assess, especially in early stages of convergence, prompting for experimental diversifications. Over longer periods of time both resource divergence and convergence may occur, e.g. due to technological changes in general.

The changing resource bases for different product generations or versions may be similarly analysed. A company operating in a product area may have to offer its customers both an old and an upgraded new product generation for some time, but then eventually have to scrap or divest the old generation. Scrapping obsolete competences is often associated with considerable difficulties, since a number of people, including managers, will be threatened thereby, trying all kinds of defensive behaviour, essentially resulting in organizational inertia (or core rigidities in the terms of Leonard-Barton, 1995), costs and delays. This is not least the case when old technical competencies (technologies) embedded in engineering subcultures have to be phased out (see below). Scrapping resources also involves scrapping some old relations, i.e. scrapping some relational capital, which is difficult. For example, scrapping some customer relations, built up through single-minded corporate campaigning about 'listening to our customers', leading to bias for current ones, is difficult and costly in the short run but even more costly in the long run if not undertaken (see Christensen, 1997).

A company wanting to enter the product area is not plagued with these costs, but if it is a new start-up company it must, on the other hand, acquire all necessary resources if it wants to independently launch a new product generation. An existing company, operating in other product areas but attempting to diversify into the product area under consideration with a new product generation, typically based on some new technology, must also acquire new resources but can at the same time draw on some of its old resources insofar as the diversification attempt is resource-related.

Thus, depending upon the resource acquisition cost, the resource scrapping cost, and the synergies between the new product generation and existing resources, either the start-up company (e.g. for mobile

B = Resources needed for a new product generation
= Start-up company's resource need

A = Existing resources for a company
with an old product generation

C = Existing resources for a company
trying to diversify into the product area

Note:

The comparative advantage of A *vis-à-vis* C corresponds to A's unique part of the resource overlap with B, i.e. the part of A's resource overlap with B which is not within C's resource overlap with B (i.e. in set-theoretic symbols (A∩B)\C). The figure indicates that C has a greater comparativeadvantage than A (for the time being).

Figure 7.6   Resource bases (including technology bases) for an incumbent (A), a start-up (B) and a product diversifier (C)

handsets or palmtops), or the existing company (e.g. in the telecom industry) already operating in the product area, or the existing company (e.g. in the computer industry) diversifying from outside into the product area will have a relative cost advantage; see Figure 7.6.

Critical abilities in management of technology and product diversification

The question is now how the economic benefits can be reaped by proper management of these dynamic shifts in inputs and outputs, or in other words these diversification processes (including divestment). Some general observations on managing technology assembly will first be given. Then some lessons from a few cases may serve as guidelines for further management thinking on the complex and situation-specific issues of diversification. The first case concerns how the Swedish telecom giant Ericsson successfully managed the shift or transition in the technology base for its telecom switching products, i.e. a case of product-related technology diversification. The second case deals with how the Swedish auto and aerospace company Saab attempted to leverage several of its numerous military-related technologies through internal technology transfer to a number of new product areas, collected in a special high-tech group called Saab Combitech. This is a case of mainly technology-related product diversification. (For further details of the cases, see Granstrand and Sjölander, 1990.) Both cases point at the criticality of managing conflicts, especially conflicts between subcultures associated with different technologies. This issue will therefore be dealt with specifically.

Managing technology assembly

As seen above, technology-related product diversification typically involves procuring some new resources while drawing on some existing technologies. Procuring new technologies can be done in various ways – by in-house R&D, by alliances or acquisitions on external technology markets, or simply through technology intelligence. Either strategy requires specific management abilities, e.g. in cooperating with lead users, competitors, suppliers or universities. External sourcing requires, in general, technology forecasting (foresighting), identifying, valuing, accessing, transferring and integrating new technologies, the latter often encountering difficulties like NIH-effects. At the same time, internally available technologies have to be internally identified, transferred and adapted to the new product, which may very well encounter difficulties, not least in a large corporation. The saying: 'Wenn Siemens wusste was Siemens weiss' is indeed relevant here.[10] Sometimes it may even be simpler (faster, cheaper) to source a piece of technology externally, than to go and find it in large, diversified organizations like Siemens, Philips or General Electric and then to overcome internal technology-transfer barriers.

All in all there is a *technology assembly problem*, or more generally *a competence or knowledge assembly problem*, to deal with in technology-related product diversification. This also holds true for product-related technology diversification. In the latter case, however, there is also the problem of managing obsolete resources, and in particular competences and technologies that are embedded in managers and personnel. Their self-interests produce not only inertia, active resistance and political maneuvering but also distortion of information, often even without guile. Top managers and board members are dependent upon internal expertise in judging new product and technology prospects, and all expertise is framed in their own competence. (This is why it is sometimes risky to promote a technologist or scientist, who has successfully specialized in one specific area, to a position as general technology manager.) As diversifying competence for an individual is difficult (costly) and time-consuming, to say the least, an important goal discrepancy or principal–agent problem arises between the board (principal) and the internal expertise (agent). It is then important for top managers and the board to complement internal expertise and judgments with external ones, e.g. in form of external technology audits, technical due diligence, scientific advisory boards, or technical alliance advisors. However, this possibility is limited by secrecy needs (sometimes corporate boards are simply very leaky and top management cannot bring the issue to the board) and by a highly specific and uncertain situation with limited availability of experts.

Managing product-related technology diversification into digital switching in Ericsson[11]

For over a century Ericsson, as a fairly specialized but highly internationalized company in telecom, has managed a number of transitions into new technologies successfully (with some exceptions), pertaining to both switching and transmission of phone calls. The transition into computerized (stored program control) switching in the 1950s to 1980s was particularly successful, leading to the so-called AXE system which provided a strong technological platform for subsequent development of mobile communications (voice and data), in turn very successful as has been widely recognized. The latter development was then a case of technology-related business diversification (with several new products – base stations, handsets, etc.) as well as a case of a technological transition from wired (cable) to wireless (radio) transmission in the access part of a telecom network (besides the transition from copper cable to optical fibre in the trunk lines of the network).

In the case of managing a series of technological transitions, several critical managerial abilities could be identified in Ericsson. Firstly, is the ability to perform environmental scanning (including technology and competitor scanning, intelligence and forecasting) and to produce technological, industrial and market forecasts. Secondly, the ability to assess the proper rate, direction and form of strategic competence diversification is critical. There is a long process, perhaps 20–30 years, from the first signals of an emerging technology (e.g. discovery of semiconductivity) to the commercial success of a new product generation based on it. All the time the technology develops, technological options proliferate and the competitors' technological approaches and positions change. When and how to introduce the new technology (if at all), and when and how to exit the old technology, are crucial timing decisions. The experience in Ericsson suggests that the building of competence for these decisions ought to be made at the outset in an experimental manner, without a precise business plan and involving good technologists, young and old. (The latter may be difficult if the product with the old technology is simultaneously successful on the market.)[12]

A third critical ability in connection with technological transitions is the ability to handle conflicts. It is almost axiomatic that technological transitions involve conflicts. This should be recognized as natural rather than pathological in the organization. Some conflicts derive from confrontations between different professional subcultures associated with different scientific and technological disciplines involved in a transition. Sometimes, as in the Ericsson case, these conflicts could be mitigated by a strong corporate culture and/or a consensus-seeking problem-solving engineering culture. Some conflicts are associated with power struggles among managers, whose power is based on knowledge in a certain technology. Some conflicts have good effects, e.g. increasing motivation as in some 'guerrilla' development work ('skunk work') in a large company, but conflicts may often turn out to be disastrous. Probably the different conflicts in Ericsson's long-standing competitor ITT during the latter half of the 1970s went far enough to delay R&D work on its System 12 competing with the AXE. For several reasons, managers often avoid dealing with conflicts until it is too late, when the conflicts have become overly person-oriented rather than issue-oriented, productive communications break down, tensions and struggles prevail, resources are wasted and speed in decision-making is lost.

Fourthly, organizational ability is important in connection with technological transitions. The new always runs a risk of being killed by the old. To organize the work on the new technology, separately from that on the old, in a semi-autonomous organization has often proved to be a viable organizational solution. It is not only a way of separating the new from the old but also gives possibilities of combining the advantages of large and small organizations. In the Ericsson case, the formation of Ellemtel, a joint venture company with the Swedish telecom operator (later named Telia) as a lead user, proved to be highly successful and done at what seems in retrospect the right time.

A fifth managerial ability concerns how to work with parallel approaches in R&D, and when and how to divest or redirect some approaches and concentrate R&D resources on a major design direction for a new product generation. At the same time, increasing R&D costs, increasing possibilities to combine different technological options (due to a general accumulation of S&T advances), and rather constant R&D times (as in the Ericsson case) increase the importance of this ability.

Managing internal technology transfer in Saab Combitech

Saab is a large European civil and military aircraft manufacturer. In a corporate restructuring in the 1980s, Saab Combitech was formed as a large subsidiary, housing a number of technologies and products outside but related to core businesses, for the purpose of diversification, cross-utilization and cross-fertilization (combination) of technologies. This in turn required in-house technology transfer and technology integration or combination.

Combining technologies in R&D work involved the problem of how to manage professional subcultures. It was then of importance that these subcultures rested on some commonalities in communication, values, problem-solving approaches, etc., that is to say, that there was some kind of overarching professional culture and corporate culture. The development and sustenance of a corporate culture were facilitated by common historical roots and traditions of various businesses, and by coherence in vision, goals and explicit strategies. This was even more true in a multinational setting in which there were national culture differences as well.

It was, moreover, important that a well-conceived technology transfer policy was implemented with support by the various business managers. The experience from Saab-Scania Combitech also pointed to the need for incorporating strategic perspectives and responsibilities into the technology transfer function, together with operative and tactical ones. This was facilitated by a CTO or a Vice President Technology with joint staff/line functions, having direct executive responsibilities for group strategic projects, ventures and new technology-based firms together with staff responsibility for supporting the CEO and the various business managers in the strategy development process.[13]

Finally, developing managerial abilities in an MTC such as Saab Combitech took time and needed a great deal of experimentation. This can hardly be done if the overall profitability is low or poor. Therefore, healthy businesses, projects and ventures are needed at the outset.

Managing conflicts among engineering subcultures

The culture associated with S&T is sometimes presumed to be homogeneous, but is in fact heterogeneous with several subcultures, not seldom in conflict with each other. Scientists and technologists certainly share some basic values and beliefs about the benefits of their work and their methods and what is legitimate in thinking and language.

However, at the same time, differences in these respects between disciplines, as well as between generations, are marked. Such differences within an overall S&T culture seem to produce intermittent reorientations rather than smooth, cumulative evolution. Individual scientists and technologists build up conceptions that ossify and obstruct intellectual reorganizations. Science and technology groups are formed on the basis of similarities in educational background and shared conceptions and language. Individuals tend to socialize in at least one group, their social skills improve, they become tied to interests, and they defy fundamentally new conceptions. As a result, disciplines expand and contract, amalgamate (fuse) and split up (diversify), and this is accompanied by generation changes, breakthroughs of new knowledge and, not least, by conflicting interests.

S&T subcultures are typically associated with S&T professions, such as chemists, biologists, mining engineers, mechanical engineers, electrical and electronics engineers and physicists. These categories correspond to the structure of graduate education and, to some extent, to the structure of industrial branches or sectors (which graduate engineering education is supposed to serve). The formation of subcultures also seems to take place largely during graduate education or in the early years of professional life when much of an individual's professional 'Weltanschauung', language and base for socialization is formed. The subcultural features formed during graduate education are often reinforced when the young professional goes into a corporation, due to the structural correspondence between universities and different sectors of industry. The inertia of the educational system in universities then tends to produce a strong and enduring sectoral barrier to change in industry.[14]

There are several determinants behind the formation of cultures and the association of an individual with different cultures pertaining to different segments of his/her life situation. The strength of this association differs between individuals and also changes with time. A high learning capacity makes a professional less dependent upon discipline-oriented knowledge as acquired by formal education, and may therefore permit him/her to be more problem-oriented and less inclined to associate with a certain professional culture. A university researcher may feel associated with S&T in general, but with academic research in particular and even more with academic research in his/her field. Problems in connection with too weak an association of university researchers with the culture of industrial R&D are often witnessed.

The association of a culture with a corporation and its change is of main concern here, especially change associated with professional subcultures. On the one hand, a corporation is associated with different cultures through its personnel. On the other hand, a specific corporate culture is often formed, which may retain its basic characteristics even if turnover of personnel is high. Since a culture reduces variations and uncertainty for its members, it may be instrumental in coordination and communication. A culture may also be instrumental in preserving a power structure. Management has possibilities to influence language, ideology, beliefs and myths in the corporation and thereby influence the corporate culture to the benefit and convenience of managers themselves. Thus, there are several motives behind the formation of a corporate culture. However, a culture may also act as a barrier to change.

Changes of professional subcultures in three corporations studied are summarized in Table 7.1. One can discern a number of factors of primary influence behind such changes, although it is extremely difficult

Table 7.1 Examples of subcultural transformations in business histories in 1960s–1970s

Change involving a subcultural transformation	Factors of primary influence
Astra	
Transition from a chemistry orientation to a biology orientation	Corporate origin Top and R&D management behaviour Recruitment Technological change
Boliden	
Integration of chemistry into the mining orientation	Top management behaviour Recruitment and promotion Corporate strategy Technological change
Alfa-Laval	
(a) Integration of economics into the engineering orientation	Top management behaviour Recruitment
(b) Transition from component orientation to systems orientation	Corporate strategy Internal conceptualizers Technological and market change Product troubles
(c) Integration of electronics into the mechanics orientation	R&D management behaviour Independent subsidiary action Recruitment Technological change

Source: Adapted from Granstrand, 1982

to separate such factors and assess their influence. The most frequently encountered factors are, on the one hand, technological and market changes and, on the other hand, top management behaviour, corporate strategy, recruitment and promotion. The latter group of factors directly involves top management. This indicates that top management plays a primary role in cultural change in the corporation and that strategy formation, recruitment and promotion are important instruments in bringing about such change. In this sense a top manager in a large corporation may act in an important manner as a 'cultural entrepreneur'. This does not always have to be the case, though. In some cases a corporate managing director has hindered or slowed down a cultural change initiated internally or externally.

Concerning the instruments for bringing about a cultural change, strategy formation, recruitment and promotion certainly are important. These instruments may, of course, be used in different ways. Thus, for example, Boliden promoted a mining man as head of a new chemical division of the corporation to be able 'to lift it up' in the corporate power structure. Astra relied heavily on recruitment of new competence, which was natural considering the total dominance of chemists at the time. (It is a fundamental fact that a specialized professional in one field cannot be converted into a specialized professional in a different field overnight or even over some years.)

A cultural entrepreneur may use other instruments as well. To restructure communications through organization and location is a tangible way of acting. He may also act in a more intangible way on the level of fundamental elements in a culture, such as influencing language and values, creating symbols and rituals, strengthening ideologies and nurturing myths.

However, the dynamics of cultural change as discussed here involves more factors than just a cultural entrepreneur, a concept which is often used in a too simplified explanation. Although there are instruments for management which influence a culture, it would be naïve to consider a culture as something that can be created and managed totally at will. Cultural change has, for instance, a prehistory in which external changes and internal conflicts are influential. The whole process of change, which may last over some decades, is characterized by disorder and uncertainty and the outcomes may vary. Starting from the situation of a dominant culture in a corporation, with a new culture emerging, four types of outcome may be discerned:

- amalgamation of cultures;
- transition to new dominance;

– ordered coexistence;
– rejection of emerging culture and regression to old culture.

Of the above, amalgamation (for instance, at Alfa-Laval), transition (for instance, at Astra) and the role of new generations of professionals are important. A new generation may change and amalgamate values and beliefs previously associated with two subcultures or disciplines, and a new generation may be needed to subdue an old subculture. Ordered coexistence of two subcultures (e.g., at Boliden) may be accomplished both by hiring new professionals with weaker subcultural association and by structuring organization and management.

Summary and conclusions

Multi-technology management

Diversification into new types of businesses and resources is an old phenomenon and an inherent feature in corporate evolution, subjected to too much controversy as well as to fashion-oriented management. Despite this, diversification has only fairly recently been analysed in the literature, with inconclusive results as to the impact of product diversification on economic performance. However, more recent research has focused on a new type of diversification into multiple technologies, i.e. technology diversification, which so far has proven to be strongly associated with growth of sales as well as with growth of R&D expenditures and external technology sourcing, especially when combined with product and market diversification. As a result, products become increasingly multi-technology ('mul-tech' rather than 'hi-tech'), and corporations develop into MNC/MPC/MTC combines.

In order to reap the economies involved in technology diversification, a number of critical management abilities have been identified, hitherto only through case studies. Thus critical abilities in multi-technology management are to manage technology assembly, technology transitions, technology transfer and conflicts. Conflicts among managers and personnel are deeply involved in innovation and diversification into new technologies, not least conflicts associated with engineering subcultures. In contrast to 'hi-tech' management, 'mul-tech' management therefore has to focus on sourcing, assembling and exploiting an ever-changing portfolio of various technologies for customer-oriented business development – rather than to focus on in-house R&D of a narrow range of proprietary advanced technologies, which possibly may be over-performing for many market segments and applications.

Managing diversification dynamics

Some general conclusions regarding successful diversification management can finally be formulated. First, at strategic level, technology-related product diversification as well as its converse, product-related technology diversification, must be clearly recognized as a venue towards growth and profitability, but with strong emphasis on relatedness involving clear economies of scale, scope, speed and space. Often these two types of diversification are best managed in a dialectic fashion, i.e., one giving rise to the other in a sequence rather than concurrently, in order to reduce risks. For instance, a product may require new technologies for new features and enhanced performance in order to meet new competition. Once these – probably expensive – technologies have been acquired and integrated, one must ask whether there could be an opportunity for technology-related product diversification. If so, still more technologies may be needed in a next phase and the diversification process continues, often over long periods of time, which requires sustained diversification strategies. Of course, uncertainty and entrepreneurialism may lead to temporary overdiversification and business failures, but the diversification–specialization pendulum must not be allowed to swing to extremes. This is very much a strategic challenge to top management and the corporate board, since commitments and sunk costs create inertia in the organization, at the same time as short-sighted pressures from investors and others, particularly in downturns, create a momentum for divestment decisions, difficult to reverse. The issue is then not so much what is the core business or the core competences, but how distributed competences can be enhanced, leveraged and integrated for developing new valuable businesses (see Granstrand *et al.*, 1997). To formulate a simple but powerful vision for the direction of long-term diversification in the corporation is often helpful. Good examples are the C&C (Computers and Communications) vision of NEC and Toshiba's E&E (Energy and Electronics) vision. However, it must also be kept in mind that despite its long-term nature, the economic lifetime of such a vision is limited.

Managing quasi-integrated corporate innovation systems

Second, at structural level, the suitability of the divisionalized organizational structure is commonly recognized for large, diversified corporations. With technology-related business divisions operating on a short-term P/L account, a rationale arises for centralizing some R&D

and technology acquisition operations. In addition, internally competing technologies may have to be organizationally separate to some degree, just as some new business development activities may have to, in order not to be stifled by dominant business divisions and day-to-day operations. The suitability of such an organizational structure with semi-autonomous units for R&D on radical new technologies, new business development and corporate venturing is by now fairly well recognized. However, there is a wide spectrum of quasi-integrated structural solutions and strategies for such units, regarding at what level they should be organized, how economic performance should be evaluated, how they should source ideas, technologies and ventures internally and externally, preferred entry and exit stages and modes, preferred interfaces with the rest of the organization, management reporting and accountability, etc. To elaborate beyond this call for awareness, though, would be to exceed the scope of the present chapter.[15]

Corporate entrepreneurship

Third, at a more operational level, technology management for diversification must have a commercial and entrepreneurial orientation. Technology has to be managed as an asset that can be built up (procured) in various ways, not only through traditional in-house R&D but also through alliances and various forms of external sourcing, requiring commercial skills. The technology asset can also be exploited in various ways, not only through traditional downstream investments in production and marketing but through alliances, spin-offs, divestment and technology marketing. These latter strategies have become increasingly attractive since the strengthening of IPRs and financial markets in the 1980s. Technology exploitation therefore has come closer to corporate venturing, thus calling for commercial skills beyond merely buying technology and interfacing R&D with marketing people in a traditional way. This is probably the most important type of extension of traditional R&D management into modern technology management.

Notes

* Parts of the material in this chapter are also published in Cantwell *et al.* (2004).
1. The resulting diversity of firms and products is actually bewildering; see e.g. Petroski (1994) and Sanderson and Uzumeri (1997) for good illustrations at product, line and variant level. In a large MNC with general-purpose products such as bearings or separators, having a variety of user situations in various industries and countries, thousands and thousands of product variants occur in perhaps hundreds of product and component areas.

2. The companies were Alfa-Laval (engineering), Astra (pharmaceuticals), Boliden (mining), Iggesund (pulp and paper), KemaNobel (chemicals), Philips (electronics), SKF (engineering) and Volvo (engineering).
3. 3M, Astra, ABB, Canon, Digital Equipment, Honda, Kyocera, Matsushita, Motorola, Nec, Sandoz, Sony, Toshiba and Toyota.
4. BASF, Bayer, Electrolux, ESAB, DuPont, Ford, Glaxo, General Motors, Hitachi, IBM, KODAK, Thone Poulenc, Pharmacia, L'Oréal, Nobel, Ericsson, Unilever, Volvo and Xerox.
5. Sumitomo, Sanyo, Merck, Nippon Steel and Siemens.
6. General Electric, Aerospatiale, ICI, FAG, Thomson CSF, Olivetti, Texas Instruments and Philips.
7. This finding has later been confirmed also by Gambardella and Torrisi (1998) for 32 of the largest European and US electronics firms.
8. Incidentally no reference is made to technology diversification in the surveys of diversification literature by Ramanujam and Varadarajan (1989) and Montgomery (1994), nor in general surveys of strategy literature, e.g. Hitt *et al.* (2001).
9. For this type of analysis the concept of technological distance has been developed; see Granstrand (1994).
10. The saying is sometimes attributed to the former chairman of Siemens, Karl-Heinz Kaske, but its origin is unclear within Siemens (which in itself illustrates the saying).
11. This section builds on a series of about 30 interviews in Ericsson during the mid-1980s, reported in Granstrand and Sjölander (1990).
12. See also Chapters 5, 6 and 7 in this volume for structured approaches to improving these two critical managerial abilities. Methods and tools for managing emerging technologies and the 'fuzzy front end' of the innovation process are also presented in Chapter 16.
13. See further Chapter 12 in this volume on the virtues of having a CTO on the top management team, as is widely practised in Japan.
14. This circumstance may partially explain the phenomenon of innovation by invasion as described by Schon (1967), that is, how whole sectors of industry are invaded by new technologies outside their traditional fields.
15. See also Chapter 12 in this volume on quasi-external acquisition of know-how and Chapter 11 on various forms of external technology marketing.

References

Ansoff, H.I. (1957), 'Strategies for diversification', *Harvard Business Review*, 35, 5, pp. 113–24.
Cantwell, J., A. Gambardella and O. Granstrand (eds) (2004), *The Economics and Management of Technological Diversification*, London: Routledge.
Chandler, A.D. (1962), *Strategy and Structure: Chapters in the History of the American Industrial Enterprise*, Cambridge, MA: MIT Press.
Chandler, A.D. Jr (1990), *Scale and Scope – The Dynamics of Industrial Capitalism*, Cambridge, MA and London, England: Belknap Press of Harvard University Press.

Christensen, C.M. (1997), *The Innovator's Dilemma: When New Technologies Cause Great Firms to Fail*, Boston, Mass.: Harvard University Press.

Gambardella, A. and S. Torrisi (1998), 'Does Technological Convergence Imply Convergence in Markets? Evidence from the Electronics Industry', *Research Policy*, 27, 6, pp. 445–63.

Gemba, K. and F. Kodama (2001), 'Diversification Dynamics of the Japanese Industry', *Research Policy*, 30, 8, pp. 1165–84.

Gort, M. (1962), *Diversification and Integration in American Industry*, Princeton, NJ: Princeton University Press.

Granstrand, O. (1982), *Technology, Management and Markets*, London: Frances Pinter.

Granstrand, O. (ed.) (1994), *Economics of Technology: Seeking Strategies for Research and Teaching in a Developing Field*, Amsterdam: North-Holland.

Granstrand, O. (1998), 'Towards a Theory of the Technology-Based Firm', *Research Policy*, 27, 6, pp. 465–89.

Granstrand, O. and C. Oskarsson (1994), 'Technology diversification in MUL-TECH corporations', *IEEE Transactions on Engineering Management*, 41, 4, pp. 355–64.

Granstrand, O. and S. Sjölander (1990), 'Managing Innovation in Multi-technology Corporations', *Research Policy*, 19, 1, pp. 35–60.

Granstrand, O., P. Patel and K. Pavitt (1997), 'Multi-technology Corporations: Why They Have "Distributed" Rather than "Distinctive Core" Competencies', *California Management Review*, 39, 4, pp. 8–25.

Granstrand, O., E. Bohlin, C. Oskarsson and N. Sjöberg (1992), 'External Technology Acquisition in Large Multi-Technology Corporations', *R&D Management*, 22, 2, pp. 111–33.

Hitt, M.A., R.E. Freeman and J.S. Harrison (eds) (2001), *Handbook of Strategic Management*, Oxford: Blackwell.

Jaffe, A.B. (1989), 'Characterizing the "Technological Position" of Firms, with Application to Quantifying Technological Opportunity and Research Spillovers', *Research Policy*, 18, 2, pp. 87–97.

Kodama, F. (1986), 'Technological Diversification of Japanese Industry', *Science*, 18, 7, 233, pp. 291–6.

Leonard-Barton, D. (1995), *Wellsprings of Knowledge: Building and Sustaining the Sources of Innovation*, Boston, MA: Harvard Business School Press.

Markides, C.C. (1995), *Diversification, Refocusing, and Economic Performance*, London, England and Cambridge, MA: The MIT Press.

Montgomery, C.A. (1994), 'Corporate Diversification', *Journal of Economic Perspectives*, 8, 3, pp. 163–78.

Nelson, R.R. and S. Winter (1982), *An Evolutionary Theory of Economic Change*, Cambridge, MA: The Belknap Press.

Oskarsson, C. (1993), 'Technology Diversification – the Phenomenon, Its Causes and Effects', PhD dissertation, Department of Industrial Management and Economics, Chalmers University of Technology, Göteborg, Sweden.

Patel, P. and K. Pavitt (1994), 'Technological Competencies in the World's Largest Firms: Characteristics, Constraints and Scope for Managerial Choice', STEEP Discussion Paper No. 13, Science Policy Research Unit, University of Sussex.

Pavitt, K., M. Robson and J. Townsend (1989), 'Technological Accumulation, Diversification and Organisation in UK Companies 1945–1983', *Management Science*, January 35, 1.

Penrose, E. (1980), *The Theory of the Growth of the Firm*, Oxford: Basil Blackwell, 1959 (citations are drawn from the 2nd ed.).

Petroski, H. (1994), *The Evolution of Useful Things*, New York, NY: Vintage Books, Random House Inc.

Ramanujam, V. and P. Varadarajan (1989), 'Research on Corporate Diversification: A Synthesis', *Strategic Management Journal*, 10, pp. 523–51.

Ravenscraft, D.J. and M. Scherer (1987), *Mergers, Sell-Offs, and Economic Efficiency*, Washington, DC: The Brookings Institutions.

Rumelt, R.P. (1974), *Strategy, Structure and Economic Performance*, Cambridge, MA: Harvard Business Press.

Sanderson, S.W. and M. Uzumeri (1997), *Managing Product Families*, Chicago: Irwin.

Schon, D.A. (1967), *Technology and Change: The New Heraclitus*, New York, NY: Delacorte Press.

Scott, J.T. (1993), *Purposive Diversification and Economic Performance*, New York, NY: Cambridge University Press.

Yamaji, K. (1994), 'Market Economy and Intellectual Property Oriented Management', Speech at LES International Conference in Beijing, 7 May.

Part III

Competence: Building Up and Exploiting Technology Assets

Executive Summary

Ove Granstrand and Arie Nagel

Technological changes have always been a major source of threats and opportunities for company survival and wealth. However, it was not until a generation or so ago that company costs and benefits of R&D and new technology started to be accounted for explicitly in industry, instead of being hidden away from top management attention in the overhead costs. As R&D and technology costs and benefits have magnified and become more observable, the management attention paid to them has grown and the perspective shifted sideways, outwards and upwards in the organization space. The focus has thereby moved from engineering management to R&D management and further to technology management and arguably even further to knowledge management. The focus on technology management is likely to broaden further, since in most cases, few if any management activities today are free from technology considerations.

As a consequence of this widening focus on technology, at least three pairs of glasses have to be used by managers in order to obtain a comprehensive perspective on technology:

1. Strategic glasses;
2. Financial glasses;
3. Commercial glasses.

Part III of the book discusses these three perspectives. Viewing technology strategically means recognizing technology and business visions, such as NEC's vision that computers and communications would converge. It also means recognizing the linkages between technologies and company objectives, and being able to formulate technology strategies to support different business strategies. Strategic glasses also enable a long-range view to be taken and compensate for possible short-sightedness in addressing only current customer demands, or other types of myopia.

Technology should be regarded as a provider of competitive edge and growth, rather than just an operational tool.

With financial glasses the technologies mastered and controlled by the company are viewed as a portfolio of capitalizable assets that could be acquired, improved and exploited through various strategies. In particular, R&D is not seen as an expense but as an investment, building on existing competencies and investing in new ones.

The commercial glasses protect against the blindness induced by the sheer brightness of R&D engineers, scientists and inventors and help to identify the shades of future customer needs and the paths to market. They also help the manager stand in the shoes of a technology salesman and see a range of alternatives to technology exploitation other than through traditional product sales, e.g. through venturing, partnering or licensing. The commercial glasses could also be turned around, to help to see from a buyers' point of view the commercial alternatives to in-house R&D. This could be a variety of ways to buy new technologies on different technology markets or to source them through alliances or intelligence operations.

The chapters in Part III contribute to providing different aspects of these views.

Chapter 11 in particular provides commercial glasses for both technology buyers and technology sellers by zooming in on new tasks for marketing and how these tasks should be organized and how top management can get involved.

Chapters 10 and 12 provide particular lenses for commercial glasses, focusing on technology intelligence and alliances respectively, in order to cope with the rapidly changing technological and market environments. Several companies have developed a Technology Intelligence System. This system has to collect and organize relevant data in order to support strategic technology management decision-making – an important role for top management. Strategic alliances can no longer be considered as second-best options compared to internal development and mergers and acquisitions. The make-buy-or-ally decision has become a key managerial consideration.

Chapter 13 focuses on in-house R&D, and charts the development of this function over time and the nature of the evolving challenges being confronted. In recent years this activity has increasingly involved collaborations with outside organizations, and the chapter contributes to each of the three views under discussion.

Chapters 10, 11, 12, and 13 also provide lenses for the strategic glasses. Each chapter deals with particular strategies for technology acquisition and exploitation. These strategies vary according to how strongly they depend on external market transactions, links to technology intelligence in Chapter 10, licensing in and out in Chapter 11, to alliances in Chapter 12 and finally internal R&D in Chapter 13.

By means of strategies such as these, the value of the technological assets of the company is built up, which leads us to the lenses for financial glasses, provided in Chapters 8 and 9. Chapter 8 deals with various systems and approaches for technology valuation, prioritization and control. In this chapter various methods of assessing technology assets are presented, from real options to the use of the balanced score card.

Chapter 9 explores the mechanisms for protecting profit margins and extracting rents by applying intellectual property rights (IPRs). In doing so, the value of technology assets can be leveraged and turned into intellectual capital (IC). In the new type of economy IC tends to dominate the capital structure of most firms, turning the spotlight on intellectual capital management for value creation. IPR protection has become much more powerful as a competitive weapon since the 1980s. This prompts the question of how to manage IPRs strategically and how to link IP strategies as value-creating strategies for company strategies, previously disconnected from each other during a weak IPR regime. In order to help find answers to these questions, the chapter also provides lenses for strategic glasses through which steps on a strategy ladder can be seen, leading from IP strategies through product, technology and innovation strategies to business and corporate strategies. This strategy connection is important for value creation.

Overall, Part III provides a comprehensive set of perspectives for viewing and understanding the value that technological assets can generate for a business.

Ten key questions for the Board

1. Do we have the means to evaluate our technology portfolio?
2. Are we able to monitor the quality of our technology decision making?
3. Do we have a well-formulated IP strategy that links to our business strategy?
4. Are we actively creating shareholder value from our IP portfolio?
5. Does our technology intelligence system provide key information for boardroom decision making?
6. Have we established specialist activities for technology marketing?

7. Do technology marketing issues get raised at board level?
8. Are we making appropriate use of alliances in the quest to acquire new technologies?
9. Have we structured the business to be responsive to the changing competitive landscape?
10. Have our R&D activities adapted to a changing business climate?

8

How to Evaluate Technology Performance: Tasks and Structure of Technology Performance Control

Hans-Helmuth Jung and Hugo Tschirky

Overview

Nowadays, technologies represent a major growth factor for most enterprises. This fact forces enterprises to consciously develop technology strategies in order to include technology-related aspects in the business strategy. Enterprises can successfully realize their technology strategies, operationalized with the help of technology projects. These technology projects encompass different technology decisions such as make or buy, and keep or sell. A question arises concerning the value, that is the increase in value of all of these technology projects and their performance. This important question appears during the planning phase of technology projects; but it also appears continuously during the revision and adaptation of strategic technology decisions.

Introduction

The continuous control of technology strategy implementation is affected by uncertainty and risk. For example, an unexpected incorporation of new product technologies into competitor's products can make current technology decisions obsolete. Competing with the current product technology also requires new process technologies in order to improve the margin or defend the market share. Moreover, the depreciation through cannibalization effects, set off by technology substitutions, can only be calculated in relation to the technology portfolio of the enterprise.

The task of a technology management control system (TMCS) must therefore be to ensure that technology projects are carried out. This means controlling the progress of the planned technology projects as well as checking if the goals are achieved. A TMCS should check whether the planned technology projects are redundancy-free with other technology projects and check them with the strategic projects for redundancy as well. This also includes the reconsideration if the planned projects are compatible with the technology strategy and business and resource strategies as well as with company and technology policy.

Why does a technology-based enterprise need a TMCS if it has already installed an R&D management control system? In the case of make-decisions involving R&D projects, an R&D management control system is needed to ensure successful project completion. In this context, the R&D management control system can be seen as an operational instrument. The above described tasks of control within the whole portfolio of technology projects shows that it is not enough to control only the R&D department. This can include departments such as the supply department, especially when the level of internal R&D and manufacturing is low. In this case, a TMCS must work closely with the sourcing management in addition to R&D management.

Furthermore, during the planning phase, a TMCS can support management by providing information about the planned technology projects. In particular, TMCS can provide the required support through the evaluation and prioritization of these technology projects. This means that control structures, processes and methods can also be used within the planning phase for evaluating and prioritizing technology projects.

Design of a technology management control system

Mission and goal

The *mission* for the TMCS is defined as:

> Bringing the technology management control system into the enterprise's management system.

In order to realize this mission, two conditions must be met: the first condition is to bring technology issues into management control systems. The second condition is to provide compatibility with technology management. Taking into consideration these two conditions, the *major goal* of designing and implementing the TMCS is:

> Processes, methods and structure of the technology management control system must be compatible with technology management and the enterprise's management control system.

Design of tasks and organization

Based on Simons' strategic management control approach (1995), the TMCS is designed in a way so that they are compatible with technology management as well as aligning with enterprise's management control system.

The four technology control levers

Each element of the technology control systems has a different purpose in controlling the technology strategy (the various levers of technology control are shown in Figure 8.1 about their purpose, control focus and control of the technology strategy):

- The *Diagnostic Technology Control System* is the essential instrument for transforming planned technology strategy into realized technology strategy. It focuses attention on goal achievement. The diagnostic technology control system relates to technology strategy as a *Plan*. The diagnostic technology control system allows management to measure outcomes and compare results with technology goals.
- The *Interactive Technology Control System* is different from the diagnostic technology control system. It gives management an instrument to influence the experimentation and opportunity-seeking that may result in emergent new technology decisions. This system relates to the technology strategy as *Patterns of Action*.

	Purpose	Control Focus	Control of Technology Strategy
Technology Beliefs System	Empower and Expand Search Activity	Vision / Mission	Perspective
Technology Boundary System	Provide Limits of Dissipating Resources and Risks	Strategic Technology Fields	Position
Technology Diagnostic Control System	Control of Planned Technology Strategy	Plans and Goals	Plan
Technology Interactive Control System	Stimulate and Guide New Technology Decisions	Strategic Uncertainties	Patterns of Action

Figure 8.1   Relating the four technology control levers to technology strategy
Source: adapted from Simons, 1995: 156

- The *Technology Beliefs System* inspires both planned technology strategy and new technology decisions. It provides guidance and inspiration for opportunity-seeking. This system relates to the technology strategy as a *Perspective*.
- The *Technology Boundary System* ensures that planned technology strategy as well as new technology decisions fall within the defined strategic technology fields and within acceptable levels of technological risk. This system controls technology strategy as a *Position*.

As noted earlier, the four systems are nested: each offers some measure of guidance or control to the technology strategy process, but each system is used in different ways for different purposes. These different usage patterns are critical in leveraging scarce management attention to maximize management's impact.

The system for controlling technology strategy and performance

The four levers of control, described above, are integrated into a dynamic system for controlling the technology strategy. Figure 8.2 presents the system, which is an adaptation of Simons' strategic management control approach (1995: 154), originally based on Mintzberg's (1978) concept of Patterns of Strategy Formulation. The system should provide the understanding of technology management controls in technology-based

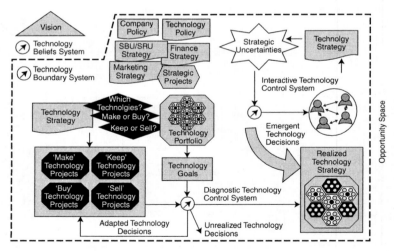

Figure 8.2   Technology management control system
Source: inspired by Simons, 1995: 154

enterprises in a systemic way and give answers concerning the two research questions so that the TMCS can be discussed without specifying the degree of systematization.

The TMCS is achieved through the technology beliefs system, the technology boundary system, the diagnostic technology control system and the interactive technology control system jointly working to control both implementation of planned technology strategy and the formation of emergent new technology decisions.

The technology beliefs system empowers and expands opportunity-seeking. The technology boundary system sets the rules of technological risk. Together, the technology beliefs and the boundary systems frame the strategic technology fields for the enterprise. The diagnostic technology control system focuses attention on the implementation of planned technology strategy, which is compared with the technology goals. The interactive technology control system expands and guides the opportunity-seeking that may result in the emergence of new technology decisions. Together, the technology diagnostic and interactive systems guide the implementation of technology strategy and approve it for adaptation to new technology decisions.

The system and its elements presented in Figure 8.2 will be verified in the next section. The case outlining the four levers of the TMCS will be shown. Due to the fact that it was not possible to find an enterprise in which all three kinds of technology decisions were simultaneously being carried out, this case deals with the keep-or-sell-decision.

Solution for technology management control system

Infineon technologies

After the IPO at the New York and Frankfurt Stock Exchanges, the Siemens Semiconductor Business became Infineon Technologies on 1 April 1999. After experiencing rapid growth for many years, Infineon had a turnover of over 7 billion euros in the fiscal year 2000. According to Dataquest, this made Infineon one of the top ten players in the semiconductor industry.

Infineon is made up of five product divisions: Wireline Communications, Wireless Solutions, Security and Chipcard ICs, Automotive & Industrial and Memory Products. The product divisions can be grouped into two areas of activities: memory components and logic components.

R&D is decentralized for all five product divisions. Production consists of two major manufacturing steps with facilities available in all of

Infineons key markets. Notably, the two manufacturing steps are the so-called Frontend, where electronic circuits are etched on silicon wafers, and the Backend, where these wafers are cut, bonded, packaged and turned into ready-made chips.

Corporate frontend

While the product division Memory Products has its own Frontend, there is a Corporate Frontend (CFE) for the remaining four product divisions. Until recently, this CFE has manufactured every product technology required by the product divisions, regardless of volume or profitability. In other words, while the product divisions were continuously optimizing their product portfolios, the optimization of CFEs technology portfolio was non-existent.

By the end of September 2000, CFE had over 100 technologies in production and 50 more were being developed in R&D. Facing a shortage in capacity, optimizing the technology portfolio became a strategic issue for Infineon.

Technology portfolios

The semiconductor industry is a very dynamic, cost intensive and extremely cyclical business. It is therefore imperative for semiconductor companies to have a clear technology strategy. Companies lacking a good technology strategy are at risk of growing uncontrollably during cyclical upturns and running into serious problems when demand crumbles.

Having realized this a few years ago, Infineon's CFE started a project to calculate market attractiveness and technology attractiveness of technologies based on a set of Key Performance Indicators (KPIs). The result of the project was an automated instrument that can calculate the position of each technology in a portfolio illustration, similar to McKinsey's 3 x 3 matrix. The technologies are represented by bubbles whose diameter is relative to the technology's turnover.

By early 2001, it was possible for Infineon to visualize the planned technology performance over a five-year period – by pressing a button. In order to facilitate strategic decisions even further, similar technologies were combined into technology portfolio groups and displayed on the same chart – the technology portfolio.

Having combined the four dimensions; market attractiveness, technology attractiveness, sales information and time, the chart was still missing one strategically important dimension: the technology's profitability.

Before starting the project as described above, Infineon had to classify its technologies. The company developed a technology catalogue, where it differentiates between several hierarchical levels of technologies. When speaking about technologies, the company always refers to Process Groups. Every process group has specific electrical parameters and design rules. This level of distinction has been found to be significant for strategic planning. Similar process groups belong to a so-called Platform Technologies which are at the highest level of aggregation. Technology portfolios form a level in between.

Action research at Infineon: technology performance measurement

After having stated the need for a technology profitability measurement, Infineon's CFE conducted an initial study on how to calculate the new key performance indicator (KPI) with the available data.

Technology gross margin

Starting position   The study showed that it was not possible to use the Economic Value Added (EVA) method that was being used at Infineon to calculate, for example, a business unit's performance. The problem was that the capital costs could not be calculated easily. While the assignment of working assets was found to be negotiable, the assignment of the fixed assets to specific technologies was practically impossible due to a high-level manufacturing inter-connection. It seemed easier to calculate the operational result. Looking at business units (BU), Infineon was already using two profitability measurements: Profit & Loss (P&L) and Gross Margin per Business Unit (GMBU). The formula for the GMBU is (Figure 8.3 shows the cost blocks built to calculate GMBU at Infineon):

$$\text{GMBU} = \text{Sales} - \text{Frontend Costs} - \text{Backend Costs}$$
$$- \text{Additional Cost of Sales}$$

As a result of the study, it was decided to define a gross margin per technology, rather than to calculate the P&L per technology, mainly because it seemed difficult at that moment to attribute some of the product costs, general & administration costs and marketing & sales costs to a technology with the available data.

Tailor-made solution   The calculation formula for the new key performance indicator Gross Margin per Technology (GMTE) was defined as

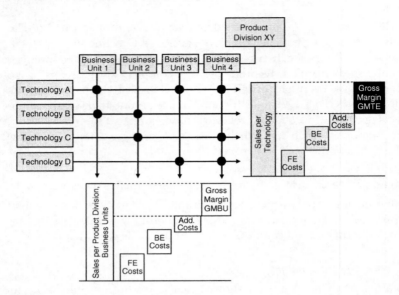

Figure 8.3   GMTE versus GMBU

follows (see Figure 8.3):

$$GMTE = Sales - Frontend\ Costs - Backend\ Costs$$
$$- Additional\ Costs\ of\ Sales$$

Reasons for this definition were that the new measurement includes the complete production costs of a technology and thus an indication of the performance of operations. Furthermore, the formula can be seen as a logical step towards a future calculation of the P&L per technology and its analogy to the existing GMBU made it suitable and acceptable to all involved.

Some might say that the GMTE should not include backend costs because the measurement is used to evaluate CFE's technologies. This seems wrong because chip costs in the backend are influenced by the CFE's technology (size of chip, structure size, etc.) and backend costs significantly influence the overall profitability of a technology. More importantly, however, it is necessary to understand that the basis of data for the calculation of the GMTE is the business units' products, including for example, backend costs that are aggregated to the respective technology. Finally, by leaving out backend costs in the formula, the new measurement could not be used to evaluate the whole manufacturing value chain, which falls under the chief operations officer's area of accountability.

After having defined the new formula, the next question was whether the absolute GMTE (€) or the cost–sales ratio GMTE (per cent) should be used in the evaluation. It is evident, that for a ranking, it is necessary to use the absolute GMTE (€) as the importance of a technology depends on its monetary return. As shown above, the GMTE (€) is equal to the margin after operations and is used to cover overhead costs (R&D, M&S, G&A). The GMTE (per) on the contrary, is an isolated KPI that is unsuitable for a ranking. To calculate the GMTE, various data sources are necessary.

Technology ABC Analysis

The KPI GMTE (€) can be used for various evaluations such as the profitability of technologies compared to structure size, wafer size, etc. It is also possible to examine overall technology performance for the total of Infineon's logic business, for each business unit or other organizational units. An instrument that can be used for almost all of these evaluations is the Technology ABC Analysis, explained below.

Underlying concepts. The Lorenz curve is a graphic representation showing the degree of inequality of a frequency distribution in which the cumulative percentages of a population (for instance, taxpayers and firms) are plotted against the cumulative percentage of the variable under study (for instance, incomes and employment). A straight line rising at an angle of 45 degrees from the start on the graph will indicate perfect equality. For instance, if 10 per cent of firms employ 10 per cent of the total labour force, 20 per cent of firms employ 20 per cent of the total labour force, etc. (linear relationship). However, if there are a large number of small firms which employ few people and a small number of large firms employing many people, the distribution will be unequal.

In economics, the method is often used to evaluate items (both on a value or quantity basis) of a sales mix in order to distinguish the monetarily important from the less important.

Infineon's benefit. Applying the Lorenz curve to Infineon's GMTE (€), derived from the BU's plan data, gives an insight into each technology's overall importance. In order to generate the graph shown in Figure 8.4, technologies were first sorted by GMTE (€). Each data point of the curve was calculated by adding the number of technologies and the

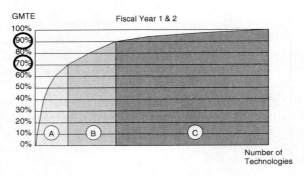

Figure 8.4   Technology ABC Analysis

GMTE (€). The ABC-borders were defined so that A-technologies made up 70 per cent of the cumulative GMTE (€), B-technologies 20 per cent and C-technologies 10 per cent.

Looking at different planning intervals (for instance, fiscal years 1–2 and fiscal years 3–5) it could be shown that Infineon would be able to reduce the total number of technologies (as a result of its technology portfolio method). According to Infineon's planning, it would reduce the number of A-technologies significantly while boosting the return at the same time.

Based on its technology portfolio, Infineon's management makes decisions about when a technology should be phased out. Combining the ABC method with information from a Phase-Out Calendar, the Phase-Out Decisions from the profitability point-of-view can be verified.

Technology trend sectors

To fully understand the profitability of a technology it is also important to take a look at its sales–cost ratio GMTE (per cent). As stated above, the GMTE (per cent) is not suitable as a stand-alone KPI and has to be shown, for instance, relative to sales.

Underlying concepts.   To demonstrate the trend of a technology, it is possible to plot the yearly GMTE (per cent) and sales figures in a graph as shown in Figure 8.5, for two technologies and two fiscal years. Since the product of GMTE (per cent) and sales are equal to GMTE (€), it is also possible to plot curves of constant GMTE (€) through each data point. As can be seen in Figure 8.5, the two sample technologies have the exact same GMTE (€).

Theoretically, it can be said that a company is indifferent to how the GMTE (€) is achieved. It will accept trade-offs between sales and GMTE (per cent) along the Isovalor Curve, as it describes a constant gross margin – thus the same amount of money (Tschirky, 1998: 349). A simplification of the Figure 8.5 is achieved, when the GMTE (per cent) is plotted against the GMTE (€) directly, instead of against sales. In this case, the Isovalor Curves become straight lines (see Figure 8.6).

It seems that the information about sales is lost in this illustration. Since the GMTE (€) is the product of GMTE (per cent) and sales, it is clear that on the perpendicular line for GMTE (100 per cent) the GMTE

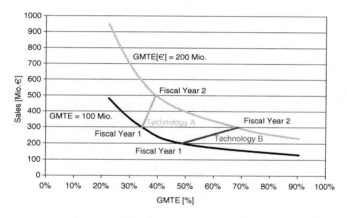

Figure 8.5 *GMTE*-trend chart (gross margin [%]-sales [€]-diagram)

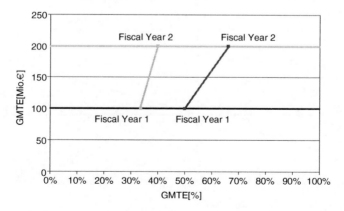

Figure 8.6 *GMTE*-trend chart (gross margin [%]-*GMTE* [€]-diagram)

(€) equals sales and for GMTE (0 per cent), the GMTE (€) is always zero. Thus, by drawing a straight line through the origin and a particular data point, the sales value for this point can be shown at the perpendicular intersection with the GMTE (100 per cent). Furthermore, it is important to note that all straight lines through the origin signify constant sales.

Interpretation of technology trend sectors.   In order to evaluate the trend of a given technology, it is necessary to draw three straight lines through the first data point in which the sales are constant, a perpendicular line signifying constant GMTE (€) and a horizontal line signifying constant GMTE (€).

The three straight lines produce six different possible trend sectors. As will be shown, the sectors can be reduced to four. Figure 8.7 illustrates what has been explained so far.

The trend of a technology is derived by looking into which sector a technology is developing from fiscal year 1 to fiscal year 2. For example, the technology shown in Figure 8.7 has an S1-trend. Looking at the sales constant first, it is easy to understand that the trend above the line signifies a growth in sales, a trend below this line would signify a drop in sales. The trend above the GMTE (€) constant tells us that the technology is going to generate more money and less below the constant. This leaves the GMTE (per cent) constant to be explained. The GMTE (per cent) shows the interdependence of sales and cost of production. If this ratio

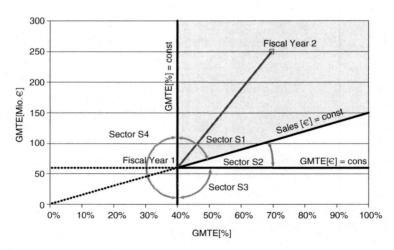

Figure 8.7   Technology trend sectors
Source: Jung *et al.*, 2002

changes over time, possible reasons are rising (sinking) production costs or falling prices on the market. This is true because the GMTE (€) consists mainly of variable costs – thus there is a linear correlation between costs and production volume.

Like most companies, Infineon is also predicting a decline in production costs over time. Therefore, a change in GMTE (per cent) has to be interpreted as follows: when prices stay stable (or rise) the GMTE (per cent) will grow. If prices fall at the same speed as production becomes cheaper, the GMTE (per cent) will remain stable. Logically, if prices fall faster than production becomes cheaper, the GMTE (per cent) will fall. Falling prices indicate that the products of this particular technology are subject to intense competition on the market. It is for this reason that all of the sectors left of the GMTE (per cent) constant are summed up into only one trend sector (S4). Thus, the trend of a technology can be classified with the technology trend sectors as follows (Figure 8.8):

Trend Sector	Sales	GMTE[€]	GMTE[%]
S1	Rising	Rising	Rising
S2	Falling	Rising	Rising
S3	Heavily Falling	Falling	Rising
S4	Rising/Falling	Rising/Falling	Falling

Figure 8.8   Trend sector classification

Norm decisions

Technology trend sectors can be used to define norm decisions respective to profitability. It is necessary though to consider the technology's overall importance for Infineon's Logic units. This can be achieved by including the results of the preceding technology ABC analysis.

The findings can be visualized by plotting the ABC thresholds. The values of the thresholds correspond to the point in time of the first data point. Figure 8.9 gives an overview of the norm decisions for all possible trends. The concluding Figure 8.10 explains how the norm decisions were derived for A-Technologies.

ABC-Analysis GMTE Trend Norm Decisions		
A-Technologies	S1	Push
70% cumulated contribution to GMTE	S2	Marketing Activity/Product Switch
	S3	Marketing Activity/Cash out
	S4	Selective (Market Leader?)
B-Technologies	S1	Push
20% cumulated contribution to GMTE	S2	Cash out
	S3	Cash out/Phase out
	S4	Phase out
C-Technologies	S1	Watch (Potential?)
10% cumulated contribution to GMTE	S2	Phase out
	S3	Phase out
	S4	Phase out

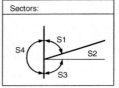

	Trend	Sales	GMTE[€]	GMTE[%]
S1	⇑	⇑	⇑	
S2	⬇	⇑	⇑	
S3	⬇⬇⬇	⬇	⇑	
S4	⇕	⇕	⬇	

Sectors:

Figure 8.9   Norm decisions

Technology Classification	GMTE Trend	Argumentation	
A-Technologies 70% cumulated contribution to GMTE	S1	Push	All indicators point upwards. The full potential of this economically important technology is not yet exhausted.
	S2	Marketing Activity/ Product Switch	Sinking sales indicate that the technology is loosing its importance. The development of succeeding technologies (products) and marketing activities have to be reviewed and the development of new succeeding technologies be considered.
	S3	Marketing Activity/ Cash out	Both sinking sales and sinking GMTE [ ] indicate that no more investments into this technology should be made (design-in-freeze). If it exists, the succeeding technology should be fostered.
	S4	Selective (Market Leader?)	Depending on its market position this technology should be cashed out (market leader) or phased out.

Figure 8.10   Norm decisions (A-Technologies)

Embedding the GMTE into Infineon's Balance Scorecard

In 2000, Infineon introduced the Balanced Scorecard (BSC) across the company. Infineon's BSC contains five views:

- Finance
- Market and Customer
- Internal Processes

- Innovation/Technology
- Human Resources

The introduction of the BSC was a top-down process, beginning with the top level, the BSC was split up in several business units as well as CFE (Corporate Frontend).

The various indicators that have been defined include the GMTE, which is an important variable in the balanced scorecard system. The indicator GMTE flows into the performance driver Controlling of Technology Projects, a key element of the Innovation/Technology view. In 2001, the BSC has yet to be introduced completely in CFE and the exact links between the different indicators cannot be presented. In any case, the use of the GMTE shows that it can be embedded into Infineon's management control system as an important performance variable. Therefore, it makes sense to design and implement a TMCS in the context of a holistic management control system, in this case, put into action with a balanced scorecard.

Findings from Infineon Technologies

With the introduction and evaluation of the GMTE, the profitability point of view has been brought into Infineon's technology strategy process.

Diagnostic technology control system

The diagnostic technology control system is realized through the technology ABC analysis, which is based on GMTE's data calculation and allows the CFE to measure the profitability of current technologies (Figure 8.11). Technology strategy can be checked with this instrument to determine if their planned impact can be achieved. GMTE is a typical critical performance variable, underlined with a quantitative target that becomes a technology goal, embodied in percentages. If a product technology does not achieve its margin, CFE's management can decide to phase out the technology. Naturally, the GMTE is not only the basis for decision-making, but it represents a valuable quantitative figure apart from the qualitative figures such as market or technology attractiveness. When deviations occur, they can be adapted, for example, by increasing the marketing activities of product divisions and in the case of strong deviations, the premature phase out of technologies. The action taken depends strongly on the results of the technology ABC analysis. Management is easily able to check the GMTE with the balanced scorecard system.

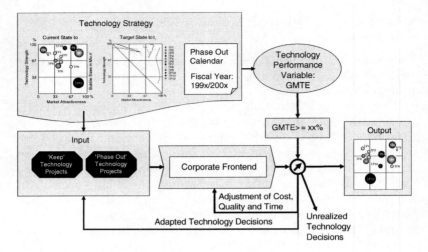

Figure 8.11   Diagnostic technology control process at Infineon

Interactive technology control system

The instrument of technology trend sectors at Infineon, as described earlier, shows a typical interactive technology control system. This instrument combines GMTE with market forecasts, and allows the CFE's management to identify the rationale behind current technology decisions. Moreover, with this instrument, strategic uncertainties that existed during the planning period can be watched and CFE's management can pro-actively steer technology decisions. Based on GMTE and the set of norm decisions, CFE's management is able to react before deviations occur (Figure 8.12). Compared to the diagnostic technology control system in which the ABC analysis can be considered as a feedback system, the interactive technology control system has the character of a feed-forward system. In other words, the instrument of technology trend sectors with pre-defined norm decisions enables management, in addition to its planned technology strategy, to make new technology decisions.

Technology beliefs and boundary systems

The old mission of the CFE was to manufacture every technology required by the product divisions, regardless of volume or profitability. In other words, while the product divisions were continuously optimizing their product portfolios, the optimization of the CFE's technology portfolio was non-existent. Through the new mission, the CFE is forced

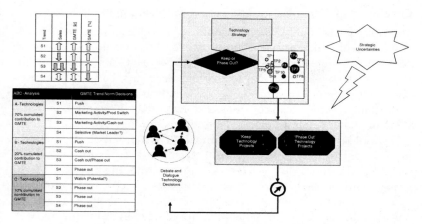

Figure 8.12   Interactive-technology control process at Infineon

to optimize their technology portfolio in the same way as product divisions and the CFE unit. This means that on the one hand, the CFE is not allowed to incur losses. On the other hand, the company's policy requires the CFE to cater for the needs of product divisions. Thus, the strategic technology fields in which the CFE must be active are predetermined. The CFE management must therefore negotiate with product division managers over forecasted product life cycles, quantities of wafers, and market development. For example, silicon chip products used in the automotive industry must be available over eight to ten years. It makes no sense to produce a few of these silicon chips every year, because the economy of scale cannot attain the accrual costs. Therefore, an economical batch size must be evaluated by the CFE and coordinated with the product division before the technology can be phased out. The produced batch of chips will then be transferred to the stock room at Infineon or to the customer. The CFE now has the permission to negotiate such issues with the product divisions.

The example points out that the CFE is embedded in the tension between corporate goals and the needs of product divisions. The beliefs and boundary systems enable the CFE management to handle these tensions either by using the opportunity space to fulfill the needs of product divisions. Both boundaries define the space within which the CFE can look for possible opportunities. One of the CFE management's tasks is to optimally remain within this scope.

Conclusion of technology management control system

Technology ABC analysis and technology trend sector analysis enable management to make their technology decisions on a financial basis. In contrast to financially based short-term decisions, it has been impossible until now to make long-term technology decisions, based on financial data. With the use of technology ABC analysis and technology trend sectors, management can control technology strategy quantitatively and therefore has a better foundation for new technology decisions.

Technology ABC analysis, based on GMTE is a useful diagnostic technology control system that gives management permission to control technology keep- or divest-decisions. Furthermore, the diagnostic technology control system allows a comparison of key strategic technology figures such as the number of wafer starts per year, yield rate, or the defect density rate per wafer. Consequently, the CFE's management could balance several technology decisions, which were planned in another way before implementing this instrument.

Infineon uses the technology trend sectors to define norm technology decisions from the profitability point of view. Therefore, monetary relevance of technologies is placed in the context of a holistic enterprise, based on the technology ABC analysis. Infineon can set ABC barriers for GMTE. In this case, Infineon uses current technology data for Fiscal Year 1, which represents basic data for a trend assessment. Because of the predefined norm decisions of technologies, management is able to quickly make new technology decisions in this way. Firstly, planned technology decisions can be reviewed, and secondly by changing premises, decisions can be rethought. Used in this way, the method of technology trend sectors is a mix of technology diagnostic and interactive technology control systems. Together with technology beliefs and boundary systems, CFE's management can balance the technology portfolios, measure the technology-related issues and take corrective actions.

The four levers of the technology control system are not used at the same intensity for each technology decision; the control focus and its appropriate instruments to be used can change over time. Methods such as technology trend sectors are seldom used and have an ad hoc character.

As with any new measurements, implementation can be difficult because people fear the findings. In the case of the GMTE it is important that the new control system will not primarily be used to evaluate the business unit's different performance with the same technology, but rather to make the CFE more profitable. In the case of Infineon, thanks to an open-minded middle management and the CFE's clear communication, the implementation of the new KPI caused no major problems.

References

Jung, H.-H., N. Atanasoski and K. Pulch (2002), 'Technology Performance Measurement: Action Research at Infineon Technologies', Proceedings of R&D Management Conference, Leuven/Belgium, 8–9 July.

Mintzberg, H. (1978), 'Patterns in Strategy Formulation', *Management Science*, 24, 9, pp. 934–48.

Simons, R. (1995), *Levers of Control: How Managers Use Innovative Control Systems to Drive Strategic Renewal*, Boston: Harvard Business School Press.

Tschirky, H. (1998), 'Konzept und Aufgaben des Integrierten Technologie-Managements', in H. Tschirky, S. Koruna (eds), *Technologie-Management: Idee und Praxis*, Zürich: Industrielle Organisation.

Tschirky, H. (1999), 'Auf dem Weg zur Unternehmenswissenschaft? Ein Ansatz zur Entsprechung von Theorie und Realität technologieintensiver Unternehmen', *Die Unternehmung*, 53, 2, pp. 67–87.

Tschirky, H., H. Brodbeck and B. Birkenmeier (1995), 'Neue Entscheidungsstrukturen eines Integrierten Technologie-Managements', *Die Unternehmung*, 49, 2, pp. 107–23.

9
From R&D/Technology Management to IP/IC Management

Ove Granstrand[1]

Overview

The emergence of the pro-patent era in the US in the 1980s is symptomatic of a transition towards intellectual capitalism. As a consequence IP issues have entered the agendas of strategic management in industry at large, while previously handled by specialists in the periphery of management attention. As a result there are often missing links between IP strategies and business strategies. This chapter presents a conceptual framework for IP strategies, technology strategies and business strategies which can be used to link these levels of strategic management. In particular the chapter illustrates various patent strategies in technology space and over time, together with some results from a study of corporate practices in Japan. Finally, the chapter introduces the wider notions of multiprotection and total IP strategies as an approach to analysing all elements of a business and how to match them properly with all available IPR types. The ultimate function of strategic management of IP is then to build up the total value of an IP portfolio as part of the company's intellectual capital. For this purpose, distributed intellectual capital management is proposed, requiring in turn a closer integration of technology, law and economics.

The emergence of the 'pro-patent era'

In order for a capitalistic economic system to operate properly, it is of decisive importance that markets for labour, capital, products, services, etc. are functioning. However, markets for ideas, knowledge, information and intellectual products in general have difficulties with functioning in principle. It is basically very difficult to sell or otherwise exploit an idea without disclosing it in such a way that others can essentially use it without paying properly. From society's point of view, an underinvestment in creative work and knowledge production may then result, since creators and innovators do not get sufficiently rewarded by profits from exploiting their creations on proper markets. To compensate for the deficient functioning of such markets, technology markets in particular, a system of intellectual property rights with patents, trademarks, trade secrets, copyrights, design rights, etc. has been created by society.

Patents are granted as a temporary monopoly right which functions as an incentive both for disclosure of technical information and for investments in generating and diffusing marketable technical inventions – granted then as an attempt to improve the efficiency of the capitalistic economic system. Alternative government policy measures for similar purposes may work more one-sidedly, e.g. public technology procurement that strengthens demand, or R&D tax deduction schemes that reduce the cost of supplying R&D. Such policy measures are usually nationally oriented and may have either strong or weak effects.

Until the 1980s, the patent system had been considered by industry to have weak economic effects on a broad average (chemicals and pharmaceuticals being one exception), resulting in weak management attention. In 1982 a new court, the US Court of Appeals for the Federal Circuit (CAFC), specializing in patents, was created in the USA. At roughly the same time, but by and large for independent reasons, US antitrust policies changed in favour of strengthening the enforcement of patent rights. In parallel, US industry and US politicians started to push forcefully for a general strengthening of the IP system since US industry was perceived to have difficulties in protecting and exploiting its R&D investments in view of the competitive successes of several Asian economies, Japan in particular. A new era thus emerged, referred to as the 'pro-patent era', for various reasons and with far-reaching consequences. This development can be seen as an important symptom of the transition towards intellectual capitalism, and it has focused wide attention upon patents, intellectual property rights and intellectual capital matters in general.

The economics and management of intellectual property on the whole (thus including patents, trademarks, trade secrets, copyrights, etc.) have then changed considerably since the early 1980s. Both the use and abuse of the patent and litigation systems increased, and prompted the eruption in the mid- to late-1980s of what some people referred to as 'patent wars', notably between the USA and Japan.

The importance of patents as a means for a company to exploit new technologies has increased, as have the resources that companies devote to IP protection. Patenting and licensing have become more strategically managed, including a shift to more offensive rather than defensive patenting in a 'patent arms race'. Several US and many Japanese companies have been particularly active in building up patent portfolios and accumulating skills in using the patent system, including using patent information for technology and competitor intelligence.

The rising value of intellectual property

During the emergence of the pro-patent era of the 1980s, the economic value of patents increased in various ways. The probability of winning a court case as a patent holder increased, as did the patent damage claims (Granstrand, 1999; Sirilla *et al.*, 1992). From being a relatively minor business issue on average, patents started to gain significance.

Not only patents have increased in value and sometimes reached astonishingly high levels.[2] Astoundingly high monetary values are also attached to trademarks. Although the valuations are very uncertain, they still illustrate the possible magnitude of intellectual capital in the form of trademarks.[3] The total value of the eight highest-valued trademarks in 1992 amounts to 132 BUSD, which is in the range of GDP for a small country. Trademark values typically increase (unless they are mismanaged). The value of know-how, trade secrets and knowledge in form of human capital in general is also difficult to measure, but there are indications that such values have increased as well.

Conceptual framework for IP strategies

As the values associated with the market exploitation of intellectual properties increase, the need to foster and manage the development of these creations as well as protect their rights on an international market grows proportionately. In response to the realization of the importance of intellectual property in today's global market, different strategies have been deployed in order to reap the benefits. However, the integration of coherent IP and technology strategies with business strategies is not a simple matter and some kind of conceptual framework is necessary (although not sufficient).

For many economic theorists, management has paradoxically been somewhat of a big, dark box, perhaps even bigger than the black box of technology used to be. An important approach to exploring this box is to represent the management factor by the formulation of generic strategies, taken in a broad sense of target-related controlled courses of organizational action. Strategies can be formulated at various managerial levels for various sets of activities, and needless to say there are many possible typologies of generic strategies.[4] Figure 9.1 gives an overview of some general types of strategies for a technology-based firm (TBF). These strategy typologies also serve as a conceptual framework for IP strategies.[5]

Through notably strong economies of four kinds, that is, economies of scale, scope, speed and space (the 'four Ss') associated with the

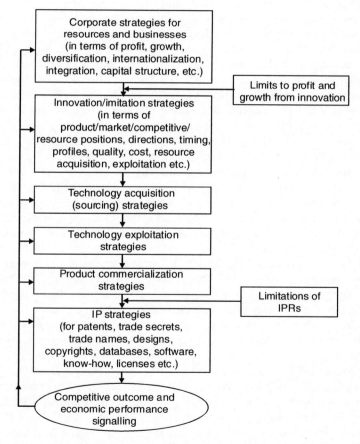

Figure 9.1 Types of management strategies for the technology-based firm
Source: Granstrand, 1999: 130, fig. 4.6

combination of different technologies and other resources, the TBF is subjected to specific dynamics in its growth and diversification and shifts in businesses and resources. In particular, a TBF tends to engage in technology diversification, thereby becoming multi-technological. As such, the TBF has incentives to economize on increasingly expensive new technologies by pursuing strategies of internationalization on both input and output markets, technology-related business diversification, external technology sale and sourcing, R&D rationalization and technology-related partnering.

In order to realize the potential economies associated with new technologies, it is crucial to formulate and execute coherent strategies at corporate, technology, product and IP levels. Figure 9.2 gives a more detailed overview of general types of strategies at technology and product business level. Note that Figure 9.2 provides a breakdown of first technology acquisition and exploitation strategies and then product commercialization strategies, which constitute a breakdown of the specific strategy 'internal exploitation'. Finally, Figure 9.2 also lists a number of patent strategies as well as possible counter-patent strategies of a competitor and subsequent litigation strategies in case the competitor infringes a patent. Figure 9.3 then illustrates the various patent strategies of Figure 9.2 in a technology landscape or space, while Figure 9.4 illustrates how a patent portfolio could be built up over a product life cycle (PLC) through continuous patenting rather than through sporadic patenting with just a few patents as has been common in the past, especially in Western companies. Strategies for other IPRs such as trade secrets and trademarks could be typologized as well, but are left out here (see further Granstrand, 2000).

Different IP strategies are linked to different product commercialization strategies. Moreover, the various strategies are mostly complementary. For example, both patents and secrets could be used to slow down competitors in order to increase market lead times in addition to focusing on speed to market. (It is actually a widely held but mostly untrue myth that a focus on market lead time can substitute for patents.)

A product business is also typically composed of several elements that could be promoted or protected by different IPRs. Altogether these conditions surrounding a business prompt the concept of multiprotection, that is, the use of not only a portfolio of patents but a portfolio of IPRs.

Patent strategies will be examined in more detail in the next section, and then the concept of multiprotection of business systems will be examined.

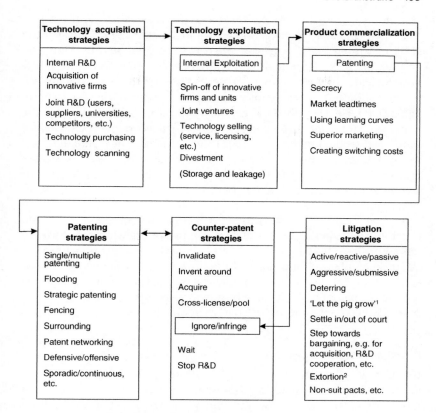

Figure 9.2 Summary of technology and patent strategies

Notes: [1] Refers to postponed filing of complaints in order to increase bargaining power. This strategy may backfire in court.
[2] Litigation used as a primary business idea for collecting damages or royalties, exercised by some inventors or patent brokers or lawyers, possibly acting on behalf of inventors on a commission basis (e.g. getting 30–50 per cent of any collectable damages). This strategy may also backfire in court.

Source: Granstrand, 1999: 236, fig. 7.9

Patent strategies

Patent strategies in general

The literature in economics and management on patent strategies is generally very thin, as was the case for technology strategies until that area grew popular in the 1980s (see Granstrand, 1982). The popularity of the strategy concept has also started to grow in the IP community. Several works on IP strategy from a mainly legal perspective have appeared; see e.g. Anawalt and Enayati (1996) and Glazier (1995). A more management-oriented work is presented by Momberg and Ashton (1986). Manuals and textbooks (as well as licensing strategies) for patenting often discuss patent strategies in terms of when (in the R&D process), where (choice of countries), why and how to patent. Patent strategies described by statistical indicators of patenting and the patent portfolios of firms and related to their economic performance have been studied by Ernst (1995). Patent strategies in Japanese industry have been studied by Rahn (1994). Various business history studies also account for patent strategies used in the evolution of an industry or a company. A recent example from the electronics industry is given in Takahashi (1994).

In these types of works, various ways are used to characterize and classify patents and patent strategies. Below, a somewhat novel way to represent these strategies, based on the concept of a technology space, the product life cycle and the technology life cycle, will be used. Patent strategies can also be defined at the level of individual patents or at the level of the patent portfolio for a business or a company as a whole. Here, patent strategies will be discussed at the portfolio level.

Patenting in technology space

In order to illustrate various patent strategies it is useful to think abstractly of a general technology space in terms of a technological terrain or technology landscape, which is gradually explored by R&D processes. Parts of the terrain with (roughly) similar R&D difficulties in terms of costs could be delineated by R&D isocost curves, in principle resembling altitude contours. Various maps of this technology landscape could be constructed, revised and improved as R&D proceeds. A patent could be represented on such maps by a circle enclosing the technical solutions in the claims of the patent. The size of the circle could also be used schematically to indicate the scope of the patent. With this type of map a number of generic patent strategies can be illustrated as in Figure 9.3, based on the configuration of multiple patents. Of course, configurations in reality are not as 'neat' as in the figure, which aims at illustrating different cases in principle. Moreover, patent strategies obviously cannot rely solely on configuration considerations, but must also take into account the actual qualities of individual patents and patent claims as well as the company situation in general (whether the company is leading or catching up, etc.) and finally the pattern of patenting

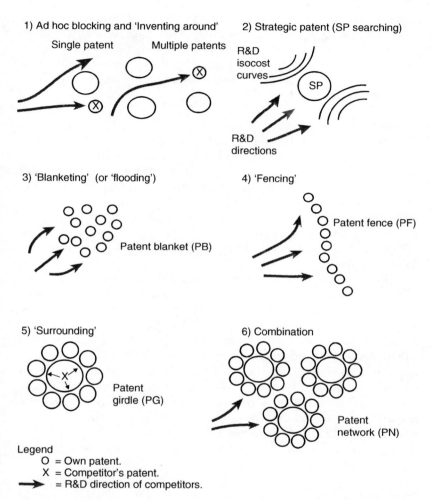

Figure 9.3 Various patent strategies in technology space
Source: Granstrand, 1999: 220, fig. 7.1

over time (see the next section). With this in mind, a number of generic patent strategies could be described as follows:

Ad hoc blocking and 'inventing around'. Typically as a result of ad hoc efforts, small resources and/or disregard of small patents and portfolio effects, one or a few patents are used in this case to protect an innovation in a special application. The possibilities to invent around are many, and R&D costs and time for inventing around are low. This strategy has been common among Western inventors, especially in small firms with limited resources for patenting, and in mechanical engineering where possibilities to cheaply invent around usually exist (in contrast to chemical engineering).

Strategic patent searching.   A single patent with a large blocking power is (somewhat ambiguously) called a strategic patent. In other words, strategic patents have deterringly high or insurmountable invent-around costs and are therefore necessary for doing business within a specific product area. This is illustrated in Figure 9.3 with R&D isocost curves, i.e. curves indicating the same level of R&D costs in the technology space or landscape (analogous to equidistance curves on ordinary maps). To continue the analogue, a strategic patent then is blocking a passage in the technology landscape, which R&D people have to pass in their search for technical solutions.

A case in point is the basic patent from 1978 of Astra-Zeneca's ulcer drug Losec (with generic name omeprazole), which has proved to be very well positioned in the chemical landscape with all its molecular variants. However, that was not known at the outset in the late 1970s and in retrospect one could say that it was a 'hit' right on target, accomplished with a mix of skills and luck. In general, when a new set of technological opportunities emerges, the landscape is clouded with uncertainty, its contours are difficult to discern, and it is difficult and time-consuming for R&D to search out the economically attractive and technologically feasible directions among all possible paths. In such a situation, it may pay off to lay out a 'blanket' or 'thicket' of patents at an early stage in the field and hope that some may prove to be strategic when uncertainty is reduced at a later stage. That is our next patent strategy.

'Blanketing' and 'flooding'.   In the case of blanketing, efforts are made to turn an area into a jungle, thicket or minefield of patents, e.g. 'mining' or 'bombing' every step in a manufacturing process (e.g. a fluid packaging process or a paper-copying process) with patents, more or less systematically.[6] Flooding refers to a less structured way of taking out multiple patents, major as well as minor, in a field. Flooding may result from quantity-oriented patenting-reward schemes among company employees as much as from a conscious company strategy. Blanketing and flooding may be used as a strategy in emerging technologies (e.g. for dental implants or superconductivity) when uncertainty is high regarding

which R&D directions are fruitful, or in situations with uncertainty about the economic importance of the scope of a patent, as described above. In special situations they may also be strategically used as a type of 'decoy patenting' in order to mislead or confuse competitors over the company's main R&D direction.

Typically, blanketing and flooding make use of the possibilities to take out patents on minor inventions from a technical point of view. Such minor patents are often frowned on by engineers and inventors and sometimes referred to as 'petty patents', 'junk patents' or 'nuisance patents'. However, such judgments are surprisingly often based on the technical characteristics rather than the possible economic importance of the patent. Minor patents can be used as nuisance patents to slow down competitors. Minor patents may also be useful in building the bargaining power of a patent portfolio. Nevertheless, it must be kept in mind that not all patents are economically justified and that a blanketing or flooding strategy is only economical up to a point.

'Fencing'. This refers to the situation where a series of patents, ordered in some way, block certain lines or directions of R&D, e.g. a range of variants of a chemical sub-process, molecular design, geometric shape, temperature conditions or pressure conditions. There is no clear-cut borderline between blanketing and fencing. As uncertainty in new technologies is reduced by R&D, the contours of the technology landscape become more clear, which opens up possibilities for more structured and economical patenting. A blanket could then be reduced to a fence without losing much blocking power. For example, a manufacturing process with new process technologies (e.g. for packaging or copying) could initially offer many configurations of process steps for which blanketing could be justified, until some specific sequences of process steps emerge as more economical for which fencing would be sufficient. In the extreme, a fence could be reduced to a strategic patent.

Fencing could be used in new technologies to block competitors, create licensing opportunities, secure design freedom for future products and protect existing ones. Fencing is typically also used for a range of possibly quite different technical solutions for achieving a similar functional result, i.e. for competing technologies or technological substitutes. It is then important for a company to try to fence off improvements in competing technologies continually over time, e.g. to erect fences for upgrades or different product generations (see Granstrand, 2000: 215, for an example). Fencing is in fact an old strategy, described already by Alfred Marshall (1994: 520 [1890].) A classic example is the way DuPont fenced in its invention of nylon by patenting a range of molecular variations of polymers with properties potentially similar to those of nylon. In this way, fencing in several dimensions may come close to systematic blanketing. (See Scherer, 1980: 451.)

'Surrounding'. Typically this is the case when an important central patent of some kind, especially a strategic patent, can be fenced in or surrounded by other patents, which are individually less important but collectively block the effective commercial use of the technology covered by the central patent, even after its expiration. Often, surrounding patents pertain to different applications of a basic invention or to different ways of producing a product or different materials in it. Surrounding can be used to get access to the surrounded technology, e.g. through cross-licensing. This is an important possibility if a competitor gets a strategic patent. Other competitors can then hope to win a second patent race for application patents that could possibly block the exploitation of the strategic patent, which in turn would create possibilities for cross-licensing. (See Spero, 1990 for an example.)

Combination into patent networks. This refers to the building of a patent portfolio in which patents of various kinds and configurations are consciously used to strengthen overall protection and bargaining power. A patent network typically evolves over time without a clear view of the configuration at the outset. It is then important to judge it in a dynamic, uncertain context, which leads us into patent strategies over time.

Patenting over time

The patenting patterns in Figure 9.3 are snapshots of the results from patenting activities over time, involving several races for patents of various types – product patents, process patents, application patents, etc. Different patent strategies over time can be considered as well. Two principal types of diagrams could be used, one showing the development over time of some economic variable (e.g. cash flow) as in Figure 9.4, and one showing some technology-related variable (typically technical performance) as in Figure 9.5. Besides this difference, Figure 9.4 shows the patent strategy of one company for one product generation while Figure 9.5 shows the patent strategies (or rather patenting behaviours) of several companies for two product generations, corresponding to two overlapping technology bases.

One product generation. Two alternative patent strategies could be illustrated in connection with the cash flow over the product life cycle (PLC)

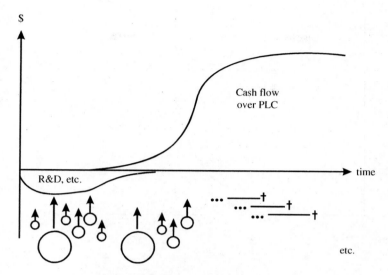

Figure 9.4   Continuous patenting and build-up of patent portfolio
Source: Granstrand, 1999: 223, fig. 7.3

of one product generation. In the first case, called *sporadic patenting*, just a few patents at key steps in the R&D process are taken out. In the second case, as shown by Figure 9.4, a conscious effort is made to build up a rich patent portfolio, and patents are applied for more or less continuously in the R&D process. This second strategy can be called *continuous or follow-up patenting* and results in the build-up of a patent portfolio for the product business in question. The portfolio is composed of a number of product patents, application patents, production process patents etc., reflecting the shifts of emphasis in R&D work in the different PLC stages. This is more costly and discloses more information, as well as requiring more astute management of patent maintenance and expiration, but gives a broader and more long-lasting protection while reducing the risk for the innovating company to be foreclosed by a fast competitor. It should also be noted that continuous patenting is somewhat along the same lines as continuous improvement or 'Kaizen'. However, continuous patenting is not only applicable to continuous improvements of a product. In developing a product of a systems nature, for example a power transmission system, many technologies are involved with patentable advances on many fronts as R&D proceeds, while the final product may represent a radical step in increased overall technical performance.

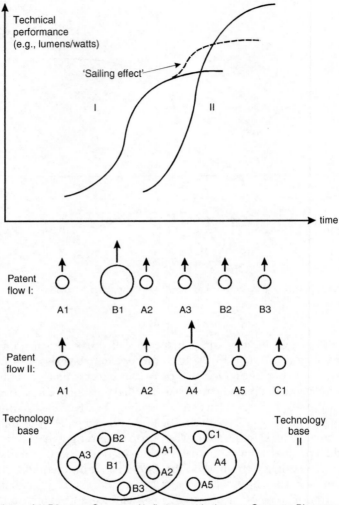

Notes: A1, B2, etc. = Company A's first patent in the area, Company B's second patent in the area, etc.

I, II = Two technical performance curves, corresponding to technology bases I and II represented by two overlapping sets of technologies, being partly protected in technology space by two patent flows over time. The 'sailing effect' refers to improvements in technical performance in response to threats from new technologies.
Circles denote scope of patents.
Arrows denote patent granting dates.

Figure 9.5 Patent strategies in the case of competing product generations
Source: Granstrand, 1999: 224, fig. 7.4

Two product generations. Figure 9.4 illustrates the patent strategies of a firm in the context of one product generation. Figure 9.5 then illustrates the patenting behaviour of different competing companies A, B and C in two competing product types or two subsequent product generations. These are predicated on two technology bases (sets of technologies), denoted I and II, with partly competing (substituting), partly complementary technologies. The shift from one product generation to the other thus involves a transition to new technologies, perhaps involving a radical innovation. The technical performance of the two product generations or types often improves over time, as shown by the schematic S-curves in Figure 9.5. A contemporary example is digital technology superseding analog in mobile telephony; an older example is that of fluorescent tubes eventually superseding incandescent lamps in terms of lumens/watts. Company B holds a major patent for technology base I and concentrates its R&D on further improvements in that area,[7] while company A builds patent positions in both technology bases. Company C is a new entrant in the area and focuses only on technology base II. Thus the competing companies have different patent shares in the different technologies for the competing product generations or product types, just as they may have different market shares. Typically, established firms with high market and patent shares for an established product generation are slow to build up strategic patent positions in a new competing technology, thereby risking the loss of market share in the new product generation. At the same time, new innovative firms get an opportunity to enter the market, which has often been the case historically in connection with a radical innovation or technology transition (see e.g. Schon, 1967; and Utterback, 1994).

Underlying investment strategies. Naturally, patenting behaviours or strategies are linked to the R&D strategies of the competing companies. For a single product generation, R&D strategies typically shift along the PLC from emphasizing product R&D to process R&D and application developments. In connection with a product generation shift involving a technology transition, general R&D and technology investment strategies and responses are:

1. Investing in improvements of the old technology in the existing product generation (yielding the 'sailing effect').
2. Investing in a new product generation based on some version of the new technology.

3. Investing in a hybrid generation, based in parts on both the old and the new technology, as a 'gap filler'.
4. Introducing the new technology in an evolutionary manner in the existing generation (e.g. piecemeal replacement of transistors with integrated circuits).
5. Abandoning the emerging technology and jumping to the next major new technology. (This is a risky strategy.)
6. Doing nothing (wait and see).

When and how to enter the new technology (if at all) and when and how to exit the old technology are thus crucial decisions for technology management.[8] It is also easy to fall behind because of a failure to build up patent positions in the emerging technology, as mentioned. Thus there are races not only for product, process and application patents for a particular type or generation of a product, but for several competing products and technologies. The old saying that in patenting the winner takes all refers to a single patent race, while in a typical technology-based business there is a multitude of patent races, hence the notion of 'patent portfolio races'. It should finally be noted that patent strategies are a reflection of R&D strategies and, to some extent, patent information is useful to outsiders in tracking down these strategies (see Brockhoff, 1992). R&D strategies can then be somewhat disguised by patent flooding or 'decoy' patenting.

Patent strategies in Japan

Several of the patenting behaviours and strategies described above were found in the Japanese corporations studied through interviews and case studies as reported in Granstrand (2000). In summary they were:

1. Patent blanketing (patent invasion of new technologies), flooding, fencing and surrounding.
2. Building of patent portfolios and patent networks.
3. Early-stage patenting, and continuous patenting, also of minor advances and variations ('Patent everything as soon as possible').
4. Increased emphasis on the quality of patents (e.g. search for 'strategic patents').
5. Patenting also for licensing out, including accessing new technologies through cross-licensing.
6. Building of patent power for deterrence, retaliation and bargaining.
7. Increased patenting in the USA.
8. Use of patents for stimulation of R&D personnel.
9. Development and maintenance of a patent culture.

Several of these behaviours and strategies have also been acknowledged by patent offices, and some of them have occasionally been reported in the literature (see e.g. Rahn, 1994). The rational aspects of these strategies should not be overplayed. Effective as many of them are, they have nevertheless evolved over time as historical products, rather than as a result of a few rational strategic decisions, as will be described below.

Evolution of strategy

For a long time, Japanese companies have emphasized the quantity of patents although well aware that the technological and economic importance of individual patents differs widely. There is also a general feeling that many Japanese patents are of minor technical and economic importance,[9] while Western patents are often more significant on an average. This may have been true in the past and is still true as far as Japanese patents in Japan are concerned. Although it may still be true as well in several technologies for Japanese patents in the USA and Europe, there are numerous studies indicating the relatively high quality of Japanese patents in many industrial sectors.[10] The strategy of extensive patenting of minor improvements in Japanese companies evolved in connection with the catch-up process in the postwar era. A careful study of patent information was necessary in order to trace useful technologies and suitable licensers, as well as to control the risk of infringing on patents of others when imitating and modifying products and processes. However, improvements were gradually made on imported technologies, aided by quality circles and suggestion systems. The urge both to improve the technology of others and to invent around the patents of others spurred small inventions, which were then readily patented. A patent was perceived among R&D personnel as a precious sign of world technical leadership. Patenting thus gained a prestigious value, probably more so in Japan than in the West. Methods such as patent mapping and patent reviews or audits were designed and developed over the years in order to cope with the patents of others and to build a patent position of one's own. Patent analysis in this way provided a 'navigational map' for both reaching and advancing the technological frontier.[11]

Historical conditions in connection with a long process of catching up and competing with the West, including strong domestic competition at the same time, have given rise to different patenting behaviours (i.e. patent 'flooding' or patent 'blanketing' and patent 'fencing'). As these behaviours have become functional for businesses, they have been more consciously refined and used, thereby gaining the status of conscious strategies. These behaviours and strategies in turn have become more and more relevant for technologically leading and innovative companies as new products and processes involve an expanding range of expensive technologies, forcing even leading companies now and then to play catch-up in some technologies. No one can afford to take (much less sustain) the lead on a broad range of technological frontiers. The IP management capabilities that Japanese industry built up during its catch-up phase also paid off in the subsequent phase of industrial development, giving Japanese industry a competitive advantage over many Western companies.

Strategic patents and licensing policies

The recognition in Japanese industry of the importance of achieving a high quality of patents has increased in recent years. This is due in part to the fact that Japan reached and advanced many technological frontiers herself in the 1980s, which led to patenting in new fields. The lawsuits from the USA and concomitant legal challenging of patents have also contributed to this recognition. The direct costs of patenting have also grown considerably, and since they are the same for both major and minor patents, any cost-cutting effort naturally aims at screening out (economically) minor patents. Finally, the adoption of a multi-claim system in Japan broadened the possibilities to increase the quality of a patent application.

Efforts have been made in Japan to focus more on the quality of patents and to increasingly obtain what are called 'strategic patents'. Broadly speaking, a strategic patent is a patent of decisive importance for someone wanting to commercialize a technology in a product area.[12] In other words, a strategic patent creates inhibitive costs for anyone wanting to invent around it.

Hitachi is a case in point here, as shown in Table 9.1. The clear definition of 'strategic patent' and the clear, quantified objectives for acquiring such patents are noteworthy. Such patents can be acquired through one's own R&D or through external acquisition. If successful over a number of years, such a patent strategy can lead to the build-up of substantial patent power for Hitachi with the possibility to block hundreds of product areas and companies.

Canon has a policy that a strategic patent[13] should be acquired before commercialization starts in a new business area. The acquisition can occur either through Canon's own efforts or through licensing in. If this cannot be ensured, the area is not entered. In addition, Canon wants to be the sole innovator in at least one respect. This latter policy of Canon

Table 9.1   Example from Hitachi of patent policy and objectives ('The third term campaign to increase strategic patents' as of 1992)

1. *Contents*	
Action policy	• Enhancing quality of patents (integrating business and patent strategies)
Basic measures	• Specify rivals and acquire five cases of strategic patents for each major product item's technology.
	• Strengthen activities to acquire basic patents that capture in advance the markets for future needs of society.
Specific examples of measures	• To establish patents on a sales point that allows the company to defeat others
	• PAS[1] and special R&D project aimed at acquiring leading-edge patents

2. *Level of strategic patent* and no. of cases annually certified (summary)**

Level	Corporate Target	Salient Points of Certification
Gold	25 cases	Basic invention top level in the world
Silver	75 cases	Basic invention top level in Japan
Copper	200 cases	Inventions that can be aggressively used as a sales point for Hitachi's mainstay products

Notes: * Strategic patents mean basic and inevitable patents that must be used by our company and others in major products of the present and future.
[1] PAS = Patent strategy system.

Source: Documentation provided by Hitachi

is not typical for Japanese companies. Many companies rely upon the possibility of obtaining a license from a strategic patent holder. For example, Canon invested heavily in the commercialization of the ferroelectric liquid crystal (FLC) technology for flat panel displays, while many other companies were watching by and large, relying upon getting a license from Canon should FLC prove viable in the end. Relying upon the possibility that a license will be obtainable from someone who succeeds in a field is not an uncommon strategy among large companies. The current and possible future technological interdependencies among large companies account for this type of delicate and risky trust.

A certain industrial and nationalistic codex also comes into play, especially regarding licensing on foreign markets, but its importance should not be overplayed. In the early 1990s many leading-edge companies in

Japan had an 'open licensing policy', meaning that every technology is in principle available for others to license if the terms are 'right'. Hitachi, for instance, declared in the early 1990s that it had an open policy, making all patents available for licensing. NEC claimed that it seldom refused to sell a license and perceived no risk in creating a new competitor with a single license. However, in the mid-1990s some of these companies questioned and modified this open licensing policy, thereby taking a step towards more selective licensing. Still, the technological interdependence between products and between companies forced clusters of companies to license fairly openly among themselves to avoid retaliation.

Licensing policies may of course differ among companies. In general, since the Betamax–VHS systems battle between Sony and JVC Matsushita in the late 1970s and 1980s, there has arisen a recognition of the importance in some cases of building groups or families of companies through liberal licensing in order to support a new product or business system.[14] This may be part of a business strategy to combine the promotion of buyer diffusion (i.e. market penetration) with the control of seller diffusion, i.e. the spread of the technology among competing and/or cooperating producers.

Licensing policies may also be declared open on other grounds: for image-building, for cross-licensing, for royalties, etc. In general, the decision to license out or not is a matter of pricing. The cost of negotiating a single licence agreement is increasing, however, which induces companies to enter more broad-based licence agreements, perhaps also more multilaterally than bilaterally. This may stimulate new patterns of cooperation and competition, such as systems competition, i.e. competition between families of cooperating companies, linked to different technical systems.

The search for strategic patents in a new technology creates a race among companies. There is also a second race for the surrounding patents taking place in order to fence in any conceivably strategic patent. These surrounding patents are often linked to production processes or to different applications and may be identified through a systematic application analysis.[15] The surrounding patents may then be used by competitors when bargaining about the original strategic patent. In the extreme case, the strategic patent may not be able to be used without infringing a surrounding patent. To avoid this situation, the strategic patent holder is also compelled to search for surrounding patents. However, failure to pursue follow up patenting in this and other situations has been common among Western firms, large as well as small. The traditional engineering attitude has been to apply for a patent only in the case of inventions with high technical qualities. Technically minor inventions, to which category many application patents and surrounding patents belong, have been downplayed and patenting has often been ignored. There has also been a belief, not least among inventors and small firms, that a single good patent is sufficient to protect a new business. Firms may also lack resources and management attention concerning patenting. Circumstances like these have resulted in the ignorance of follow-up patenting and in failure to build up patent portfolios over time.

The outcome of this second patent race determines, in principle, the distribution of bargaining power among the competing companies and their prospects for cross-licensing. To obtain surrounding patents is thus a case of fencing out or fencing in, depending upon whether the surrounding patent holder is the holder of the strategic patent or not. This is a stereotypical example but it illustrates the interdependence of patents. For instance, it should be noted that the two patent races do not necessarily follow upon each other neatly in time. An old patent may become one of the surrounding patents to a strategic patent over time. Since many companies start to explore a new field early and take out patents with parallel R&D approaches, the interdependencies among companies and patents might become quite complicated. Such interdependence is likely to become more important in the future as the number of technologies related to a product increases.

General counter-patent strategies

When confronting a blocking patent, a number of strategic responses are possible, as shown in Figure 9.2.

Similar response strategies apply when confronting blockages by a patent blanket or a patent fence, etc. For example, when entering a new business a patent map may show a jungle of patents, in which case a company may allow its IP department the right to veto any further R&D in that area, or at least bring the matter to the attention of business management. Such patent clearance procedures become important as patents and technological interdependencies proliferate.[16] Needless to say, it is also important to pursue them early in the R&D process,[17] as well as important to make R&D management responsive to patent clearance. In relation to the validity search, one should note that such a search cannot be made conclusive in principle, unless a patent is litigated. Ultimately it is the courts who decide on validity, which introduces a chance element into patent clearance – as well as in patent enforcement, as is dealt with next.

Litigation strategies

Infringement monitoring in a large international corporation with a large, diversified product and patent portfolio may in fact be difficult, especially if products go into the production processes of customers. To pay off, infringement monitoring costs must not exceed expected benefits from patent enforcement, involving probabilities of deterrence, detection, favourable settlements by courts or otherwise, and damages or licensing payments. If this is not the case, patenting may not pay off either.

If infringement occurs or there are substantial grounds for suspicion, various strategies for legal enforcement of patent rights could be employed. Litigation strategies can be characterized in general terms, such as offensive/defensive, just like patent strategies; but it is difficult to make a structured list of legal strategies that preempts all available possibilities in various legal systems. Before choosing an offensive litigation strategy one should also assess the risks of retaliation, which in addition to risks of counter-litigation include risks of losing some business.

Litigation processes also contain many stages and contingencies, from the filing of complaints to the ultimate appeals. Formal decision analysis using decision trees with subjective probabilities may be a useful tool for analysing such decisions as well as patent strategy decisions in general. However, it must be kept in mind that reality is often not easily cast into structured frameworks such as these.

Multiprotection and total IP strategies

During the 1980s a trend towards dealing with IP in a more comprehensive way emerged in Japanese 'best-practice' companies. This was reflected both in how policies and strategies were formulated and in how IP-related activities became organized in the company.

There are many types of intellectual property or assets in a company – patents, trade secrets, trademarks, etc. There are also many ways to create these assets jointly in connection with a particular business. These different ways are mostly complementary and raise the total asset value when used in combination. Thus it is justified to talk about the importance of creating *multiprotection systems* and *total IP strategies*.[18] This idea seems quite natural and acceptable to people in industry. Nevertheless, patent matters dominate when dealing with IP. This is often reflected by work specialization, as well as by terminology, in a manner that is deceptive. The governmental organizations are called 'Patent Offices', consultancy firms are often called 'Patent Bureaus', experts are called 'Patent Attorneys', associations are called 'Patent Associations', company departments are called the 'Patent Department' with a 'Patent Manager' and company policies are called 'Patent Policies'. In such circumstances it is easy to pursue an unbalanced approach to IP matters, perhaps placing too much emphasis on patents and too little on trademarks, trade secrets, copyrights and designs, and above all neglecting complementarities among different IP elements.

If IP matters should be treated more comprehensively, how much more comprehensively? And if IP matters are important, what is the proper role of IP management in technology management, business management and corporate management? The question of how to 'size' and position IP management in the company is highly relevant. Intellectual resources, including general competence as well as technology, are pervasive throughout the whole corporation, but pervasiveness in itself is not an argument for putting IP management in the centre of the whole company organization. There are many pervasive activities in a company that should from time to time be placed at the centre of attention by means of organization, campaigns, culture building, management policies, management fads, etc.

Multiprotection is not only practised among leading Japanese companies. In fact, leading US companies have developed such practices long ago. Coca-Cola, for example, has skilfully built up and maintained multiprotection. The recipe for the Coca-Cola soft drink is a well-protected trade secret, as is well known.[19] A patent has a limited lifetime, while a secret can possibly last forever, at least in theory. This is especially important for products with long lifetimes, which in turn may result from slow-moving customer preferences or slow-moving product technology. The machinery for the process technology, including the distribution process (e.g. vending machines), has been systematically analysed and protected by patents. The unconventional Coca-Cola bottle has design protection and the Coca-Cola name and logo have trademark protection.[20] The IPRs are strongly and systematically developed and promoted by R&D and marketing activities, etc. and enforced by infringement monitoring and legal action. It is not an accident that Coca-Cola has maintained one of the most highly valued trademarks in the world (see 'The emergence of the "pro-patent era"' above), although its value was not initially clear to the company.[21]

Selecting and securing property rights for various elements constituting a business is not enough for multiprotection. The rights have to be enforced and infringers have to be deterred. IBM, for example, has pursued a very hard-nosed enforcement and litigation policy over the years through frequent litigation and the pursuit of the legal process to fruition, despite the legal costs and the prospect of losing (see Mody, 1990). Thus IBM has apparently considered it more important to win a war than to win every battle.[22] In this way IBM has kept competitors and inventors wary about infringement. IBM has also sustained its IPR-consciousness, which has been combined with a licensing policy, sometimes a quite generous one (although partly due to antitrust decrees).[23]

Japanese companies, on the other hand, have traditionally avoided litigation and court settlements.[24] This is well known, even to the extent that some inventors and companies accuse Japanese companies of infringement in order to have them settle for a licence rather than risk going to court. However, things are changing and many Japanese companies are becoming more litigious, at least when they are attacked. For example, when Motorola sued Hitachi in 1989 for infringing upon a number of Motorola's patents, Hitachi counter-sued Motorola for infringing upon Hitachi's patents. As a result, the court in effect stopped the sales of the corresponding products of both Motorola and Hitachi, a court decision that apparently hurt Motorola more than Hitachi (see Anawalt and Enayati, 1996: 342). This also illustrates the retaliatory power of large patent portfolios as well as the vulnerability of being a large, diversified hi-tech litigator.

A business can be broken down into various constituent elements and product technologies that could be covered by various IPRs, resulting in an IPR package or multiprotection system for the business. In principle, this corresponds to an analysis of the elements in Table 9.2.

Different IP types sometimes substitute for each other at the business component level. The typical example is that patent protection and secrecy protection substitute for each other for a particular invention. In general, however, the different IP types can also be used to complement or reinforce one another. Altogether, the different business elements or components in Table 9.2 form a *business system* in a product area. A business system with its business components thus encompasses products and their components and technology bases, together with the other elements in Table 9.2. This concept thereby focuses on the total set of intellectual resources or intellectual capital needed to make a customer offering and conduct a business deal.

Table 9.2 Analysing the business system for multiple IP protection

Business element/component	IP type (example)
1. Business idea	Trade secret
2. Business plan/model/method	Trade secret, patent
3. Product technology (equipment, materials etc.)	Patents, utility models, licenses, trade secrets, trademark, design
4. Production/process technology	Patents, trade secrets, licenses
5. R&D results	Trade secrets, patents, database rights, licenses
6. Component technology	Maskwork protection, patents, trademark, defensive publishing
7. Application technologies	Patents, utility models, licenses, trademarks
8. Complementary products	Patents, trade secrets, database rights, copyright
9. Substitute technologies	Patents, licenses
10. Systems configuration	Open information, defensive publishing, copy lefting
11. Software, orgware, data	Patents, copyright, trade secrets, database rights
12. Auxiliary services	Trademarks, trade secrets
13. Distribution technology	Patents, utility models, trade secret
14. Marketing concepts	Copyright, open PR information, patents, trademarks, designs
15. Packaging	Designs, trademarks
16. Company and business names, logos, slogans and symbols ('company aesthetics')	Trademarks, copyright, designs

Source: Granstrand, 1999: 224, table 7.5

At the level of a business system the various IPRs should be complementary as a rule, forming effective multiprotection as a means for commercialization and enhancement of the business. The value of the total IP portfolio to a company is built up in principle by the various value components of various IPRs in various business systems of the company. There are then significant complexities and difficulties involved in assigning meaningful values to individual IPRs, values which, moreover, may not be additive as a rule. Nevertheless, the ultimate function of strategic management of IP is to build up the total value of an IP portfolio through proper (optimal) use of various strategies.[25] Hence, there is a close connection between IP management and intellectual capital management, the latter being concerned with the wider concept of intellectual capital, comprising also human capital and relational capital, besides IP.

For a multi-business corporation there is a further need to coordinate IP protection across businesses (i.e. regarding company logos, trademarks, etc. and licensing). Multiprotection in a multi-business corporation then necessitates the formulation of company-wide IP policies.

Distributed intellectual capital management

IP constitutes a vital part of a company's intellectual capital (IC), other parts being human capital (competence, skills, etc.) and relational capital (network capital, organizational capital), although there are several ways to decompose and account for IC. IC in turn typically dominates over physical and financial capital in the total capital structure of a company in the new type of capitalist knowledge economy (intellectual capitalism).

As IC becomes increasingly important to firms and countries, it is natural to ask what the proper managerial responses would be, which of course is a mega-dollar question. One could consider extensions of the IP organization as one response. However, a formal organization with departments, committees, managers, specialists and so forth is insufficient. The arguments in the quality-management movement of the 1980s against sole reliance on such an organizational response apply in the main to this context as well. Extensions and transformations of corporate culture then have to be considered a second response, likely to be complementary to the first response. Just as the patent organization could be extended to an IP organization, which could further be extended to an IC organization, perhaps ultimately encompassing the whole firm if it becomes sufficiently IC-based, the patent culture could be transformed into an IP culture and perhaps further into an IC culture. Needless to say, cultural change is far from something that can be managed at will. However, cultural change can be influenced to various degrees by managerial action. Having some kind of patent culture already is thus a good starting point. Extending it to be more comprehensively IP-oriented means extending the property dimension. A further extension from IP to IC means adding a value dimension, and broadening the concern from mere property protection to rent control or rent protection and the acquisition, development and exploitation of IC on the whole. In principle, then, managerial actions have relevance for building an IC culture as well, although there will be additional difficulties, e.g. in clashes between the company and a wider range of groups of people with strong concern about their individual IC or their professional group's IC.

Moreover, cultural formation and change take time, often too much time in the fast pace of contemporary business. Thus, a third type of managerial action may be called for. This is what could be called distributed management, which refers to a corporate-wide focused reorientation with responsibilities distributed at management levels and no central responsibility except that vested in top management. Mostly such an organization is implemented swiftly on a broad front in order to get momentum in mobilizing and motivating the organization, besides saving time. It thereby becomes one out of at most a few corporate-wide concerns. Often a similar reorientation is implemented in many companies across industries at about the same time. Its form can be labelled a corporate campaign, a crash programme or the like, and its content a managerial or organizational innovation, a management revolution or the like. It could also be a short-lived management fad, especially if it fails. Attempts to make too many corporate reorientations at the same time also considerably weaken their prospects of success.

There have been several such reorientations in the corporate world in the recent past, with various rationales behind them and a fair amount of success on average. Thus, there have been reorientations focusing on inventory levels, total quality, lead times and core competencies. The foci of these reorientations or movements have had certain shared features, which can be seen as requirements or facilitators for successful reorientations. Foci such as inventory levels, total quality, and lead times:

(a) are concrete in character;
(b) can penetrate a wide range of activities in and around the organization;
(c) have a potential for visible improvements;
(d) can attract realistic expectations in a situation susceptible to organizational change;
(e) exert a direct and credible (and positive) influence on basic and acceptable objectives and visions of the organization.

These requirements could very well be fulfilled by IC-related activities. Thus, IC could be the focus of a reorientation through distributed management. As with any form of distributed management, there are two main rationales. One is that the activities or operations actually focused upon become improved. The second rationale is that many other types of related activities become improved in the process. This might superficially seem a side-effect, but may in fact be the most important effect. By focusing on lowering inventory costs at all stages (through Kanban, etc.) the whole production and distribution organization could be improved, since its slacks and deficiencies are then likely to surface. By securing and increasing quality in a broad sense, a certain innovativeness in the organization could be improved. By lowering lead times, both improved efficiency and innovativeness across R&D, production and marketing functions could be attained, at least in the short run. By focusing on core competences, being by definition valuable, widely applicable and difficult to imitate, these could be improved and exploited more efficiently, while at the same time increasing the awareness of the strategic value of IC. By focusing further on IC and its dynamics, the IC management could be improved at all levels in the corporation, while at the same time improvements in overall efficiency and innovativeness are likely. Anyone with experience in intellectual work knows that it has a tremendous potential for productivity improvements. At the same time there are managerial challenges, e.g. in achieving a closer integration at all organizational levels of technology, law and economics – a difficult trio to manage.

Notes

1. Much of the material in this chapter draws on Granstrand (2000).
2. A list of the most highly valued patents in the world is not readily available. Such a list would most probably include the patents behind the top-selling pharmaceuticals. The best-selling pharmaceutical worldwide in 1997 was the ulcer drug Losec, developed and patented by the pharmaceutical company Astra in 1978. Astra management has estimated the value (discounted to 1978) of the basic patent to fall in the range 15–30 BUSD, which is of the same magnitude as the most highly valued brand names.
3. Valuation of trademarks may be done in several mostly subjective ways, all of which produce uncertain results. (For an overview, see Aaker, 1996.) The astounding magnitudes of trademark values do not result from valuation errors although the precise figures may be in error. Trademarks may be kept valid permanently, and their value is built up over time through various means, primarily through advertising and positive exposure to consumers. They are thereby subjected to increasing returns or cumulative advantages, although volatile. Thus old, consistently well-managed trademarks for consumer mass markets could be expected to accumulate the highest values, although there are exceptions like Intel, being a relatively young company (formed in 1968) with a component product. The dominance of US trademarks among the highly valued ones is noteworthy, with trademarks such as Marlboro and Coca-Cola on top, each valued at more than 40 BUSD in 1995. The most valuable Japanese trademark is Sony, valued at 8.8 BUSD in 1995, and thereby ranking 15th.

4. See also Chapter 5 in this volume, which describes a generic strategy process model, focusing on a typology of steps in the process of strategy formation. For a similar typology of technology strategies as presented here, see Chapter 11 in this volume. See also Chapter 6 for a typology of strategies specifically for coping with disruptive technological changes.

5. This framework can be used to gather actual data on company strategies. For examples, see Granstrand *et al.* (1992) and Granstrand (2000).

6. Various military terms and analogies are used among patent practitioners.

7. Cf. the so-called 'sailing effect', which refers to improvements in late stages of a maturing technology. These improvements are mainly made in response to a perceived threat of a new technology. The expression was derived from the performance of sailing ships, which was boosted in response to the arrival of ships powered by steam engines (see Graham, 1956).

8. Short/long-run costs/benefits of various technology acquisition and exploitation strategies must be taken into account. Technology acquisition costs depend in turn on the extent of the company's technology overlap or competence fit with the new technology base. See further Chapter 6 in this volume.

9. It is important to distinguish between technical and economic aspects when talking about the level, importance, quality or 'size' of an invention, technical advance or innovation. Although there may be a positive correlation between a high level of invention (i.e. technical quality) and its economic importance, the correlation may be weak and there may be many economically important but technically minor inventions, as well as many economically unimportant but technically major inventions.

10. A commonly used indicator of patent quality is citation rate, despite its many flaws. The quality of Japanese patents is indeed high in many industrial sectors, using this indicator. See Granstrand (2000).

11. Information gathered through personal communication with Mr S. Saba.

12. Some also use the terms 'essential patent', 'basic patent', 'generic patent' or 'inevitable patent'. However, certain such terms are also used in other senses.

13. Naturally it is often not clear at once whether a patent is strategic or not, and the perception of a patent being strategic may have to be revised in light of later technological developments.

14. The Betamax–VHS battle has been widely reported. It now qualifies as a classic case of the importance of strategic licensing. Oddly enough, and far less well known, is that the technological interdependence was such that had Sony won the battle, JVC would still have been rather well off through collection of royalties from Sony.

15. An alleged case of this is described in Spero (1990), in which Mitsubishi was accused of having fenced in a strategic patent held by a small US firm, with the purpose of acquiring it through cross-licensing. (The article represents the small firm's view of the case.)

16. For a good illustration of the legal complexities involved, see Merges (1994).

17. Patent clearance was unfortunately performed too late in the standardization work of the GSM system for mobile communications (see Granstrand, 2000).

18. This does not necessarily imply that IP activities should be centralized. However, in a decentralized IP organization, the need for comprehensive IP

policies and strategies is even more emphasized. The term 'multiprotection system' has been suggested by Dr A. Mifune.

19. Note that conventional food recipes are not protectable by patents, although early patent-like protection in Venice during the 15th-century Renaissance, as well as in Sybaris in ancient Greece, originally gave protection to recipes of famous chefs. This does not necessarily mean that the Coca-Cola recipe is not patentable (at least as a medicine in principle), or that Coca-Cola's preference for keeping it a trade secret is due to uncertainty about patentability.

20. The bottle has received US trademark protection as well, which was the first example of a three-dimensional trademark.

21. According to Professor F.M. Scherer the early development of the Coca-Cola image was quite accidental, and only after some time did the company realize what a valuable asset they had and then took aggressive steps to protect it.

22. Note that although 'hot' patent wars may break out now and then, the common patent war is 'cold', with on-going deterrence and negotiations.

23. For further readings about IBM in these respects, see Mody (1990) and Grindley and Teece (1997).

24. This has been true for many US companies too.

25. Compare with Chapter 8 in this volume, describing portfolio approach to technology valuation. The IP risks, e.g. regarding litigation, should also be taken into account. For the importance of IP risks in general, see Chapter 18 in this volume.

References

Aaker, D.A. (1996), *Building Strong Brands*, New York: Free Press.

Anawalt, H.C. and E. Enayati (1996), *IP Strategy: Complete Intellectual Property Planning, Access and Protection*, New York, NY: CBC (Clark, Boardman, Callaghan).

Brockhoff, K.K. (1992), 'Instruments for patent data analyses in business firms', *Technovation*, 12, 1, pp. 41–58.

Ernst, H. (1995), 'Patenting strategies in the German mechanical engineering industry and their relationship to company performance', *Technovation*, 15, 4, pp. 225–40.

Glazier, S.C. (1995), *Patent Strategies for Business*, 2nd edn, London: Euromoney Books.

Graham, G.S. (1956), 'The ascendancy of the sailing ship 1850–85', *Economic History Review*, IX, 1, pp. 74–88.

Granstrand, O. (1982), *Technology, Management and Markets*, London: Frances Pinter.

Granstrand, O. (1999/2000), *The Economics and Management of Intellectual Property – Towards Intellectual Capitalism*, Cheltenham: Edward Elgar Publishing.

Granstrand, O., E. Bohlin, C. Oskarsson and N. Sjöberg (1992), 'External technology acquisition in large multi-technology corporations', *R&D Management*, 22, 2, pp. 111–33.

Grindley, P.C., and D.J. Teece (1997), 'Managing intellectual capital: licensing and cross-licensing in semiconductors and electronics', *California Management Review*, 39, 2, pp. 8–41.

Marshall, A. (1994), *Principles of Economics*, London: (Originally published 1890.) Macmillan – now Palgrave Macmillan.

Merges, R.P. (1994), 'Intellectual property rights and bargaining breakdown: the case of blocking patents', *Tennessee Law Review*, 62, 1, pp. 75–106.

Mody, A. (1990), 'New international environment for intellectual property rights', in Rushing and Brown (eds), *Intellectual Property Rights in Science, Technology, and Economic Performance: International Comparisons*, Colorado, CO: Westview Press, ch. 10, pp. 203–39.

Momberg, D., and A. Ashton (1986), *Strategy in the Use of Intellectual Property. A Guide to Managing Business' Most Valuable Asset*, Hong Kong: Gerundive Press.

Rahn, G. (1994), 'Patentstrategien japanischer Unternehmen', *Gewerblicher Rechtsschutz und Urheberecht, Internationaler Teil*, 5, pp. 377–82.

Scherer, F.M. (1980), *Industrial Market Structure and Economic Performance*, Chicago, IL: Rand McNally.

Schon, D.A. (1967), *Technology and Change*, New York, NY: New Heraclitus, Delacorte Press.

Sirilla, G.M., G.P. Edgell and A.R. Hess (1992), 'The advice of counsel defense to increased patent damages', *Journal of the Patent and Trademark Office Society*, 74, 10, pp. 705–28.

Spero, D.M. (1990), 'Patent protection or piracy – A CEO views Japan', *Harvard Business Review*, 68, 5, pp. 58–67.

Takahashi, T. (1994), *Intellectual Property Rights and Corporate Strategies: One Aspect of Competition in the U.S. and Japanese Electronics Industry*, Tokyo: Nomura Research Institute.

Utterback, J.M. (1994), *Mastering the Dynamics of Innovation*, Boston, MA: Harvard Business School Press.

10
Technology Intelligence System: Benefits and Roles of Top Management

Pascal Savioz and Hugo Tschirky

Overview

In order to cope with the rapidly changing technological environment, several companies have established the so-called Technology Intelligence (TI) Systems. The goal is to collect, analyse, disseminate and utilize information that is relevant to the company and will improve decision-making quality. In doing so, a company faces, in particular, two challenges: to what extent should the TI systems be organized and how should it be organized? Planning is a great concern of top management, thus top management are prime users of an intelligence system. The question is however, how is top management involved in the system?

In this chapter we discuss the elements of a TI system. This is followed by a discussion of the various roles top management plays within the intelligence system. Furthermore, examples in companies of different sizes illustrate various forms of organization of the system and the varying roles of top management. We conclude with a discussion of the possible differences.

Introduction

An awareness of the company's technological environment in a time of rapid change seems to be crucial for success in technology-based companies. These changes may become significant threats when disregarded by the company's management, but changes may also become valuable opportunities if predicted early. The growing awareness of, and the will to take advantage of, opportunities, has led numerous companies to develop a broader interest in the field of TI. The purpose of TI is to support decision-making in technological and general management considerations. Thus, top management becomes directly involved in a TI system.

Organizing TI as a system

Several empirical studies have shown that TI is pursued systematically, unsystematically, or partially systematically in practice (to name a few: Ashton and Klavang, 1997: 3; Reger *et al.*, 1998: 8; Lichtenthaler, 2000: 248; Groom and David, 2001: 18). However, in order to discuss the different elements of TI, one must be able to describe a TI system (without specifying the degree of systematization). A management system can be entirely reflected looking at Figure 10.1. There is value creation throughout the TI Process of need formulation, collection, analysis, dissemination and application of relevant information. Therefore, these activities can be interpreted as primary or direct activities of value creation (cp. Durand *et al.*, 1997: 209). However, in contrast to the production of goods, the result of these TI activities, i.e. the generated intelligence, only becomes valuable when it is applied in order to improve decision-making. Decision-making is improved when the quality (in content and timing) of information is improved in order to reduce uncertainty (Savioz, 2001: 284). The indirect activities enable the primary activities. For a TI system, these enablers consist of: TI management, TI mission and goals, TI structure and TI tools.

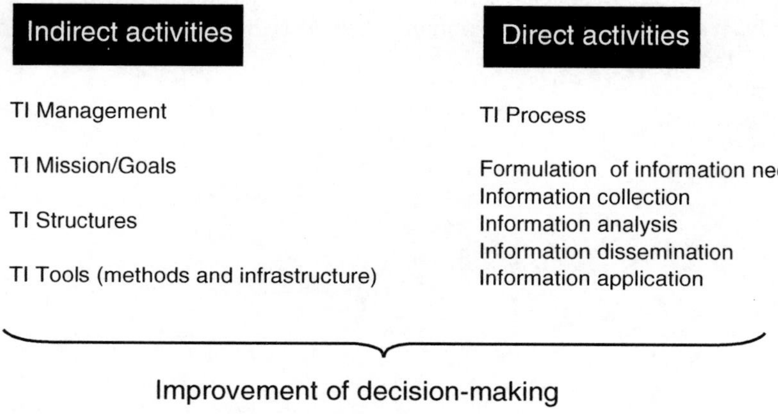

Indirect activities	Direct activities
TI Management	TI Process
TI Mission/Goals	Formulation of information need
	Information collection
TI Structures	Information analysis
	Information dissemination
TI Tools (methods and infrastructure)	Information application

Improvement of decision-making

Figure 10.1   Direct and indirect TI activities

These elements of the TI system are briefly described in the following:

TI process

The TI process consists of five steps or activities: explicit or implicit formulation of information need, information collection, information analysis, information dissemination and information application (Figure 10.2). However, it is not a step-by-step process, but a parallel assembly of diverse interacting TI activities with blurred limits. The need for information can occur at any level of the company, and the intelligence produced can be applied at any level as well. Thus, the TI process serves decision-makers, i.e. top management, but also engineers who are confronted with daily 'little' decisions. Such a view can be called 'organizational intelligence' (Gerybadze, 1994: 133). The way companies handle these activities depends on the nature of need, time horizon, competencies, size and company culture.

TI management

Since management organizes the system, it has a higher status than the process. Nevertheless, it is an indirect activity in the value creation process because it enables direct activities. Management of TI includes designing, directing and developing elements of the system (cp. Tschirky, 1998: 216). Following McDonald and Richardson (1997: 131) the tasks in the design stage are interviewing management and other relevant personnel to get intelligence needs, followed by a prioritization of needs and technological areas. Then, resources should be assigned (i.e. monitoring and assessment specialists, a system manager and IT infrastructure). Lastly, the system should be organized. In the directing and development stages, the main tasks are to train people, to adapt and to expand the system.

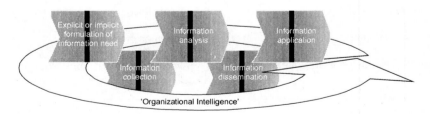

Figure 10.2 TI activities in the TI process understood as 'organizational intelligence'

TI mission and goals

TI mission and goals define the purpose, and therefore the required output of the TI System. TI mission should always be related to business mission and strategy. In fact, they influence one other: since TI activities should be based on business mission and strategy, the latter might change with insights obtained from TI. This phenomenon is a veritable chicken-and-egg problem. The interaction between business mission and strategy and TI mission is represented in Figure 10.3.

The observation area always has a time and a content dimension. Depending on strategy, the organization puts the focus on a particular area of observation. While 'followers' seem to focus on technologies and developments in the present or the near future, and in existing or familiar businesses ('keeping abreast'), 'leaders' seem to pursue observation beyond this area ('looking-ahead').

TI structures

TI structures describe how TI activities are assigned to different units and people, and how they are organized. There are various ways to coordinate TI activities. In a broad study Lichtenthaler (2000: 248) observed three forms of coordination: the structured, the informal and the project-oriented coordination (Figure 10.4).

In fact, Lichtenthaler observed in his study that all these types of coordination are run in parallel in most companies. A problem could be the fact that formal and informal activities are sometimes redundant. However, these diverse possibilities of distribution and coordination of

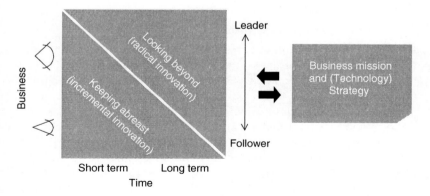

Figure 10.3   TI mission in interaction with business mission and strategy

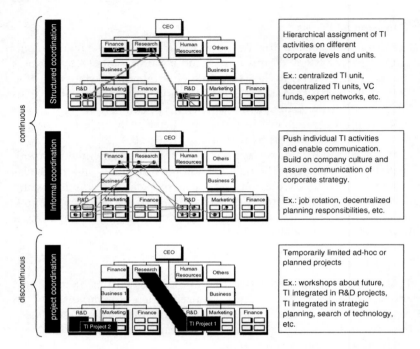

Figure 10.4 Structured, informal and project-oriented coordination of TI activities

Source: adapted from Lichtenthaler, 2000: 248

TI activities show in some way that anything is possible (and indeed practised).

TI tools (methods and infrastructure)

Until now, the discussion of TI has been limited to content and people. Just a few words have been said about the tools that support TI activities. Tools may be understood as TI methods that support the technical infrastructure.

The literature provides a wide range of methods used for TI. A central question is: which method should be used in which case? Factors influencing the application may be technology strategy (Gerybadze, 1994: 136), environmental complexity and uncertainty of the industry (Balachandra, 1980: 164; Lichtenthaler, 2000: 332), time focus (Reger *et al.*, 1998: 12) and complexity of the method itself (Krystek and Müller-Stewens, 1993: 202). Figure 10.5 gives an idea of some methods.

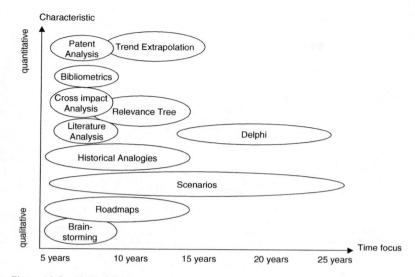

Figure 10.5 TI methods

Sources: adapted from Reger *et al.*, 1998: 12 and Lichtenthaler, 2000: 41

Over the past few years, the potential of information technologies has grown enormously, and with this, the potential usefulness of the TI process. With the exception of need formulation and intelligence application, Information Technology supports the process at any stage (collection, analysis, dissemination). Thus, Information Technology remains a supporting tool which facilitates several tasks, without replacing human thinking (Fröhlich, 2000: 199). Hohhof (1997: 262) lists computer support roles as follows:

- To provide access to secondary information for both intelligence system analysts and intelligence system users,
- To identify and distribute primary information,
- To organise information for retrospective retrieval and provide access to other internal information sources,
- To facilitate the Intelligence analysis process, and
- To distribute intelligence products to system users.

TI in the board room

The previous chapters showed basic elements of a TI system. In this chapter, we will explain the role of top management in a TI System. To do

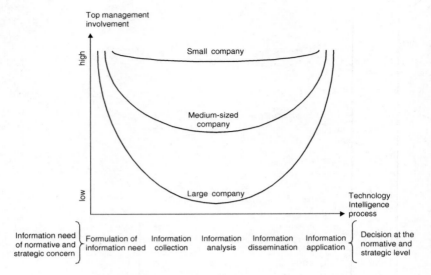

Figure 10.6   Top management involvement in different TI activities

so, we accept top management's main activities at the normative and strategic levels (see a discussion in Tschirky, 1998: 225). Thus top management is more involved at the front- and back-end of the TI process. However, in smaller firms they may also be involved in the 'operational' task of TI. This tendency is illustrated in Figure 10.6.

The statements and recommendations in this chapter emerge from the authors practical experience through action research and interviews in numerous small, medium-sized and large companies all over the world, and lessons obtained from recent literature.

Top management as TI 'users'

The most obvious role of top management is the user role. They normally need highly relevant information to take strategic decisions. A decision situation can be both: proactive or reactive (Savioz, 2001: 280). While the first situation asks for deliberately collected information to optimize a predictable (planned) decision, the latter may occur if any collected information generates a (unplanned) call for action. This implies that the TI system should be designed for both situations.

In large firms, top management may, on the one hand, 'feed' the TI system with explicitly formulated information needs. Many large companies run a formalized TI system with specialized TI units. Thus, top management can address their needs, for instance monitoring a specific technology, directly to this unit, and they can expect to receive the desired information in a reasonable time span. This corresponds to a 'command-deliver' logic and is appropriate for proactive decisions. On the other hand, top management can formulate a kind of framework, for instance by defining an area of interest, in which any or specialized TI workers are to act upon. In this case, TI workers have a kind of 'entrepreneurial status', the power to decide how to collect information, and whether the gathered information is important to top management. In both cases, command and/or framework, there is a need to build a sound TI system which is very expensive. In addition, top management has to have a great deal of trust in the information delivered because top managers do not necessarily have the scientific/technical background to interpret the results.

In smaller companies, top management normally has to take decisions similar in nature to larger companies. However, they cannot afford to build such expensive systems with specialized TI units and workers because of their restricted resources. Communication between top management (as users) and those employees who collect, analyse and deliver the information is very direct, and therefore more efficient than in large companies. In addition, top managers are often very familiar with science and technologies, and they can interpret the results in order to improve their decision quality considerably.

Top management as technology intelligence 'workers'

As noted above, instead of just using the output from the TI system, top management can also be involved in the value-creating process of TI activities. This is particularly true for small and medium-sized enterprises. There are several reasons for this: firstly, since there are fewer employees, top managers should also fulfil operational tasks. The literature refers to this in terms of entrepreneurship (Dess *et al.*, 1999: 85). Secondly, top managers normally have an excellent network of scientists and opinion leaders in their business. These prime sources of information should be considered when collecting information. Thirdly, since top managers of smaller firms are often scientists themselves, they have the best knowledge about issues faced by employees. Certainly the biggest challenge is to balance TI activities with other important management tasks, requiring the delegation of certain activities to other employees.

It is difficult to determine just from company size what specialized TI team makes sense. Certainly it depends on the nature of the business (particularly technology life-cycle and status in the value chain), firm growth, internal organization and company culture. This underscores the fact that TI system design is very specific to each company.

Top management as TI 'promoters, coaches and supervisors'

In order for TI system to be implemented successfully, it is necessary that top management give their full commitment to it, regardless of company size. Otherwise, the implementation project runs the risk of failing because the people involved may not regard it as highly important. In addition to top management's commitment, at least one of them should act as a promoter of the TI system.

Someone in the company has to coach the TI system, especially the TI process if it is formalized. It makes sense to delegate this coordinating task to a special person or unit in larger firms. In small companies, however, this is the concern of top management. They should be concerned about designing, directing and developing the TI system, which does not mean that they have to fulfil all tasks. In contrast, in larger companies, the coaching role shifts to a supervisory role, usually performed by top management.

Examples

Three TI systems in companies with different sizes are illustrated in this chapter. There will also be a short discussion of the role of top management.

TI at Zeptosens (small company)

Zeptosens is a Swiss start-up company that began its operations in March 1999. A multidisciplinary team with a scientific background in physics, chemistry and biology provides the skills and know-how to develop analytical solutions to solve detection and monitoring requirements in life sciences. Zeptosens has no turnover at present, R&D expenditures are very high. Approximately 15 people work for Zeptosens, most of whom are scientists with a PhD.

Zeptosens implicitly runs a TI system. 'Technology Watch' (Figure 10.7) appears as a regular agenda item at their weekly meetings, which involve all employees. The Technology Watch deals with three basic questions: firstly, is there an existing or emerging technology that could solve an actual problem of Zeptosens (problem in search of technology)? Secondly, is there a problem outside the company that could be solved

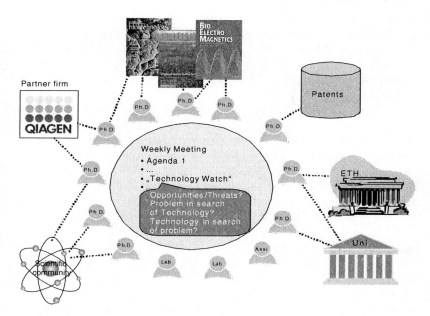

Figure 10.7 Elements of TI at Zeptosens

with one of Zeptosens' technologies (technology in search of a problem)? Thirdly, are there other potential opportunities and threats in the technological environment? To answer these questions, each employee has to do specific tasks, i.e. to read some allocated scientific journals, to scour patent databases, to network with the scientific community (e.g. with universities) and partner firms. In this way, each employee has an entrepreneurial responsibility. An enormous advantage of such a 'forced' exchange of trends about the technological environment and the emerging ideas lies in the increased organizational knowledge base and resulting potential innovations.

This is probably one of the most optimal solutions for 'organizational intelligence'. Top management is fully involved in the TI process at every stage. In fact, there is no difference between top management and other employees with regard to TI in this start-up company.

TI at Straumann (medium-sized company)

The Institute Straumann is a fast growing Swiss medical technology company in the field of implant dentistry. Straumann works in close collaboration in R&D with the International Team on Oral Implantology (ITI), a world-wide non-profit association with most opinion leaders in the business of Straumann. Turnover at Straumann is US$113 million, of which about 9 per cent is spent on R&D (exclusively done in Switzerland). Straumann employs more than 500 people world-wide, about 40 people work in R&D.

Straumann explicitly runs a formalized TI system since 2000. The following discusses several elements of this system (Figure 10.8).

The TI system directly interacts with the *business mission and strategy*. The business mission and strategy define the TI mission and therefore the observation area. Corresponding to the observation areas described below, two initiatives have been taken: the 'screening' that deals with the 'keeping abreast' area, and the 'Opportunity Landscape' that deals with the 'looking beyond' area.

The *'screening'* is 'to lead to effective and efficient decision-making before product development by systematic evaluation and documentation of any technological trend'. The process follows a Stage-Gate logic with a filtering and a bundling function. About six screening core-team members (mostly heads of technical departments) meet twice monthly to discuss and decide whether an input in the screening process should be followed up. If so, an ad hoc and short-term evaluation

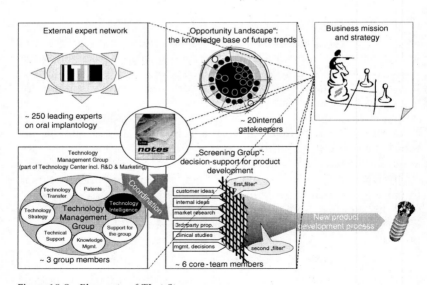

Figure 10.8   Elements of TI at Straumann

project team with internal and, if necessary, external experts is established to conduct a detailed examination. Any input and decision is well documented.

The *'Opportunity Landscape'* is the knowledge-base of future trends. In fact, all issues that are or might be relevant to the company's future, in the context of business mission and strategy, are closely tracked by so-called gatekeepers. There are 20 gatekeepers at Straumann. Their mission is to gather, analyse and disseminate any relevant information about trends within this issue. They have an entrepreneurial responsibility and should act reactively as well as proactively. The output of the Opportunity Landscape is two fold: on the one hand, any other process in the firm, for instance the screening process, can be nurtured by insights from the gatekeepers. Since future as well as current issues are tracked, anybody in the firm can return to this organizational knowledge-base if advice is necessary. On the other hand, in an annual cycle, top management can adapt the business mission and strategy with learning obtained from the Opportunity Landscape, and hence redefine the issues in it (for a detailed description of the Opportunity Landscape, see Savioz and Blum (2002)).

An *external expert network*, the ITI, is a very important source of information about trends in the field of oral dentistry. This 'external knowledge-base' interacts with the screening process and the Opportunity Landscape.

Coordination of the elements described below is one main task of the *Technology Management Group*. A member of this group is the common denominator of the Opportunity Landscape's gatekeepers, the screening core-team members and top management. Next to this coordinating task, this group is also responsible for other concerns in relation to technology. Since these concerns are very complex, the members of the group manage them collegially, in order to profit from the individual's strengths. In addition, they can consider more tasks than there are people, which counters the resource restrictions.

Finally, a common *IT platform*, i.e. Lotus Notes, supports communication and ensures coordinated database management.

There is a distinctive interaction between the TI system and top management. Top management takes on every role described before: they are users since the TI system is closely related to business mission and strategy, and vice versa. For strategic decisions, e.g. new product development decisions, they can revert to the screening or the gatekeepers.

In addition, some top managers are directly involved in the TI process: the head of R&D is a member of the screening core-team, three top managers are simultaneously gatekeepers, and some are members of the ITI.

When it was designed, the TI system at Straumann had top management's full commitment. The promoter of the design and implementation project was the head of R&D. Today, the system is coached (coordinated) by the technology management group. Top management plays the role of the supervisor on most occasions. However, communication is favourable, thus any change in the system is possible on an informal basis.

TI at Daimler-Benz (large company)

Daimler-Benz is a diversified organization, mainly active in the fields of passenger cars, commercial vehicles, aero engines and services. Before the merger with Chrysler, Daimler-Benz employed 300,000 people, who helped to generate approximately US$58 billion in sales. About 7.9 per cent was spent on R&D, with a clear separation between research and development. Research is divided in four key areas and one central group 'technology'.

Daimler-Benz runs a formalized TI system at two levels (Lichtenthaler, 2000: 187). The first is at the corporate level, the other at the divisional level. TI at the corporate level is much more important at Daimler-Benz, and supports the divisions. TI activities are coordinated centrally in the group 'technology'. Some elements of TI at the Daimler-Benz's corporate level are presented in Figure 10.9 and described below.

The *technology monitoring unit* in the central group 'technology' builds the core element of the TI system. The mission of this unit is to inform the board about the central research department, the general technology management and research and business units about external and internal technologies and technological trends. At the same time, the Technology Monitoring unit organizes and coordinates various other TI activities, and builds the competence centre for TI methods.

A *network of internal 'gatekeepers'* from the four research areas represents the main users of the intelligence. But at the same time, they are a primary source of technological trends. These gatekeepers are decision-makers in their research fields, as well as other experts in the field.

The *circle member group* is an international network with about 150 experts, who link Daimler-Benz with trends from top universities, and with technologies that are not covered by the internal gatekeeper

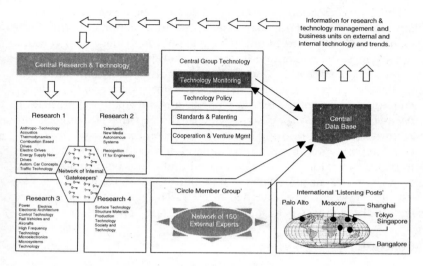

Figure 10.9   Elements of TI at Daimler-Benz

network. Each external expert has an internal scientific representative who ensures communication between the experts and Daimler-Benz. The Circle member group meets twice a year to remain informed about the long-term business strategy and future fields of interest. Their meetings are organized and coordinated by the Technology Monitoring unit. In addition to the regular meetings, there are spontaneous meetings between experts and researchers at Daimler-Benz. The Circle member group is the 'scanning' TI element at Daimler-Benz.

To monitor specific technologies, Daimler-Benz installed several *international listening posts* at the so-called hot spots. They are located in Palo Alto, Moscow, Tokyo, Shanghai, Singapore and Bangalore. Their mission is to track technological and market trends in poorly understood technology clusters (e.g. Palo Alto) and markets (e.g. Shanghai). The biggest challenge seems to be the coordination between information need formulation, typically from the headquarter in Germany, and the information collection at the listening posts. The Technology Monitoring unit is in charge of this coordination. In addition to the monitoring function, the listening posts also have other tasks, depending on the competencies present at the specific location (e.g. software development at Bangalore).

The communication between TI players is guaranteed by a sound *IT infrastructure* with a central database. In fact, information from the TI elements are directly entered into the database. Top management consults this database continuously for strategic planning and decision-making purposes. Lang (1998: 153) speaks about 'information channelling'.

The role of top management in the TI system at Daimler-Benz is clearly and uniquely that of the user. Top management formulates information needs by way of business strategy. Their link to the TI system is the Technology Monitoring unit in the central group 'technology'. This organization represents a typical TI 'command-deliver' pattern, which seems to be necessary for a centrally managed multinational company. However, Daimler-Benz undertakes some actions to extend and complete the existing TI system with other decentralized TI elements, and to organize decentralized processes to support the corporate TI process.

Conclusion

The definition of a TI system, as well as top management's roles within it and the system's interaction with other management processes form the main part of this chapter. TI should be understood as a supporting system with which to improve management's decision-making quality. Several elements, like an appropriate organization and useful tools, enable the value creating TI process.

Three examples illustrate how a TI system might be organized, and the implication for the board room. The example of Zeptosens shows that even a very small start-up company is able to run a TI system, if adapted to their requirements and limitations. Since this start-up company has very limited resources, they cannot afford to designate extra TI workers. In fact, everybody at Zeptosens is a TI worker, especially 'top managers'. Because they are most familiar with current and potential technologies, and because they are normally strongly integrated in the scientific community, they are very close to sources of relevant information. In addition, based on their scientific background, they can quickly act on the (self-)generated intelligence. In fact, this example shows a very 'small' TI system.

A 'bigger' and more organized solution for a TI system is shown in the example of Straumann. While on the one hand there is a bigger, but always restricted resource potential (i.e. more specialists, and therefore more diversified knowledge), there is on the other hand also a greater need to be formally organized because of more complex structures. The solution at Straumann is interdisciplinary and among diverse hierarchical levels. In fact, the TI system at Straumann is based on the best available competencies within the company. Therefore, top management is still active in some activities at the operational level of TI. However, there is one person who coordinates the Opportunity Landscape and the screening process, and thus, the TI system. Of course such an organization needs additional financial resources (estimated at 3 per cent of R&D expenditures at Straumann). But this is justifiable given the importance of a TI system.

The example of Daimler-Benz shows a TI system that is considerably different to that of smaller companies. In fact, the organization, the coordination and other activities take place without the direct involvement of top management. The role of top management is to give a TI framework by means of the business mission and strategy, and to use insights from the TI system for their daily strategic work. An enormous advantage of such a well structured and far reaching TI system is that this company has access to relevant first-hand information from anywhere in the world. But this is very expensive, and therefore only a few companies in the world are in a position to install such a system.

To conclude, any company should and can run a TI system. Top management plays an important role. Firstly, they have to be committed to such a system. Otherwise the TI system would not work effectively. Secondly, the system should be designed to cater for the needs of top management. However, following the idea of the 'organizational intelligence', it should also fulfil the needs of other decision-makers. Thirdly, the smaller the company, the greater the requirement for top management involvement in operational TI activities.

References

Ashton, W.B. and R.A. Klavans (1997), *Keeping Abreast of Science and Technology: Technical Intelligence in Business*, Columbus, Ohio: Batelle Press.

Balachandra, R. (1980), 'Perceived Usefulness of Technology Forecasting Techniques', *Technological Forecasting and Social Change*, 16, 1, pp. 155–66.

Dess, G.G., G.T. Lumpkin and J.E. McGee (1999), 'Linking Corporate Entrepreneurship to Strategy, Structure, and Process: Suggested Research Directions', *Entrepreneurship, Theory and Practice*, Spring, pp. 85–102.

Durand, T., F. Farhi and C. de Brabant (1997), 'Organizing for Competitive Intelligence – The Technology and Manufacturing Perspective', in W.B. Ashton and R.A. Klavans (eds), *Keeping Abreast of Science and Technology: Technical Intelligence in Business*, Columbus, Ohio: Batelle Press, pp. 189–210.

Fröhlich, O. (2000), 'Konzept und Anwendungsmöglichkeiten von Business Intelligence', *Controlling*, 4, 5, pp. 199–209.

Gerybadze, A. (1994), 'Technology Forecasting as a Process of Organisational Intelligence', *R&D Management*, 24, 2, pp. 131–40.

Groom, J.R. and F.R. David (2001), 'Competitive Intelligence Activity among Small Firms', *S.A.M. Advanced Management Journal*, 66, 1, pp. 12–20.

Hohhof, B. (1997), 'Computer Support Systems for Scientific and Technical Intelligence', in W.B. Ashton and R.A. Klavans (eds), *Keeping Abreast of Science and Technology: Technical Intelligence in Business*, Columbus, Ohio: Batelle Press, pp. 259–79.

Krystek, U. and G. Müller-Stewens (1993), *Frühaufklärung für Unternehmen: Identifikation und Handhabung zukünftiger Chancen und Bedrohungen*, Stuttgart: Schäffer-Poeschel.

Lang, H.C. (1998), *Technology Intelligence: ihre Gestaltung in Abhängigkeit der Wettbewerbssituation*, Zürich; Industrielle Organisation.

Lichtenthaler, E. (2000), *Organisation der Technology Intelligence: eine empirische Untersuchung in technologieintensiven, international tätigen Grossunternehmen*, Zürich: Dissertation ETH Zürich Nr. 13787.

McDonald, D.W. and J.L. Richardson (1997), 'Designing and Implementing Technology Intelligence Systems', W.B. Ashton and R.A. Klavans (eds), *Keeping Abreast of Science and Technology: Technical Intelligence in Business*, Columbus, Ohio: Batelle Press, pp. 123–55.

Porter, M.E. (1985), *Competitive Advantage: Creating and Sustaining Superior Performance*, New York: Free Press.

Reger, G., K. Blind, K. Cuhls and C. Kolo (1998), *Technology Foresight in Enterprises: Main Results of an International Study by the Fraunhofer Institute for Systems and Innovation Research (ISI) and the Department of R&D Management*, University of Stuttgart.

Savioz, P. (2001), 'Intelligence zur Entscheidungsunterstützung in High-Risk-Projekten', in O. Gassman, C. Kobe and E. Voit (eds), *High-Risk-Projekte: Quantensprünge in der Entwicklung erfolgreich managen*, Berlin: Springer, pp. 279–300.

Savioz, P. and M. Blum (2002), 'Strategic Forecast Tool for SMEs: How the Opportunity Landscape Interacts with Business Strategy to Anticipate Technological Trends', *Technovation*, 22, 2, pp. 91–100.

Savioz, P., A. Heer and H. Tschirky (2001), 'Technology Intelligence in Technology-based SMEs: System Design and Implementation', *Proceedings of the Portland International Conference on Management of Engineering and Technology* (PICMET), Portland, 29 July–2 August.

Tschirky, H. (1998), 'Konzept und Aufgaben des Integrierten Technologie-Managements', in H. Tschirky and S. Koruna (eds), *Technologie-Management: Idee und Praxis*, Zürich: Industrielle Organisation, pp. 193–394.

11

Technology Marketing: A New Core Competence of Technology-Based Enterprises

Jean-Philippe Escher and Hugo Tschirky

Overview

Even in the area of technology, firms are increasingly contracting in from external sources, or contracting out their own work to third parties. This involves the areas of licensing, R&D cooperation, production and OEM briefs and commerce in technologically demanding components and part-products. The activities, which we call, 'Technology Marketing', depend on new processes and concepts. Why? Because known marketing methods do not sufficiently address the unique knowledge-defined nature of technologies. This chapter seeks to answer the questions: What new tasks does technology marketing embody, how should technology marketing be organized and to what extent is top management involved in technology marketing tasks?

Technology markets: a premise of technology marketing

In the 1970s, after the gold-seeking diversification, technology-based enterprises were forced to concentrate on their core technologies and to externally source-out technologies that were less important strategically. In many technologically sophisticated products, the range of technologies was simply too large for a single firm to develop internally its entire need (Grindley and Teece, 1997: 9). This rising technology demand triggered the beginning of a technology market place.

In recent years, the once buyer dominated market place has become simultaneously more and more driven by technology sellers. Strong technology providers have realized that they could get higher returns on investments, in a given time, by exploiting their technologies externally. This means that technologies not only serve to empower the companies' own products, but also serve as external market objects. Still a lot of enterprises are refusing to exploit their technological knowledge externally for fearing of losing their crown jewels or simply because they are unaware of this opportunity.

The existence of a booming technology market place is also illustrated by the existence of service providers such as technology brokers, consultants and insurance products. The function of these companies is to assist the market players in their efforts to find suitable partners in a foggy market place and to avoid uncalculable risks. Nonetheless, all these service providers cannot deny that an efficient system of intellectual property rights is a prerequisite for flourishing technology markets. This aspect is highlighted in Chapter 9 'From R&D/Technology Management to IP/IC Management' by Ove Grandstrand.

Technology marketing: the second level of company trade activities

In order to understand the wide variety of options in the procurement and use of technologies, the *trilogy of strategic technology decisions* is a useful tool. Introduced in Chapter 2 'Bringing Technology to the Boardroom', the trilogy consists of the three fundamental strategic technology decisions 'Which Technologies', 'Make or Buy' and 'Keep or Sell' (see Figure 2.9). The 'Keep' and 'Buy' options include all types of cooperation in the development of product or process technologies, as well as all conceivable forms of utilizing and commercializing external R&D and production process technologies.

In the future, companies will be faced with significantly more 'buy or sell?' decisions than before. The next question then arises: with what form of business are these buy and sell businesses best achieved? For the moment, in the interest of comprehensiveness, we will define the professional buy-and-sell process as 'technology marketing'.

Figure 11.1 illustrates both forms of technology marketing and of traditional marketing. It presupposes that traditional marketing also *formally* covers *many of the company's acquisition and exploitation-oriented activities*. This presupposition is compatible with the marketing concept as, for example, described by Kotler and Bliemel (1999: 16): 'Marketing is a process within the economic and social structure via which individuals and groups satisfy their needs and desires by manufacturing, selling and trading products and other things.' Obviously marketing has a connection with, for example, the acquisition and exploitation activities. A type of cooperation whereby, partners are simultaneously

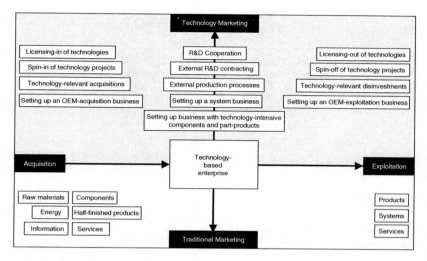

Figure 11.1 Various forms of technology marketing

both customers and providers is common business. Classical marketing, however, deals only superficially with the application of this within acquisition marketing; its focus is on exploitation markets (Weinhold, 1991). Access to a more comprehensive partnership, however, provides new approaches in problem-solving and ways of achieving success for customers, in partner systems involving customers or dealers, or in key account management (Belz, 1998: 257, 360, 440). Such arrangements affect comprehensive forms of cooperation in business to business marketing in general or in terms of complex activities (e.g. investments, financial services, etc.).

Therefore, the task of technology marketing is to, explicitly and with equal weight, integrate acquisition and exploitation activities. Considerable synergies may arise between these areas. Many know-how partnerships exist quite happily without large amounts of cash flow and still provide sustainable advantages to the parties involved. This is already the case in the buy-and-sell activities: they extend well beyond the licensing of technologies to include the establishment of partnerships in the area of external R&D and production activities. These partnerships cover R&D cooperation, the researching of technology-strategic relevant acquisitions and disinvestment, as well as the entry into OEM procurement and exploitation business, the grouping of partners for the business of modules and systems, and the setting up of

Table 11.1   Basic differences between traditional marketing and technology marketing

Determining factors	Traditional marketing	Technology marketing
Purpose	Increase competitiveness Improve ROE	Optimize technology potential Set up alliances and networks
Target groups	Product, service, system user	CEO, CTO, R&D specialists Production management Original equipment manufacturers (OEM)
Market segmenting (examples)	According to various criteria: geographic, geodemographic, psychographic, behavioural End-users, product users, key and smaller customers	Technology products to be substituted Similar process functions New product and process functions Core competence strategies and readiness to outsource Production capacities
Marketing instruments: Market performance Price and conditions Market administration Distribution	Products, services, systems Price according to market rules Advertising, purchasing stimuli, sales Distribution channels	Know-how, patents, prototypes, projects Case-specific pricing Reputation among specialists Situation-specific technology transfer, conferences, technology broker
Body of knowledge	Marketing (and technology)	Technology and marketing

Source: Tschirky, 1998: 303

business in technology-intensive components and interim products. Table 11.1 illustrates the very different sequences of events in technology marketing as compared to traditional marketing.

The strategies involved are different. Traditional marketing is oriented towards competitiveness; technology marketing may be primarily concerned with the financial and access-oriented optimization of technology potential, or with the targeted creation of a network that provides relevant technology knowledge. There are also significant differences with regard to the competencies required for successful technology marketing, for which expert technology knowledge concerning technology trends, technology development and application and production are vital. Both types of marketing, however, have the same goal: to increase the firm's profitability.

The issue of market segmentation is similar. While traditional marketing makes use of geographic or behavioural (etc.) criteria, technology marketing focuses on various forms of technological criteria. Thus it may be reasonable to conduct market grouping according to substituting technologies (e.g. is so-called 'Bubble-Jet' technology capable of replacing quartz printing and laser technology, partially or wholly?). Or it may be useful to consider (this is a cross-industry question) which product functions may be achieved by certain technologies (e.g. in the case of a highly efficient soldering technology, suitable for the manufacture of vacuum containers, the potential market segment lies not in the variety of vacuum apparatus but in the number of products whose manufacture requires the production process function of binding metals securely).

Traditional marketing deals with describable products, systems and services whose prices are set according to market rules and which reach the customers by market means and via real distribution channels. Technology marketing, in contrast, primarily involves complex knowledge, the value of which is difficult to estimate, but becomes known via its reputation and whose distribution takes place in the form of situative technology transfer.

These differences reflect company tasks in fully separate market areas. Figuratively speaking, technology marketing involves what is carried out on the 'second level of company activities' (see Figure 2.10).

Strategic objectives of technology marketing

By selling or buying technologies externally a company can pursue different strategies simultaneously. Due to their complexity, strategic objectives have to be defined in order to set clear guidelines for future decisions like the choice of suitable technology partners and the most favourable form of technology trading. Furthermore, technology marketing could affect the technology potential substantially and could have a strong positive or negative impact on a company's competitive advantage. Therefore technology marketing strategies have to be aligned to the business strategy, technology strategy and intellectual property strategy. For further information to this issue compare Granstrand's Chapter 9. The following text will present the main strategic objectives and exemplary cases of technology trading businesses.

Reasons for technology acquisition

Faster development

The main drivers of external technology acquisition are, first, the ever present pressure of time – development delays must be avoided at all costs – and secondly, the need to make efficient use of resources, i.e. to make the best possible use of a given R&D budget.

Instead of building up technological know-how internally, licensing-in is a proper way to get access to already externally available technological know-how in order to bring products faster to the market. This short-term policy is not suitable as a substitute for long-term strategies. As long as the in-licensed technologies affect technology fields, which do not lie in business decisive areas, this action is appropriate.

Cost and risk reduction

The second strategic objective of external technology acquisition is to reduce cost and risk of R&D investments. Building up in-house technological know-how is time and resource intensive and is always accompanied by technological uncertainty. This means that a company has to balance technological and financial risks of its R&D investments regarding the strategic importance of the technology to its business, available resources and commercial potential. External acquisition is favoured in two cases: firstly, if the technology is not strategically relevant and secondly, if investments bear a high technological or financial risk. In the latter case a company could enter into a strategic alliance to share the risk of technological and financial failure; in the first case the company could rely on externally available technologies that have already proven their functionality by licensing them in.

Learning from others

A widely persued strategic objective is to learn from others by accessing their technological know-how. This option is used by many companies with the intention of building up their own technological competencies or determining their competitors' strengths and weaknesses concerning technological know-how. This could take place in many different forms: longterm alliances, co-development, buying competitors' products, etc. Regarding the building-up of new competencies, companies do fall back on a broad and well-cultivated research network (Bucher *et al.*, 2001). In this aspect a reliable longterm strategic alliance is a mutual goal, where both partners can benefit from each other.

Reasons for technology exploitation

Faster access to external technology sources

A very effective way to benefit from its achievements in R&D is to exploit technologies externally, in the form of R&D cooperation and cross-licensing, in order to acquire external technologies. The proposed technology could increase the interest of potential technology providers to bring in their technological know-how. Another aspect is concerned with financial resource limitations. Firms that are high net users of others' patents have a choice. They must increasingly pay royalties, or they must develop their own portfolios in order to bring something to the table in cross-licensing negotiations (Grindley and Teece, 1997: 8).

Additional profit

One objective is to obtain value from the firm's intellectual property (IP), in the form of its patent portfolio, by generating royalty income (Grindley and Teece, 1997: 16). Of course, all of this is net income (Rivette and Kline, 2000). It is easy to realize that well-managed external technology exploitation could contribute substantially to the company's growth of shareholder value. Other aspects of significant interest are higher return on investments in R&D or strengthening the technological position of the enterprise through additional investments in research programmes.

Foster a technology network

Technology intensive enterprises maintain a strong technology network. The enterprise benefits in many ways from a strong technology network, especially concerning technology marketing. A company generally prefers to sign a technology transaction contract with already known business partners. The partner's internal procedures are familiar and the company has built up a confidential relationship (Bidault and Fischer, 1994). The risk of failure diminishes and transaction cost decline. However, the success of external technology exploitation depends on such a network (Bidault and Fischer, 1994) and is a proper tool for maintaining or even fortifying the network.

Faster learning in R&D

The performance progress of a technology in correspondence with the accumulated means invested in it follows an S-curve. It is worth asking whether it is possible to influence this process. In other words, would

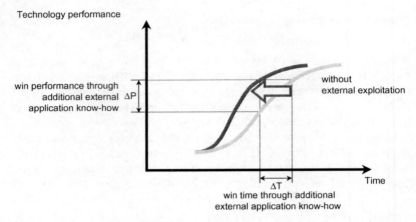

Figure 11.2   Time winning effect of the R&D learning curve phenomenon on the S-curve of a technology

it be feasible to develop an *R&D learning curve* analogous to familiar production-process learning curves (see Figure 11.2)?

An approach to this issue has been elaborated by Teichmann (1994) (Tschirky, 1998: 242). His starting-point was the premise that an important learning process also takes place in the R&D area. He refers to the number of applications that are realized in the course of technology improvement.

An example is the improvement of speech recognition technology in telecommunications applications bringing it up to the level of 100 words. According to Teichmann's thesis this level could be reached more quickly if applications are first realized at the level of technology involving just a few words (e.g. elevator programming). From these applications, knowledge may be gathered which will stimulate increases in R&D performance.

Improvement of reputation and image

Another important aspect is the improvement of the enterprise's reputation and image through external technology exploitation. By projecting the image as a strong technology provider, with an outstanding R&D unit, the enterprise will probably promote its reputation considerably. Considering this aspect, the external technology exploitation will have a positive impact on the level of traditional product markets.

Practical examples of technology marketing activities

Companies are already demonstrating, in various forms, how they acquire and utilize technologies. There are many different examples.

Honda example

Honda Motor Co. and General Motors Corp. commented on their recent agreement as follows: 'There is no precedent in the auto industry for two companies that differ so much in size and corporate culture to maintain close cooperative relations without capital ties' (*Nikkei Weekly*, 6 December 1999). The core of future intensified cooperation is to mutually exchange key technologies. As a complementary extension to its present offering in drive technologies, Honda will receive diesel motors from Isuzu Motors Ltd (a GM company); and Honda will make its own low-emission technologies available (in the latter area, Honda is a leader, as indicated by its development of a 'Zero-level Emission Vehicle' (ZLEV)).

This agreement may also be interpreted in the light of long-term technology strategy: it is estimated that fuel-cell technology – also a key technology being developed at Honda – will be ripe for commercialization from the year 2004. After this, it is predicted that traditional fuel-burning technology will very quickly become unimportant. For this reason, Honda seized the opportunity, while it was still possible, to make use of accumulated know-how concerning low-emission drives. At the same time Honda has focused its efforts on fuel-cell technology, supported by the cooperation with GM.

CERN example

The European Laboratory for Particle Physics (CERN) is, at present, being forced to make budget cuts (*Neue Zürcher Zeitung*, 4 July 1998). In 1980, 3,800 people were employed, today the number is 2,800, and in the year 2005 it will be 2,000. In order to address the current demand for technologies, in spite of this restructuring, industry has been appealed to cooperate in development projects under an initiative entitled 'Call for Technology'. According to this cooperative model, CERN will provide its accumulated technological and scientific expertise, while its industrial partners will deliver specific development know-how and personnel and material resources. Already, several firms of various sizes have made use of this opportunity for technology transfer. In many cases, a major attraction of the arrangement is the possibility of obtaining new technological expertise and using it to launch new products on the traditional market.

A typical example is the small firm Lemo SA in Ecublens, which specializes in electronic plugs. As early as the end of the 1950s Lemo developed a miniaturized plug for co-axial cables for CERN. A world standard emerged from this development, and today the company has a product range of over 40 models, used in particle physics as well as in telecommunications and medical electronics. In the meantime, Lemo's offering to CERN has extended significantly, today involving a turnover of around Sfr. 300,000, with products ranging from high voltage plugs to miniaturized plugs for glass fibre technology. Cooperation with CERN and the know-how it has gained there has so far generated profits of around Sfr. 100 million for Lemo.

IBM example

An agreement has recently been made between IBM Corp. and Acer (Tapei, Taiwan) based on an $8 billion technology transfer deal (EETTimesOline (eet.com), 6 July 1999). According to the deal, Acer will, for the next seven years, for its own servers, desktops and note-book computers, take over usage rights from IBM in the area of hard disc drives and network and display technologies. In return, IBM will purchase $1.3 billion worth of 13.3 inch LCDs, manufactured by Acer using IBM production technologies (already transferred by a regulated licensing agreement in the previous year). In this context, collaboration is planned to cooperatively develop products which will be distributed by Acer in Asia and the Middle East.

Other similar agreements have been made with Dell, EMC, Apple and Nintendo. With the help of such OEM alliances, the number of which has steadily grown since 1993, IBM can spread its internally developed technologies much faster than would be possible via its own product range.

At the beginning of 2000, it was announced that IBM, with its 2,756 patents, stood at the top of the list for patents granted in the USA in 1999 (*The Financial Times*, 12 January 2000). Gerald Rosenthal, Vice-President of Intellectual Property and Licensing, describes IBM's patent policy as follows: 'We do not intend to use patent portfolio to prevent companies from using our technologies as long as they are willing to pay the license fees. Our patent portfolio not only generates large license revenues but is also a strategy in terms of winning new businesses.' Indeed, at present, IBM's annual intake from licences amounts to around $1 billion. In 1999, in addition, turnover of technology group components brought in more than $30 billion. IBM makes use of its strong patent position through cross-technology licensing agreements with other computer manufacturers, selectively allowing direct access to its technology know-how. IBM invests over $5 billion in research and development annually.

IBM not only benefits from royalties – it often gets paid by a back flow of the licensee's application know-how. In comparison to the production learning curve, IBM is decreasing along the R&D learning curve by accumulating early technology experience, resulting in a shorter time to market. This matter is in complete agreement with the statement of Tony Baker, director of business development for IBM Technology Group: 'We've learned that we can bring our technology to market faster via IBM products, IBM subsystems [by] selling technology to OEM customers.' (EETTimesOnline (eet.com), 6 July 1999).

Nelm example

Nelm AG is an enterprise based in the Ticino, the Italian part of Switzerland, specializing in quality electronic production. It was founded in 1973 and in 1976 was taken over by Cerberus AG as a subsidiary, originally with the task, complementary to main production in Volketswil, of manufacturing large series of fire and intruder detectors. During the 1980s, Nelm AG progressively underwent a successful strategic change (J. P. Thiébaud, 2000). This involved the extension of core competencies enabling the firm to provide a broad spectrum of services to other companies, such as product and manufacture engineering, component procurement and process planning, conductor plate manufacture, electronic assembly and quality control, and finally supply chain management (Brumm, 1992). To this end, in 1987 the Altimex Network was created as a technology pool for electronic manufacture. It consists of Altimex AG, focusing on project management, engineering, product design, and procurement and logistics, and Nelm AG; manufacturing is concentrated in the latter, which is today in a position to fill both prototype and large series orders.

Nelm employs around 500 people at present. Half of the firm's business involves filling manufacturing orders from the Cerberus division of the new (1998) Siemens Building Technologies, and the other service orders for third parties.

This successful in-sourcing strategy involves a specific form of technology transfer: production process technologies mastered by Nelm AG are made available to other firms. This, however, takes place not via the transfer of technical knowledge and facilities but via the materialized products of the technologies used. Such an explicit definition points to the fact that, in the case of Nelm AG, the 'commercial units' are technologies, traded in their applied form.

Functional integration of buying and sales

Suitable structures are required to implement active technology marketing. It might be thinkable, analogous to usual organizational forms, to set up buying and sales units for technology businesses also. In the case of technology marketing activities it is found that this would not be suitable for the following reasons.

Upon closer inspection, it becomes apparent that the three decision-making areas represented in Figure 2.9 of Tschriky's chapter despite their varying subject-matter, have a significant amount in common. Each of the three areas should be based upon at least three areas of information. These include, firstly, information concerning the current status of functionality, as well as performance and application aspects of those technologies which are important to the enterprise at a given point in time or might be so in the future. Secondly, information is needed about the future development of these technologies and the presumed advent of new technologies. Thirdly – and of increasing urgency – information is required which covers, case-wise, the current state of development and use of product and process technologies in other firms.

In other words, the competence required for processing and running acquisition and exploitation-related technology business is more or less identical. For this reason technology marketing activities ask for a structure, which integrates both buying and selling tasks. As companies of all sizes are under pressure to find external solutions to information-gathering, it is also expedient to allocate to this unit and the responsibility for the design and running of an appropriate information procurement system. Here one speaks of 'technology intelligence'. (For further information compare Chapter 10 by Savioz.)

Our proposal is to set up an organizational unit, entitled 'Technology Intelligence and Marketing' (TIM), which has the following tasks (Tschirky, 1998: 324):

- Establishment and maintenance of intensive contacts with internal technology bearers and external technology experts.
- Systematic patent analyses.
- Set up and operation of a 'technology intelligence' system oriented towards all company-relevant technology fields.
- Creation of 'technology road maps' of core technologies.
- Compilation of experiences in the establishment and operation of technology cooperation and strategic alliances.
- Initiation of technology business and the project responsibility for carrying it through.

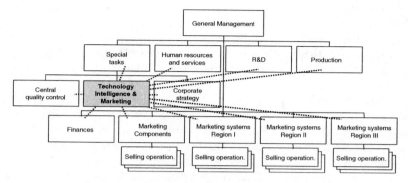

Figure 11.3 Structure of the Technology Intelligence and Marketing unit in the organization chart of an industrial company
Source: Tschirky, 1998: 323

- Periodic elaboration of technology strategy.
- Organization of interdisciplinary functions to promote decision-making.
- Elaboration of information in the area of technology assessment.

In terms of personnel, TIM should be supported by a core team involving (depending on the size of the firm) a small number of experts. In addition, the part-time collaboration in TIM tasks of all company units affected by technology decisions should be foreseen (see Figure 11.3). This would result in a company-wide standard information level regarding technology matters and increase identification with results. It would seem logical to place TIM under the supervision of the CTO (Chief Technology Officer) or the general management member responsible for technology.

Example: the new technology options of Schulthess Maschinen AG

Schulthess Maschinen AG, a middle-sized firm in the machine industry, pursues a niche strategy and focuses its product offering primarily on high-quality washing machines. The production of high-quality products requires investment in modern production plants, however, comparatively low turnover means that available production capacity is not fully utilized.

In search of ways to better utilize its available and unused production capacity, the company is concentrating on the acquisition of external production contracts. While the marketing activities surrounding technologies in most firms primarily concern product technologies, at Schulthess the emphasis is on the marketing of production process technologies. It must be noted, however, that no technology leaves Schulthess: external parties may only make contractual use of its technologies internally.

Schulthess Maschinen AG has its production concentrated on its core competencies – the processing of fine sheet metal, steel and casting material, surface treatments and assembly – and has systematically expanded and optimized them. Supporting these competencies are around 20 production process technologies with marketing potential.

The goal of Schulthess' technology marketing activities is to establish solid partnerships with companies, for which it carries out production contracts, thereby ensuring that its internal plant is better utilized. In this context a long-term contractual relationship is advantageous. The search for appropriate partners is not only exclusive to Schulthess' own branch of industry: one of the company's great advantages lies in its range of offerings in a comprehensive value creation chain.

Evaluation of the technology portfolio

The question concerning which production process technologies are actually suitable for marketing, in the sense of fulfilling external production contracts, must firstly be investigated via a comprehensive evaluation of all the individual technologies.

Here, developing an overview of the production process technologies available in the firm rather in the form of a technology portfolio is unavoidable. As displayed in Chapter 2 (see Figure 2.11) the use of the dynamic technology portfolio bears a significant advantage compared to conventional portfolios including information about yet to be deployed 'new technologies' and 'obsolete technologies'.

Figure 11.4 takes this into account by positioning the process technologies of Schulthess in a dynamic technology portfolio. The technology-attractiveness is the marketability including technological relevance and technology demand aspects. Whereas the technology strength is the enterprise's technology position by means of financial and know-how resources compared to the strongest competitors.

In this dynamic technology portfolio, several key technologies are included, covering those already in use and those requiring future resources. It is obvious that technologies in the upper right of the portfolio are highly marketable, but also bear the risk of damaging the competitive advantages of Schulthess. The company's task is to

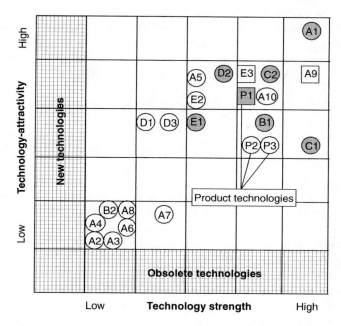

Figure 11.4 Dynamic technology portfolio of Schulthess Maschinen AG

balance potential opportunities and risks. At the same time, this type of representation provides an overview of technologies that have residual commercial value eventhough abandoned by the company.

The application of a dynamic technology portfolio is very advantageous for Schulthess in making an inventory of production process technologies for application by third parties. At this point new production methods that are under discussion may also be brought in as 'new technologies'.

Criteria for a technology marketing strategy

Other decision-making criteria come into play for Schulthess in addition to the criteria surrounding the technology and market position of production process technologies. Firstly the question arises as to how far the revealing of core competencies inherent in the marketing of its production process technologies endangers the company's competitive capabilities. Core competencies, in this context, are concerned with abilities available at only a few companies, which generate additional benefits to customers and are not, or are only in a limited sense, capable of imitation or substitution. In completing production assignments for third parties this danger is minimal. Schulthess masters these production technologies marvellously. In fulfilling external contracts it usually deploys those production process technologies identified as core competencies only for the manufacturing of the product functions of the contracting party.

In addition, in order to take on external production contracts, sufficient plant capacity must be available. On the average Schulthess' production resources are only used at about 70 per cent capacity; thus in some areas, the firm is able, if needed, to increase its production capacity considerably. The expenditure and internal costs generated by these technology marketing activities should be known factors, and must never exceed the profits generated by the arrangement.

Flexibility is a further important decision-making criteria: conversion and preparation time in production, and personnel expenditure on external contracts, need to be kept to a minimum; the completion of an external contract naturally has an indirect connection with Schulthess' core business. In this sense semi and fully automatic production technologies demonstrate a high level of flexibility, and are for this reason the most suitable for deployment in external production contract assignments.

If regarded as dependent on the above criteria and their expression, technology marketing strategies may be applied to production process technologies in the context of external contract assignments. Here the marketing dimension is determined by the external contracting party:

- *vertical*: the production contract either precedes or follows in the value creation chain.
- *horizontal*: the contracting party comes from the same branch of industry and may be a competitor.
- *lateral*: the contract assignment is carried out for a party from a different branch of industry.

For Schulthess, the opportunity to begin technology marketing activities in all dimensions is emerging, i.e. within the value creation chain as well as within or outside of the branch of industry. In some cases, however, it is expedient to follow a selective procedure in contract acquisition from partners within the value creation chain and/or from parties outside the industry. This strategic policy is especially applicable in the area of production process technologies whose technology effects are important for Schulthess' competitive capacity.

Conclusion

The phenomenon of external technology acquisition has been given a lot of attention in theory and practice over the last few years. So far research has been limited to an analysis of the situation of the buyer in the technology trade. In this chapter it is argued that only through integrated consideration of the trilogy of technology decisions, especially the integrated analysis of procurement and sales of technologies, effective technology decisions can be made. To support the buying and selling of technologies, a new type of marketing that goes beyond traditional marketing is needed. This new discipline of technology management, called technology marketing, is focused on the acquisition and exploitation markets of technologies. Through its integrated approach, technology marketing generates new strategic options. To ensure that these options can be realized, structural solutions for the functional integration of technology buying and selling are needed. As a whole this research shows that the new field of technology marketing will become more important, in practice and theory, over the next couple of years. Further research to develop this area cannot be ignored.

References

Belz, Ch. (1998), *Akzente im Innovativen Marketing*, St Gallen: Thexis.

Bidault, F. and W. Fischer (1994), 'Technology transactions: networks over markets', *R&D Management*, 24, 4, pp. 373–86.

Brodbeck, H., B. Birkenmeier and H. Tschirky (1995), 'Neue Entscheidungsstrukturen des Integrierten Technologie-Managments', *Die Unternehmung*, 49, 2, S. p. 109.

Brumm, G. (1992), *Konzept eines Synergie-Verbunds mehrerer unabhängiger Unternehmungen*, Internal document, Nelm AG.

Bucher, Ph., B. Birkenmeier, H. Brodbeck, J.-Ph. Escher and P. Savioz (2001), *Management Principles for Evaluating and Introducing Disruptive Technologies: The Case of Nanotechnology in Switzerland*, presented at the R&D Management Conference, Dublin.

Grindley, P. and D. Teece (1997), 'Managing intellectual capital: licensing and cross-licensing in semiconductors and electronics', *California Management Review*, 39, 2, p. 8.

Kotler, Ph. and F. Bliemel (1999), *Marketing-Management*, Stuttgart: Schäffer-Poeschel Verlag.

Rivette, K. and D. Kline (2000), *Rembrandts in the Attic – Unlocking the Hidden Value of Patents*, Boston: Harvard Business School Press.

Thiébaud, J. P. (2000), Statement, Director of Nelm AG, 13 January.

Tschirky, H. (1998), 'Konzept und Aufgaben des integrierten Technologie-Managements', in Tschirky, H. and Koruna, S., (eds), *Technologie Management: Idee und Praxis*, Zurich: Verlag Industrielle Organisation.

Weinhold, H. (1991), *Marketing in 20 Lektionen, 21. Auflage* (St. Gallen *et al.*: Fachmed).

12

Changing the Rules of the Game: Strategic Alliances, the New Competitive Weapon

Geert Duysters, Arie Nagel and Ash Vasudevan

Overview

The rules of the competitive game are changing in an unprecedented way. The conventional stable environment has been replaced by a new competitive environment characterized by rapid technological change, increasing patterns of globalization, and competitors who no longer emerge from familiar corners. The combination of these factors has led to a situation in which firms are increasingly challenged by the need for complementary assets and know-how, and the need to develop a capability for changing the rules of the game. After a brief discussion on these specific changes, this chapter explains how to develop such a capability. We argue that the capacity to deal with the changing rules can best be met by allying with complementary companies: the need for multiple competencies drives companies towards cooperation. Finally, a number of presciptions are given that enable managers at all levels to determine their readiness to deal with their chaotic global business environment. This enables them to take a lead in changing the rules of the game. This should prove to be a core asset to companies that hope to survive in discontinuous, non-linear and intensely competitive marketplaces.

Changing the rules

One industry after another has seen the emergence of revolutionaries who are constantly changing transaction processes and users' experiences by introducing new products that meet the unarticulated needs of the customers. As a result, the playing field has become wider and more importantly boundaryless, bringing in players with multiple

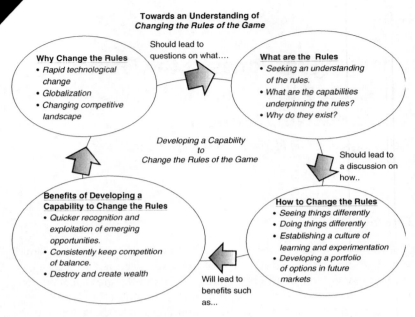

Figure 12.1 Towards an understanding of changing the rules of the game
Source: Thomson Financial

competencies and perspectives to shape the needs of the customers and to serve them.

The challenge for organizations is to find the means by which they *can develop a capability for changing the rules of the game*. In order provide an explanation of what we mean by changing the rules of the game, we begin by examining the core issues surrounding it: why change the rules, what are the rules, and how to change the rules. Figure 12.1 summarizes the ensuing discussions.

As Hamel and Prahalad (1994) pointed out, it is not so much that companies compete on products, but on the knowledge and skills underlying the R&D, production and marketing skills associated with contemporary products. These are called competencies and if these competencies are unique to one company and at the same time recognized by the market place, they are described as 'core competencies'. To us it seems that these should be the ones as described above: the capability to deal with the choice between make, buy or ally. Also Hamel and Prahalad described that 'the rules of the game' constantly change. As such, it is important for organizations to develop the capability of recognizing these changes in preliminary stages and to deal with it. How to do this is the subject of the second part of this chapter.

Why do the rules change?

Three prominent factors that directly challenge the conventional, stable view of the past and increase the need for companies to proactively seek change have emerged:

- *Rapid Technological Change.* We see a trend towards shrinking product life cycles and the rapid introduction of new products and services based on technologies that have enabled companies to increase their efficiency and productivity. While technology has dramatically impacted on the ability of firms to provide cutting-edge products and services at competitive prices, it has also greatly enhanced the power of the customer to make informed decisions about their eventual purchases. The age of mass standardization – be it of products, services, or marketing – has been replaced by mass customization. This dramatic change has been brought about largely by developments in computing and communications, which have seen significant advances in power, memory, and speed of transmission. Technology is empowering and will continue to empower customers by defining why – they need products or services, how – they prefer to receive them, when – they receive them, and how much – they will pay for them. Customer loyalty is now a fleeting phenomenon not to be trifled with. Unlike the past, when locational and emotional constraints served as convenient mechanisms by which companies could depend on the loyalty of their customers, today's burgeoning world of internet commerce has diminished such conveniences. Now, more than ever, businesses cannot afford to take their customers for granted, because access to their competitors is 'just a click away'.
- *Globalization.* Tele-communications have facilitated transactions and communications between geographically dispersed locations. Simultaneously other forces of globalization have made the competitive playing field in most industries larger than ever, with players from different countries entering the fray with divergent strategies, but with a converging and common intent: to be global leader. The previous notion that the economic system is a collection of independent national markets isolated from one another, is being replaced by the notion that diverse national markets are now merging into one huge global marketplace.

- *Changing Competitive Landscape.* The rise of the internet, accompanied by the ongoing convergence of industries, has led to a situation in which competition no longer comes from familiar corners, but increasingly from unfamiliar, hitherto unexpected, places. Typically from outside the industry, bringing in new thinking, new attitudes, new market-shaping concepts, and most importantly, new price/performance capabilities. In this environment, it is now very hard to determine who the competitors are.

As explained above, the business environment is becoming very complex. Changing the rules of the game is becoming an important capability that a company must nurture and institutionalize, if it is to survive in the current marketplace. But what are rules of the game and who makes them?

What are the rules?

Understanding the rules, and the capabilities that underpin those rules, questioning the rules and seeking new ways of changing the rules, these should be at the core of every firm's competitive effort. Such an emphasis will enable your company to benefit from the incessant flow of new products and service ideas, to identify new market opportunities, and to determine the company's capabilities and the collaborators needed to exploit them. But who makes the rules?

Underpinning any rule is a superior competence or capability, typically based on two kinds of knowledge: technological knowledge that includes knowledge of the different components and the links between them, and market knowledge that includes knowledge of distribution channels, product applications, new markets, and customer expectations, preferences, needs, and wants. Challenges to the prevailing rules may emerge from both fronts. New entrants may come in with a new technology, evoke fundamental changes in the knowledge that underpins the products or services, introduce new products and services with competitive cost, performance, and/or quality advantage, and render the prevailing paradigm useless (e.g. electronic watches, internet, electric car, the PC). This process is also referred to as *technological discontinuity* and may either be competence enhancing or competence destroying. On the other hand, a market innovation may lead to a competitor offering the same product or service, or an incrementally different product or service, through a completely different medium, thereby transforming the customer experience. This is called a *market discontinuity*, because it introduces fundamental changes in the way consumers acquire knowledge, make purchasing decisions, purchase the product or service, experience the functionality of the product and thereby satisfy their needs.

To understand this, it is important to consider it in the context of a paradigm, which typically includes a set of explicit and tacit rules that emerge to define and influence the behaviour of those within the paradigm and those outside of it. These rules can differ from industry to industry. For instance, while the key to success may be prime location for retailing, extensive advertising in athletic shoes, it may be mass customization for the computer industry. Who establishes the rules? Typically those companies that make extensive technological and market commitments and are able to spot opportunities, exploit them and occupy scarce positions better and faster than their competitors. Changing the rules of the game typically involves a radical change to the prevailing paradigm, accompanied by a radical transformation in the consumption experience.

How to develop the capacity to change the rules of the game?

It is important to explore how a company can consistently be a source of new ideas, new rules, and new wealth-creation opportunities. During our research and interviews with executives from leading companies caught in the melee of digital competition, some surprising yet simple rules have emerged, which when adopted, can lead to the generation of new ideas and new perspectives for changing the rules of the game. So what are some of the rules governing change in a business context? Based on our research, the following simple rules were identified:

- *Seeing things differently.* It is very important to develop a vision for your business and industry, frequently revisit the assumptions of your business model and question their relevance over time, especially when you are successful. When was the last time you invited a group of people to discuss the underlying principles of your business model, and questioned them? To generate new insights into your business model and proactively understand what these concepts are, it is very important to foster a climate that encourages new perspectives and ideas.
- *Doing things differently.* While recognizing the need for new perspectives and ideas is the first and most crucial step towards competing in an environment of change, it is useful only if accompanied by action. Many organizations feel the need for change, but do not

follow through the steps to actually accomplish it. Remember that an organization is a system of interconnected entities and that even small changes can lead to widespread performance-enhancing opportunities. For instance, ensuring the digitization of information and transactions within the organization can lead to dramatic improvements in productivity. It is important to question the assumptions behind your business model all the time, especially when you are successful. That is the time when incumbents get complacent – 'Nobody can beat us at this game ... we invented it'. This is when those practising the prevailing paradigm are most reluctant to change, because they can hide their fears by making a wonderful case for rejection: 'The numbers are great. Everybody likes our product or service. Why mess with something good?' Not thinking of change, especially when you are successful, is perhaps one of the most-likely reasons for future failure.

- *Establishing a culture of learning and experimenting.* Organizations are embedded in orthodoxies that dictate what they should do, as opposed to what they can do, and sometimes what they would like to do. While they require effort, learning and experimenting do foster change and now, more than ever, organizations should seek ways to make learning and experimenting part of their culture. Learning involves the constant interaction and flow of communication between employees within the organization. Companies that want to embrace change and create the future must rely on the collective intelligence and wisdom of their people. Sharing knowledge and learning go hand in hand. One of the most powerful ways to learn is through tolerating mistakes and learning from them. 3M is a leader because it consistently fosters a culture of innovation among its employees coupled with a tolerance for mistakes. Encouraging 'outside the box' thinking is also critical for fostering creativity and generating new insights. Solutions or unique insights into problems may often exist outside your discipline. Sometimes it is what they don't know, rather than what they do, that intrigues people from outside, and leads them to ask simple and seemingly naïve questions. The discovery of warm superconductors is credited to Dr Alex Mueller, an IBM research fellow at Zurich, who had no background in the superconductor paradigm but had an insight into the properties of ceramic materials that revolutionized the superconductor industry. Seeking solutions from outside your paradigm, or 'managing the white space', as Motorola refers to it, is a very important managerial imperative if a company wants to create the future.

- *Developing a portfolio of options in future markets.* To take the lead in changing the rules of the game, it is important to foster a culture of innovation, new ideas, and new perspectives within the organization. It is also important to develop a portfolio of options to successfully respond to unfolding events, especially when those events are likely to destroy your current competencies. This still begs the question, why options? As argued before, today's discontinuous, non-linear and continually changing economic environment is forcing companies remain consistently at the cutting-edge of technological and market knowledge developments or else face the risk of fading into oblivion. Most innovations in today's markets are products of several distinct technological and market inputs. Unfortunately, no single firm has either the breadth or depth of competencies to be at the cutting edge on both fronts. For instance, auto manufacturers are now faced with the daunting challenge of being at the cutting edge of knowledge development in fields such as microelectronics, robotics, systems integration, consumer finance, ceramics, engineering plastics, and electrical storage and propulsion. Even if they attempt to build such a base, the advantage of breadth is often offset by lack of depth and a focus on the successful exploitation of certain key competencies. To remain competitive, firms are faced with the challenge of developing their own core competencies, but also be in a position to have access to the core competence of other firms within and outside their industry through key strategic linkages. In today's global markets in which technological progress is extremely rapid, boundary spanning strategic alliances have become an important factor for the overall competitive position of a company. Even the largest organizations cannot afford to develop all their new products, new technologies or new markets by themselves. The amount of capital needed and the risks involved in engaging solely in large-scale in-house development programmes is simply too high to be acceptable. Therefore, over the past decades, we have witnessed an unprecedented growth in the use of alternative forms of organization, like the more traditional mergers and acquisitions, and todate a fast growing number of strategic alliances (see Figure 12.2).

Growing number of cooperations

Within five years from now, the value of alliances is projected to be in the range of $30–50 trillion (Booz-Allen and Hamilton, 2000). As a result,

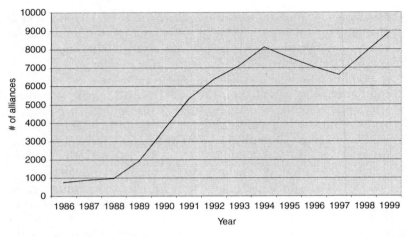

Figure 12.2   Number of newly established strategic alliances per year (1986–99),
3-year moving averages

Source: Thomson Financial

the traditionally independent self-contained organization seems to have
evolved into an organization that replaces part of its internal growth by
growth through mergers, acquisitions and strategic alliances. The rise of
these particular forms of organization has created many opportunities for
companies, while at the same time posing major threats to these same
organizations. Mergers and acquisitions and strategic alliances have been
instrumental in many firms' ability to access new markets and to absorb
new technologies; however, these activities have an extremely high failure rate. Ironically, the more worries expressed in the literature about the
viability of these modes of organization, the higher their growth rate. In
spite of the reported failure rates of up to 70 per cent, strategic alliances
and mergers and acquisitions have never been more popular. Hence the
need for it must be enormous.

In his inaugural lecture, Duysters (2001) argues that:

- Innovation can no longer be seen as the sole outcome of internal
  accumulation of know-how. In today's turbulent business, environment innovation comes about by the interplay of two distinct but
  related factors: endogenous innovation efforts and (quasi) external
  acquisition of technology and know-how.
- Strategic alliances can no longer be considered as second best compared to stand-alone alternatives or mergers and acquisitions. We will

argue that strategic alliances can provide flexible and efficient, fast-to-build solutions for the acquisition of new technologies in today's turbulent environment.

External and quasi-external acquisition of know-how

Over the past decades, firms have constantly struggled to deal effectively with their rapidly changing environments. Especially in high-tech industries, costs of research and development have rocketed, whereas steep learning curves and ever shortening product and technology life cycles have reduced the time to recoup these costs significantly. These developments stimulate firms to share development costs and to reduce lead times for their innovative products. A reduction in lead times allows organizations to pre-empt emerging markets and enables them to move faster down the learning curve. Furthermore, the ongoing complexity of products and technologies increases the need for flexibility in order to respond quickly to changing market needs and to new technological opportunities. The emergence of the network economy has not only accelerated these forces but also established a whole new business paradigm that rendered a number of existing skills and know-how useless. Whereas, for a long time, firms have relied heavily on the internal accumulation of know-how, they have come to realize that internal development is no longer sufficient to deal with their changing technological environment. A rapidly increasing number of firms seems to recognize that external technology acquisition can help them to increase their flexibility and allows them to move swiftly from one technology to another in rapidly changing competitive and technological settings.

In Chapter 6, Durand explains what the basic strategic options of a firms are when facing technological change.

Benefits of developing a capability for changing the rules of the game

As we have argued above, taking the lead in changing the rules of the game should be at the core of a company's competitive effort, if it has any hope of surviving in discontinuous, non-linear and intensely competitive marketplace. Developing an internal capability to change the rules of the game will enable companies to exploit opportunities and occupy scarce positions better and faster than their competitors. By constantly fostering a culture of learning and experimenting, generating new visions, new perspectives and new market shaping concepts, companies can and will be able to consistently recognize and exploit emerging opportunities, occupy scarce positions, and keep their competitors off balance. This will increase their potential to be at the forefront of both wealth creation and wealth destruction.

Managerial prescriptions from the above

With knowledge and understanding of the 'why', 'what' and 'how' of developing the capacity to change the rules of the game, we can consider some recommendations that will enable managers at all levels to determine their readiness to deal with the even more chaotic global business environment. Moreover these rules come in the forefront of changing the rules of the game:

- *Rules are made to be broken.* Yesterday's rules are likely to be today's memories and establishing tomorrow's rules should be today's dreams. It is better that it is your company simultaneously making and breaking the rules than it is your competitor or some other company from another industry. It is better to be arrogant about breaking rules than preserving them. Trivoli Systems do just that. They have created a team of marketers and developers called *'the courtyard gang'* who are expected to create scenarios and identify means by which Trivoli Systems could be put out business. Evaluate the rules within your company and industry frequently. What kind of knowledge underpins the rules? Is it technological or market, or both? How can the rules be changed?
- *Facilitate communication within the organization.* Constantly monitor to spot and eliminate any *'one stop shopping'* within your company. Creativity exists in all organizations. It is just a matter of unlocking the door that shuts in traditions, culture and conventions and shuts out change. The use of cross-functional teams comprising of people of both genders and different ages, and keeping the team composition dynamic will greatly enhance the potential to break the complacency barrier and prevailing company orthodoxies. Invest in changing the architecture of your building if you feel it hampers communication between divisions and across functions.
- *The challenge for competing in the uncertain world with an unclear future is finding a strategy that includes constantly identifying options, making choices, acting, and making adjustments.* No resource is a constant in your value network. Determine the technological and marketing

options taken by your company. Does your company emphasize one more than the other? Are the options taken simply to preserve the company's current competitive position or are they expected to trigger technological and market discontinuities? Remember that innovators don't just study the marketplace as defined by others; they also scout for opportunities among current non-buyers to try to understand what keeps them out of the market. An important factor in changing the rules of the game is to be able to consistently challenge the defining characteristics of the market, as defined by your company and by others.

- *Organize sessions to consider the unthinkable.* Start a conversation about the future with your employees, customers, and alliance partners. A willingness to take risks is an important criterion for changing the rules of the game. Broadly speaking, what capabilities – both technological and market – are you going to need to develop new products and services? Where are you positioned in terms of those requirements? Are you getting the entire organization involved in a conversation concerning where the company should be, or are you and a group of managers going into retreat and making such decisions?

- *The pace of change in most businesses is accelerating, and decision-makers must be able to deal with movement and chaos as a permanent condition.* You cannot escape the dual and conflicting demands posed on your firm. Duality is here to stay. Pulling you in one direction will be your need to establish stable patterns through planning, structuring, and control to improve the performance of your existing paradigm and maintain a focus on current marketplace realities. Pulling you in the opposite direction will be forces of instability, such as experimentation, learning, and innovation, which are expected to generate insights into new and necessary capabilities, as well as potential new products, services, and emerging opportunities that are likely to destroy your current sources of strength. Chaos ensues as a consequence of these dual forces. As the famous psychologist Karl Weick observed, 'Chaotic action is preferable to orderly inaction'. It is important to learn to accept the wisdom of concurrently learning and acting in the face of not knowing and change. Yahoo thrives at chaotic action. They rely primarily on their speed and ability to adapt to changing market dynamics. It is this ability that has enabled them to launch products that are not fully functional and yet beat their competitors to the finish line. Thus, it is better to embrace the chaotic environment and be proactive in seeking opportunities for technological and market discontinuities. Passiveness will increasingly become a serious weakness, leading to a disappearance of wealth-capturing opportunities.

- *It is important to recognize that experimentation, innovation, and individual initiatives are no longer sources of instability.* This has to be deeply institutionalized as an essential ingredient of the organizational culture, buried in the normal routines and behavioural patterns within the organization. There has to be a commitment to thinking and acting for change. The necessity to change is no longer a second-order derivative of competition, where the company waits until an imminent threat to the current sources of success is visible. It has to be a first-order condition; the company has to be proactive and set the pace of change. Learn, adapt, change, and evolve, but don't expect to fully know where you are going. Experimenting with new paradigms enables companies to develop repertoires of internal and external configurations that can be used to spot and exploit technological and market discontinuities.

- *Reward customers, employees, and partners for participating in knowledge creation, discovery, and sharing.* It is important to foster teamwork and collaboration beyond the boundaries of the organization to include customers and your network partners.

Conclusions

After 40 years, Marshall McLuhan's vision of the emergence of the 'Global Village' has finally been realized in this new economic era. Hundreds of millions of people can now interact, and share information with each other in real-time.

To survive in today's economy, firms are forced to offer integrated flexible solutions to their customers, which can be easily achieved by teaming up with a number of competent partners. Firms cannot afford the time-consuming and difficult integration activities required by mergers and acquisitions. In turbulent environments, innovative capabilities could become obsolete by the time the integration process has finished. In fact, eight out of ten executives believe that alliances will become the prime vehicle for corporate growth.

However, engaging in quasi-external means of technology acquisition is not enough. Firms also have to organize for innovation. It is important to recognize the signs of decay and take proactive measures to initiate change. A chaotic condition, with its underlying features of unpredictable behaviour and patterns, is the only constant in today's ever-changing economic landscape. Two choices are likely to emerge in this context: be bold and innovative, or simply strive to maintain the status quo. Being bold, taking options, and constantly questioning the assumptions of success is going to be the *sine qua non* of monitoring new business opportunities, conceiving new product and service ideas and changing the rules of the game. To the rest of the companies that aren't bold, aren't taking options, and aren't questioning the assumptions of their success, look at the daily newspapers. You may find yourself mentioned in a news article as yet another company that was blindsided by new entrants. You may even find yourself caricatured in a news article in a cartoon in the *Wall Street Journal*, but not for your noteworthy accomplishments.

References

'Accenture: Dispelling the Myths of Alliances' (2000), *Outlook*, Special Edition.

Afuah, A. (1998), *Innovations Management*, Oxford University Press.

Bailey, J. (1997), *The Emergence of Cybermediaries*, Cambridge, Mass: MIT.

Barker, J.A. (1993), *Paradigms: The Business of Discovering the Future*, HarperBusiness.

Booz-Allen and Hamilton (2000), *The Allianced Enterprise: Breakout Strategy for the New Millenium*, Los Angeles: Booz-Allen and Hamilton.

Buckley, P.J. and M. Casson (1988), 'A Theory of Cooperation in International Business', in F.J. Contractor and P. Lorange (eds), *Cooperative Strategies in International Business*, Lexington, Mass.: D.C. Heath.

Contractor, F.J. and P. Lorange (1988), *Cooperative Strategies in International Business*, Lexington, Mass.: D.C. Heath.

De la Sierra, Cauley (1994), *Managing Global Alliances; Key Steps for Successful Collaboration*, Addison-Wesley.

Draulans, J., A.P. de Man and H. Volberda (1999), 'Alliantievaardigheid: een bron van concurrentievoordeel', *Holland/Belgium Management Review*, 63, January, pp. 53–9.

Duysters, G. (2001), Inaugural Speech, Eindhoven University, June.

Duysters, G., A.P. de Man and L. Wildeman (1999), 'A Network Approach to Alliance Management', *European Management Journal*, 17, 2, pp. 182–7.

Duysters, G. and J. Hagedoorn (2000), 'A Note on Organisational Modes of Strategic Technology Partnering', *Journal of Scientific & Industrial Research*, 58, pp. 640–9.

Duysters, G. and J. Hagedoorn (2001), 'Do Company Strategies and Structures converge in Global Markets?', *Journal of International Business Studies*, 32, 2.

Gulati, R., 'Alliances and Networks' (1998), *Strategic Management Journal*, 19, pp. 293–317.

Hagedoorn, J. and G. Duysters (forthcoming), 'External Appropriation of Innovative Capabilities: The Choice Between Strategic Partnering and Mergers and Acquisitions', *Journal of Management Studies*, 39.

Hamel, Gary and Yves L. Doz (1998), *Alliance Advantage: The Art of Creating Value Through Partnering*, Harvard Business School Press.

Hamel, G. and C.K. Prahalad (1994), *Competing for the Future*, Harvard Business Press.

Kelly, K. (1997), 'New Rules for the New Economy', *Wired*, September.

Lawrence, P.R. and J.W. Lorsch (1967), *Organisation and Environment*, Boston: Harvard Business School Press.

Luehrman, T.A. (1998a), Investment Opportunities as Real Options, *Harvard Business Review*, July–August, pp. 51–67.

Luehrman, T.A. (1998b), 'Strategy as a Portfolio of Real Options', *Harvard Business Review*, September–October: 89–99.

Negroponte, N. (1995), *Being Digital*, New York: Vintage Books.

Salter, C. (1999), 'The Agenda: April', *Fast Company*, p. 135.

Shapiro, C. and H.R. Varian (1998), *Information Rules: A Strategic Guide to the Network Economy*, Boston, Harvard Business School Press.

Spekman, R.E. and L.A. Isabella (2000), *Alliance Competence: Maximizing the Value of Your Partnerships*, New York, John Wiley.

Vanhaverbeke, W., G. Duysters and N. Noorderhaven (2001), 'A Longitudinal Analysis of the Choice between Technology Based Strategic Alliances and Acquisitions in High-Tech Industries: The Case of the ASIC Industry', working paper.

13

New Challenges for R&D Management

Jeff Butler

Overview

The concepts we use to think about R&D must be refreshed and reinterpreted in the context of how businesses now operate, how industries are restructuring and how R&D activities are being organized to meet new requirements and promote new opportunities. The links between business strategy, technology strategy and R&D and innovation strategy are not fixed. Innovative businesses can exploit the dynamism of these relationships.

R&D management systems must be pro-active in order to embrace the challenges that are emerging. These challenges must be addressed by all the members of the senior management team, not just by R&D managers, and will also concern suppliers, customers, users and collaborators. R&D is being organized as a diffused activity that transcends industry sectors. Knowledge is being traded. R&D is becoming a service industry. Technology users are becoming increasingly sophisticated and are often themselves engaged in collaborative R&D activities.

The chapter examines these changes and their implications for managers. Directors of all sizes of companies must consider how the responsibilities of managers need to be assigned. The ways in which R&D activities are organized and how R&D management is evolving are described. An analogy with a familiar puzzle is suggested as a way of distinguishing operational and strategic levels of challenge. A framework for considering how to respond to these challenges is briefly introduced.

Introduction

The ways in which R&D activities are organized, the purposes and the kinds of activities that are organized , where they are organized and by whom they are carried out, have all changed significantly in recent years. As industries restructure and advanced economies progress towards a knowledge-based society and as we learn to innovate in many different ways, in service industries as well as in manufacturing industries, our understanding of what R&D should be performed, what it has become in the modern economy and what as a result is needed in R&D management, must change. This new understanding must reflect what is currently happening in R&D in universities and other organizations as well as in businesses. It must reflect what is happening in science and technology and in society at large. It must take into account how innovations might be introduced quickly and frequently and could sometimes be significant and cause technological or business discontinuities; in other words there must be a readiness to plan strategically in volatile commercial environments.

It is not sufficient simply to understand the present conditions in which R&D is managed and the directions in which it is changing. In addition, managers must prepare flexibly for an uncertain future. In the future, even more ambitious and challenging roles for R&D could emerge.

The relationships between R&D management, innovation management and technology management are dynamic, because of external influences on businesses and because of our evolving understanding of how technology can be used strategically. Innovative businesses will exploit this dynamism.

Instead of R&D being managed as a functional department, or as a business process (i.e. as part of the innovation process), R&D is now being managed 'as a business' and knowledge and know-how are being traded in 'technology markets'.[1] Businesses are trying to distinguish themselves by finding a new niche in the value chain. It is possible to use R&D to support this strategy and some R&D responsibilities can be devolved to other companies in the supply chain. As a result of companies redefining themselves in this way there are R&D implications and some companies are choosing to become R&D-based businesses.

New concepts and tools are emerging. Developments in the theory and practice of R&D management should be symbiotic and R&D should support innovation. Independently, innovation can lead to new ideas and opportunities to stimulate R&D activities, and new ways of organizing R&D. R&D needs to be used more extensively for transformational innovation as well as for incremental innovation. Managers need to convince investors and other stakeholders that R&D can fulfil this potential. A few years ago, a challenge for business was to manage R&D effectively in order to be a successful innovator. Now an additional challenge t\ business is to innovate successfully in order to perform and exploit R&D effectively.

There are many different challenges that confront managers in planning, funding, controlling, leading and inspiring R&D activities. R&D management embraces all of these requirements. Some challenges concern all the senior management team, not just R&D managers. Some challenges concern suppliers, customers and collaborators. The theory and practice of R&D management also faces challenges. Challenges arise from operational and strategic issues and from the consequences of managing change at an accelerating pace.

A review of conference themes and journal papers[2] would reveal the various issues and challenges that have been confronted by R&D managers and the tools and techniques used to address them. These are outlined below.

An overview of challenges

Challenges faced by R&D managers have included:

- responding to a disruptive technology;
- adjusting to a merger or acquisition;
- the need to rapidly expand or contract an R&D team;
- the privatization of government laboratories.

These kinds of challenges are induced by specific external events that may surprise the organization; at that point in time the R&D manager may have little control over the situation. Failing to respond positively and successfully to such events may seriously deplete current R&D efforts or future R&D capability; the role of R&D in the organization must be defended so that the ability of the business to perform effectively is not impaired.

In contrast, there are events or trends where appropriate management actions will strengthen R&D performance. The challenge here is to recognize the opportunity quickly enough and to respond to it comprehensively. This response may concern R&D managers over relatively long periods and can be driven either by the entire business or by the R&D department in isolation. The result might be an improvement in R&D effectiveness or in surrounding business processes, such as the innovation process. These challenges include:

- the introduction of TQM;
- managing the effects of globalization;

- the internationalization of R&D;
- managing the interfaces between R&D and other functions;
- increasing speed to market.

There are some concerns that managers have addressed intermittently for several decades and these might be regarded as fundamental to R&D management:

- justifying R&D budgets;
- demonstrating the effectiveness of R&D;
- maintaining reputation;
- recruiting and retaining staff;
- managing uncertainty and complexity.

Each of these individually is a continuing challenge for which there is no single solution. The tasks are never finally completed but good R&D management will probably address them all collectively and success will then be mutually reinforcing and consolidated. However, the nature of each task is changing, and there are different perspectives on how each task might best be managed. The responsibilities for these tasks are continuously rearranged as businesses reconfigure themselves, and new tools and techniques are emerging.

Learning to manage

Managers strive continuously and incrementally to improve practices. Often, these attempts are inspired by a new insight or concept or management philosophy and in recent years there has been an increasingly rapid turnover in such initiatives. Some, such as options pricing and R&D portfolio management, apply specifically to R&D management but many are relevant to the whole business. R&D might follow rather than lead other departments in adopting or reacting to each new approach:

- technology gatekeeper and product champion;
- R&D portfolio management;
- continuous improvement;
- core competence analysis;[3]
- outsourcing;
- business process engineering;
- the virtual organisation;
- using IT effectively;
- benchmarking;
- performance measurement;
- options pricing and options thinking;

- collaboration and networking;
- knowledge management;
- technology portfolio management;
- the balanced scorecard;
- the valuation of intangible assets.[4]

Readers may consider that some of the above concepts and approaches are now 'permanently' established in business management rather than being transient phenomena. For example, effective IT management is now essential in most businesses. However, in general there have been waves of enthusiasm for new techniques. Most, if not all of the above topics, have been introduced one by one. Sometimes a new technique has become fashionable before the effects of the previous technique were fully implemented or appropriated.

As a result of the sequences of management emphasis, in R&D management and in business management more generally, the vocabulary of R&D management has gradually changed. Some new terms have been introduced, some terms have become dated or redundant, some have been adapted, some have survived intact. But, there is still a legacy that can constrain how managers perceive situations.

Academic researchers tend to lose interest in how quickly and effectively businesses are adopting particular techniques. Consultants find new approaches to promote. There is a challenge for R&D management to become more progressive and innovative and to champion new approaches.

How and where R&D is organized

The Industrial Research Institute (IRI)[5] surveys its member companies in the USA annually to learn what challenges R&D managers are facing, how these challenges are prioritized and how R&D expenditures are being allocated. It claims that its 260 or so members carry out 75 per cent of the industrial R&D in the USA. In Europe, the European Industrial Research Managers Association (EIRMA)[6] has about 150 large company members and claims a similar percentage of the total industrial R&D activity in the region. Trends in how these expenditures are allocated is monitored in the surveys and a much more diffused pattern of R&D activity is emerging than has traditionally been the case. This is not just evidence of more companies being involved in R&D activity but also evidence of a more complex pattern of activities and relationships and more fundamental changes in why and how R&D activities are being organized. In Korea there is a certification scheme that recognizes the existence of R&D capability and facilities in a company and consequently it is indicated that there are over 10,000 companies with R&D centres.[7] In the UK the R&D Scoreboard, published by the DTI, shows the range of R&D expenditures across several sectors but there is in addition a complex pattern of trade between companies, in materials, components, technology and services, that is measured as sales turnover rather than R&D expenditure but nevertheless is a factor in innovation progress.

R&D is not just organized in laboratories and workshops. It is also organized inside manufacturing departments, on construction sites, in software houses and design studios and partly in marketing and sales offices. It is not just organized in manufacturing companies or technology-intensive businesses but in a wide range of businesses including those in the service industries. A diverse range of objectives is associated with this range of 'sponsors' or 'customers' for R&D. But most importantly, since the early 1990s R&D activities have increasingly been organized in networks and collaborative ventures rather than within the boundaries of a single firm. These trends are reflected in declining corporate budgets for in-house basic research and a stronger focus on using in-house R&D for shorter-term needs. R&D activities span a wide range of intellectual and practical activities that generate knowledge, new businesses and new industries. Much R&D is identified via an opportunity to incrementally improve existing products, processes and services and is driven by business needs rather than scientific or technological advances. R&D sustains existing businesses by improving the design, use and reliability of products, the efficiency of processes and the quality and delivery of services. In short, it increases customer or user satisfaction and helps companies to compete. It is a feature of most industries, from defence to banking and from civil engineering to pharmaceuticals.

Various sets of statistics such as the UK R&D Scoreboard and OECD data show that R&D is a significant investment for many industries. It is also a significant activity in the public sector – in universities and research and technology institutes. The latter are technology providers and the former are technology clients but the difference between the two sectors is becoming blurred as industry more extensively awards contracts and sponsors research in universities and as government departments are restructured into agencies and private companies. Industry also becomes more specialized and an increasing number of technology transactions between firms are necessary. Governments in several European member states are seeking an increase in the percentage of R&D funded by business so that statistics will benchmark favourably with the USA, Japan and some of the highest levels in Europe (such as Finland). This is intended to stimulate the European economy and its innovation systems so that the Lisbon 2000 EU Summit objectives will be met by 2010. A target of spending 3 per cent GDP on R&D has been suggested.

But the increasing externalization of R&D activities makes it more difficult to recognise what R&D should be supported by a particular business. In addition to benchmarking aggregate statistics, policy makers should analyse the distribution of R&D expenditures across businesses, and what it is used for. The methods of measuring R&D and other technology transactions need to be refined (the valuation of intangible assets might make this more sophisticated) and how supply chains and value chains are being reconfigured and how this has an effect on technology and R&D strategy should be examined.

Companies strive to find a niche within their value chain. The nature of R&D evolves as a result of businesses reconfiguring, repositioning and redefining themselves. Related or interdependent R&D activities can be distributed across several companies. Some companies (such as Intel and Cisco) have used venture capital to invest in established businesses as a way of reducing risks in early stage technologies and as a strategic approach to organizing part of their overall R&D effort. Thus it is not immediately clear how to define what the purpose of R&D is in any given company. 'Perhaps R&D is not the most meaningful description of the activity which takes place in business. Commercialisation of science might be better. The confusion here is between the description of function and process. R&D's function is to create options for new products and processes, while the process of R&D involves a network that spreads far beyond the confines of the company.'[8]

The direct connection between the R&D strategy and the technology strategy of a business has changed in the last decade and we need to look at the technology strategy needs of consortia, alliances, networks and supply chains rather than just individual companies to understand fully the purpose of R&D activities and how they might best be advanced.

R&D has become more multi-disciplinary and has shifted from processes based on discovery and experimentation (e.g. chemicals and early pharmaceuticals industry)[9] to processes based on design and knowledge assembly. R&D has in general become more dispersed as well as externalized. Now, in some subject areas, we talk about 'communities' of researchers who are held together only by a common interest or capability but not by employment contracts or collaborative agreements. Open source thinking (derived from the way in which Linux and other software has been developed and made available) involves end users implicitly as 'volunteer' R&D workers:

> InnoCentive is a new business venture of Eli Lilly and Company, a leading innovation-driven pharmaceutical corporation. Through its e.Lilly division, Eli Lilly and Company is exploring new models of scientific innovation that use the power of the internet to create and enhance networks.
>
> The impetus for InnoCentive was to create a new paradigm for scientific research and collaboration. By breaking down the traditional laboratory doors, InnoCentive opens up an exciting new world of scientific collaboration. A dynamic open-source approach where solution seekers – well respected global corporations – can reach beyond their traditional R&D facilities and tap into more of the brightest scientific minds in the world.[10]

How R&D management is organized

The theory and the practice of R&D management have both evolved over several decades. How we manage R&D depends on how we interpret various concepts. The concept of organizing R&D work into projects is very dominant – so dominant it is almost inconceivable how we might do it otherwise. Much work has focused on decision-making to determine which projects should be pursued and how they should be managed. Projects have specific objectives and can be financed according to the importance, likelihood and urgency of achieving those objectives. Thus, project selection, project termination, R&D programmes and portfolio management are central to the way that R&D has been organized and R&D management thinking has advanced. These concepts have been used to control overall R&D expenditures. Much R&D management literature has been concerned with the financial control of projects – reducing risks for corporate investors and sponsors and allocating resources. There are other management topics that must be addressed in order that projects can be completed successfully – human resources, operational management, facilities management, quality management, and environmental and ethical concerns. The characteristics of projects – the difficulty and uncertainty of the proposed work, the timescale, how multidisciplinary it needs to be, etc. – influence the optimum team composition and the dedication and creativity that will be required. There is still much more that needs to be understood about these factors.

Trends may be reducing the central importance of projects and project management as the way in which R&D activities are organized and managed. Learning company principles, options thinking, the concept of technology capabilities and the diffusion of R&D activities across networks are all reducing the central importance of projects and making knowledge management and technology exploitation more important:

> There are deep forces in the economy. They will challenge conventional notions of what it takes to be successful in R&D. R&D VPs will need to reflect deeply on their role in the corporation, and what the new realities imply for them and their function. The fact of the matter is that in about one-third of U.S. industry there is no correlation between R&D spending (as a fraction of sales) and changes in shareholder return. In another third, there is a negative relationship (over a 30-year period); this group includes semiconductors, computer hardware and software, and telecommunications. In only one-third of U.S. industries, including pharmaceuticals, chemicals and paper, has there been a positive long-term relationship between R&D spending and shareholder return.
>
> R&D heads are thus challenged to examine their assumptions, to think harder about what really does lead to competitive success and to shareholder returns in their industries, and to turn their energies to these tasks. At the same time, corporate CEOs will be challenged to learn to think of the value that R&D brings to the corporation because it represents the best option for successfully playing in an uncertain future. This, too, will be a transformational change for most corporations.[11]

We often organize work into work packages with tightly specified deliverables. This reduction in the tolerances for uncertainty has changed the traditional characteristics of R&D activity. Experimentation becomes less important and existing knowledge is accessed more frequently. Work packages become orders and contracts for specialized teams and businesses. We use options thinking (derived from options pricing theory) to decide what work should progress and we search for ways of commercializing technologies as a core strategy rather than ad hoc bonus.[12] These approaches give more flexibility and creativity about the methods of finance than would normally be allowed in a conventionally managed project. We set up new businesses to outsource components of R&D work or even to do R&D work 'as a business'. For R&D-based businesses or technology intensive companies, R&D activity is the ongoing business rather than a means towards improving business. For many other companies that are involved in diffused R&D activity, the work is done because there are contracts to be obtained.

R&D-based businesses might be financed by venture capital and the success of the investment is decided by the longer-term viability of the business and how easily it can be realized via an IPO or acquisition. This changes the rules of the game about how projects or activities should be managed and how success will be evaluated. Knowledge and accumulating intangible assets become more important: 'Increasingly, R&D will be the "make" option in a "make or buy" world. More technology will be available for license or exchange than ever before, and internal R&D departments will have to compete effectively with these external sources.'[13]

R&D was regarded as a function and then some years later as part of a business process – the innovation process. This evolution has now been extended towards the notion of R&D being organized 'as a business'. In retrospect, this can be described as fifth generation R&D management.[14] In the early 1990s, there was keen interest in technology strategy and integrating technology strategy with business strategy[15] and it was acknowledged that organizations needed to have complementary assets in order to appropriate the benefits of R&D. It could be argued that the importance of the technology strategy is diminishing since R&D can now be organized in a diffuse way. R&D generates knowledge and businesses must be entrepreneurial enough to find ways of exploiting it.

A summary of the evolution of how R&D has been organized is shown in Table 13.1. The periods shown in Table 13.1 are indicative rather than authoritative[16] and did not terminate abruptly but overlapped considerably since some companies are more progressive than others. The increasing pace of change can be seen in this table but not all industries progress at the same pace.

We can consider management of R&D to have evolved through seven phases (see Table 13.2). Phases 1–5 are now well established or have expired whereas phases 6 and 7 are just emerging.[17]

R&D management has often been responsive to business pressures but could alternatively have adopted a more aggressive stance. There needs to be dynamic and creative interaction between technology-push and

Table 13.1 The evolution of management concepts and approaches

Management emphasis	Application period
R&D as a function – corporate and government laboratories	1960–80
R&D focused on current business and market needs	1972–95
Interfaces between departments – R&D/ production and R&D/marketing. Matrix management.	1975–85
R&D serves innovation as a business process. Project teams and concurrent engineering	1990–98
Networks of collaborating organizations including business–business and university–industry projects	1995–2002
Core competences	1995–99
The virtual R&D organization	1996–2000
R&D 'as a business'	1999–2001
Knowledge management	2000–02
e-business, e-R&D, e-science	2000–04

market-pull and now between R&D opportunity and business innovation, so that emerging technological possibilities educate markets and articulate latent needs whilst social and environmental needs define technological options and sustainable business trajectories:

> We are dealing with a globally networked ecology, feeding off discoveries and developments in molecular biology, genomics, computational sciences, physics and microrobotics.... Today's R&D must seek, find and fuse disparate technologies emanating from the global science base.[18]

How R&D activities can be better organized

The suggestion in this chapter is that managers can address better all the challenges of R&D management by using a coherent framework for technology management. This is preferable to incremental and sequential advances that focus on the latest business pressure or management buzzword.

A framework that is suitable for all sizes of companies and all levels of technology intensity is suggested below. It allows relationships between different management responsibilities to be analysed so that the impacts

Table 13.2   The evolution of R&D management

Period & Phase of R&D management evolution	Main attributes of the period
1950–72 1. R&D for corporate business (or public sector) purposes (1st generation R&D management – a linear model)	Curiosity and discipline-based activities in relevant technology areas. Technology-push a dominant influence. Centralized corporate laboratories progressing towards matrix management across scientific disciplines and technology project teams.
1972–90 2. R&D for customers – the government department or business division. (2nd generation R&D management)	Market-driven activities with decentralized laboratory facilities. Business units more closely linked to programmes. R&D as a cost centre.
1990–2001 3. Business-driven R&D[19]	Commercial attitudes Quality focus. The specifics of user needs (and customization) becoming more important than best averages market definition. 3rd generation R&D management[20] R&D strategy and technology strategy are closely connected.
1993–2002+ 4. Collaborative networks	5th generation management model[21] emerging Networks and consortia. Strategic alliances.
1999–2002+ 5. R&D 'as a business'	R&D projects made viable through sponsorship and collaborations, not just relevance to new product introductions. Contracting out. Outsourcing. R&D as a profit centre. Knowledge is strategically exploited via consultancy services and IP is 'traded' (IBM and Dow are advanced proponents of this approach)

Table 13.3   (Continued)

Period and Phase of R&D management evolution	Main attributes of the period
2000–02+ 6. R&D via business start ups, knowledge intensive service businesses (R&D based businesses) and enterprise developments	Project proposals written as a business plan Spin-off companies from university and other incubators. R&D often funded by venture capital, orientated towards new business development opportunities. Knowledge and expertise is valuable and is recognized via equity or company acquisition. 5th generation management model firmly established
2004+ 7. R&D activity parallels the growth of knowledge-intensive business services	Extended 5th generation models. Intangible assets fully recognized. R&D, innovation and technology management are integrated. A new model of R&D management is required?

and importance of those interfaces on R&D, innovation or technology management requirements can be assessed. Because it looks at the whole business and not just the R&D management function or the innovation process, it can also facilitate an analysis of interactions between businesses so that R&D activities organized in or on behalf of one organization can be supported by complementary assets in another. A cluster of firms or several firms working together in a sector or a particular value chain could be treated as a virtual organization and the framework could be applied across this organization in the same way as if being applied to a single organization.

The framework is based around a matrix or relationship diagram (see Straker 1995),[22] and is similar to the matrices used in quality function deployment (QFD) where what needs to be done is shown on the horizontal axis and how it can be done is shown on the vertical axis. Thus, for example, financial responsibilities (essential in all businesses) are primarily assigned to the finance department, who monitor and control using accountancy techniques, but other departments can influence financial performance (not least the quality and operations departments). Strategy is primarily the responsibility of the director of strategy (if the company has such a person) or the chief executive and main board of directors, but it can be influenced significantly by the external

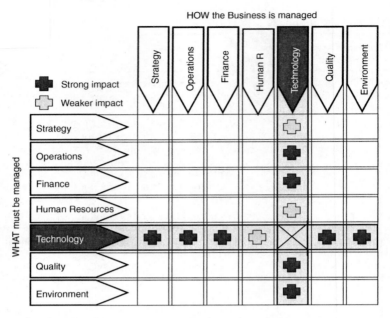

Figure 13.1   Technology management in a business context

Source: J. Bessant *et al.*, *TEMAGUIDE : A Guide to Technology Management and Innovation for Companies* (Madrid: Fundacion COTEC para la Innovacion Tecnologica, 1998)

environment of the company and the opinions of stakeholders such as customers, suppliers, employees and financial analysts. It can also be significantly influenced by technology opportunities and so the strategy of the business and strategic technology matters of the business are closely interdependent. Operational technology matters may have a closer affinity with quality management and operational management responsibilities.

The strength of particular relationships between responsibilities can be indicated numerically, or by a plus or minus or zero sign in each cell. The distribution of these strengths will be different from company to company and the process of discussing and deciding the values will probably be intrinsically useful. It is not essential that all cells be completed if the framework is being used for a particular purpose, such as a focus on technology management. The matrix is illustrated in Figure 13.1. The plus symbols in this diagram are purely illustrative. The strength of all other cross-impacts can be determined by each management team analysing the systems and culture in their own organization.

The framework in Figure 13.1. is deliberately provocative. Firstly, managers must think hard about WHAT must be managed in each row and HOW it CAN or SHOULD be managed in each column. There may be an imperfect match, for various reasons, and managers might disagree about how responsibilities should be allocated. The responsibilities overlap and merge, hence managers must work as an integrated team. Secondly, the framework does not have a marketing responsibility shown explicitly; this invites inputs from all managers (including product designers and quality managers) who might have an influence on the image and reputation of the company or who might collect commercially useful information. Thirdly, the environmental responsibility is not just about ecological issues but is much broader to include consumer related responsibilities (and hence some marketing) and other stakeholder issues. Operational responsibilities include logistics (sales, delivery and service support) and some marketing activities. The interdependency of several responsibilities will become apparent as the composition of these elements is explored. This provocative presentation ensures that a fresh perspective is adopted on what a business must do.

This framework was devised to show the importance of technology management in a business, and to introduce and encourage the use of several technology management techniques such as creative problem solving or technology watch (see TEMAGUIDE).[23] It was not designed to represent how or where R&D activities take place. To identify how R&D activities are fitted into the framework it is necessary to think more deeply about activities that support current business needs and activities that support the development of future capability, as indicated below.

The framework is explained in TEMAGUIDE as a conceptual model focused on business processes rather than functional responsibilities and is supported by a second model, a learning cycle model, similar to other learning or quality management models (see Figure 13.2.). This has five elements – Scan, Focus, Resource, Implement and Learn. R&D activities can help a company to scan its technology environment, or to focus on the most promising technology opportunities, and support the other elements of the model.

The loop is also representative of innovation processes. If there is a desire in the organization to improve its position or performance then

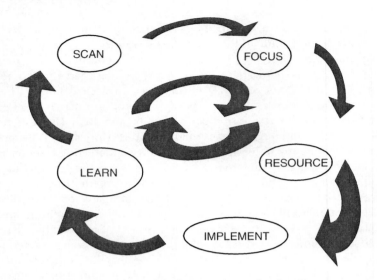

Figure 13.2   A learning cycle model of innovation and technology management capability

Source: J. Bessant *et al.*, *TEMAGUIDE : A Guide to Technology Management and Innovation for Companies* (Madrid: Fundacion COTEC para la Innovacion Tecnologica, 1998)

the learning cycle model,(Figure 13.2), can be applied at each cell in Figure 13.1. A number of opportunities to improve the business will be identified as a result of applying the framework and challenging the relationships behind each cell. R&D activities are identified by scanning and focusing and R&D management is represented as a learning experience (rather than a control process).

An extra dimension can be considered. Each cell in the matrix can be decomposed into smaller elements. Each can be related to the innovation or learning cycle model. Three elements can be suggested – (i) a need to sustain existing business activities (ii) a need to develop a future capability (iii) a need to monitor progress (see Figure 13.3). R&D contributes to the business in the following respects: (i) it has a role to play in sustaining existing business activities (ii) it develops future capability (iii) it can be used to monitor progress. Technology management in particular owns these responsibilities and can execute them by identifying suitable R&D activities. In case (i), R&D supports incremental innovation and fulfils a number of other tasks such as testing, quality control investigations, safety and reliability and production process

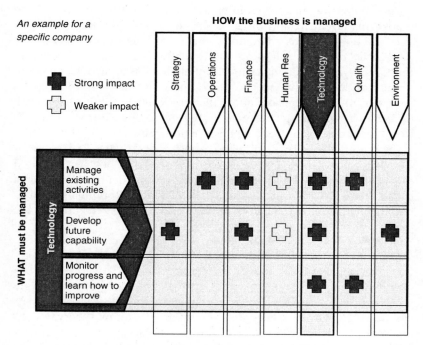

Figure 13.3 Decomposing the technology management relationship to reveal R&D and R&D management opportunities

Source: J. Bessant *et al.*, *TEMAGUIDE : A Guide to Technology Management and Innovation for Companies* (Madrid: Fundacion COTEC para la Innovacion Tecnologica, 1998)

improvements. In case (ii), it leads towards more strategic innovation and is a method by which expertise is acquired or grown organically. In case (iii), R&D provides the expertise to understand how and where competitors are progressing. What has just been explained for the technology cells of a company is applicable to all the other management responsibilities (strategy, finance, human resources, operations, quality and environmental) and the three elements – now, future and monitoring progress – can stimulate the identification of R&D opportunities and requirements. So R&D is given an organizational learning dimension and role, not just a technology dimension. Using this approach, R&D is not just associated with innovation initiatives as if they are events but is associated with incremental and strategic change as an organizational learning process. The learning cycle model (Figure 13.2) reinforces that process.

The framework encourages an analysis of interactions between technology management and other aspects of a business. R&D does not need to be regarded as a function, which was how R&D was originally organized (and which does not easily fit the dispersed R&D activities found in contemporary situations) but emerges as an activity that will support or develop any aspect of the business, including its services.

Readers may be suspicious about the practical value of this framework in their own organization, especially after such a quick introduction (see the original document for more information). However, it is hoped that its presentation here will stimulate a fresh look at what R&D is, what R&D is becoming, how it relates to business needs and how it can be used more effectively and be organized differently. In particular this might be useful where R&D is focused on social, behavioural, economic, organizational and information sciences, or on the skills associated with creative industries.

Hitherto much of R&D management theory and practice has been associated with the 'traditional' domains of science and technology (chemical physical, biological and their interdisciplinary derivatives such as optronics, genomics, bioinformatics, nanotechnology) but increasingly into the future it can be expected also to be associated with psychology, emotions, art, virtual spaces and communities, gaming theory, etc. to reflect the focus on intangibles in product design and service delivery and also to facilitate efficient workplace learning. For example, some businesses in the chemical industry have shifted progressively towards specialty chemicals that need a deeper understanding of consumer preferences and this can stimulate fundamental research into tastes, odours, tactile sensation and geographical and cultural variations. Software for knowledge management, pattern recognition, multimedia design and simulation are powerful tools with research applications; they also have a potential to improve workplace learning and thus the effectiveness of R&D or knowledge based workers.

Another framework for examining R&D activities is a 2×2 matrix called the innovation uncertainty map.[24] This is one way of looking at a snapshot of projects in a portfolio. The use of this framework encourages a view of project management that first emphasises the characteristics of the projects and the kinds of employees and skills and expertise that might be required. Some firms consider their portfolio to be managed within a pipeline or funnel – sometimes referred to as the innovation funnel. As the names suggest, this is an analogy based on chemical industry concepts and there is a bottleneck or resource constraint implicit in the model. The innovation pipeline facilitates stage-gate project

management.[25] As projects progress from experimental
study through to commercial exploitation they typical
ingly larger investments. Thus, the commercialization o
restricted. The technology strategy of a business usually re
to those that the management team believes it can succe _____ .ion,
depending on the complementary assets of the business. The funnel
model is a familiar concept and is still used and is powerful for many
purposes, especially in a single firm context, but does not adequately represent what is happening between companies when knowledge is being
traded and assembled and different organizations are being connected.
To better represent the latter, the author of this chapter has proposed a
digital model of R&D and/or innovation, based on the analogy of signals passing down optical fibre. In such a model, there can be sufficient
bandwidth (i.e. finance and human resources) to permit the unrestricted
development and application of ideas. What becomes more important
in such a model is how businesses and other organizations connect –
what do they need to know about each other in order to collaborate
successfully. Various sources of finance can be approached if there is a
business case. Good technology can be commercialized by finding new
partners or by licensing and spinning out new businesses or by creating
new organizations. The implications for technology strategy, for styles
of R&D management and for the 'virtual' or expandable resources that
might be needed at various stages, including the exploitation stages, are
very significant. This is a model of what is actually happening in and
around contemporary R&D activities.

Conclusions

Throughout this chapter, R&D has deliberately been referred to as an
activity rather than a management function or a business process. The
words projects, programmes and portfolio were avoided where possible
since they have connotations associated with R&D being managed as an
internal function to satisfy a single company technology strategy. The
term 'project' tends to suggest a single fixed objective and justification.
Instead, it is necessary now to recognize the wide range of purposes that
R&D can fulfil and the various ways in which R&D can be organized;
the vocabulary of R&D management needs to be refreshed to avoid confusion and limited vision. It is believed that the words 'R&D activity'
better describe how knowledge is being generated, assembled, developed
and applied when R&D is diffused across several organizations. Each

:eholder in dispersed R&D activities has a different perspective and a different reason for being involved. Unless an appropriate vocabulary is used to describe the modern mode of organizing R&D and the new wider range of R&D activities, then R&D management will be constrained by a set of inadequate concepts, tools and models and businesses will under-perform.

All managers in a business must embrace R&D management – it is not just the operational control of projects, it is not just an internal consequence of the technology strategy. It is a business opportunity. There are some workers who have informal R&D management responsibilities, including the scientists, technologists and entrepreneurs involved in doing R&D work. R&D management is no longer an administrative duty or a functional management responsibility.

There are new tools and concepts being introduced. R&D activities and R&D management are dynamic. There is a tendency to chase buzzwords in a search for instant solutions and improvements. To discourage such a sequential pursuit, a coherent framework for technology management has been presented. This framework puts R&D management into a technology management and business management perspective.

The challenges of R&D management are not just the many specific challenges that make R&D activity interesting and difficult but also elusive strategic challenges – to use R&D effectively and entrepreneurially as an integral part of business strategy. As stated earlier, a challenge now is not just to make R&D succeed in order that innovation and hence the business might succeed, but to make the business innovative so that R&D activities will succeed. It is a challenge for R&D management as a professional discipline to promote itself enthusiastically and confidently so that it will be self-sustaining and will play a full part in a knowledge-driven society.

The analogy of Rubik's Cube

To illustrate the objective of this chapter, as has just been outlined, an analogy can usefully be introduced. Consider the Rubik's Cube puzzle.[26] This puzzle can be frustrating and addictive. Average players amuse themselves and learn how to manipulate the cube faster and faster; this requires manual dexterity. But no progress towards a solution is made just by faster and more furious manipulation. To become an expert, players must learn how to recognize patterns. Instead of just chasing 'buzzwords' to improve R&D performance incrementally, a more holistic approach needs to be adopted.

Actions

Managers should:

- Review how the role of R&I
  in related technology area
  alliances etc. Ensure that
  and understanding of the
  review should extend to re
  institutes, customers and
- Identify and discuss R&
  believed that the capab
  knowledge (either for e
  nesses) then pursue tho͟sᷛ͟ ͟ᵒᵖ͟ᵖ

  are being traded in 'markets' in a variety of ways, including ͟ᵇ͟ᵘ͟
  incubation. As a result, R&D projects can be justified as business plans
  when they might not have been viable as internal projects.
- Review the existing business and technology strategy and consider if
  it accommodates the full potential and scope of R&D opportunity.
  This may require a fresh look at the role of the business in its various
  value chains. Is it sufficiently ambitious? Redefine the role of R&D
  accordingly and communicate that new purpose.
- Use alternative business models (such as spin-off incubation, licensing or new supply-chain relationships) as a way of stimulating creative approaches to the identification of R&D project opportunities.
  Does the organization have R&D expertise that is underutilized or
  undervalued? It may need a revised business strategy to develop and
  exploit its full potential.
- When considering the benefits of joining a collaborative R&D project
  as a partner or contractor, consider in particular how expertise and
  capability will be enhanced and what this might imply for the future
  business models and strategies that might become necessary. The
  existing business strategy may need to be revised or extended to
  respond to volatile commercial environments and suddenly R&D
  might need to contribute more ambitiously and to exhibit vision and
  leadership; expertise and access to expertise are valuable resources that
  are now being developed and exploited in new ways.
- Value knowledge highly. Monitor developments in accounting practices and strategic management (including, for example, options
  thinking, the balanced scorecard and intangible assets) to articulate
  and communicate the value of knowledge more effectively.

Use R&D management
benchmarking) to leve
to focus on effectiv
more added valu
- Find creative
  expect all w
  strategy
  will re
  ciat

(and R&D performance measurement and
rage knowledge (internally and externally) and
ness and business impacts. These aims will create
e than a focus on efficiency and productivity.
ays of financing R&D project opportunities. Do not
orthwhile activities to be related closely to the technology
f the business. Consider how the proposed R&D portfolio
alue the business (using options thinking and concepts asso-
d with intangible assets). Incorporate the ideas and benefits in a
vised technology strategy.
Consider alliances and other methods for financial and management
support, not just for scientific or technical support.

- Get involved via collaborations and contracts in a wider range of R&D
  related activities. By this route, companies that have no internal R&D
  activities might progressively extend their capabilities.
- Regard R&D management as an integral part of technology
  management – not just a branch of technology management.

Notes

1. Arora, A., Fosfuri, A. and Gambardella, A. (2002), *Markets for Technology: the Economics of Innovation and Corporate Strategy*, Cambridge MA: MIT Press.
2. For conferences see The EIRMA Conference (www.eirma.org) and The R&D Management Conference (www.radma.org) and for journals see *Research Technology Management* (www.iriinc.org) and *R&D Management* (www.blackwellpublishers.co.uk)
3. Prahalad, C. K. and Hamel, G. (1990), 'The Core Competence of the Corporation', *Harvard Business Review*, May/June.
4. Mouritsen, J. (1998), *Intellectual Capital Accounts: a New Tool for Companies*, OECD.
5. www.iriinc.org
6. www.eirma.org
7. White Paper on 'Industrial technology', Korean Industrial Technology Association, www.koita.or.kr
8. Sir William Castell (CEO, Amersham plc), 'R&D in the new global economy', p. 6 in *The 2001 R&D Scoreboard, Commentary and Analysis*, DTI Future and Innovation Unit, London, www.innovation.gov.uk/finance
9. Mitchell, G. R., 'Industrial R&D strategy for the Early 21st Century', *Research Technology Management*, Jan. Feb. 2000, 43, 1, pp. 31–5.
10. www.InnoCentive.com
11. Foster, R. N., 'Managing Technological Innovation for the Next 25 Years', *Research Technology Management*, Jan. Feb. 2000, 43, 1, pp. 29–31.
12. Jolly, V. J., *Commercializing New Technologies*, HBS Press, Boston, Mass, 1997.
13. Foster, R. N., op. cit.

14. Rothwell, R. (1992), 'Successful Industrial Innovation: Critical Success Factors for the 1990s', *R&D Management*, 22, 3, pp. 221–39
15. Coombs, R. and A. Richards, 'Technologies Products and Firms' Strategies', *Technology Analysis and Strategic Management*, 3, 1991, pp. 77–86, 157–75
16. Tables 13.1 and 13.2 were constructed by the author of this chapter on the basis of experience in the field but without any systematic survey
17. See note 16 above.
18. Castell, op. cit.
19. See Ganguly, A., *Business-driven Research & Development – Managing Knowledge to Create Wealth*, Macmillan Business, London, 1999.
20. See Roussel, P., Saad, K. N. and Erickson, T. J., *Third Generation R&D*, A.D. Little, 1991.
21. See Rothwell R., op. cit.
22. Straker, D., *A Toolbook for Quality Improvement and Problem Solving*, Prentice Hall, London, 1995.
23. TEMAGUIDE, *A Guide to Technology Management and Innovation for Companies*, Bessant, J., Brockhoff, K., Butler, J., Ernst, H., Pearson, A. W. and Ruiz, J., (eds) Fundacion COTEC para la Innovacion Tecnologica, Madrid, 1998.
24. See Hauschildt, J. and Pearson, A. W. (eds), *Means and Innovation Management, Creativity and Innovation Management*, 3, 3, Sept., 1994, pp. 162–6.
25. Cooper, R., 'Third Generation New Product Processes', *Journal of Product Innovation Management*, 11, 1, pp. 3–14 and Cooper, R., *Winning at New Products*, Kogan Page, London 1988.
26. Named after the inventor Rubik, a Rubik cube is made up of smaller cubes, each with different coloured faces. The smaller cubes are connected and cannot be removed from their position in the larger cube. There are nine coloured squares on each large face. The puzzle solution requires that the smaller cubes be turned until each face of the large cube is a single colour.

Part IV

Innovation: Fostering and Managing the Innovation Process

Executive Summary

Cornelius Herstatt

The development of new products and services is crucial for the survival and growth of firms. Fostering and managing innovation processes efficiently is a key success factor. In the following chapters we focus on the management of innovation processes from different perspectives. We examine the process of innovation itself with a focus on the early phases; the generation of breakthrough-ideas for radical innovation using internal and external sources; knowledge management and organisational support for innovation; and finally, risk management issues associated with technology driven innovation.

Part IV consists of five chapters. Chapter 14 explores the challenge faced by large and successful firms to remain innovative. Besides individual competence, the organizational competence needed to develop new products and services is becoming more and more important. This issue is addressed by presenting the case of a large, highly profitable firm, which over the years lost its ability to innovate, especially when it came to new products, even though being extremely efficient in its operations. The concept of organizational competence is discussed in the context of the competence-based management literature and a model is presented. On that basis, the case study is revisited and some theoretical as well as practical implications are identified.

Chapter 15 gives an overview of innovation process models, including classical sequential approaches, stage-gate models and simultaneous process models. Pros and cons of these models and their applicability and value for innovation practice are discussed.

The early phases of the innovation process (the so-called 'fuzzy front end' of innovation) turn out to be extremely difficult to manage in practice, and high failure rates ('innovation-flops') can be related to insufficiencies during these early phases. The appropriate management

ns crucial, since major business opportunities
nsiderable amount of the development costs
scusses the various attempts to systematically
tive and dynamic part of the innovation pro-
nat support up-front activities are presented and
newness of the product or service innovation is

innovation, today's companies have to develop
entry poini.   :al innovations in order to survive in the long
run. However, the identification of such innovations is a difficult task,
often associated with significant risks. How can companies systematically develop concepts for radical innovations by relying on market
research? Chapter 17 will discuss this question and conclude that concentrating on the question *whom* to address as the information source
for radical innovation is more important than *how* to methodologically
support the search process.

Breakthrough or radical innovation very often implies high risk for the
innovating company. In order to understand such risks better, a reference
framework as part of the formal risk assessment process is necessary and
helpful. Chapter 18 describes the development and use of such a framework, for diagnosing risks in technology-based projects. This specific
risk reference framework consists of 12 main risk categories and 142 connected critical innovation issues. The model presented in this section has
been developed for a global company in the fast moving consumer goods
industry.

An awareness of both the future market demands and technological developments is crucial for successful product development. Besides
the 'external' view, companies have to carefully manage their internal
sources. Engineers and entrepreneurs are considered, worldwide, to be
essential sources of innovation (radical and incremental).

Overall, Part IV of the book provides both practical and theoretical
perspectives on the development and sustenance of an innovative culture within organisations. This is critical to maintaining a healthy flow
of new products to market – the future lifeblood of all businesses.

Ten key questions for the Board

1. Do our organizational routines and attitudes foster collaboration and
   innovation – or are we just focused on efficient operations?
2. Do we have a clear model of our innovation process?

3. Is our innovation process geared to the kind of innovation we are seeking (e.g. radical versus incremental) and does it identify the role of technology development?
4. Do we have methods and tools to manage the 'fuzzy front end' of the innovation process?
5. Are we making an assessment of the market and technological uncertainty of our innovations and using appropriate tools?
6. Can we identify a group of experts to help us develop radical innovations?
7. Do we have a process to work with 'lead-users' in idea generation and concept development?
8. Are the risk factors associated with our product innovation identified and assessed?
9. Given the global nature of our company, are we aware of the impact that cultural differences can have on performance?
10. Are our engineers in close contact with the market?

14
Promoting Innovation in Organizations Unable to Innovate
Thomas Durand

Overview

This chapter addresses the issue of documenting the ability of an organization to develop new products, paradoxically adopting the perspective of incompetence. The chapter presents the case of a large, highly profitable firm, which over the years lost the ability to innovate, especially when it comes to new products, even though extremely efficient in its operations. The concept of organizational competence is discussed in the context of the competence-based management literature and a model is presented. On that basis, the case study is revisited and some theoretical as well as practical implications are identified.

Introduction

This chapter addresses the issue of documenting the concept of competence in organizations, by adopting the perspective of incompetence. The rationale for this chapter stems from three preliminary comments:

1. The competence-based management literature has focused much attention on learning, i.e. knowledge and competence building, much less on the real nature of competence itself. Much has been described about the process of learning in organizations, i.e. about the flux, much less about the accumulated stock resulting from the flux, namely the competence base of the organization.

   The main reason for this may have to do with the difficulties encountered in grasping and describing the real essence of organizational competence.

2. A corollary feature of the competence-based literature in management is the lack of empirical work. This point is quite striking. At this

stage, too little has been done to document and illustrate the existing theoretical contributions around the concept of competence; not to mention empirically testing the validity of the whole theoretical constructs of the resource-based view or the competence-based theory. It seems to us that this has to do with the difficulties of operationalizing the concept, which again relates directly to the specific nature of the concepts at hand.

3. The whole argument behind the competence-based theory is designed to apply for organizations. Yet, many contributions tend to implicitly or explicitly extrapolate what is known for individuals, extending this knowledge to the organizational level. This is actually one of the key elements of the epistemic challenge posed to management researchers by this still emerging concept of competence.

Although clearly debatable, these three comments tend to reinforce each other. In turn, they led to the idea behind this chapter: 'If you cannot tell them what they are good at, tell them what they are incompetent at'. If it seems so difficult to describe competence, what about incompetence? The literature lacks empirical work: why not attempt to empirically describe incompetence? Competence for individuals is significantly more documented than organizational competence: why not approach and describe the incompetence of an organization?

A research project was launched to further explore this line of inquiry. A case study was conducted in a large firm, which over the years has lost the ability to innovate, especially when dealing with new products.

In this sense, the company is clearly 'incompetent' compared to its major competitors. The company is (still) highly profitable, efficient in its operations but, when it comes to designing, developing and bringing new products to the market place, the company is evaluated as helpless, incapable, i.e. incompetent, by its own top management.

The research project was designed and conducted to analyse and document the reasons behind this inability to innovate.

The methodology relied on in-depth interviews with key players within the organization. This led to a diagnosis of the situation and in turn to an empirical exploration of the innovation-related incompetence of the firm.

The case study is presented first in this chapter. It aims to show what organizational incompetence may be. Some form of incompetence is thus illustrated and documented concretely. The paper then briefly presents a framework model of competence, built around three dimensions (knowledge, know-how and attitudes), pointing out both the specificities and linkages of these three interdependent elements of competence.

On that basis, the case study is revisited, analysed and discussed in relation to the framework model presented. Incompetence is then discussed in the context of the model. Some theoretical and practical implications are then identified, including a development around the theme of unlearning. Suggestions are also made for further investigation.

The chapter concludes by advocating for more empirical work to help establish a self-sustained, documented theory of competence in management.

The case of Antinnova Inc

The context

Antinnova Inc is a division of a publicly owned multinational corporation, with its business in consumer goods. It has sales of €2 billion. The division operates primarily in Europe. Antinnova is a leader in its markets and owns widely recognized brands.

Antinnova designs, mass-manufactures and sells its products through various distribution channels. Marketing and advertising is an essential component of the business.

The whole industry is currently going through significant technological changes associated with a scientific revolution, which occurred some years ago. Thus, in addition to its 'development' department, Antinnova has its own research centre with scientists recognized as experts in their field.

In a stagnant oligopolistic market, with a few smaller players focusing on niches, Antinnova has a long track record of high profitability. The company is well respected in its industry. Yet, the top management at Antinnova is well aware of the difficulties faced by the organization when it comes to developing new products. Most of the products launched in the last 5 years have either resulted in failures or have generated limited sales, significantly below expectations. More recently, the rate of development of new products has even slowed down. This is a major problem for the management of Antinnova, as the proclaimed strategy is precisely to try to innovate in this stagnant market, in order to achieve growth. 'The only other option would indeed be to fight for market shares through a price war. Since we are the market leader, that would in fact hurt the profitability of Antinnova before anything else' says the CEO. Innovation, and more specifically product innovation, is thus a strategic priority for the firm.

The top management has some difficulties in grasping what is going wrong within the organization but clearly considers that Antinnova, even though profitable and efficient, has developed some form of incompetence in the area of product development.

A global assessment of such a condition can be made intuitively. The position as a leader in a stagnant market obviously does not help the innovation processes because the everyday environment is by no means stimulating. In addition, the experience of various players within the organization tends to function as a dampening mechanism, reinforcing the organizational inertia as most unconventional signals coming from the market place are in fact filtered, neglected and even rejected, instead of being used to regenerate the cognitive frames. The individual and collective representations prevailing within the organization have been shaped over the years and entrenched in the organizational structures and routines. The context is in a sense frozen, with established settings for inter-functional processes and inter-individual interactions, with pre-defined budget sizes, pre-assigned roles in the decision processes, recognized and tacitly accepted positions in the implicit hierarchy, etc. Any attempt to innovate means renewing the way the participants view the situation. This is seen as potentially modifying the status quo and interpreted as a perverse attack against existing tacit rules and established territories. Countermeasures are immediately at work, stemming from dogmatic visions, carelessness or territorial concerns. The counter-attacks are obviously supported by the good performance of the business. Financial results are used to justify inaction. In such circumstances, the very same conditions which led to success in the past, may now be leading to failure. In a way the organization generated its own auto-destructive mechanisms and its own blindness. The organization forbids its member from pointing at its potential failings and restrains them from questioning the collective behavior. New market opportunities requiring renewed representations cannot be accommodated to the 'proclaimed vision' and the firm is condemned to loop back within its established stagnant path, unable to break the vicious circle. We thought that it would be interesting to go beyond that global intuitive assessment. Our research project thus selected this context, in order to conduct an exploration of what was identified *ex ante* as a case of organizational incompetence.

Thirty in-depth interviews over a 3-month time span were conducted with managers in all major functional departments (marketing, research, development, manufacturing, human resources) as well as with top managers. Some of them were met several times.

Major findings

The interviews show that the representation of the concept of innovation is not shared among employees at Antinnova. Some managers primarily advocate process innovation, to cut manufacturing costs. Others claim that 'incremental adaptation of existing products is essential', as the priority is to fit the continuously changing demand. Others reject 'me-too' products as 'non-innovative imitations' which cannot bring significant competitive advantage; in turn, they advocate for radical innovation based on 'real research projects'.

In other words, right from the beginning, there is a clear misfit around the key word used by the top management when attempting to promote innovation. The meaning of the concept of innovation thus varies according to where one sits and what territory one covers. Everyone looks at some bits and pieces of the concept, ignoring the holistic view. No one seems to remember the real potential of the integrated perspective, combining the resources, the competence and the representations, as a way to renew the collective dynamics.

Antinnova's *research centre* is located at the division headquarters. The scientific revolution which took place upstream of the business led to hiring scientists involved in basic research in order to understand and transfer these new scientific developments into technological applications. These experts are thus connected to the international scientific community. They tend to deny any real ability of the top management at Antinnova to understand and evaluate their work. They tend to think of evaluation in terms of peer review. They have been accustomed to define their own research agenda, based on their own view of the 'real' research needs of the company (the top management explicitly recognized, in private with us, how difficult it is to assess the relevance of the research projects which are submitted for approval). As a consequence, the monitoring of ongoing research projects is limited and deadlines are uncertain and flexible.

The interviews clearly show that leading researchers have a tendency to look down on the development engineers (the former have PhDs while the latter hold engineering degrees) and do not give much credit to the requirements communicated by marketing. In addition, they are detached from the world of manufacturing.

Paradoxically, despite these distant feelings for their colleagues from other departments, the researchers at Antinnova desperately wanted recognition and respect from the rest of the organization. This should not be regarded as a contradiction but more as the same symptom of lack of trust and poor working relations between the research centre and the other functions. It must be said clearly that no positive sign coming from the rest of the organization in the direction of the research centre could be observed during the course of our investigations.

The *marketing* department at Antinnova is the leading player and behaves as such. Marketers at Antinnova are more concerned with advertising campaigns to sustain their brands than with new product developments. Virtually no strategic marketing is conducted. Much of the focus of Marketing has to do with sales and communication issues. They view product innovation as 'difficult and costly in our [supposedly] mature market'. The marketing department claims that they have good working relations with the engineers from the development department. The truth of the matter is that the *modus operandi* between Marketing and Development reflects a situation of domination, the latter obeying the former. Marketing views the research centre as 'operating on another planet, and happy to stay there'. There is simply no contact whatsoever between Research and Marketing. Strangely enough the 'NIH' syndrome, usually known to strike in research units, is obviously at work within the marketing department. 'Any new idea submitted to Marketing from any-one else is immediately rejected'. In addition the normal career path of a marketer in the whole Group of Antinnova means that he/she should not spend more than 18 to 24 months in the same position in the same division. Therefore, this causes a high turnover within the corresponding marketing departments, impacting the types of innovation which marketers promote. Such a short time span means incremental, i.e. cosmetic, innovations dealing with minor functionalities and marginal but visible adaptations of the product, e.g. changes in packaging. Anything else goes beyond the 'normal' scope of a 'normally' ambitious product manager. We clearly made the point by analytically reconstructing the list of all product development briefs coming from Marketing over the last three years. 'After five years of moving things around, we usually end up with a design of the product looping back to what it was before; the problem is that in the meantime, Marketing has forced us to reorganize our manufacturing lines several times to cope with their cosmetic adaptations' as the manufacturing manager puts it.

Development does not understand why Marketing and Research would have to talk to one another. Development engineers feel that any marketing need should be expressed to them, thus leaving it for Development to translate the marketing briefs into research needs, whenever they feel that it is necessary. Development insists that process innovation is key for manufacturing costs and thus as important as product innovation. The most striking point is that Development runs the Development Committee with an objective of efficiency. Every person involved in product development indeed takes part in this monthly committee, but little discussion goes on during the meeting as the Development manager has arranged all decisions to be made ahead of time by the General Manager. The development committee is thus extremely efficient, essentially making decisions already made elsewhere, without any real challenging of ideas, 'hence saving a lot of lengthy, although really important discussion!' as someone joked about it. While innovation requires creativity, interaction and iteration, Development views product development projects as processes to be managed and run efficiently. Development is thus short term and efficiency oriented. Nevertheless, Development engineers express anger and frustration because Marketing does not pay enough attention to the proposals and ideas emanating from technicians.

Manufacturing has been under enormous pressure to rationalize operations out of a decreasing number of plants where the productivity gains have been spectacular over the years. Their innovative thrust obviously goes for process improvement and productivity. From that perspective, they appreciate the support of Development. Manufacturing has tried to establish some linkages with Research as they wish to prepare actively for the implementation of new production technologies stemming from the scientific revolution affecting the industry. Their working relations with Marketing are minimal and rather difficult, given the continuous flow of marginal product adaptations pushed by marketers, thus significantly disturbing the organization of production 'while in fact bringing little innovative value to the customers'.

Human resources mobility across functions within Antinnova is minimal. The worst situation is found at the research centre where no researcher has been in any other function at Antinnova or elsewhere. Some exceptions may be noted in other departments: the head of Development spent some years in Manufacturing as the head of one of the largest plant; one marketer was previously a development engineer. Nevertheless, these few cases do not seem to be sufficient to significantly improve the working relations across organizational borders at Antinnova.

It should be stressed here that the quality and dedication of the staff of each of the functional departments which we interviewed are not to be questioned. These are really very good people, doing their best to contribute to Antinnova's success. They are great individuals, active, dedicated and even positive thinkers, nice to deal with, but collectively unable to cooperate across organizational borders.

Stories of missed opportunities are many. 'A few weeks after I arrived as the new marketing manager, I organized a meeting with researchers. I did not do it again. These guys are strange'. On another occasion, Development carefully prepared proposals to be submitted at the yearly key strategic planning meeting. 'We did not get any feedback on what we suggested, except a vague comment about keeping the focus on the core business'. Eighteen months before we conducted our own investigation, the CEO decided to organize a creativity programme, with various working groups across the organization, to collect and assess ideas for new products. Thirty-two interesting items were pre-selected, out of which eight priority themes were chosen. The CEO gave these a top priority on the agenda. Nevertheless, no one interviewed on the issue of innovation mentioned this process to us; except the CEO. We subsequently found out that no significant progress had been made on most of the 8 priority themes, every team 'being too busy with other priorities'.

Summary of findings on Antinnova's incompetence

The major findings of our research at Antinnova show an organization dedicated to efficiency in all respects, including efficiency in product development, but ignoring of the needs for informal interaction and creativity. All internal players are extremely busy ('busy being busy') with no or little time and interest to listen to anyone else from other departments. Each member of the organization is entrenched in his/her own logic, according to his/her functional position. Each function is convinced and claims that they understand the underlying strategic dynamics of the business better than others do. Over the years, the degree of trust among staff and managers from the various departments has deteriorated to a minimum.

Antinnova is a rather rich company with significant resources. The organization is not proactive but reactive, with a tendency to follow innovations developed by competitors (me-too products), willing to bet a significant amount of resources for every product launch, especially for advertising campaigns despite the high risks involved. The organization is obsessed by large and costly projects. Smaller ideas are rejected. The organization is thus becoming extremely conservative and perfectionist, fearing the risk attached to any product launch when so much is at stake.

In addition, incentive mechanisms, including financial compensation, are centred on individual performance and tend to be short-term-oriented. Therefore, they do not reinforce solidarity and collective work with a longer term perspective. Despite all its zeal to advocate for innovation within the company, Antinnova's top management is unable to balance the internal forces at work within the firm. Everyday decisions are made at all levels of the organization to allocate resources, time and energy, resulting in a clear tendency towards short term performance and defence of territory rather than new developments and collective endeavours in search of new sources of profitability.

Top management actually pays much attention to operational performance and short term cost cuts. Through their everyday behaviour, top managers thus tacitly express the reality of what they expect. In turn, they contradict their claims about the allegedly vital importance of innovation, thus reinforcing the distrust on the matter. Since no visible and significant change appears in the management's way of dealing with priorities, since no clear signal is sent and *a fortiori* received about a renewed representation of the firm's strategic agenda, then no change in behaviour can be achieved from the rest of the staff.

All this led to very little capacity to accept iteration and interaction in the product design. Antinnova's competence to compete operationally has created an incompetence to compete entrepreneurially. In other words, this company has slowly built an internal culture, an organizational structure and routines which made it unable to launch new products successfully. This company has built a strong incompetence base for itself. One may call it 'in-built incompetence'. And this incompetence is built to last. At least until the company runs into difficulties.

Let us now turn to a model of organizational competence which can serve as a theoretical basis to analyse and discuss the case of Antinnova.

A model of competence

We start by reviewing briefly the competence-based perspective as it stems from the economics and management literature, before presenting a model of organizational competence integrating and articulating what we view as the main underlying dimensions of the concept. This model will then make it possible to revisit the case study presented and thus address the issue of incompetence.

The resource-based view and its corollary, the competence-based perspective

The resource based theory of the firm arose after Penrose's (1959) work, later developed by Rumelt (1984), Wernerfelt (1984), Barney (1986a,b),

Collis (1991), Amit and Schoemaker (1993), Grant (1996) and several other authors. This perspective very rightly pointed out that the firm's performance is not just the result of the external environment in the competitive game (Porter's five forces, the external positioning, etc.); the firm's performance also varies according to the way resources are tapped and leveraged by the organization to satisfy client needs in the market place.

Interestingly enough, the resource based view of the firm did not really stimulate interest among practitioners until Prahalad and Hamel (1990) published their core competence piece, as Wernerfelt (1995) suggests. In Prahalad and Hamel's terminology, to be 'core', the competencies have to meet three criteria, namely (1) offer real benefits to customers, (2) be difficult to imitate and (3) provide access to a variety of markets.

The heart of the matter has to do with the uniqueness of the various re-combinations of core competencies which the firm may achieve, to design, manufacture and distribute products and services to the customers on the market place. A higher level resource bundling process is thus at work to create an offer which may be attractive to and valued by the clients, McGee (1995).

This clearly stresses that a unique combination of core competencies can indeed generate a real competitive advantage. In addition, Prahalad and Hamel suggested re-thinking strategy in terms of competence rather than organizational SBU's.

In turn, the resource based view led to a knowledge-based perspective (Conner and Prahalad, 1996; Kogut and Zander, 1996). At the same time, an attempt was made to build a theory of competence-based strategy. The term competence is used here to broaden the concept of resource, building on the resource-based perspective.

The Prahalad and Hamel (1990) core competencies lead to Hamel and Heene (1994) and Sanchez *et al.* (1996) as well as to the Heene and Sanchez (1997) and Sanchez and Heene (1997) volumes.

As Durand (1998) puts it: 'in medieval times, alchemists were seeking to turn base metals into gold. Today managers and firms seek to turn resources and assets into profit. A new form of alchemy is needed in the organization. Let's call it competence.'

We follow Heene and Sanchez who advocate that the emerging competence theory has something more to offer than the resource based view, bringing into the picture this 'organizational alchemy', which is necessary to properly leverage available resources and assets.

In any case, the line of reasoning behind the resource/competence based view of the firm remains essentially as follows: the firm taps resources and assets and combines these into products and services for the clients through ad hoc management processes taking place within the organization. We choose to use the generic word competence to describe these capabilities for combining, bundling and integrating resources into products and services, what Heene and Sanchez (1997) called the integrated coordinated deployment of resources and assets.

Some of these competencies are distinctive enough to be labelled core competencies, i.e. leveraging specific sets of capabilities and assets which give the firm a potentially significant and sustainable competitive advantage over its competitors. In contrast some inability to achieve a part or all of this may be distinctive enough to be labeled incompetence.

Let us now try to clarify what we mean by the concept of competence.

A model of organizational competence built round three generic forms of competence: knowledge, know-how and attitudes

From research on education, we propose (see Durand, 1998) to borrow the three key dimensions of individual learning: knowledge, know-how and attitudes, following Pestalozzi (1797) who referred to 'head, hand and heart'.

Knowledge corresponds to the structured sets of assimilated information which make it possible to understand the world, obviously with partial and somewhat contradictory interpretations. Knowledge thus encompasses the access to data, the ability to recognize them as acceptable information and to integrate them into pre-existing schemes, which obviously evolve along the way.

Know-how relates to the ability to act in a concrete way according to predefined objectives or processes. Know-how does not exclude knowledge but does not necessitate a full understanding of why the skills and capabilities, when put into operation, actually work. Therefore, know-how, in part, relates to empirism and tacitness.

Attitudes are too often neglected in the resource based view as well as in the competence based theory of the firm. This may be due to the traditional lack of interest of economists in behavioural and social aspects, although Barney (1986b), Fiol (1991) or Leonard-Barton (1992) have touched upon this aspect. We believe that behaviour, and even more so identity and will (determination) are essential parts of the capability of an individual or an organization to achieve anything. This is a matter of choice in defining concepts. We argue that a dedicated organization, eager to succeed, is more competent than a demoralized, passive one with exactly the same knowledge and know-how.

These three dimensions are the generic axes of our competence model. Figure 14.1 illustrates some sub-dimensions, worthy of interest, around these three principal axes, including the distinction between techniques (essentially empirical) and technology (partly explained scientifically), or between know-how, know-what and know-why (Sanchez, 1996).

Going one step further, one should recognize that management is not necessarily capable of acting along these dimensions. Standard managerial levers are different in nature:

- *Strategizing* (strategic thinking leading to a strategic vision, a strategic logic thus relating to the 'know why', strategy deployment and strategic decision making). This relates to the knowledge (know-what and know-why) dimension.

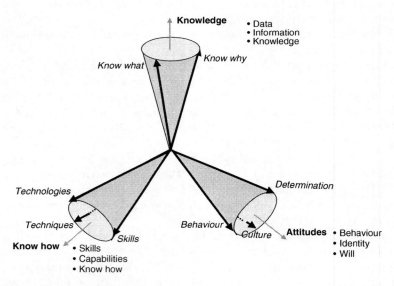

Figure 14.1 Three dimensions of competence
Source: Durand, 1998

- *Organizing* (the organizational structure as well as management processes). This relates more to the 'know how' dimension.
- *Motivating* (i.e. setting up incentives but also coaching, encouraging positive thinking and behaviour, promoting dedication and will). Therefore, this relates to the 'attitudes' dimension. This raises the issue of the interaction between managerial tasks and competence building and leveraging. The links are obviously not so direct. How can management operate on the same wavelength (according to the same dimensions) as the competence base in order to better build and leverage competence? This important issue will be discussed later in this chapter, focusing on the case of Antinnova.

The model also refines the heart of the concept of competence, the 'organizational alchemy' as we call it, which has to do with the coordinated deployment of resources and assets. Indeed, while Heene and Sanchez (1997) actually associate their coordinated deployment function solely to the management processes, the model extends the concept of competence to integrate the cultural identity, the strategic vision and the organizational structure. The identity (the shared values, revealed by the rites, taboos and beliefs) functions as a cement holding the organizational pieces together, at least as efficiently as any other coordinating and integrating mechanism. Similarly, a shared vision also contributes to the coordinated deployment of strategy, channelling of people's energy, motivation and commitment. Finally, the organizational structure is also a key element of the same coordinated deployment of assets and capabilities.

In other words, in our model, the content of the coordinated deployment concept is reviewed and broadened to encompass four elements: the management processes, the identity, the strategic vision and the structure. This is shown in Figure 14.2. In so doing, our model clearly relates to Strategor's (1997) *tetrahedron* of strategic management.

This integration actually helps go beyond the fuzziness of alchemy towards the idea that if the competence building processes cannot necessarily be fully monitored within the firm, at least the management can act to create the organizational conditions which will facilitate the development and deployment of collective capabilities.

The model also includes the question of competence building. In a way, competence is a stock accumulated as a result of an ongoing flux of learning, thus reinforcing and enlarging the competence base of the organization. Table 14.1 extends to know-how and attitudes, what Durand (1992) described for knowledge building, suggesting a sequence of stages

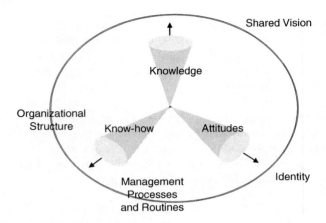

Figure 14.2   Coordinated deployment
Source: Durand, 1998

Figure 14.3
Source: Durand, 1998

Table 14.1   Parallel learning processes and stages

Knowledge	Know-how	Attitudes
Data Reception	Action	Interaction
Information	Skills and capabilities	Behaviour, culture, will
Knowledge	Know-how	Attitudes
Expertise	Expertise	Expertise

Source: Durand (1998)

from data and information, to knowledge and expertise, as shown in Figure 14.3.

Indeed, know-how is built through action which shapes skills and techniques. Similarly, attitudes are shaped through interaction when individuals conform to group or organizational behaviour, adopt the same cultural values and share the same basic commitments. Table 14.1 illustrates the parallelism which prevails in the way learning mechanisms

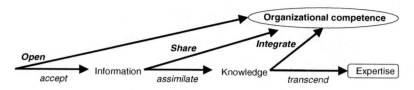

Figure 14.4
Source: Durand, 1998

operate for each dimension of the model. In this sense, learning stems from information, action and interaction.

However, one may add a layer to this sequential representation. Recognizing that competence is not just a set of non-related elements of knowledge but also means interaction and integration, the model may be complemented as in Figure 14.4.

A second competence building mechanism appears requiring openness, sharing and integration. These three elements counterbalance the natural tendency of human activities for differentiation, which leads to segmented knowledge. We further suggest that both mechanisms, i.e. both paths, operate simultaneously. The first path deepens the knowledge while the second one recombines and extends the associated potential for the organization, in a holistic way, beyond differentiation.

Expertise actually requires going one step further. Expertise needs some form of 'quantum jump' in competence together with an integration of the three generic forms of competence which we discussed. Figure 14.5 illustrates this idea graphically, detailing the learning processes for each dimension of the model of competence.

At this stage, it is important to note that the pre-existing stock of competence (the knowledge base, existing skills and identity) significantly affects the learning capabilities. It may operate as a booster for a fast build up competence. It may also transform itself into a source of bias and inertia, hindering any real new learning. History indeed matters. The 'installed base' counts. This is also shown graphically in Figure 14.5. For each axis, the dotted arrows loop back on the pre-existing competence base, which in turn influences new learning. The result of learning is not just a function of the learning process. It also depends on the pre-existing competence base.

This holds particularly true when the installed base of competence aims at cost reduction and efficiency, whereas the new competence required emphasize creativity and innovation.

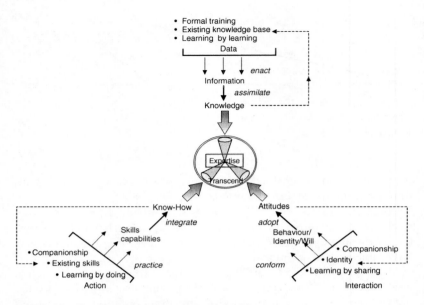

Figure 14.5   The dynamics of competence building

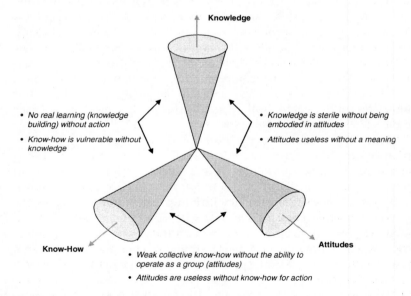

Figure 14.6   The three dimensions of competence that are interdependent

One final feature of our model of competence has to do with the idea that learning takes place for the three generic dimensions of the model, in a simultaneous and interdependent way. See Figure 14.6. Knowledge building stems from exposure to and reception of external data which has to be accepted as information and integrated into frameworks. Know-how is built through action. Attitudes are shaped through interaction in companionship. Nevertheless, the three parallel modes of building up competence operate in an interrelated, simultaneous way. This extends what Senge (1990) advocates, following Piaget: learning needs action.

A more detailed discussion of the model can be found in Durand (1998). The intent and focus of this chapter require us to turn to the issue of incompetence, and revisit the story of Antinnova.

Revisiting the case study: from competence to incompetence

The model presented above is aimed at describing competence, using an integrated set of three generic and interdependent dimensions. Yet, the model may also be helpful for describing what incompetence is about, thus in turn helping to grasp the concept of competence from the opposite perspective, as a mirror image.

Incompetence at Antinnova

One of the most striking aspects of the Antinnova case is probably the contrast between (a) the quality and dedication of the company staff members and (b) the lack of trust and cooperation among managers from different functional departments. The knowledge of the organization regarding markets, client needs, competition, technologies, etc. is actually remarkable (although it could be improved). Similarly, the available skills within the organization at Antinnova are without doubt at the forefront in the industry (advertising campaigns, lean manufacturing operations, etc.). But, when it comes to collective practices on new product development, Antinnova is just not capable.

Before anything else, one should recognize that there is indeed a contradiction between (1) well-established, efficient routines and (2) innovation processes requiring some form of destruction. This is a question of rhythm, objectives or focus. The cognitive capabilities, the behaviour or the degree of openness needed are obviously different. However both are essential for an organization to survive and for individuals to contribute to this success.

The knowledge and functional know-how at Antinnova are most probably not the problem. The problem comes from the 'know-how to work together' on non-routine tasks. We would argue that attitudes constitute the basis of incompetence of the Antinnova organization for product development.

In this instance, attitudes annihilate the knowledge and skills of the company. It is not a matter of rare resources or assets which could be (or not be) acquired on the market from suppliers. It is not a question of a piece of equipment or a technological process for which the blue print would be missing. Instead, it is a question of coordinated deployment of resources and assets, going beyond management processes. The management processes are not the problem *per se*. The trouble emanates from the way the members of the organization play against the management processes.

We argue that the past and current cultural behaviour of this company has grown into an organization fit for productivity and efficiency but unfit for creativity and innovation. Teams work hard under pressure but antagonism and lack of trust result in a streamlined but sterile product development process. How can innovation projects be treated under similar time pressure as operations? The development committee and the way it is run are just the tip of the iceberg. It reflects the real nature of the culture prevailing at Antinnova. This culture is at least twofold. On the one hand, the dominant values have to do with productivity and efficiency, not creativity and trial and error. On the other hand, historical fights and oppositions have generated a culture of suspicion and lack of openness to ideas and suggestions of others.

It sounds like the cats and dogs story. If cats and dogs have been known to hate and fight each other for ages, it does not mean that dogs are unable to live peacefully with other dogs or with other animals. The same holds for cats. Some cats and some dogs can actually get along pretty well. It is just a question of starting life on a different basis. But, when a puppy first meets a cat, the puppy usually learns the lesson once and for all (obviously, the same holds for kittens the other way around). Re-forming this early training is known to be difficult.

In such instances, trying to convince, explaining what the common goals are, deploying the strategy, arguing, may not prove sufficient, or even relevant. A cognitive response to this type of incompetence is just not adequate. This would focus on a wrong dimension of the competence base, the knowledge axis of the model.

Conversely, the 'soon-to-be classical' literature on competence would propose re-engineering the management processes, typically adapting the structure and re-engineering the product development process. Yet, we argue that, in this instance, implementing new management processes may not do the job either. The incompetence which we identify, at Antinnova in this instance, is embedded in the heart (not in the hand) of the organization. It is a matter of identity and culture which are rooted deep down in the collective behaviour of the organization.

The disease may actually be even more difficult to treat. Indeed our model suggests that the pre-existing competence base for each of the principal axes of the competence model acts as a filter, shaping and limiting any new learning. This holds especially true for the identity of an organization which is known to constitute a major source of inertia. In that sense, the model presented suggests that the incompetence encountered in the case of Antinnova is of a different nature than what conventional managerial wisdom would indicate. This in turn would lead to recommend a different kind of managerial action.

All in all, the case of Antinnova thus illustrates how one single missing link among the three generic elements of competence (knowledge, know-how and attitudes) could affect the performance of an entire organization. Because of a major deficiency on one key dimension, namely attitudes, the whole ability of the company to innovate gets destroyed. In addition, the classical managerial levers discussed previously, (a) strategizing (formulation and communication of strategy which in this instance means explaining the importance of product innovation) and (b) organizing (both the structure and the management processes) are most probably ineffective, as they have so far proven to be for the top management of Antinnova. Even the 'motivating' part (c) is not enough, as it may sound as rhetoric to the staff.

Instead, what our model suggests for Antinnova would be a different tack: what is needed is some attempt to transform the culture of the organization in order to generate new attitudes more compatible with the specific needs of innovation. However, transforming the identity involves unlearning part of the existing cultural base. This raises the issue of unlearning, which is most probably the core issue in the Antinnova case.

In order to be able to generate new learning and some form of unlearning, in a context where the pre-existing competence base leads to deny and reject new representations, one way may be to organize the contextual conditions which would make it possible for entrenched routines to appear insufficient. Therefore, one key element is to make sure that the new context does not render the previous representations and routines fully obsolete, but only partially unfit to cope with new challenges. Indeed, the former and the new representations, as well as the former routines (operations oriented) and the new processes (innovation focused) have to function simultaneously, if not harmoniously. If the change is to be successfully introduced into the firm, this is actually just one of the challenges posed to management. How to design the new processes in a way that the individuals can cope with the rhythm, the time scale, the pressure of both the normal operations and the newly required innovative processes?

One of the best triggers for such a change may be to use some external force, suddenly presented as a major threat to the firm. Creating a feeling of urgency may thus be used as a catalytic shock onto the organization.

The external challenge may then help build a shared feel for the timing and the nature of the potential response, as well as a shared view of the resources and solidarity needed. Therefore, the challenge functions as a cement used to repair the organizational construct, which in a way had eroded over the years. This is illustrated in Figure 14.7. When the organization is severely opposing change, as in the case of Antinnova, the external shock may even have to be overplayed in order to create and diffuse a symbolic feeling of danger throughout the organization. Paradoxically, it is as important to try to create an atmosphere of fun, rediscovering how to work closely again as a group, in a context where individual competition is (at least for a break) considered to become secondary given the importance of what has to be done jointly to cope with the challenge faced by the organization.

We argue that one additional trick may be to start by setting-up reasonable objectives in order to build trust and confidence in the collective

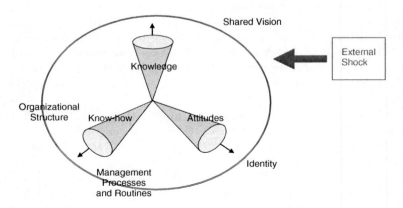

Figure 14.7   Coordinated deployment

strength of the organization working as a group. Once this is achieved, some form of self-organizing may start: more ambitious responses may then be looked for to respond to the threat identified.

The Antinnova case may in a way be summarized as follows:

- the attitudes in the organization are not united enough to permit product development processes to function smoothly (deficient organizational behaviour);
- the culture prevailing at Antinnova makes it extremely difficult for the organization to reform itself. Productivity in operations, efficiency in project management and antagonism among functional departments are dominant values (too strong an inadequate culture, which is unfit to what is needed to innovate);
- the strategy adopted by the top management at Antinnova represents a 'U-turn' for the organization which has been under enormous stress for productivity over the previous years, thus becoming good at running lean operations, much less at innovating (asking the organization what for it cannot deliver).

We have argued that, in such an instance, the use of a catalytic shock may be the best way to help the organization unlearn and relearn. This raises the issue of unlearning.

Unlearning

From an empirical study of 20 projects on product and process developments, Leonard-Barton (1992) derives an interesting idea: she points out that core competence may become core rigidities when change affects the type of competence required. Interestingly enough, in such instances, learning means unlearning first.

Hedberg (1981), Nystrom and Starbuck (1984), Durand (1992), McGill and Slocum (1993), and Rumelt (1995), Bettis and Prahalad (1995) have all addressed the same issue of obsolete competence and unlearning. When past experience and accumulated competence are obsolete and constitute an inertia, it is essential to unlearn before any new learning takes place.

Yet, unlearning is neither a natural nor an easy move for an organization. This is actually one of the most difficult task of management. Seen from the perspective of our model of competence, this may be achieved in two complementary ways. On the one hand it is a matter of making sure that the existing competence base fades away, e.g. through human resources mobility, retraining, deploying strategy, reorganizing the structure, re-engineering the management processes, etc. On the other hand, it is also a matter of promoting new learning, escaping from the bias generated by the pre-existing competence base, as illustrated by the dotted, loop-back arrows in Figure 14.5. New information, new action and renewed interaction are the best ways to overcome the inertia of obsolete competence. The organization has to move from single-loop to double-loop learning. Yet, we argue that the three key dimensions of our model of competence do not present the same ability to resist change. More specifically, we argue that unlearning the culture of the organization is more difficult than discarding an obsolete know-how, which in turn is more difficult than discarding a useless piece of knowledge. In that sense, our model of competence is clearly asymmetrical.

In the case of Antinnova, this leads to the recommendation that the sequence of managerial action should be to treat the problem of inadequate culture first, before trying to reorganize the product development process and deploy the strategy. This is illustrated in Figure 14.6. Obviously these three elements of action have to take place in a coordinated way. However, it would probably be irrelevant to continue what the top management of Antinnova has been doing for years unsuccessfully: it is hopeless to try to convince the staff about the relevance of the new strategy and the importance of innovation. Reorganization alone would not seem more appropriate at this stage. The urgent task is most probably to help the managers and staff within each of the functional departments to unlearn their antagonism, in order to enable them to work

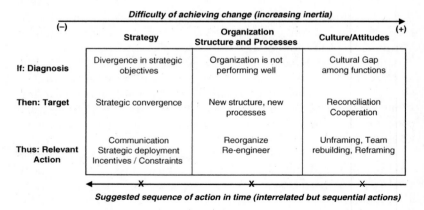

	Strategy	Organization Structure and Processes	Culture/Attitudes
If: Diagnosis	Divergence in strategic objectives	Organization is not performing well	Cultural Gap among functions
Then: Target	Strategic convergence	New structure, new processes	Reconciliation Cooperation
Thus: Relevant Action	Communication Strategic deployment Incentives / Constraints	Reorganize Re-engineer	Unframing, Team rebuilding, Reframing

Difficulty of achieving change (increasing inertia)

(−)   (+)

Suggested sequence of action in time (interrelated but sequential actions)

Figure 14.8   Dimensions of the diagnosis and relevant levers for managerial action

together again on a basis of trust and confidence. The problem is essentially cultural. It is embedded deeply in the heart of the organization. One should probably aim at unfreezing the situation, unframing the players to have them rebuild their modes of interaction on a different basis. It is a matter of team rebuilding. Before this is done, no significant change should be expected at Antinnova regarding innovation. We have argued that this may be achieved through the use of some form of a catalytic shock emanating from the outside and presented as a major threat to the organization.

Summary

We have started with three preliminary comments about the management literature on competence, (a) pointing out the focus of past research on learning while relatively less attention has been paid to describing the stock of competence itself, (b) recognizing the overall lack of empirical contribution on competence and (c) suggesting that the concept of organizational competence is more than a simple extension of individual competence. On that basis, we have indicated that the objective of this chapter is to attempt to document, empirically, the concept of organizational incompetence (in the case of product development), one way of grasping the concept of organizational competence.

Then, we started by presenting the case study of Antinnova. This highly profitable firm, leader in its markets, has been unable to develop new products successfully in the recent years, thus showing a clear incompetence in innovation-related matters. We have described the main findings of our field investigations, showing how the firm has built itself an internal culture and organizational routines fit for productivity and efficiency but unfit for creativity and innovation. Then, we explained a model of competence, as a way to analyse the incompetence of the Antinnova company. Firstly, we have briefly reviewed the literature dealing with the resource-based view and the competence-based perspective. We have then presented our model of competence built around three key dimensions (knowledge, know-how and attitudes). We have broadened the concept of coordinated deployment of assets and resources, what we call the 'organizational alchemy', to include not only management processes but also the identity, a shared vision and the organizational structure.

We have also seen that managerial levers (strategizing, organizing, motivating) only indirectly relate to the three generic dimensions of our model. We have then introduced the dynamics of competence building into the model, discussing the importance of the pre-existing competence base which influences the flow of new learning. We have finally suggested that the three generic dimensions of competence in our model are interdependent, reinforcing each other as learning takes place simultaneously in all directions through information, action and interaction.

Based on the model, we have then revisited the case study. Since the core problem of the Antinnova organization is not an issue of a missing piece of knowledge or know-how but has to do with attitudes and behaviour, we have suggested that it thus requires more than strategy deployment or process re-engineering to treat the problem.

We have seen in greater detail the nature of the incompetence of Antinnova when it comes to product development and have discussed the implications of this diagnosis for potential managerial action.

All in all, practitioners may wish to recall from the case of Antinnova that it may not be sufficient to explain the strategy at length. It may not be sufficient either to reorganize for innovation, through some form of restructuring or re-engineering of the management processes. When the culture of a company is strongly (although tacitly) opposing innovation, some other managerial approach is needed to treat the disease. Cultural change is the issue. This may be done by overplaying an external shock. It may also be achieved through a process of 'un-freezing' the main player in the organization, thereby encouraging them to participate in changing attitudes to innovation.

References

Amit, R. and P.J. Schoemaker (1993), 'Strategic Assets and Organizational Rent', *Strategic Management Journal*, 1, pp. 33–46.

Arrow, K.J. (1962), 'The Economic Implications of Learning by Doing', *Review of Economic Studies*, 29, pp. 155–73.

Atkinson, A.B. and J.E. Stiglitz (1969), 'A New View of Technological Change', *Economic Journal*, 76, pp. 573–8.

Barnes, J. (1984), 'Cognitive Biases and their Impact on Strategic Planning', *Strategic Management Journal*, 5, pp. 129–37.

Barney, J.B. (1986a), 'Strategic Factor Markets: Expectations, Luck and Business Strategy', *Management Science*, 32, pp. 1231–41.

Barney, J.B. (1986b), 'Organizational Culture: Can it be a Source of Sustained Competitive Advantage?', *Academy of Management Review*, vol. 11.

Bettis, A.R. and C.K. Prahalad (1995), 'The Dominant Logic: Retrospective and Extension', *Strategic Management Journal*, 16, pp. 5–14.

Carlson, (1995), personal communication.

Collis, J. (1991), 'A Resource-Based Analysis of Global Competition: the Case of the Bearing Industry', *Strategic Management Journal*, 12, pp. 49–68.

Conner, K.C. and C.K. Prahalad (1996), 'A Resource-Based Theory of the Firm: Knowledge Versus Opportunism', *Organization Science*, 7, 5, Sept.–Oct.

Davenport, T.H. and L. Prusak (1998), 'Working Knowledge. How Organizations Manage What they Know', Harvard Business School.

Dosi, G., D. Teece and S. Winter (1991), 'Toward a Theory of Corporate Coherence', in G. Dosi, R. Gianetti and P.A. Toninelli, (eds), *Technology and the Enterprise in a Historical Perspective*, Oxford University Press.

Durand, Th. (1992), 'The Dynamics of Cognitive Technological Maps', in P. Lorange, J. Roos, B. Chakravarty and A. Van de Ven, (eds), *Strategic Processes*, Blackwell Business, Apr.

Durand, Th. (1997), 'Strategizing Innovation: Competence Analysis in Assessing Strategic Change', in A. Heene and R. Sanchez, (eds), *Competence-Based Strategic Management*, John Wiley.

Durand, Th. (1998), 'The Alchemy of Competence', in C.K. Prahalad, G. Hamel, D. O'Neil and H. Thomas, (eds), *Strategic Flexibility: Managing in a Turbulent Environment*, John Wiley.

Durand, Th., E. Mounoud and B. Ramanantsoa (1996), 'Uncovering Strategic Assumptions: Understanding Managers' Ability to Build Representations', *European Management Journal*, 14, 4, pp. 389–98.

Durand, Th. and Silvia Guerra-Vieira (1997), 'Competence-Based Strategies When Facing Innovation. But What is Competence?', in H. Thomas and D. O'Neal, (eds) *Strategic Discovery: Competing in New Arenas*, John Wiley.

Fiol, M. (1991), 'Managing Culture as a Competitive Resource: an Identity-Based View of Sustainable Competitive Advantage', *Journal of Management*, vol. 17, no. 1.

Grant, R.M. (1996), 'Prospering in Dynamically-competitive Environments: Organizational Capability as Knowledge Integration', *Organization Science*, vol. 7, no. 4, July–Aug.

Hamel, G. and A. Heene (eds) (1994), *Competence-Based Competition*, John Wiley.

Hambrick, D. (1989), 'Putting Top Managers Back into the Strategy Picture', *Strategic Management Journal*, Summer Special Issue, 10, pp. 5–15.

Hedberg, R. (1981), 'How Organizations Learn and Unlearn', in *Handbook of Organizational Design*, edited by P.C. Nystrom and W.H. Starbuck, Oxford University Press.

Hedlund, and Nonaka (1992), 'The Dynamics of Knowledge', in *Strategic Processes*, edited by P. Lorange *et al.*, John Wiley.

Heene, A. and R. Sanchez (eds) (1997), *Competence-Based Strategic Management*, John Wiley.

Kogut, B. and U. Zander (1996), 'What Firms Do?: Coordination, Identity and Learning', *Organization Science*, 7, 5, Sept.–Oct.

Leonard-Barton, D. (1992), 'Core Capabilities and Core Rigidities: a Paradox in Managing New Product Development', *Strategic Management Journal*, 13.

Lowendahl, B. (1997), 'Strategic Management of Professional Service Firms', Handelshojskolens Forlag, Copenhagen Business School Press.

Lundvall, B.A. (1988), 'Innovation as an Interactive Process: from User-Producer Interaction to the National System of Innovation' in G. Dosi *et al.* (ed.), *Technical Change and Economic Theory*, Frances Pinter.

Marino, K.E. (1996), 'Developing Consensus on Firm Competencies and Capabilities', *Academy of Management Executive*, 10, 3, pp. 40–51.

Mc Gee, J. (1995), Communication at the Third International Workshop on Competence-Based Competition, Ghent, Nov. 1995.

McGill, M.E. and J.W. Slocum (1993), 'Unlearning the Organization', *Organizational Dynamics*, pp. 67–78, autumn.

Moscovici, S. (1988), 'Notes Towards a Description of Social Representations', *European Journal of Social Psychology*, 18, pp. 211–50.

Nystrom, P.C. and W. Starbuck (1984), 'To avoid Organizational Crisis, Unlearn', *Organization Dynamics*, 13.

Penrose, E. (1959), *The Theory of the Growth of the Firm*, Blackwell.

Pestallozi, J.H. (1797), 'Mes recherches sur la marche de la nature dans l'évolution du genre humain', Payot Lausanne (ed.) Traduction Michel Soétard.

Prahalad, C.K. and G. Hamel (1990), 'The Core Competence of the Corporation', *Harvard Business Review*, pp. 79–91.

Rosenberg, N. (1972), *Technology and American Economic Growth*, edited by Armouk, New York.

Rumelt, R.P. (1984), 'Towards a Strategic Theory of the Firm', in R. Lamb, (ed.) *Competitive Strategic Management*, Prentice-Hall.

Rumelt, R.P. (1995), 'Inertia and Transformation' in C.A. Montgomery, (ed.) *Resource-based and Evolutionary Theories of the Firm*, Boston: Kluwer Academic Publishers.

Sanchez, R. (1996), 'Managing Articulated Knowledge in Competence-Based Competition', in R. Sanchez, A. Heene and H. Thomas (eds), *Dynamics of Competence-Based Competition*, Elsevier.

Sanchez, R. and A. Heene (1997), 'A Systems View of the Firm in Competence-Based Competition', in R. Sanchez, A. Heene and H. Thomas (eds), *Dynamics of Competence-Based Competition*, Elsevier.

Sanchez, R., A. Heene and H. Thomas (forthcoming), 'Towards the Theory and Practice of Competence-Based Competition', in R. Sanchez, A. Heene and H. Thomas (eds), *Dynamics of Competence-Based Competition*, Elsevier.

Schneider, S. and R. Angelmar (1993), 'Cognition in Organizational Analysis: Who's Minding the Store?', *Organization Studies*, 14, pp. 347–74.

Schwenk, C. (1984), 'Cognitive Simplification Processes in Strategic Decision-making', *Strategic Management Review*, 5, pp. 111–28.

Schwenk, C. (1988), 'The Cognitive Perspective on Strategic Decision-making', *Journal of Management Studies*, 25, pp. 41–55.

Senge, (1990), *The Fifth Discipline*, Century Business.

Strategor, (1997), *Stratégie, Structure, Décision, Identité – Politique Générale d'Entreprises*, ouvrage collectif, InterEditions.

Stubbart, C. (1989), 'Cognitive Science: a Missing Link in Strategic Management Research', *Journal of Management Review*, 10, pp. 724–36.

Teece, D.J. and G. Pisano (1994), 'The Dynamic Capabilities of Firms: An Introduction', International Institute for Applied Systems Analysis, Laxenburg, Austria.

von Hippel, E. (1976), 'The Dominant Role of Users in the Scientific Instrument Innovation Process', *Research Policy*, 5.

Wernerfelt, B. (1984), 'A Resource-Based View of the Firm', *Strategic Management Journal*, 5, pp. 171–80.

Wernerfelt, B. (1995), 'The Resource-Based View of the Firm: Ten Years After', *Strategic Management Journal*, 16.

15
Innovation Process Models and Their Evolution

Cornelius Herstatt and Birgit Verworn

Overview

In practice as well as in management research, process models are an important element of innovation management to standardize or describe innovation processes. The literature presents numerous process models, which are difficult to overlook. This raises several questions: What is the benefit of standardized innovation processes? Why are there different process models? Is there 'one best way'? This chapter attempts to introduce people involved in innovation management to process models. With this purpose in mind, we give a brief review of the emergence and advancement of innovation process models in two parts of the world (the Anglo-American and German-speaking world), highlight pros and cons and discuss the implications for current innovation practice. In order to achieve this, we focus on models which had a significant effect on practice or research.

As one might expect, we conclude that there is no ideal process which guarantees company success. In practice, process models are used as a management tool to standardize development activities, thereby to enhance the effectiveness and efficiency of new product, process or service development projects. In this way, they contribute to the overall company success.

Introduction

Today, new products or services are launched at an increasingly faster rate. Therefore, innovation management has become important for enhancing the effectiveness and efficiency of new product development. For a technology-based enterprise, the capability to absorb technical knowledge from universities and research institutes is crucial. Studies indicate that, in small and medium sized enterprises in particular, insufficient skills in innovation management hamper the absorption rate of technical knowledge. High-class innovation processes are regarded as a key success factor for (Legler *et al.*, 2001: 141) overcoming this issue.

Conceptual models which describe the development and commercialization of new products are an essential element of innovation management. The literature features numerous process models that describe how companies develop or should develop new products or services. Virtually every management handbook provides a process model for visualizing product development activities. Empirical studies in the field of innovation management represent activities observed in the form of process models. Companies develop process models to standardize their innovative efforts. This raises the question, why there are so many different process models. Is there a generally accepted model? This chapter tries to answer this question by reviewing the evolution of process models and implications for current innovation practice.

In the following section, we give an overview of design and application aspects of process models for innovation projects. 'Process models in the USA and Canada' describes different generations of process models, emanating from the English-speaking part of the world. This is followed by a section focusing on process particularities in the German-speaking area and what can be learned and adopted from German innovation processes. Due to the large quantity of literature on innovation processes, we select exemplary process models which are used by companies or which we think exerted influence on research. This selection does not claim to be complete. The penultimate gives examples of innovation processes in practice. A brief summary of the discussion on process models for innovation projects is given in the final section.

Process models: fields of application

A way of classifying innovation process models is to distinguish them in terms of objectives. So far, process models have been categorized as descriptive versus normative (Cooper, 1983a: 6). Normative models are often derived from practical experience, case studies or quantitative studies analysing successful new product development. Approaches found to be successful are condensed in an ideal process model. Examples are described by Cooper (1983a: 7), Cooper and Kleinschmidt (1990: 45), Kuczmarski (1992: 163), Rosenau (1996: 79), and Ulrich and Eppihger (1995: 14). Normative models can provide the basis for process clarification and systematization in companies. In this case, process models fulfil the function of a management tool (see e. g. Bernasco *et al.*, 1999: 124; Cohen *et al.*, 1998: 3; Cooper and Kleinschmidt, 1991: 137; 1994: 24; Hughes and Chafin, 1996: 97, O'Connor, 1994: 185). In contrast, descriptive models evolve from empirical studies and are not intended to advise managers. Their objective is to describe and evaluate actual practice (e.g. Cooper, 1983b: 1). Handbooks or lectures about innovation management for students provide further flow diagrams. In this didactic context, they are intended for visualizing innovation processes for educational or didactical reasons (e.g. Clark and Wheelwright, 1993: 90; Crawford, 1994: 26; Pleschak and Sabisch, 1996: 24; Tidd *et al.*, 1998: 255).

Figure 15.1 summarizes the types of process models described above. Individual process models may have diverse objectives and therefore belong to more than one of these subgroups. As indicated by the arrows in Figure 15.1, in some cases, process models of one subgroup represent the basis for models belonging to another subgroup. For instance, management tools are often derived from normative process models. Although the scheme is not a strict classification with independent categories, we think it might be helpful for dealing with the large quantity of process models found in the literature.

Besides the objective of a process, there are several other reasons explaining the existence of innumerable models. The literature often provides multiphase models which break the new product development

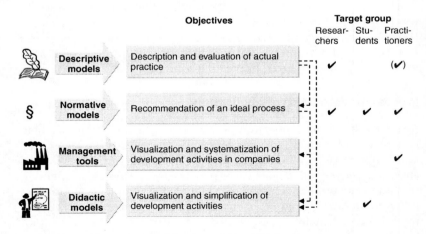

Figure 15.1   Objectives of process models (own depiction)

process into sequential tasks. They differ in terms of the objective, level of detail and the main focus chosen. The lower the level of detail, the higher the compliance with other models and real new product development processes. On the other hand, models with a low level of detail may lack specificity. Explicit process models have a higher explanatory power, although they may be confined to special branches or types of firms. Apart from the purpose of a process model, it has to be well-balanced in terms of reduced complexity and excessive specialization.

Process models in the USA and Canada

First-generation innovation processes

In the North American area, Cooper distinguishes between several generations of process models (Cooper, 1994: 4). The first-generation 'phase-review-processes' were developed by NASA in the 1960s. Phase-review-processes were intended as a management tool. Development was broken into sequential phases to systematize and control work with contractors and suppliers on space projects (see Figure 15.2). Inputs and outputs for each phase were defined and a management review was held at the end of every phase to decide on the continuation of a project ('go-no-go'). Thus, former ad hoc activities were standardized. Phase-review-processes were, for example, adopted by the US military and firms like Hewlett Packard. As phase-review-processes were engineering driven, one of their major advantages was the reduction of technical uncertainty. In addition, the phased approach ensured that tasks were completed. This could cause delays, due to the fact that activities were put on hold until every task supposed to be finished before the next management review was completed. Another shortcoming of the phase-review-processes was that they only covered the development

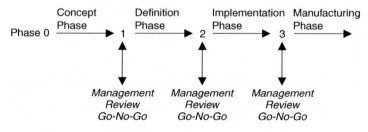

Figure 15.2   Phase-review-process
Source: Hughes and Chafin, 1996: 92

phase and not the complete innovation process from idea generation to launch. Marketing activities were neglected. The discussion on phase-review-processes are summarized by Cooper (1994: 4) and Hughes and Chafin (1996: 90).

Although some companies still use phase-review-processes, we cannot recommend this out-dated approach to current innovation practice.

Second-generation innovation processes

The second-generation of North American process models resulted from empirical studies on success factors for new product development (e.g. Myers and Marquis, 1969; the British SAPHO studies by Rothwell *et al.*, 1974), in particular from the Canadian NewProd studies by Cooper (see Cooper, 1979; Cooper, 1994; Cooper *et al.*, 1984).

While Myers and Marquis (1969) used a descriptive process model to arrange their empirical results (see Figure 15.3), Cooper and Kleinschmidt (1990: 45) merge critical success factors in a normative model. Myers and Marquis process model is a conceptual framework for research. In contrast, Cooper's normative process models can be the basis for standardized innovation processes in companies.

Cooper and Kleinschmidt identified a standardized approach for development projects, which they calls 'game plan', as a critical success factor (1986: 84; 1990: 44). Figure 15.4 shows a typical second-generation stage-gate-process.

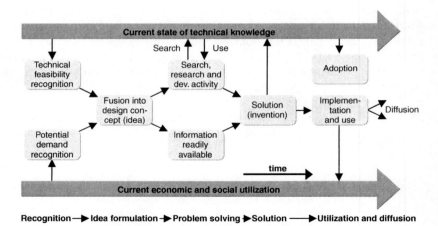

Figure 15.3 Descriptive process model
Source: Myers and Marquis 1969: 4

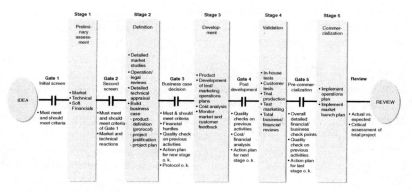

Figure 15.4   Typical second-generation stage-gate-process
Source: Cooper and Kleinschmidt, 1990: 46

The product development process starts with an idea originating from basic research, customer-based techniques, and creativity techniques (Cooper and Kleinschmidt, 1990: 45). At gate 1, the idea is evaluated according to 'must meet and should meet criteria' such as strategic alignment, feasibility or fit with company policies. Stage 1 is a quick and inexpensive assessment of the project in terms of market, technology, and financials. After passing a second gate, a detailed investigation follows during stage 2. The output is a business plan, a basis for the decision at gate 3. Stage 3 contains the actual development of the product and a marketing concept. The deliverable of this stage is a product prototype. Gate 4 ensures that the developed product is consistent with the definition specified at gate 3. In-house product tests, customer field trials, test markets, and trial productions are typical activities during the validation stage 4. Gate 5 decides on production start-up and market launch, a follow-on from stage 5. The objective of a terminating review is to compare actual with expected results and assess the entire project.

Second-generation stage-gate processes resemble first-generation phase-review-processes but overcome some of their disadvantages. Again, the innovation process is broken into discrete stages. However, in contrast to the phase-review-process, a stage-gate-process integrates the engineering and marketing perspectives. Decisions at the gates are made by multifunctional teams, according to well-defined go/kill criteria. In addition, the stage-gate-process covers the whole innovation process from idea generation to launch. The process is not strictly sequential, and parallel activities are permitted to speed up the process (Cooper, 1994: 5; Cooper and Kleinschmidt, 1990: 45).

A major advantage of the implementation of stage-gate-processes in a company is the systematization of an often ad hoc development. The innovation process is transparent for all functions involved, and a common understanding is shared. This facilitates communication within the project team as well as with top management (Cooper and Kleinschmidt, 1994: 29). Several authors give advice on the implementation of stage-gate-processes in companies (e.g. O'Connor, 1996: 101; Rosenau, 1996: 84). Stage-gate-processes were and are used as a management tool by many large companies such as IBM, 3M, General Motors and Northern Telecom. Empirical studies indicated that firms using a stage-gate approach were more successful than firms without a standardized innovation process (Cooper and Kleinschmidt, 1990: 44; 1991: 139; Whiteley *et al.*, 1998: 16). In a benchmarking forum with companies using a stage-gate-process, O'Connor identified seven challenges to the implementation of a stage-gate-process in a company:

- process optimization and validation;
- gaining top management commitment and involvement;
- structured decision-making;
- developing NPD (new product development) leaders and high-performance teams;
- training critical skills and knowledge;
- portfolio optimization;
- linking and positioning the process (O'Connor, 1996: 192).

Figure 15.5 shows a process model by Ulrich and Eppinger similar to that of Cooper. They, too, regard process models as an important management tool and present their own normative model (1995: 14). The activities each function carries out during the development of a new product are described. The noteworthiness of this model is its interdisciplinary point of view. Every function is weaved into each phase of the development process.

To summarize, second-generation stage-gate-processes had a strong influence on research as well as on practice. They have been and are the basis for the standardization of innovation processes in companies. They can still be applied, if development time is not very critical or if innovation projects require a sequential progression.

Third-generation innovation processes and beyond

Coopers normative third-generation stage-gate-models strive for more flexible processes (Cooper, 1996: 472). Third-generation stages and gates are not strictly sequential and less stringent than second-generation stages and gates. They are rather guidelines than strict rules on how to operate and adapt to the level of risk inherent in a project (see Figure 15.6). To speed up the product development process, transitions

Mission Statement	Phase 1 Concept Development	Phase 2 System-Level Design	Phase 3 Detail Design	Phase 4 Testing and Refinement	Phase 5 Production Ramp-Up	Product Launch
Marketing						
	• define market segments • identify lead users • identify competitive products	• develop plan for product options and extended product family	• develop marketing plan	• develop promotion and launch materials • facilitate field testing	• place early production with key customers	
Design						
	• investigate feasibiliy of product concepts • develop industrial design concepts • build and test experimental prototypes	• generate alternative product architectures • define major sub-systems and interfaces • refine industrial design	• define part geometry • assign tolerances • choose materials • complete industrial design control documentation	• do reliability testing, life testing and performance testing • obtain regulatory approvals • implement design changes	• evaluate early production output	
Manufacturing						
	• estimate manufacturing cost • assess production feasibility	• identify suppliers for key components • perform make-buy analysis • define final assembly scheme	• define piece-part production processes • design tooling • define quality assurance processes • begin procurement of long-lead tooling	• facilitate supplier ramp-up • refine fabrication and assembly processes • train work force • refine quality assurance processes	• begin operation of entire production system	
Other functions						
	• finance: facilitate economic analysis • legal: investigate patent issues	• finance: facilitate make-buy analysis • service: identify service issues		• sales: develop sales plan		

Figure 15.5   Normative process model

Source: Ulrich and Eppinger, 1995: 15

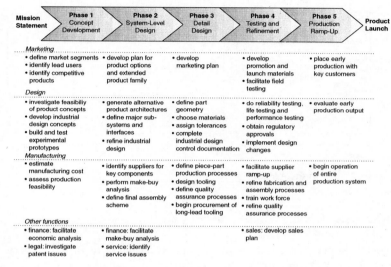

Figure 15.6   Third-generation stage-gate-process

Source: Cooper, 1996: 479

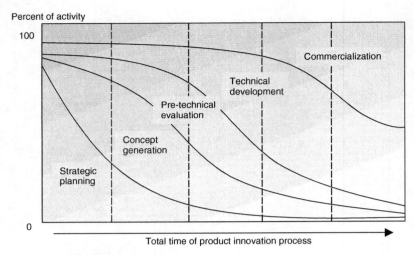

Percent of activity

Figure 15.7   Simultaneous development phases
Source: Crawford, 1994: 27

between stages are smooth and tasks are increasingly performed in parallel (Cooper, 1996: 472).

The third-generation stage-gate-process is closer to reality and therefore the effort to implement it in a company is smaller.

From the 1980s up to now, besides further improvements by Cooper, several other normative process models and management tools have been developed. The majority tries to overcome delays caused by a sequential approach to the innovation process. Parallel activities were regarded as a powerful way to reduce development time. Figure 15.7 gives an idea of parallel phases instead of sequential phases in new product development processes.

A widespread approach used by many well-known companies, including General Motors, Chrysler, Ford, Motorola, Hewlett Packard, and Intel, is called concurrent engineering or integrated product development. Concurrent engineering is defined as the simultaneous design and development of all the processes and information needed in new product development (Swink, 1998: 104). The focus is on improving product manufacturability and quality while reducing development cycle time and cost by resolving product, process, and organizational issues at earlier stages (Deszca *et al.*, 1999: 614; Swink, 1998: 103). For example, manufacturing process designers start developing tooling and manufacturing processes in close collaboration with product designers before the

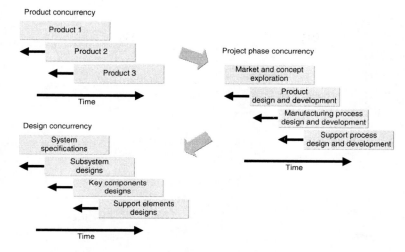

Figure 15.8 Different types of concurrency
Source: Swink, 1998: 114

product specifications are completed. Thus, project phases overlap. In addition, Figure 15.8 shows two other types of concurrency, product concurrency and design concurrency. An example of product concurrency is the development of a first and a next generation of a product in parallel. Design concurrency enables parallel system level and component level design (Swink, 1998: 113).

To maximize the effectiveness of concurrent engineering, it has to be customized to the respective company. Further, it should be evaluated as to what activities could be processed simultaneously. Factors such as programme priorities (e.g., cost, quality, and timing), the level of innovation and the technical risk, influence the concurrent engineering programme design (Swink, 1998: 111, 112). The involvement of corporate-level management is regarded as a key to the successful implementation of concurrent engineering. To increase the probability of success, top management should: '(1) elevate the project, (2) elucidate goals, (3) eliminate barriers to integration, and (4) elaborate concurrent engineering processes' (Swink, 1998: 113).

Figure 15.9 shows a further example of a process model developed as a management tool for a company. In this company, an existing stage-gate-process was superseded by a so-called 'value proposition cycle' (Hughes and Chafin, 1996: 90). This approach tries to make the new product development process more flexible and enhance efficiency and

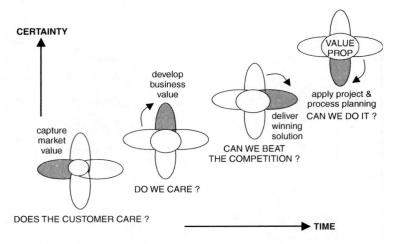

Figure 15.9 Value proposition cycle
Source: Hughes and Chafin, 1996: 93

effectiveness through 'continuous learning, identifying the certainty of knowledge, building consensus, and focusing on adding value to customers and end users' (Hughes and Chafin, 1996: 91).

The value proposition cycle consists of four iterative loops to identify the market value, develop the business value, deliver a solution superior to competition and plan the process. The enlarging centre in Figure 15.9 illustrates the increase in created value. As the team continuously traverses the loops, it can react to changes more quickly, enabling a continuous learning process, which Hughes and Chafin, (1996: 94) left out in Cooper's stage-gate-models.

Besides attempts to generate more flexible process models, recent studies apply a contingency approach to process models (e.g. Balachandra and Friar, 1997: 285). They question the existence of critical development activities that must be done similarly regardless of environmental, company or other project characteristics. Song and Montoya-Weiss, (1998: 125), for instance, survey the impact of product innovativeness on new product development activities. Their results suggest that there are performance-critical development activities in every new product development. Nevertheless, they also provide empirical support for the notion that the emphasis on single activities should be adapted to the level of product innovativeness (Song and Montoya-Weiss, 1998: 132): 'The key difference in the determinants of new product success between really new and incremental products is the

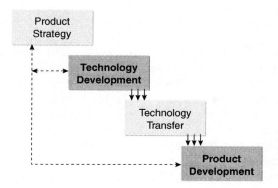

Figure 15.10 Technology and product development process

impact of strategic planning and business and market opportunity analysis activities' (Song and Montoya-Weiss, 1998: 130). While a detailed business and market opportunity analysis contributes to the success of incremental product development, it is counter-productive for the development of really new products (Balachandra and Friar, 1997: 282). In a separate section of this book about the 'fuzzy front end', we discuss typical questions to be asked by companies to identify the degree of innovativeness of a project. The innovation process and focus on single activities should be adapted to the outcome of this self-assessment.

One can go even further and suggest adopting a technology development process prior to the actual new product development process (see Figure 15.10). These two processes are linked by a technology transfer step.

The objective of the technology process is to develop a technology to a point where feasibility is demonstrated. The technology transfer step consists of three elements:

- programme synchronization to synchronize the technology development and product development programmes;
- technology equalization to broaden the project's technical scope to consider supporting technologies besides the already developed core technology;
- technology transfer management to transfer knowledge between the technology development and product development team.

A preliminary technology development process prior to the product development process was observed in case studies (e.g. Kobe, 2001: 72, 185).

To summarize, process models in the USA and Canada are influenced strongly by Cooper's phased stage-gate-process derived from the NewProd studies. In the 1980s and 1990s numerous companies implemented phased process models to standardize their innovation processes. Recent studies on innovation processes try to create more flexible process models which overcome insufficiencies of a phased approach. Concurrent engineering reduces development time by overlapping tasks. Current innovation practice can profit from both sequential stage-gate-processes and concurrent engineering approach depending on the nature of the tasks. The degree of innovativeness of a project for a company should be assessed as it strongly determines the usefulness of applying any process model. If the application field of a new technology is not known, a technology development process prior to the product development process may be required. In this case, emphasis should be placed on the transfer process, from technology to product development.

Process models in the German-speaking area

This section looks at innovation process particularities in the German-speaking world. Literature on innovation management in that area also quotes Cooper's stage-gate-process. Almost every handbook on innovation management contains process models that illustrate the innovation steps. We select two examples from Thom, (1992: 9) and Pleschak and Sabisch (1996: 24). Thom's scheme was selected because it had a strong influence on the German literature in innovation management. Pleschak's model was chosen because we consider it as typical and particularly comprehensive for the German-speaking area (a further example is presented in the next chapter of this book about the 'fuzzy front end' of innovation). In addition, we introduce a normative process model by Ebert *et al.* (1992: 148) which highlights a distinctive feature of most of the German new product development process-models: the use of two documents which could be translated into requirement specification ('Lastenheft') and functional specification ('Pflichtenheft'). The requirement specification contains the needs and requirements of the users. These user needs are translated into technical specifications, documented in the functional specification (Sabisch and Wylegalla, 1999: 30).

Phases of the innovation process		
Main phases		
1 Idea generation	2 Idea acceptance	3 Idea implementation
Specification of the main phases		
1.1 Definition of the search field	2.1 Idea evaluation	3.1 Realization of the new idea
1.2 Idea detection	2.2 Preparation of implementation plans	3.2 Sale of the new idea to target customers
1.3 Idea proposal	2.3 Decision on one implementation plan	3.3 Check on acceptance

Figure 15.11 Scheme of the innovation process
Source: Thom, 1992: 9

One of the most frequently quoted schemes of the innovation process in the German literature is shown in Figure 15.11. It was developed by Thom at the beginning of the 1980s. The idea centres on the three main phases of idea generation, idea acceptance, and idea implementation.

In contrast to Thom's scheme, the process model by Pleschak and Sabisch (1996) goes into detail (see Figure 15.12). It intentionally includes the possibility of project termination during every stage of the innovation process due to the rejection of an idea, or technical or economical failure similar to Cooper's gates. The early detection of failures is particularly important for technology-based companies in a fast-changing technical environment. It is not unusual that unforeseen technical problems emerge during the development or over optimistic estimates cannot be reached. If such signals can be detected early and conclusions are drawn, resources can be saved (Balachandra and Friar, 1994: 30).

While German process models presented so far are redolent of English process models, the process model shown in Figure 15.13 points out a particularity in the German-speaking area: the compilation of requirement specifications ('Lastenheft') and functional specifications ('Pflichtenheft'). The requirement specifications are based on results from market research. They contain the needs and requirements of the users. In functional specifications, user needs (in a user-oriented language) are translated into technical specifications (in a technical-oriented language) (Boutellier and Völker, 1997: 92). The functional specifications

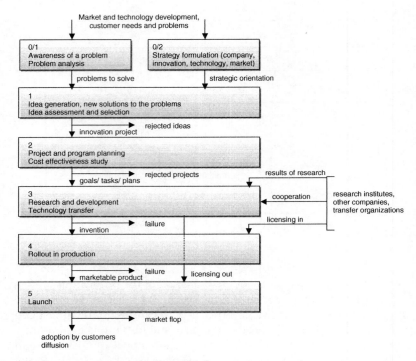

Figure 15.12   Process model including failures
Source: Pleschak and Sabisch, 1996: 24

should include a project overview, economic and technical goals and information concerning the environment of the project (Boutellier and Völker, 1997: 94). The translation of customer attributes into engineering characteristics resembles a management tool developed in Japan, namely QFD or Quality Function Deployment (for details, see Hauser and Clausing, 1988: 69). A study indicates that almost every German company, at least in some industrial sectors, uses functional specifications and almost half of the companies use requirement specifications (Sabisch and Wylegalla, 1999: 30: 51). Usually, requirement specifications are generated by marketing, and functional specifications by the development department.

To summarize, most process models referred to in the German literature resemble Cooper's stage-gate-process. The standardized utilization of requirement and in particular functional specifications discriminates new product development processes in the German-speaking area from

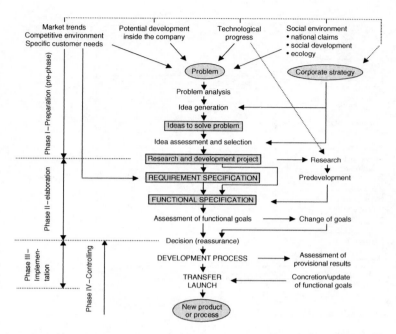

Figure 15.13 Process model including requirement specification and functional specification

Source: Ebert *et al.*, 1992: 148

other countries. This is at least true for traditional industrial sectors. We reckon that this might be different for newer areas like biotechnology or the service sector. The use of the two standardized documents can enhance customer orientation and prevent over-engineering and could therefore set an example for innovation processes in companies in other regions.

Innovation processes in practice

Finally, we present four examples of the successful systematization of innovation processes in practice. Three examples describe innovation processes in technology-based US companies. The fourth example is a systematic innovation process successfully implemented in a German manufacturer of cigarette machines. This example shows the use of requirement specifications ('Lastenheft') and functional specifications ('Pflichtenheft') in a stage-gate-process.

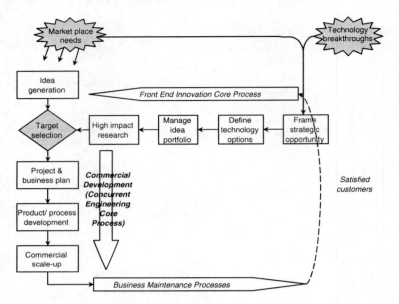

Figure 15.14   AlliedSignal's innovation process
Source: Smith *et al.*, 1999: 23

Figure 15.14 shows the AlliedSignal's innovation process (Smith *et al.*, 1999).

AlliedSignal is a technology-driven company with three core business sectors: Aerospace, Automotive, and Engineered Materials. The early invention stage is separated from the development process in order to create a fast, free-flowing, creative environment, where ideas can be developed. By contrast, objectives of the commercial development phase are speed to market and failure avoidance in a focused, coordinated, team environment.

Exxon implemented stage-gate processes in different subsidiaries (Cohen *et al.*, 1998). While Exxon Chemical Company implemented a stage-gate system similar to that proposed by Cooper, Exxon Research and Engineering Company (ERE) added two new gates to precede the Exxon Chemical Company process (see Figure 15.15). These gates address the need for basic research, wherein knowledge-building is required to convert general ideas into focused, specific technical ideas or concepts.

Finally, Figure 15.16 shows a combination of a stage-gate process and requirement specifications ('Lastenheft') and functional or product

EXXON CHEMICALS PRODUCT INNOVATION PROCESS

ERE TECHNOLOGY ADVANCEMENT SYSTEM

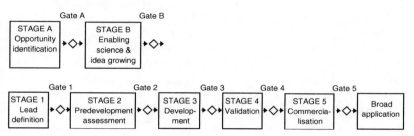

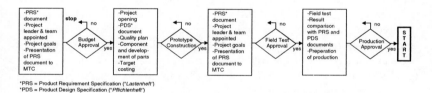

Figure 15.15   Exxon's innovation processes
Source: Cohen *et al.*, 1998: 35

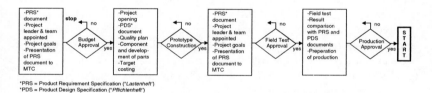

Figure 15.16   Innovation process of a German manufacturer of cigarette machines (own depiction)

design specifications ('Pflichtenheft'). This process was successfully implemented by a German manufacturer of cigarette machines.

In this section, we showed how three companies successfully structured their innovative activities. Yet, differences between innovation processes make clear that there is no standard innovation process which can be implemented in every company. By contrast, company specifics and the kind of innovation projects have to be considered. For the Exxon Research and Engineering Company, e.g. where products with a high degree of technical novelty are developed, additional stages and gates for basic research were added to Cooper's process model.

Summary

This chapter discusses process models as a tool to standardize innovation processes. The literature presents numerous process models which are difficult to overlook. We gave a brief review of the evolution of process models in two world-regions and presented examples of successful implementation of systematic processes in technology-based companies in both regions. We tried to select models which had a significant effect on practice or research. Our selection is of course highly subjective given the vast number of process models described in the literature.

In North America, Cooper's stage-gate-process gave direction to the spread of sequential process models in practice. Recent approaches like concurrent engineering try to synchronize activities and reduce time-to-market. Cooper also stimulated the emergence of standardized processes in the German-speaking world. Yet, a particularity in this area is the utilization of requirement specifications and functional specifications. These two documents contain user needs which are translated into technical specifications, thereby enhancing customer orientation and preventing over-engineering.

Overall, we claim that neither 'one best way' nor a generally applicable process model exists. In fact, various process models make sense simply because they address different objectives or problems or have a different focus. We propose making a rough distinction between descriptive models, normative models, didactic models and process models used as a management tool. Process models, used as a management tool, should take into account the newness of the product and the technology embodied in a firm. Radical innovation projects require a different approach compared to incremental innovation projects. If the technology is completely new to a firm, a technology process prior to the product development process may be required, together with an adequate transfer process between them.

References

Balachandra, R. and J.H. Friar (1997), 'Factors for Success in R&D Projects and New Product Innovation: A Contextual Framework', *IEEE Transactions on Engineering Management*, 44, 3, pp. 276–87.

Balachandra, R. and J.A. Raelin (1984), 'When To Kill that R&D Project', *Research Management*, 27, 4, pp. 30–3.

Bernasco, W. *et al.* (1999), 'Balanced Matrix Structure and New Product Development Process at Texas Instruments Materials and Controls Division', *R&D Management*, 29, 2, pp. 121–31.

Boutellier, R. and R. Völker (1997), *Erfolg durch innovative Produkte*, München: Hanser.

Clark, K.B. and S.C. Wheelwright (1993), *Managing New Product and Process Development – Text and Cases*, New York: The Free Press.

Cohen, L.Y., P.W. Kamienski and R.L. Espino (1998), 'Gate System Focuses Industrial Basic Research', *Research Technology Management*, 7–8, pp. 34–7.

Cooper, R.G. (1979), 'The Dimensions of Industrial New Product Success and Failure', *Journal of Marketing*, 43, 3, pp. 93–103.

Cooper, R.G. (1983a), 'A Process Model for Industrial New Product Development', *IEEE Transactions on Engineering Management*, 30, 1, pp. 2–11.

Cooper, R.G. (1983b), 'The New Product Process: an Empirically-Based Classification Scheme', *R&D Management*, 13, 1, pp. 1–13.

Cooper, R.G. (1994), 'Third-Generation New Product Processes', *Journal of Product Innovation Management*, 11, pp. 3–14.

Cooper, R.G. (1996), 'Overhauling the New Product Process', *Industrial Marketing Management*, 25, 6, pp. 465–82.

Cooper, R.G. and E.J. Kleinschmidt (1986), 'An Investigation into the New Product Process: Steps, Deficiencies, and Impact', *Journal of Product Innovation Management*, 3, pp. 7–85.

Cooper, R.G. and E.J. Kleinschmidt (1987), 'Success Factors in Product Innovation', *Industrial Marketing Management*, 16, 3, pp. 215–23.

Cooper, R.G. and E.J. Kleinschmidt (1990), *New Products – the Key Factors in Success*, Chicago: American Marketing Association.

Cooper, R.G. and E.J. Kleinschmidt (1991), 'New Product Processes at Leading Industrial Firms', *Industrial Marketing Management*, 20, pp. 137–47.

Cooper, R.G. and E.J. Kleinschmidt (1994), 'Screening New Products for Potential Winners', *IEEE Engineering Management Review*, 22, 4, pp. 24–30.

Crawford, C.M. (1994), *New Products Management*, 4th edn, Boston: Irwin, Burr Ridge.

Deszca, G.H. Munro and H. Noori (1999), 'Developing Breakthrough Products: Challenges and Options for Market Assessment', *Journal of Operations Management*, 17, pp. 613–30.

Ebert, G.F. Pleschak and H. Sabisch (1992), 'Aktuelle Aufgaben des Forschungs – und Entwicklungscontrolling in Industrieunternehmen', in H.G. Gemünden and F. Pleschak (eds), *Innovationsmanagement und Wettbewerbsfähigkeit*, Wiesbaden: Gabler.

Hauser, J.R. and D. Clausing (1988), 'The House of Quality', *Harvard Business Review*, 66, 3, pp. 63–72.

Hughes, G.D. and D.C. Chafin (1996), 'Turning New Product Development into a Continuous Learning Process', *Journal of Product Innovation Management*, 13, pp. 89–104.

Kobe, C. (2001), 'Integration der Technologiebeobachtung in die Frühphase von Innovationsprojekten', Dissertation No. 2550 at the University of St Gallen.

Kuczmarski, T.D. (1992), *Managing New Products – the Power of Innovation*, 2nd edn, London: Prentice-Hall.

Legler, H., G. Licht and J. Egeln (2001), 'Zur Technologischen Leistungsfähigkeit Deutschlands', Gutachten im Auftrag des Bundesministeriums für Bildung und Forschung.

Myers, S. and D.G. Marquis (1969), 'Successful Industrial Innovations', National Science Foundation Tech. Rep. NSF 69-17.

O'Connor, P. (1994), 'Implementing a Stage-Gate process: a Multi-Company Perspective', *Journal of Product Innovation Management*, 11, 3, pp. 183–200.

O'Connor, P. (1996), 'Implementing a Product Development Process', in M. D. Rosenau Jr *et al.* (eds), *The PDMA Handbook of New Product Development*, New York: John Wiley, pp. 93–106.

Pleschak, F. and H. Sabisch (1996), *Innovationsmanagement*, Stuttgart: Schäffer-Poeschel.

Rosenau Jr, M.D. (1996), 'Choosing a Development Process That's Right for Your Company', in M.D. Rosenau Jr. *et al.* (eds), *The PDMA Handbook of New Product Development*, New York: John Wiley, pp. 77–92.

Rothwell, R.C. Freeman and A. Horlsey *et al.* (1974), 'SAPHO Updated – Project SAPHO Phase II', *Research Policy*, 3, pp. 258–91.

Sabisch, H. and J. Wylegalla (1999), 'Pflichten – und Lastenhefte für Innovationsprojekte', *Technologie & Management*, 48, 1, pp. 28–32.

Smith, G.R., W.C. Herbein and R.C. Morris (1999), 'Front-End Innovation at AlliedSignal and Alcoa', *Research Technology Management*, 42, pp. 15–24.

Song, X.M. and M.M. Montoya-Weiss (1998), 'Critical Development Activities for Really New versus Incremental Products', *Journal of Product Innovation Management*, 5, 2, pp. 124–35.

Swink, M.L. (1998), 'A Tutorial on Implementing Concurrent Engineering in New Product Development Programs', *Journal of Operations Management*, 16, pp. 103–16.

Tidd, J.J. Bessant and K. Pavitt (1998), *Managing Innovation – Integrating Technological, Market and Organizational Change*, Chichester: John Wiley.

Thom, N. (1992), *Innovationsmanagement*, Bern: Schweizerische Volksbank.

Ulrich, K.T. and S.D. Eppinger (1995), *Product Design and Development*, New York: McGraw-Hill.

Whiteley, R.L., A.S. Bean and M.J. Russo (1998), 'Using the IRI/CIMS R&D Database', *Research Technology Management*, 41, 4, pp. 15–16.

16
The 'Fuzzy Front End' of Innovation
Cornelius Herstatt and Birgit Verworn

Overview

The fast transformation of technologies into new products or processes is one of the core challenges for any technology-based enterprise. From the different steps of the innovation process, the early phases ('fuzzy front end') have the highest impact on project outcome. The front end influences the design and total costs of the new product or process significantly. However, the 'fuzzy front end' is unfortunately the least-well structured part of the innovation process, both in theory and in practice.

The focus of the present chapter is on methods and tools for managing the 'fuzzy front end' of the innovation process. Firstly, the activities, characteristics, and challenges of the front end are described. Secondly, a framework to arrange different methods and tools is presented: since a product upgrade requires a different approach compared to radical innovation, where the market is unknown and a new technology is applied, we believe such a framework to be useful for practitioners. Thirdly, a selection of methods and tools that can be applied to the 'fuzzy front end' is presented and allocated within the framework. The methods selected here address process improvements, concept generation, and concept testing. Finally, we present some examples of systematic front end processes in technology-based firms.

Introduction

Successfully launching new products, processes or services in the marketplace is vital for the long-term survival of any enterprise. As life cycles are shortening and the technological and competitive environment are changing fast, technology-based enterprises have to convert new technologies into innovative products and processes as quickly as possible. In parallel, they have to make sure that customer needs are met.

To cope with these challenges, the 'fuzzy front end' of the innovation process plays a key role. It determines, to a great extent, which projects will be executed. Quality, costs, and timings are usually defined at the front end. At this early stage, the effort to optimize is low and effects on the whole innovation process may be extremely high. But managers describe the front end as the greatest weakness in product innovation (Khurana and Rosenthal, 1997).

Consistently, an extensive empirical study (Cooper and Kleinschmidt, 1994) showed, that 'the greatest differences between winners and losers were found in the quality of execution of pre-development activities'. Two factors were identified to play a major role in product success: the quality of executing the pre-development activities, and a well defined product and project prior to the development phase (Cooper and Kleinschmidt, 1990). A study of Koen *et al.* (1999) identified the front end as the key-contributing factor for large numbers of really new products introduced each year.

Yet, Cooper and Kleinschmidt (1988) found that pre-development activities received the least amount of attention (only 6 per cent of dollars and 16 per cent of man-days of the total) compared to product development and commercialization stages. When product innovation success was observed, about twice as much money and time was spent on the front end stages compared to non-performing projects. Consequently, high failure rates have often been linked to insufficiencies, low management attention and poor financial support at the 'fuzzy front end'.

In the following section, we describe the 'fuzzy front end' of innovation in more detail. To arrange different methods and tools for the 'fuzzy front end', a framework is presented in the section after that. This framework differentiates innovation projects in terms of the implicit market and technical uncertainties. Based on this differentiation, the next section presents a selection of methods and tools suitable for the 'fuzzy front end' and their respective area of application. This selection does not claim to cover the whole range of methods applicable to the front end. Instead, it focuses on the one hand basic and on the other hand relatively new methods, to provide an insight into the basics and into current discussions. The methods selected address concept generation and concept testing. Finally, in the penultimate section, we present some examples of systematic front end processes in technology-based

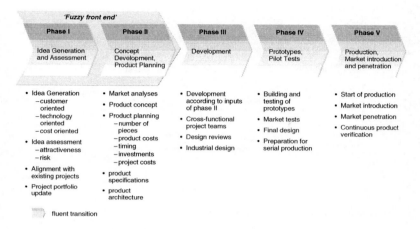

Figure 16.1 The innovation process

firms. Conclusions and a brief summary are presented in the final section.

Characteristics of the 'fuzzy front end' of innovation

In the innovation management literature, several terms are used to describe the front end of innovation, e.g. 'pre-development' (Cooper and Kleinschmidt, 1994); 'pre-project activities' (Verganti, 1997); and 'fuzzy front end' or 'pre-phase 0' (Khurana and Rosenthal, 1997, 1998). In general, the front end ranges from the generation of an idea to either its approval for development or its termination (Murphy and Kumar, 1997). Figure 16.1 describes a model of the innovation process, highlighting the front end and its activities.

As typical front end tasks include creative activities like idea generation and concept development, there has to be sufficient room for creativity. Figure 16.2 shows a typical characteristic of the 'fuzzy front end': at the beginning of the innovation process, the degree of freedom in design and influence on project outcomes are high, whereas costs for changes are low. This front end advantage is limited by the fact that the amount and certainty of information is low compared to later stages of the innovation process. Hence, sound decisions cannot be made unless necessary information is gathered during the course of the innovation process.

In the next section, we will show in more detail, the kind of information required at the front end, which depends on the kind of

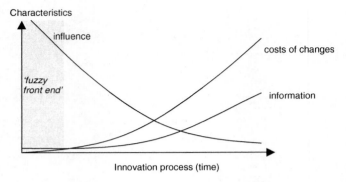

Figure 16.2 Influence, cost of changes, and information during the innovation process

Source: according to von Hippel, 1993; modified by the authors

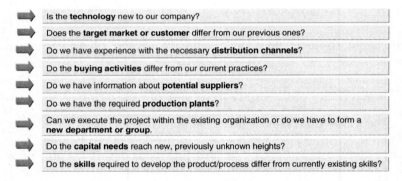

Figure 16.3 Questions determining the degree of newness of an innovation project

innovation targeted. This determines the application fields of methods and tools.

A framework of application fields for different methods and tools for the 'fuzzy front end'

As already outlined, the lack of information is a limiting factor for the front end. Therefore, the *newness* of key activities for the enterprise is a key factor to be considered when choosing appropriate methods and tools. Typical questions an enterprise has to ask itself at the beginning of an innovation project are summarized in Figure 16.3.

Methods and tools might help to fill the gap between the amount of information needed and already available. Different methods and tools require different kinds of information input to gather results. Hence, the difference between the amount of information required to perform a particular task and the amount of information already possessed should be considered when choosing an appropriate method or tool. This difference can be defined as 'uncertainty'.

As the multidimensional approach in Figure 16.3 is too complex to assign methods and tools to the respective application field characterized by a combination of these factors, a two-dimensional framework is chosen and presented in Figure 16.4. It focuses on two key factors an enterprise has to consider, namely the market and the technical uncertainty of an innovation project.

Extreme newness to a firm is implied in *radical innovation* with a high market as well as technical uncertainty (upper right quadrant of Figure 16.4). In the literature, distinctions are made between incremental and radical, 'breakthrough' innovation, or continuous and discontinuous innovation (Lynn *et al.*, 1996). There are several definitions of 'breakthrough' innovations (e.g. Rice, 1999; Song and

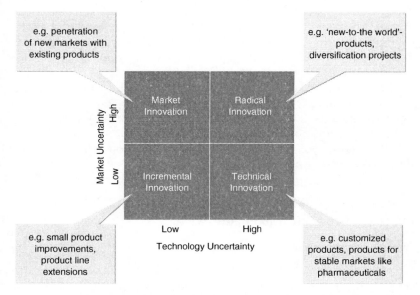

Figure 16.4   A framework of application fields of methods and tools for the 'fuzzy front end'

Source: Lynn and Akgun, 1998; modified by the authors

Montoya-Weiss, 1998; and for a detailed review see Veryzer, 1998). However, a common understanding of these terms has yet to emerge. We prefer the term radical innovation. Radical innovation means that the firm has to acquire new marketing and technological skills and cannot build on former experiences. Technology-driven innovations represent the core business of technology-based enterprises. These need not be radical innovations alone. For instance, for pharmaceutical enterprises, the market for a new drug is the number of people with the particular disease. The market uncertainty is low. These 'technical innovations' are shown in the lower right quadrant of Figure 16.4.

Although the focus of the technology-based enterprise is on technical and radical innovations, those which incorporate an existing technology should not be neglected. For example, *incremental* innovations (lower left quadrant of Figure 16.4) with a low market and technical uncertainty, like product improvements or product line extensions, could result in a considerable competitive advantage. If a technology-based enterprise concentrates solely on the development of new technologies, it could be leapfrogged by competitors, e.g. fast followers which add additional product features highly preferred by customers. Likewise, *market innovations* with a low technological and a high market uncertainty as shown in the upper left quadrant of Figure 16.4 should be considered. Turnover could be increased significantly by finding new areas of application for existing technologies and the penetration of new markets. Examples of market innovations are 'personal copiers' or food processors for home use.

To summarize, our framework for methods and tools of the 'fuzzy front end' includes market and technological uncertainty. The four combinations of these uncertainties are defined as incremental, market, technical, and radical innovation.

In the following section, we will present methods and tools supporting these types of innovations.

Methods and tools for the 'fuzzy front end' and the respective application fields

Process-related aspects

The 'stage-gate' approach

One of the major advantages of a process-oriented approach is the systematization of an often ad hoc development. The process is transparent for all departments, and a common understanding can be developed. This eases communication within teams as well as with top management.

A vast number of models to structure and systematize the innovation process are available. These models typically divide the innovation process into distinct phases and assign tasks and responsibilities to each of these phases.

Process models vary in terms of level of detail, priorities, and perspectives, e.g. market or technological. Figure 16.5 shows one of the most well known models, the so-called 'stage-gate-process'. The 'fuzzy front end' ('predevelopment activities') is here divided into four subphases, from idea generation to concept evaluation. After every stage, a gate exists, deciding on continuation or termination the project (go or no-go). The 'stage-gate'-process integrates market and technological perspectives, since activities are performed in parallel and decisions at the gates are made within cross-functional teams.

Besides this 'stage-gate'-driven process, several attempts have been made to structure the 'fuzzy front end' (e.g. Murphy and Kumar, 1997). Probably the most sophisticated process model is illustrated in Figure 16.6. Khurana and Rosenthal (1998) define the front end 'to include product strategy formulation and communication, opportunity identification and assessment, idea generation, product definition, project planning, and executive reviews'.

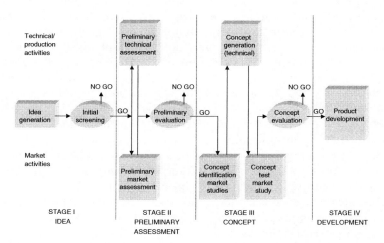

Figure 16.5 The 'stage-gate'-process
Source: Cooper, 1988: 243

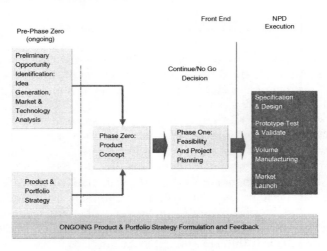

Figure 16.6   A model of the front end of the innovation process
Source: Khurana and Rosenthal, 1998: 59

The Khurana and Rosenthal approach starts with an input-stream from two different sources within the corporation, into the product concept development. The first input stream containing the steps from opportunity identification through to idea generation and market research activities is similar to Cooper's model. The second input stream includes activities like product and portfolio strategy formulation, which are typically assigned to strategic management. Khurana and Rosenthal emphasize the meaning of foundation elements, e.g. the formulation and communication of a strategic vision, a well-planned portfolio of new products, cross-functional sharing of responsibilities, and an information system. Typical result of a first qualitative screening is an idea portfolio, which has to be aligned with existing projects and the overall project portfolio.

Phase zero results in the product concept, which includes a preliminary identification of customer needs, market segments, competitive situations, business prospects, and an alignment with existing plans. In phase one, the business and technical feasibility are assessed, the product is defined, and the project is planned. Primary front-end deliverables are a clear product concept and product definition, and a detailed project plan. If a product concept is approved, the NPD (New Product Development) execution starts.

Similar to Cooper's stage-gate process model, Khurana and Rosenthal's front end model is a useful approach for visualizing and structuring front end activities, reducing the fuzziness, and easing communication. Nevertheless, a lack of flexibility due to the sequential approach of the process models has often been criticized.

Empirical studies (e.g. Cooper, 1996) show that firms using a well executed 'stage-gate' process are more successful than firms without a systematic approach and a gate-driven system. But closer observation shows that the 'stage-gate' approach has (only) proven helpful in the case of incremental innovation. And for innovations with a high market and/or technical uncertainty, a sequential and formalized approach might even be counterproductive. Several empirical studies confirm that in such cases a learning-based approach is more adequate (Lynn and Akgun, 1998; Lynn and Green, 1998; Rice *et al.*, 1998). Why? In the case of radical innovation, all corporate areas and functions have to go through extensive learning-processes and sometimes years of trial-and-errors. An example of such a trial-and-error process is General Electrics' CT scanner (Lynn and Akgun, 1998). After years of learning from the development of unsuccessful breast, head, and full body scanners, General Electrics introduced a further full body scanner and became the dominant CT supplier. In many cases, the first experiences with prototypes are negative like in the CT scanner example. The emphasis is on gaining maximum information and not on 'getting it right' the first time. As radical innovations sometimes cause high costs for years with no guarantee of success due to high uncertainties, a short term, cost-oriented evaluation at sequential gates would not allow for any 'breakthroughs'.

To summarize, a process-oriented sequential approach with evaluation gates enhances the effectiveness and efficiency of incremental innovation processes, leading to minor improvements (products and/or processes). For innovation projects characterized by high uncertainty in both dimensions (market *and* technology), a flexible, learning-based approach should be applied. Unfortunately, only little experience has been documented and reported on how to manage such processes.

'Front-loading' problem-solving

Besides structuring the innovation process, recent research in innovation management has concentrated on various approaches to shorten development times, e.g. cross-project management (McGrath *et al.*, 1992) or overlapping activities, or adequate staffing (Smith and Reinertsen, 1991). In this section, we discuss the 'front-loading' problem-solving approach and its impact on structuring and enhancing the performance of the 'fuzzy front end'.

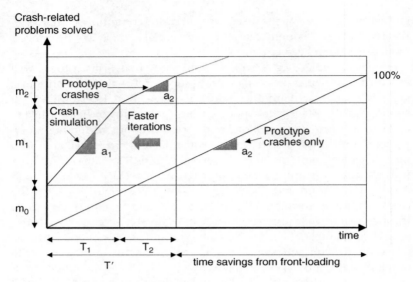

Figure 16.7   'Front-loading' problem solving for car crash tests
Source: according to Thomke and Fujimoto, 2000: modified by the authors

'Front-loading' problem-solving is defined as 'a strategy that seeks to improve development performance by shifting the identification and solving of problems to earlier phases of a product development process' (Thomke and Fujimoto, 2000). The focus is on lead-time reduction in order to enhance the efficiency of the development process.

To achieve this enhancement, two approaches are described by Thomke and Fujimoto (2000):

- project-to-project knowledge transfer, and
- rapid problem-solving.

Figure 16.7 illustrates the two approaches for car crash tests.

Firstly, the total number of problems to be solved is reduced by transferring problem-specific information from former projects (m_0). An example is postmortem reports which provide software developers with information on problems that occurred during former projects. The importance of systematic learning from past experience is supported by several studies (e.g. Verganti, 1997).

Secondly, technologies and methods shall be applied to increase the speed of problem-identification and solving. For car crash tests, the time-consuming process of building physical prototypes limits the rate of crash-tests and therefore problems solved (a_2). Computer-aided engineering tools enable the simulation of crash tests, with a higher rate of problems solved (a_1) at even lower costs compared to physical prototypes. Some problems can only be solved by physical prototype crash tests (e.g. roll-over crashes). Therefore, after a time T_1 of virtual crash tests, further physical prototype crash tests are carried out (T_2). Figure 16.7 shows potential time savings from 'front-loading' compared to physical prototype crash tests alone.

To summarize, 'front-loading' problem-solving may enhance the efficiency of the innovation process by transferring knowledge from one project to another and rapid problem solving, for example, by computer simulation. The principle of front-loading can be theoretically applied to all kinds of innovation projects. But it requires information to be available early in the process and this is more likely to be the case for incremental innovations. In addition, project-to-project knowledge transfer assumes that projects are not completely new to a firm, which limits at least this aspect of 'front-loading' to incremental, market or technical innovation.

Project planning

Another success factor identified in numerous studies is the thorough planning of a project (e.g. Maidique and Zirger, 1984; Pinto and Slevin, 1988; Rubenstein *et al.*, 1976). As most innovations are developed in the form of a project, accurate project planning can significantly increase the effectiveness and efficiency of an innovation project. In the following, a short summary of the key elements of project planning is given.

Project goals and project definition.   Different studies identify a well-defined product and project prior to the development phase as one of the success factors for new product development (e.g. Cooper and Kleinschmidt, 1990).

Project goals should be complete and well-defined. They should be aligned between all parties, in particular with the client. In addition, they should be ranked according to their importance.

Goals are part of the project definition. The project definition is a short description of the project and a basis for go/no-go-decisions. Additional elements of a project definition are listed in Figure 16.8.

Work breakdown structure.   A work breakdown structure identifies all work packages required on a project. It ensures that all tasks required to satisfy the overall projects goals are completed. The main activity is

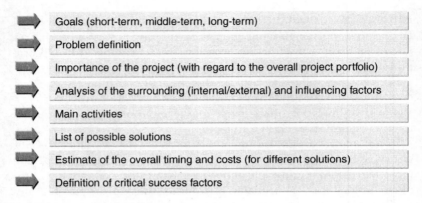

Figure 16.8   Elements of a project definition

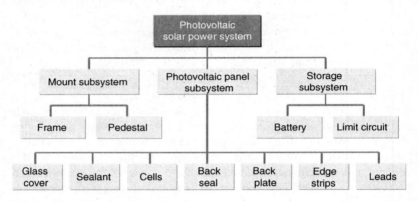

Figure 16.9   Work breakdown structure
Source: Rosenau, 1998: 72

hierarchically broken down into a number of partial activities. The smallest activities are called work packages. Work packages should be tangible, deliverable items. They should be sufficiently small so that each is understandable. The work breakdown structure is the basis for time, cost and resources estimates. Figure 16.9 shows a work breakdown structure for a photovoltaic solar power system.

Project schedule and time estimate.   The project schedule contains the duration and sometimes the sequence of single work packages defined in the work breakdown structure. Scheduling methods are milestone charts, which portray selected events, bar charts, which visualize activities as bars, and network diagrams which depict activities and their sequence and interdependencies.

1. *Milestone charts:* Milestones are critical events, which require approval or verification before further progression is made. These critical activities are depicted in a calendar bar chart.
2. *Bar charts:* Bar charts (Figure 16.10), sometimes called Gantt charts after H. L. Gantt, consist of bars which represent single activities, with their length being proportional to the time required to accomplish that activity.
3. *Network diagrams:* A network diagram links single activities with each other to portray interdependencies. Many different forms of networks diagrams are used, for example, programme evaluation and review techniques (PERT), or precedence diagramming method (PDM). Figure 16.11 shows an example of a network diagram.

Activity	J	F	M	A	M	J	J	A	S	O	N	D
A												
B												
C												
D												
E												
F												
G												
H												

Figure 16.10   Bar chart

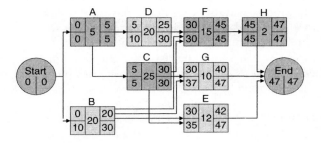

Figure 16.11   Network diagram

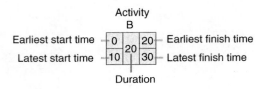

Figure 16.12   Network diagram (extract)

The earliest and latest time to start an activity, the duration, and the earliest and latest time to finish an activity are included (see Figure 16.12).

Latest timings are calculated by working backward from the end. This depiction allows the identification of the critical path (in dark grey), and the slack between the earliest and latest time to start or finish an activity.

On the one hand, network diagrams contain more information than milestone and bar charts. They display interdependencies between different activities and can illustrate the critical path and the slack. This is particularly useful if the diagram has to be adapted to changes. On the other hand, milestone and bar charts are simple to construct and easy to understand. There also exist composites of bar charts and network diagrams. Firms should select scheduling methods adapted to the respective projects and aligned with resources. In innovation practice, bar charts are preferred as they are easier to apply. In contrast, network diagrams are rarely used in firms.

Cost and resources estimates.   Costs and resources can be estimated based on the schedule. Resources are in the form of human resources, equipment, and materials. There are several reasons to consider resource allocation at the beginning of a project. Firstly, inconsistencies can be avoided, for example, the use of a particular resource on two activities at the same time. Secondly, if resources have to be shared with other projects, resource allocation provides information for the coordination of the resource between the projects.

Further tasks which should be part of a thorough project planning are the definition of responsibilities and a risk assessment. Project planning can be supported by project management software, e.g. Microsoft Project.

A thorough project planning is vital for all kinds of innovation. For radical innovations, the time, cost, and resource estimates are of course much less accurate, whereas incremental innovations can rely on experience with similar activities. Hence, project planning is a much simpler task in the case of minor or routine innovation projects compared to the case of radical innovation projects.

Eppinger has developed DSM as an attempt to design a project management procedure useful in radical innovations (see next section).

Design structure matrix (DSM)

According to Eppinger, 'product development needs a fundamentally different planning tool' (Eppinger, 2001), since generic project management approaches do not help innovation managers much. Eppinger claims that conventional project planning methods and tools, as presented in the former section, were created to plan large construction projects such as building houses. These projects are characterized by sequential or parallel tasks which do not need to be reworked. The foundation of a house is not changed after building the walls. Complex product development projects require innovation and therefore learning (feedback) loops. Network diagrams for complex product developments could run to tens or hundreds of pages and integrating changes is time-consuming.

Hence, an initiative at the MIT looked at another approach to manage iteration (http://web.mit.edu/dsm). The tool used, the so-called Design Structure Matrix (DSM) encourages useful iteration and eliminates unnecessary iteration with only marginal benefit. DSM was developed about twenty years ago, but is not widely known or used in companies. Figure 16.13 shows a simple DSM. The tasks are listed in the order

	A	B	C	D	E	F	G	H	I	J
A	*									
B	X	*					X			X
C	X		*							
D	X		X	*						
E		X	X		*		X		X	
F			X			*				
G							X	*		X
H		X		X					*	X	X
I	X			X	X	X		X		*	
J	X	X		X	X		X				*

Figure 16.13 The Design Structure Matrix
Source: Eppinger, 2001: 151

in which they are carried out. They are arranged in the same order, horizontally and vertically. Across each row, tasks are marked that supply necessary information to the task in that row. For example, task B needs information from tasks A, G, and J. All the X's below the dotted diagonal show information that is available, before the task that needs the information is started. But an X in the upper half marks a piece of information that is not available until the task that needs the information is completed. That means considerable rework might be necessary.

Besides making information flows in a product development process more transparent, DSM can be used to optimize information flows. For example, the sequence of tasks can be rearranged to reduce the number of Xs in the upper half and therefore minimize rework. Another example is the reduction of information exchange by changing the content of the tasks (Eppinger, 2001).

As already outlined, DSM is aimed at complex product development projects that require iterations. Here, it can be a substitute for conventional planning tools like network diagrams presented in Figure 16.11, since the effort to analyse information flows could be very time-consuming.

Idea and concept generation

Here we will not comment on conventional market forecasting techniques or 'creativity techniques' applied at the 'fuzzy front end' as these have been described in detail by numerous authors. Further, it has been confirmed widely by many authors (e.g. Bower and Christensen, 1995; Lynn et al., 1996; Balachandra and Friar, 1997; Lynn and Green, 1998; Song and Montoya-Weiss, 1998; Deszca et al., 1999) that conventional marketing approaches and even sophisticated analytical methods are inadequate for generating radical innovations. Instead, we present some market forecasting techniques, which claim to address this gap.

TRIZ

TRIZ or TIPS (Theory of Inventive Problem Solving) is a method for systematically solving problems. It was developed in Russia by Altschuller and his colleagues in the 1960s. It is based on the assumption that there are underlying principles for solving problems, independent of industry or product. TRIZ draws analogies to existing solutions. Altschuller identified several underlying principles by analysing numerous patents. On the basis of such principles, fundamental technical contradictions, e.g. airplane or car crashworthiness vs. lightweight vs. reduced fuel consumption, are dealt with.

An example of how TRIZ can be applied to draw analogies is the principle to open nuts: a quick pressure drop makes them 'explode'. A quick pressure drop can also be used in a different context, e.g. to remove the stalk and seeds from sweet pepper and split diamonds along microcracks (Terninko *et al.*, 1998).

During the 1980s and 1990s, TRIZ became popular in the US, sometimes under the acronym TIPS (Theory of Inventive Problem Solving). It was integrated in software solutions like Invention Machine TechOptimizer and Ideation International Innovation WorkBench. Today, companies like General Motors, Johnson & Johnson, Ford Motors, and Proctor & Gamble are using TRIZ.

Altschuller originally targeted at incremental and technical innovation (Terninko *et al.*, 1998). Although there are some recent efforts to solve other problems like management problems with TRIZ, incremental and technical innovation are the main application domain of TRIZ. Although supported by software, TRIZ is very difficult to apply and requires a lot of practice.

The lead user method

Today's customers are often stuck to existing products and are not able to envision their future needs ('functional fixedness'). The approach described in this section addresses this issue by selecting qualified customers, so-called 'lead users'. The 'lead user' method, originally developed by von Hippel, allows the identification of qualified customers and either learn from their expertise or develop new product concepts based on their insights.

The existence of innovative users who create their own solutions has been proven by several studies. Examples are 'TipEx', which was invented by a secretary in the 1950s and converted by 3M into a commercial product, or the sports drink 'Gatorade', which was developed by a trainer of a college football team. Urban and von Hippel identified innovative users in the field of computer-aided design (CAD) systems for printed circuit boards (Urban and von Hippel, 1988). Herstatt proved the existence of innovative users in low-tech fields (Herstatt, 1991), Luethje for consumer goods (Luethje, 2000). A study of innovations in skateboarding, snowboarding and surfing shows that the source for almost every basic product development was sportsmen and not the manufacturers of sporting equipment (Shah, 2000).

Hence, it seems plausible for enterprises to identify and integrate such innovative users into their innovative projects. For this purpose, MIT Professor Eric von Hippel developed a heuristic approach, the lead user method (in the 1980s). According to him, lead users can be described by two characteristics:

The first characteristic of lead user is that they are trendsetters in the respective marketplace and are already concerned with needs that the majority of the marketplace will face much later. The second characteristic covers the motivational aspect. Users only try to find solutions for issues if they can benefit significantly from the solutions. Figure 16.15 illustrates the shape of the market trend. Lead users have needs that are well ahead of the trend.

Figure 16.16 shows the process of a typical lead user project. Firstly, the direction the innovation should take is determined and goals are set.

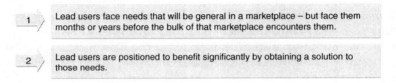

Figure 16.14   Lead user characteristics
Source: Urban and von Hippel, 1988: 569

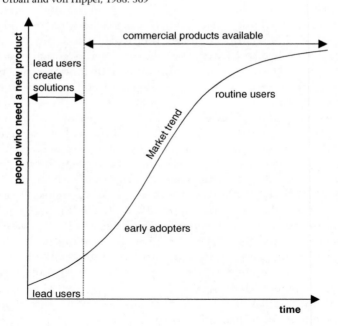

Figure 16.15   The lead user curve
Source: von Hippel *et al.*, 1999: 49

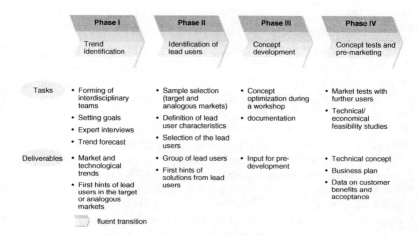

Figure 16.16   The lead user process

An interdisciplinary team with members from technical as well as marketing functions is formed. Future trends are determined in more detail by expert interviews and trend forecasting. As a result, a deeper understanding of market and technological trends emerges, enabling the team to catch first hints of lead users in the target or analogous markets. In phase II, the characteristics of the respective lead users are defined in more detail. For this purpose, a sample is chosen. The sample can include users in the target market or analogous markets. Lead user characteristics are studied in more detail. Lead users can be identified via interviews or questionnaire surveys. In addition, first solutions from these lead users can be observed and collected. During the next phase, lead users and an interdisciplinary company-internal team are brought together in a workshop lasting two to three days. After presenting the collected solutions from lead users, rough concepts are developed and the best selected. The lead users are split into smaller groups to develop the concepts in more detail. The results should be documented and tested in a wider field in phase IV. Market studies, a technical and economical feasibility study result in the output of phase IV: a technical concept and a business plan. This is the point where the lead user process flows into the conventional innovation process.

The lead user approach has been used for industrial as well as consumer goods (Herstatt and von Hippel, 1992; von Hippel *et al.*, 1999). This approach has proved useful for all types of innovation projects.

Concept testing

Information acceleration

For radical innovations, it is often not obvious who the 'true' customer may be and even if known, customers are often not able to envision their future needs, the personal computer in the seventies, for example (Bower and Christensen, 1995; Lynn and Green, 1998). Radical innovations shift market structures, require customer learning, and induce behaviour changes (Urban *et al.*, 1996). Hence, it is often extremely difficult to determine the potential market or even the potential customer.

Information acceleration is a method that places potential customers in a virtual, future environment and measures the likelihood of purchase, perceptions, and preferences. The future environment is multi-media based and often includes virtual newspaper articles, advertising, or prototypes. A customer can choose the information sources he or she would normally use to make a buying decision. This specific approach overcomes the deficiencies of conventional techniques which do not enable the customer to envision the future environment and present only a small amount of information which might not be relevant for buying decisions (Rosenberger and de Chernatony, 1995).

Unfortunately, only very few examples of applications of this marketing technique are described in the form of case studies, e.g. electric vehicles at General Motors (Urban *et al.*, 1996). This is not surprising as the costs for the application of information acceleration are very high, often exceeding $100,000 for a single application (Urban *et al.*, 1996). Therefore, information acceleration is only recommended for high-risk products requiring large capital commitments (Urban *et al.*, 1997). For such kinds of products, the risk and development time can be reduced, and product improvements can be identified earlier. Hence, similar to early prototyping described in the previous section, information acceleration is a method that can be applied in the context of a 'front-loading' approach. The benefits of information acceleration are limited to the testing of existing concepts. It does not enable customers to develop own ideas. From this perspective, information acceleration may support radical innovation but will not naturally lead to it.

Web-based conjoint analysis

Hauser and his colleagues at the MIT have developed further, less expensive and time-consuming ways in place of information acceleration, using information and communication technologies for concept testing (Dahan and Hauser, 2000). Here, we present the web-based conjoint analysis as an example of how a traditional method uses the benefits of the World Wide Web.

Conjoint analysis has been known for over 20 years and is the most used quantitative method for concept testing. Basically, in a conjoint analysis a product is decomposed into features with different characteristics for each feature. The aim of a conjoint analysis is to find out which characteristics of the features customers prefer and how much they value the features. It is a mathematical technique to reduce the amount of combinations of feature characteristics which have to be ranked or rated by customers (for a detailed description of conjoint analysis, see Urban and Hauser, 1993).

For example, an instant camera for teenagers might be represented by features such as picture quality (low, high), picture taking (1-step, 2-step), or picture removal method (manual, automatic) (Dahan and Hauser, 2000).

Virtual conjoint analysis enables concept tests to be conducted without the need for physical prototypes. On the one hand, as the costs for virtual prototypes are lower than for physical prototypes, more concepts can be tested within the same market research budget. On the other hand, there is a serious risk of sample bias from using web-based respondents. Although studies at MIT have so far indicated that virtual prototypes deliver similar results physical prototypes, this might strongly depend on the kind of product. To overcome this disadvantage, the results with virtual prototypes should be compared to a small amount of physical prototypes. As the product must be decomposed into features and the customer must be able to grasp the concept, web-based conjoint analysis is limited to incremental, market, and technical innovation. For radical innovation, we believe, this method is not appropriate.

Further methods that integrate information and communication technology are presented on a web page at the MIT (http://mitsloan.mit.edu/vc). These methods are not only traditional methods transferred to the web. For example, they additionally stimulate the communication between customers.

Examples of front end processes in practice

After the more theoretical discussion of methods and tools, we finally present two practical examples of front end innovation processes. These examples show how technology-based companies successfully structured the early phases of the innovation process.

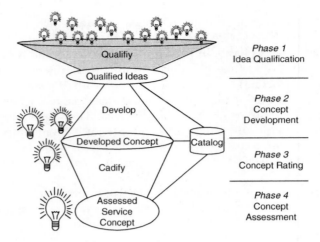

Figure 16.17   Nortel's Galileo front end process
Source: Montoya-Weiss and O'Driscoll, 2000: 146

Figure 16.17 shows an 'idea-to-opportunity front end process' developed by Nortel (Montoya-Weiss and O'Driscoll, 2000). The process was given the name 'Galileo' because Nortel intended to develop a mechanism (like Galileo's telescope) that would enable them to see the 'stars' (i.e. high potential ideas) more clearly.

The process consists of four phases: idea qualification, concept development, concept rating, and concept assessment. The primary goals of Nortel's Galileo process are to help idea generators to translate their embryonic ideas into robust concepts, and help company executives to systematically evaluate and compare concepts for investment purposes.

The second example is a front end process successfully implemented in a large German manufacturer of tools with more than 12,000 employees (Walter, 1997). The process structures the tasks of problem identification, idea generation, idea assessment and pre-development (see Figure 16.18).

Summary and conclusions

This chapter described the 'fuzzy front end' of innovation, its vital importance for the innovation process, processes, structures and methods supporting its management. A framework was presented to systematize the application fields of such processes and methods to support the

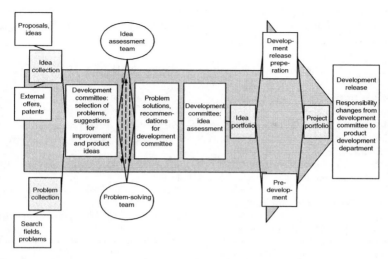

Figure 16.18   Front end process of a large manufacturer of tools
Source: Walter, 1997: 109

Area	Chapter	Method	Application			
			Incremental innovation	Market innovation	Technical innovation	Radical innovation
Process	4.1.1	'Stage-gate' approach	X			
	4.1.2	'Front-loading' problem-solving	X	X	X	
	4.1.3	Project planning	X	X	X	X
	4.1.4	Design structure matrix (DSM)		X	X	X
Concept generation	4.2.1	TRIZ	X	X	X	
	4.2.2	Lead user approach	X	X	X	X
Concept testing	4.3.1	Information acceleration		X	X	X
	4.3.2	Web-based conjoint analysis	X	X	X	

Figure 16.19   Front end methods (X = applicable with good results; X = difficult to apply)

front end. Eight methods concerned with process improvement, concept generation, and concept testing were selected and described in more detail. Figure 16.19 gives an overview of these methods and their respective application fields. They range from 'basic' methods like thorough project planning to relatively demanding marketing techniques such as information acceleration.

We cannot and shall not recommend a particular method. Instead, the degree of newness to the firm, the importance of an opportunity, and the resources of an enterprise (e.g. depending on the size), have to be taken into consideration. In addition, it might be useful to apply several methods to balance the advantages and disadvantages of using a single method, which are described above.

References

Balachandra, R. and K. Friar (1997), 'Factors for success in R&D projects and new product innovation: a contextual framework' *IEEE Transactions on Engineering Management*, 44, 3, pp. 276–87.

Bower, J.L. and C.M. Christensen (1995), 'Disruptive technologies: catching the wave', *Harvard Business Review*, 73, 1, pp. 43–53.

Cooper, R.C. (1998), 'Predevelopment activities determine new product success', *Industrial Marketing Management*, 17, 2, pp. 237–48.

Cooper, R.G. (1996), 'Overhauling the new product process', *Industrial Marketing Management*, 25, 6, pp. 465–82.

Cooper, R.C. and E.J. Kleinschmidt (1998), 'Resource allocation in the new product process', *Industrial Marketing Management*, 17, 3, pp. 249–262.

Cooper, R.C. and E.J. Kleinschmidt (1990), *New products: the key factors in success*, American Marketing Association.

Cooper, R.C. and E.J. Kleinschmidt (1994), 'Screening new products for potential winners: Institute of Electrical and Electronics Engineers', *IEEE Engineering Management Review*, 22, 4, pp. 24–30.

Dahan, E. and J.R. Hauser (2000), 'The virtual customer: communication, conceptualisation, and computation', working paper, MIT, Center for Innovation in Product Development, Cambridge, Mass.

Deszca, G., H. Munro and H. Noori (1999), 'Developing breakthrough products: challenges and options for market assessment', *Journal of Operations Management*, 17, pp. 613–30.

Eppinger, S.D. (2001), 'Innovation at the speed of information', *Harvard Business Review*, 79, 1, pp. 149–158.

Herstatt, C. (1991), 'Anwender als Quellen fuer die Produktinnovation', *dissertation*, Zuerich.

Herstatt, C. and E. von Hippel (1992), 'From experience: developing new product concepts via the lead user method: a case study in a "low-tech" field', *The Journal of Product Innovation Management*, 9, 3, pp. 213–21.

Herstatt, C. and C. Lettl (2000), 'Management of "technology-push" development projects', working paper no. 5, AB TIM, TU Hamburg-Harburg.

Herstatt, C., C. Luethje and C. Lettl. (forthcoming) 'Innovationsfelder mit Lead Usern erschliessen', working paper no. 9; AB TIM, TU Hamburg-Harburg.

Khurana, A. and S.R. Rosenthal (1997), 'Integrating the fuzzy front end of new product development', *Sloan Management Review*, Cambridge.

Khurana, A. and S.R. Rosenthal (1998), 'Towards holistic "front ends" in new product development', *The Journal of Product Innovation Management*, 15, 1, pp. 57–74.

Koen P. *et al.* (2001), 'Providing clarity and a common language to the' "fuzzy front end", *Research Technology Management*, 44, 2, pp. 46–55.

Luethje, C. (2000), *Kundenorientierung im Innovationsprozess: eine Untersuchung der Kunden-Hersteller-Interaktion in Konsumguetermaerkten*, Deutscher Universitaets-Verlag, Wiesbaden.

Lynn, G.S. and A.E. Akgun (1998), 'Innovation strategies under uncertainty: a contingency approach for new product development', *Engineering Management Journal*, 10, 3, pp. 11–17.

Lynn, G.S. and C.J. Green (1998), 'Market forecasting for high-tech vs. low-tech industrial products', *Engineering Management Journal*, 10, 1, 15–18.

Lynn, G.S., J.G. Morone and A.S. Paulson (1996), 'Marketing and discontinuous innovation: the probe and learn process', *California Management Review*, 38, 3, pp. 8–16.

Maidique, M.A. and B.J. Zirger (1984), 'A study of success and failure in product innovation: the case of the U.S. electronics industry', *IEEE Transactions on Engineering Management*, EM-31, 4, pp. 192–203.

McGrath, M.E., M.T. Anthony and A.R. Shapiro (1992), *Product Development: Success Through Product And Cycle-Time Excellence*, Boston: Butterworth-Heinemann.

Montoya-Weiss, M.M. and T.M. O'Driscoll (2000), 'From experience: applying support technology in the fuzzy front end', *Journal of Product Innovation Management*, 17, pp. 143–61.

Murphy, S.A. and V. Kumar (1997), 'The front end of new product development: a Canadian survey', *R&D Management*, 27, 1, pp. 5–16.

Pinto, J.K. and D.P. Slevin (1988), 'Critical success factors across the project life cycle', *Project Management Journal*, 19, pp. 67–75.

Rice, M.P. (1999), Starting the process – managing breakthrough innovation', *Chemtech* 29, 2, pp. 8–13.

Rice, M.P., G.C. O'Connor, L.S. Peters and J.G. Morone (1998), 'Managing discontinuous innovation', *Research Technology Management*, 41, 3, 52–8.

Rosenau, M.D. (1998), *Successful Project Management: a Step-by-Step Approach with Practical Examples*, 3rd edn, John Wiley, New York.

Rosenberger, P.J. III, and L. de Chernatony (1995), 'Virtual reality techniques in NPD research', *Journal of the Market Research Society*, 37, 1, pp. 345–55.

Rubenstein, A.H., A.K. Chakrabati, R.D. O'Keefe, W.E. Souder and H. C. Young (1976), 'Factors influencing innovation success at the project level', *Research Management*, 19, pp. 15–20.

Shah, S. (2000), 'Sources and patterns of innovation in a consumer products field: innovations in sporting equipment', working paper WP 4105, Sloan School of Management, MIT.

Smith, P.G. and D.G. Reinertsen (1991), *Developing Products in Half the Time*, New York: Van Nostrand Reinhold.

Song, X.M. and M.M. Montoya-Weiss (1998), 'Critical development activities for really new versus incremental products', *The Journal of Product Innovation Management*, 15, 2, pp. 124–35.

Terninko, J.A. Zusman and B. Zlotin (1998), *Systematic Innovations: an Introduction to TRIZ*, Boca Raton: St Lucie Press.

Thomke, S. and T. Fujimoto (2000), 'The effect of "front-loading" problem-solving on product development performance', *The Journal of Product Innovation Management*, 17, 2, pp. 128–42.

Urban, G.L. and J.R. Hauser (1993), *Design and Marketing of New Products*, New Jersey: Prentice-Hall.

Urban, G.L., J.R. Hauser, W.J. Qualls, B.D. Weinberg, J. D. Bohlmann and R. A. Chicos (1997), 'Information acceleration: validation and lessons from the field', *Journal of Marketing Research*, 34, 1, pp. 143–53.

Urban, G.L. and E. von Hippel (1988), 'Lead user analysis for the development of new industrial products' *Management Science*, 34, 5, pp. 569–82.

Urban, G.L., B.D. Weinberg and J.R. Hauser (1996), 'Premarket forecasting of really-new products', *Journal of Marketing*, 60, 1, pp. 47–60.

Verganti, R. (1997), 'Leveraging on systematic learning to manage the early phases of product innovation projects', *R&D Management*, 27, 4, pp. 377–92.

Veryzer, R.W. (1998), 'Discontinuous innovation and the new product development process', *The Journal of Product Innovation Management*, 15, 4, pp. 304–21.

von Hippel, E. (1993), *Wettbewerbsfaktor Zeit*, Moderne Industrie.

von Hippel, E., S. Thomke and M. Sonnack (1999), 'Creating breakthroughs at 3M', *Harvard Business Review*, 77, 5, pp. 47–57.

Walter, W. (1997), *Erfolgsversprechende Muster für betriebliche Ideenfindungsprozesse*, Grässner, Karlsruhe.

17
Market Research for Radical Innovation
Cornelius Herstatt

Overview

'Strong market orientation is essential for innovation success!' Although both academics and market research practitioners would generally accept this statement, the need to calibrate with the needs of the customer often results in conservative innovation strategies. Due to their focus on what is currently on offer in the marketplace, customers primarily demand so-called incremental innovations. Companies, however, want to develop entry points for radical innovations. The identification of radical innovations is a difficult task whose implementation is often associated with significant risk. It is questionable whether market research alone can allow innovation management to develop attractive areas for radical innovations and if it can also contribute to the reduction of the risk inherent in such innovations. Closer observation shows that the market research methods used today for the discovery of radical innovations, in the form of new market/technology combinations, are only partially suited. Empirical tests verify that successful innovative companies often don't use such methods, rather they involve specifically qualified, innovative knowledge carriers early on in the process, such as Lead Users or external experts with relevant knowledge from analogous markets in the search for innovations. When searching for applications for radical innovations, market researchers should initially concentrate on the question of *whom* they address as the information source. How successful the process of involving experts is, and how well supported the methodology is, depends heavily on the specific factors and conditions related to the project planning.

Introduction

Adding value in a company, via innovation, demands the identification of attractive innovation fields, the creation of new products and services as well as their successful implementation in the market. The higher the degree of innovation (market/technological), the greater the risks involved, i.e. risks that stand in the way of its successful realization. Technical, market, temporal or cost-related risks all play a role here. Well-known product 'flops' like the New Coke, the Apple Newton, the Videodisc or the Commodore computer verify that even large companies, experienced in market research, are not protected from such risks. An important goal of innovation management should therefore be to make the inherent risks associated with innovation more transparent and thus more manageable. It is here that market research plays a central role. Market research should support innovation management in two respects, in particular:

1. in the generation of the most attractive points of entry for product and process innovations, in known as well as in as yet undeveloped application fields and
2. in the reduction of the risks associated with innovations, in particular the inherent marketing risks that grow with increasing degree of innovation (Schlaak, 1999). How well equipped is market research for this task? We will examine this question in the following discussion.

In the following section we will discuss the suitability of different market research methods with particular reference to their ability to produce information for radical innovations. Then we will outline how, *despite* marked customer and/or market orientation, market research can support innovation management by developing search fields, ideas and concepts for radical innovations. The penultimate section, 4, introduces a typology of different users who can be involved in innovation projects with differing degrees of innovation. The final section, 5, addresses gaps in the research and questions that emerge from these.

The suitability of market research for the generation of radical innovations

Innovations can be basically grouped according to the dimensions 'Method' and 'Purpose', and with respect to their degree of novelty (Figure 17.1).

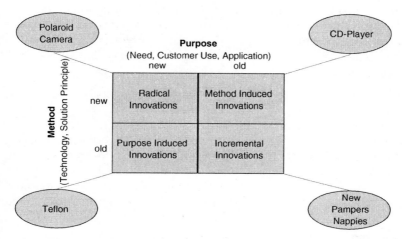

Figure 17.1 Innovations with differing degrees of novelty
Source: According to Hauschildt (1997: 57)

Radical product innovations are those that satisfy a new need through the utilization of a new technology or one not yet applied in a particular form. One characteristic of radical innovations is that the market as well as the technological uncertainty is at maximum (Lynn and Heintz, 1992). What can market research contribute to the satisfying of a new need, the recognition of a new technology and the reduction of market and technological uncertainties?

Market research is occupied in particular with the question of obtaining information for innovations. Market research is applicable where both the inherent market and/or customer needs are evident as well as (Herstatt, 1991) where, depending upon the topic in question, different methods can be applied, for example, survey techniques, observations, creativity techniques or combined processes (e.g. focus groups, video-supported observations/questioning, laboratory tests, etc.) (Herstatt and Geschka, 1991).

Practical experience shows that direct research with customers and users delivers good results for incremental innovations, whereas for purpose/method induced innovations they produce good results only occasionally and for radical innovations the results are usually unusable. Why? Conventional market research methods such as customer surveys and focus group discussions are inherently more short-term focused (oriented towards the customers of today) and due to their alignment with the existing product programme, lead to the development of small improvements in existing products. The market information need of radical innovation projects is however oriented towards the future (oriented towards customers and markets from tomorrow). Further, methodical reasons as to why the suitability of market research is limited for radical innovations are:

- Market research strives for representative statements and therefore is more focused on the average user or customer, who is scarcely able to articulate his needs or doesn't realize that they even exist.
- Market research requires a multitude of testing and therefore value is placed on the application of quantitative methods that provide a base for easier comparison. Interesting applications for new needs (e.g. new sports like kite surfing or downhill mountain biking that are followed by a small group of passionate amateur sport fans) won't be captured in this way.

Radical innovation projects demand stronger explorative and anticipatory market research methods that are capable of determining the current needs of the customer (Lender, 1991; Deszca *et al.*, 1999). Empirical test show that companies involved with radical innovation projects rarely report about the application of advanced market research methods (Herstatt *et al.*, 1999). Processes that could be applied in such circumstances, 'Empathic Design' for example, are still in their infancy (for more on this, see Herstatt and Lettl, 2000).

Burton and Patterson (1999) recommend the application of differing processes, depending on the desired level of innovation (see Figure 17.2). The empirical verification of the effectiveness of these techniques, as well as the use of the processes recommended here is still yet to be determined.

On the other hand, examination of research success factors for innovation (Kirchmann, 1994; Gruner, 1996; Lüthje, 1999) consistently reinforces how important the early involvement of customers is for the later success of the innovation (discriminating factor). The works of Lüthje (1999) and Gruner (1996) emphasize that *individual characteristics* of the people involved has a significant influence on the eventual success of the innovation projects analysed. The actual form of user involvement and the methodology applied had, however, no significant influence on the innovation success (Gruner, 1996).

However, which characteristics do (particularly) innovative users possess? Is it possible to differentiate between innovative and non-innovative users? Can the relevant characteristics be quantified, allowing producers to use them to identify innovative users early on in a development project? In order to answer these questions, one has to determine

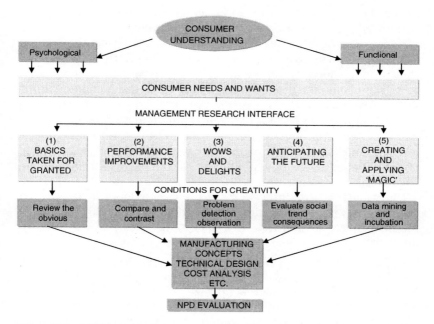

Figure 17.2 Market research for innovations with differing degrees of novelty
Source: Burton and Patterson (1999: 64)

exactly *who* it is that innovates (the source of the innovation). Von Hippel has focused on this area of research since the mid-1980s. It has been shown through his own work as well as that of his students, that it is not only manufacturers that play a crucial role in the development of innovations in varying industries, but also users ('Lead Users') and suppliers ('Lead Suppliers'). The analysis of von Hippel and others centred on incremental as well as radical product and process innovations.

It is obviously in the interest of a manufacturer to identify innovative users or suppliers early on in order to check the innovation potential of the development work and, if necessary, to channel new products and processes. The question is, how this identification process should be managed and if such users allow for identification based on specific characteristics. The Lead User model (von Hippel, 1988) gives a first indication of particular characteristics that differentiate innovative from non-innovative users: Lead Users face needs that will be common in the marketplace, but face them months or years before the bulk of that marketplace encounters them, and Lead Users are positioned to benefit significantly by obtaining a solution to those needs.

Research by Lüthje in the area of outdoor and trekking clothing showed further that innovative behaviour by the users was the result of and could be explained by the existence of a new user-need that hasn't being satisfied by the present product range of a manufacturer (Lüthje, 1999). Dissatisfaction with existing products, application knowledge and technical experience was of medium importance whilst the general motivation (e.g. pursuing economic goals) clearly played a lesser role.

This set of characteristics or properties was confirmed by Shah (2000). The idea that innovative and non-innovative users can be differentiated, and that specific characteristics play a role, appears to have been proven.

The quality of user innovations, in our opinion, still hasn't been explicitly researched. But, multiple examples of user innovations in the marketplace demonstrate that such projects can also be successfully established in mass markets (e.g. mountain bikes, surf and snow boards, the successful web software Apache, the sports drink Gatorade and many more). Through the analysis of 47 innovation projects at 3M, Morrison *et al.* (2001) found that projects that were carried out with the involvement Lead Users proved significantly more successful, in terms of turnover and degree of innovation, than projects that were internally undertaken and developed with the use of standard market research methods (e.g. focus groups with average users or brainstorming sessions) (Morrison *et al.*, 2000).

Why, however, do users become innovative at all? What knowledge with regard to the motivation of innovative users can be derived from such tests that could be of use for Innovation Management? How can such data be extracted from the market and applied?

In attempting to answer these questions, a closer look at the behavioural patterns of 'innovative users' is required. In this situation, one can continually observe the following phenomena:

1. Often innovative users and less well established manufacturers have the greatest need for innovation because:

   – a new need exists which is not (yet) being addressed by manufacturers;
   – the needs at present are very specific;
   – an entry by a manufacturer is not an attractive option as a wider market is not yet recognizable;

2. Often it is difficult and/or very expensive to transfer the required market information from users to producers as it:

- is of an experience-based nature (tacit knowledge) and, at least by users, often not considered to be relevant;
- can't be explained in 'words' (how do you teach swimming or bike riding? What is a beautiful fragrance? What is a user-friendly interface in a computer programme?)

Innovative users differentiate themselves from non-innovative users as a result of, among other reasons, their possession of new needs. Due to the fact that such new or latent needs often can't be satisfied through existing (technical) solutions and producers often aren't prepared to offer solutions for such needs, innovative users develop problem-solving behaviour in order to satisfy their needs ('Necessity is the mother of invention'). This will allow them to develop solution-related knowledge (explicit and non-explicit), relevant for manufacturers investigating such fields for innovation.

To enable the market research of a company to successfully identify these innovative users by way of specific characteristics (recognition patterns), the effectiveness and efficiency of the market research work has to improve greatly.

Identification of innovative users

A four-stage, step-wise process is described for the selection and involvement of innovative users in Figure 17.3. This model has proved useful in various practical applications (Herstatt, 2001).

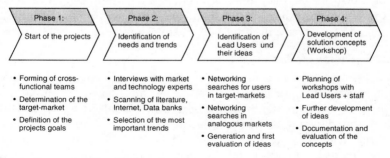

Figure 17.3 Process for the identification and involvement of innovative users
Source: Based on von Hippel (1988): modified by the author

Various applications of the process-model have shown that the set-up of the different activities within the four phases has to be aligned with the particular requirements of the project and will be greatly influenced by external variables (e.g. development dynamics in the field of innovation, time, costs and budget pressure and planning experience of the employees involved in the innovation project).

The 'Lead User methodology' as it is often incorrectly referred to is in fact not a methodology, rather more a basic framework. Degrees of freedom exist, with regard to the arrangement of the individual phases in particular (intensity, resources employed, method used). Two recent applications of the Lead User process showed, for example, that although both projects were carried out in identical product/market areas, the results presented two very different types for radical innovations. The projects were carried out by two leading manufacturers of hygiene products and in both cases the search field was identical ('Covering material for surgical operations'), see Cases 1 and 2.

Case 1: 3M

At 3M (Medical Division) the scope of the innovation project was chosen in Phase 1 of the Lead User project as the protection from infection of patients undergoing surgery. Increasing demands on hygiene, a higher resistance against antibiotics and the increasing cost pressures in clinics were identified as significant developments in the search field. With the help of a networking approach, doctors in the target market, who operate under difficult conditions (e.g. surgeons in developing countries, veterinarians) were identified. In addition, users from analogous fields were involved, for example microbiologists or make-up artists. The latter developed solutions utilizing materials that were dependable and that stick well to human skin. The results yielded improved patient coverings, a microbial-treated incision foil and a radical new approach for individual infection control, allowing the delivery of the hygienic measures, tailored to the specific needs of the patient (Thomke *et al.*, 1998).

Case 2: Johnson & Johnson (J&J)

At J&J the search field team concentrated on patient coverings and the protective clothing of operation personnel. In order to determine the future development trends in the search fields, talks were held with experts in different branches (surgeons, leading OP-nurses, hygiene experts). The project team decided, in Phase II of the project, to pursue in detail a technological trend ('surgical robotics'). During this process a group of about 20 innovative users emerged organically (surgeons as users of the robotic system, OP-personnel as those responsible for the hygiene precautions in OP, clinical engineers as those responsible for the technical evaluation and hygiene experts for infection-related questions). During a workshop, four complete and detailed concepts were worked out. For example, a gown for the covering of the surgical robot, allowing the sterility and handling problems to be removed or a complete solution that allows prevention of the mist (water drops as well as bone and blood particles) generated during the operation. All four concepts worked on by the subgroups contained products that weren't at the time in the J&J programme and until now haven't been produced by any competitor in the market place (Herstatt, 2001).

What can be taken from both these projects? The key message is that it proved fruitful to identify Lead Users early on in the project and to work together with them to develop the concept. During the course of both projects different methodologies were pursued. Also, the number and origin of the experts and the Lead Users involved, as well as the process that leads to their identification, were significantly different. Finally, the internal project teams of both were differently composed in terms of expertise and in one case were intensively coached through external consultancy.

Both these Lead User projects, along with those previously undertaken, reinforce how the early and, as far as possible, accurate identification of innovative users are very important. Once they are initially identified and are prepared to become involved with the companies, it is of secondary importance *how* the market research methodologically is organized. Why? Lead Users, by definition, have today, the needs of tomorrow. Therefore, there is no need for ingenious surveys or observation techniques to acquire the information relevant to the innovation.

Characteristics of innovative users

The innovation management of a company does not involve itself *exclusively* with applications for radical innovations *or* those for incremental. In practice, both aspects are found. In fact often it is not possible in day-to-day innovation work to keep these categories separate (projects that were supposed to lead to an improvement in a product, end as a new development; radical innovation plans are abandoned half way along the project or are transformed into an optimization project, etc.).

What types of users should the innovation management involve in what type of innovation projects? Should Lead Users, as von Hippel describes them, be involved in any project work? Are the characteristic categories determined empirically by the Lead User research to date adequate in order to recognize Lead Users prior to the start of a development project? Further research is needed in order to answer these questions.

A user typology that supports the innovation management, depending upon the need in question, in categorizing or choosing an innovative user with respect to their information contributions would certainly be useful. What would such a concrete typology look like?

We will answer this question by analysing several problems typically found in practice. For example, if ideas are sought for improving existing products and service performance, then often it is sufficient to approach 'Normal users'. *Example:* A producer of drills that are predominately used by home handymen would like to generate ideas with the aim of improving existing product features. In order to collect ideas that will be applied in a 'normal' situation, it may be enough to meet with 'Normal' or typical users.

However, the situation is different if the aim is to improve specialized for demanding aspects of product functionality. *Example:* A producer of drills that are predominately used by professional tradesmen would like to collect ideas with respect to the durability of the drill bits. In order to generate ideas relating to the improvement of such features, it is best to talk with users for whom this feature is of very *high* importance (e.g. Installation groups where the drilling machines are practically in constant use). We call them 'Extreme' users.

If a manufacturer wants to scrutinize the general effectiveness of a technology and to collect information on alternatives such as suitable technological solutions, then a possibility is to analyse analogous fields. *Example:* A producer of drills would like to understand how the problem of drilling through extremely hard subsurfaces in other, analogous fields of applications. Discussions with operators of diamond drill machines used in oil field exploration could provide significant input and impulse to innovation projects. We call these 'Analogous' users.

Are extreme and analogous users identical to Lead Users as described by von Hippel? This question is answerable when the problem-solving knowledge that is available to the innovative manufacturer has the capability to start a significant marketing and/or technological trend and possesses a broad problem-solving potential for a complete user industry. Extreme users are usually found within the user industry in question, analogous users, by definition, stem from other related application fields.

This methodological approach (user typology) proved reliable in the previously mentioned project at Johnson & Johnson. It allowed the identification of both ideas for product and process improvements as well

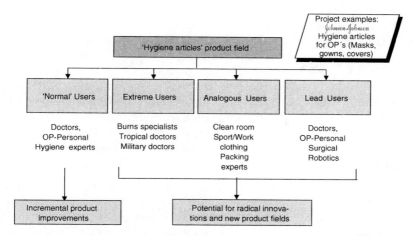

Figure 17.4   Characterization of users based on their potential contribution to the hygiene article search field

as the recognition of promising radical innovations on the basis of the previously defined user-groups ('communities') (Figure 17.4).

Search and selection process

The search process for suitable users is in itself a creative process that has to be tailored to the specific demands of the search field in question. Two basic processes can be described here:

1. *Screening approach.* With a large number of product users, a 'search pattern' can be used to test the existence of characteristics that have already been determined. For example, information available in customer data banks, customer complaints or external audit information from customer surveys. This process is suitable when the number of customers in the market is manageable and therefore a more or less complete screening of all users is possible. This approach is, in particular, suitable for collecting ideas from representative and extreme users.

2. *Networking approach.* In this case, only a few customers are included at the beginning and are questioned as to whether they are aware of other product users that have new needs or are currently actively innovative. These kinds of recommendations usually lead very quickly to particularly interesting users. A great advantage of this method lies in the fact that the team will often refer to analogous fields in which similar challenges are to be found as those in the actual search field. An

example of this is a medical imaging innovation project with the aim of diagnosing very small tumors. During the search process, not only were leading radiologists involved but also experts from the military, consulted as Lead Users. In order to identify small shapes on satellite images (e.g. weapons), pattern recognition software is often utilized in the military, where excellent results are achievable even with bad resolution. The pattern recognition system was completely new to medical imaging, until then, the primary objective of research in the industry has been to increase the image resolution. The networking approach is particularly suitable for the identification of extreme and analogous users.

Another question, which is also relevant in practical terms, is how many expert users should be involved, particularly in phases 2, 3 and 4 of the process (Figure 17.3) in order to generate a satisfactory number of innovative ideas. This aspect is yet to be explicitly, academically researched. Work by Griffin and Hauser indicates that often relatively few discussions with experts (7 discussions in a group of 30 potential experts) are enough to achieve a lasting impression of the problems and needs in user field (Griffin and Hauser, 1993).

Future trends, research possibilities and questions

Innovations can, in general, have a high risk of failure. This risk should be mitigated through systematic innovation market research. However, the theoretically based market research had scarcely been thought of as an instrument to reduce market uncertainty. The question as to what contribution existing market research methodologies can make to innovation management is not yet completely clear.

Numerous market research methodologies for the incremental innovation are available. How can market research be used in order to obtain information of strategic relevance for radical innovations in the early phases of the innovation process?

For the early phases (idea generation and concept development), the Lead User process is particularly well suited. More precisely, this is not an actual methodology, but rather a procedural guide. 'Lead Users' also includes analogous or extreme users from other related applications or fields. In the practical application of the Lead User process, numerous methodological and process decisions have to be made, that until now, have not been sufficiently well researched (e.g. the efficient identification of innovative users, the number of users to involve, etc.).

The Lead User process allows for combination of complementary need assessment methods and market research methods (e.g. Conjoint Analysis, 'House of Quality'). For researchers, the question still remains as to how the individual methods can be integrated into an all-encompassing concept for the market research of innovations.

References

Burton, A. and S. Patterson (1999), 'Integration of Consumer and Management in NPD', *Journal of the Market Research Society*, 41, 1, pp. 61–74.

Deszca, G., Munro, H. and Noori, H. (1999), 'Developing breakthrough products: challenges and options for market assessment', *Journal of Operations Management*, 17, S. pp. 613–30.

Griffin, A. and J. Hauser (1993), 'The voice of the customer', *Marketing Science*, Winter.

Gruner, K. (1996), *Kundenbindung in den Produktinnovationsprozssß*, Wiesbaden (Gabler).

Hauschildt, J. (1997), *Innovationsmanagement*, 2, vollst, Überarb. Auflage, München (Vahlen).

Herstatt, C. (1991), *Anwender als Quellen für die Produktinnovation*, Zürich.

Herstatt, C. (2001) Aufder Suche nach der radikalen Innovation, *IO-management* (9).

Herstatt, C. and H. Geschka (1991), 'Produktinnovation durch Kunden', *Die Unternehmung* (3), Oktober–Ausgabe.

Herstatt, C. and C. Lettl (2000), 'Management von technologiegetriebenen Entwicklungsprojekten', in O. Gassmann, C. Kobe, and E. Voit, (eds), *High-Risk-Projekte – Quantensprünge in der Entwicklung erfolgreich managen*, Berlin–Heidelberg–New York.

Herstatt, C., H. Geschka, D. Guggisberg, and J. Geis (1999), 'Innovationsbedarfserfassung in der Schweiz–Methoden, Erfahrungen und Tendenzen', *Die Unternehmung* (3).

Kirchmann, E. (1994), *Innovationskooperationen zwischen Herstellern und Anwendern*, Deutscher Universitäts-Verlag (DUV).

Lender, F. (1991), *Innovatives Technologie-Marketing: Grenzen der, 'konventionellen' Marktforschungskonzepte und Ansätze zur methodischen Neugestaltung*, Göttingen.

Lüthje, Chr. (1999), *Kundenorientierung im Innovationsprozess: Eine Untersuchung der Kunden-Hersteller-Interaktion in Konsumgütermärkten*, München.

Lynn, F. and S. Heintz, (1992), 'From experience: where does your new technology fit into the marketplace?', *The Journal of Product Innovation Management*, 9, 1, S. pp. 19–25.

Morrison, Pamela D., Gary L. Lillien, Kathleen Searls, Mary Sonnack, and Eric von Hippel (2001), 'Performance assessment of the Lead User idea generation process for new product design and development', working paper, WP 4151, Sloan School of Management.

Schlaak, T. (1999), 'Der Innovationsgrad als Schlüsselvariable: Perspektiven für das Management von Produktentwicklungen', Wiesbaden (DUV).

Shah, S. (2000), 'Sources and patterns of innovation in a consumer products field: innovations in sporting equipment', Sloan working paper #4105, MIT Sloan School of Management.

Thomke, S., E. von Hippel, and M. Sonnack (1998) 'Breakthrough innovation at 3M', *Harvard Business Manager* (3).

Von Hippel, E. (1988), *Sources of Innovation*, Cambridge, Mass..

18

Strategic Decision-Making About Technology-Based Projects: Development and Use of a Risk Reference Framework

Johannes I.M. Halman, Jimme A. Keizer and Michael Song

Overview

This chapter describes the development and use of a risk reference framework for diagnosing risks in technology-based projects. The risk reference framework consists of 12 main risk categories and 142 connected critical innovation issues. This framework has been developed for a globally operating company in the fast moving consumer goods industry. The development has been based on data from 114 interviews with professionals in product innovation, in-depth risk analyses carried out for 8 breakthrough projects, input from a panel with experts in product innovation, and an extensive literature review. The use of the risk reference framework as an essential part of a formal risk assessment process is explained.

Introduction

An intensified international competition, diverse and rapidly changing technologies and demanding customer expectations have made the innovation process more complex and the possible outcome considerably less certain. As a consequence, the importance of diagnosing and managing risks throughout the development process has increased accordingly. As risks are inherent in innovation, an innovation strategy based on risk avoidance cannot be a realistic option. So management must develop and apply approaches that will identify risks and develop strategies to manage them. This process will have to start in the early phases of product development, when management still has the ability to influence the course of events and make a substantial impact on the eventual outcome (Wheelwright and Clark, 1992; Cooper, 1993).

The strategic importance of identifying and managing innovation risks as a critical challenge of renewal has also been recognized in the literature (Cooper and More, 1979; Cooper, 1981). Numerous academic scholars have investigated in the last 20 years the possible reasons for new product success and failure (for an overview see Montoya-Weiss and Calantone, 1994). These investigations have yielded important findings about critical issues within product development. Although these findings may be considered as valuable clues to a more effective and efficient way of product innovation, improvement of the success rate still appears difficult to achieve in practice (Gupta and Souder, 1998). The research outcomes and recommendations – if they get through into practice – are too general in nature to offer sufficient support for risk identification and management of a particular new innovation project. An obvious reason for this is that the majority of these investigations covered a broad array of industries and as a consequence presented results as 'averages' across industries rather than specific to any one (Cooper and Kleinschmidt, 1993). To identify the risks in a particular product innovation project, besides generic, also sector, company and project specific characteristics will have to be considered. One of the ways for a company to achieve this is to apply the lessons learned from its past projects and programmes to its future projects and programmes (Hamel and Prahalad, 1991; Gupta and Souder, 1998). However, what a team or manager learns from a particular innovation project can be easily lost in the organization as a whole. To be effective, product innovation learning should be shared and stored in a form convenient to all future innovation teams within the organization (Maidique and Zirger, 1988; McKee, 1992).

In this chapter we will describe the development of a risk reference framework for product innovation projects at Unilever. This risk reference framework allows a product innovation team to relate their own project to technological, organizational, business and market related factors which have proven in the past to be potentially critical for achieving product innovation success. Unilever is a multinational corporation with worldwide sales reaching $39.6 billion, and investments in technology and innovation of around $870 million each year. This company is a fast moving consumer goods company with more than 1000 well known brands all together, consisting of a large diversity of products which can be broken down into three main categories: foods, home and personal care products.

The risk reference framework outlined in this chapter is to a certain extent company specific and thus unique. The method and the outcomes of the research process however provide a generic outline (see Figure 18.1) of how one might embed general findings about critical innovation issues from the literature within the specific context of a firm.

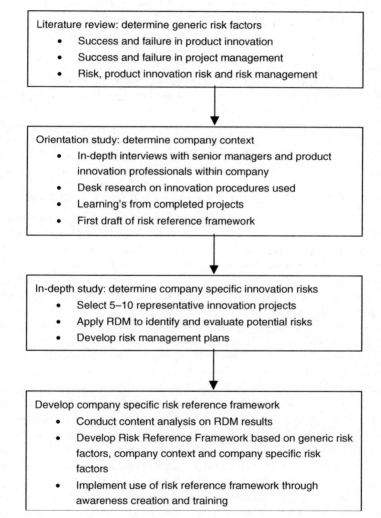

Literature review: determine generic risk factors
- Success and failure in product innovation
- Success and failure in project management
- Risk, product innovation risk and risk management

Orientation study: determine company context
- In-depth interviews with senior managers and product innovation professionals within company
- Desk research on innovation procedures used
- Learning's from completed projects
- First draft of risk reference framework

In-depth study: determine company specific innovation risks
- Select 5–10 representative innovation projects
- Apply RDM to identify and evaluate potential risks
- Develop risk management plans

Develop company specific risk reference framework
- Conduct content analysis on RDM results
- Develop Risk Reference Framework based on generic risk factors, company context and company specific risk factors
- Implement use of risk reference framework through awareness creation and training

Figure 18.1   Development of a company specific risk reference framework

The remainder of this chapter is organized as follows. In the next section we will explain our research methodology. In the section 'Analysis and results' we will clarify the basic structure of the risk reference framework, consisting of 12 risk categories and related innovation risk issues. In this section we will also present some important findings about perceptions that innovation professionals have about product innovation risk. Finally, in the discussion section, we elaborate on the theoretical and managerial implications of our research findings.

Method

Our research design consisted of a multistage combination of different methods: (1) a literature review of success and failure in project management, in general, and product innovation in particular and about risk, product innovation risk and risk management; (2) interactive development of a risk reference framework for product innovation projects; (3) in-depth risk case studies; and (4) content analysis and statistical processing of the results derived from the in-depth case studies on risk.

Literature review about success and failure in product innovation

Over the last 30 years, numerous studies have examined the determinants of new product success and identified several factors that distinguish successful products from unsuccessful ones. Early research consisted mainly of exploratory case studies. From individual cases, this research moved to groups of cases and to large surveys about successful innovations. A major advance was made in the seventies in Europe, with the pioneering Sappho Studies (Rothwell, 1972; Rothwell *et al.*, 1974) in which a pairwise comparison methodology was used to differentiate between successful and unsuccessful policies and practices by contrasting the results of successful and unsuccessful innovations. The Sappho studies were preceded by similar studies in other countries. Particularly important in this respect are the Stanford Innovation Project (Maidique and Zirger, 1984) in the USA, NewProd I, II in Canada (Cooper, 1979; Cooper and Kleinschmidt, 1987), and the success and failure studies in Japan (Song and Parry, 1997). This stream of research on determinants of new product successes and failures identified various factors that underlie new product success: product performance related factors, market factors, marketing factors (understanding the market and customer needs), synergy factors (good fit between product and marketing requirements and the resources of the firm) and organization and project management factors. Besides this first stream of research about product success and failure, two additional streams of research on product development can be distinguished (Brown and Eisenhardt, 1995). A second stream of research centres on communication, highlighting the political and information-seeking dynamics underlying the communication processes of successful innovation teams. The third research stream portrays product development as a balancing act between product vision developed at the executive level and disciplined problem solving at the project level. This last stream also stressed the important role of suppliers in the product innovation process.

We also examined the literature on project management performance and risk. Research on the determinants of project management performance has traditionally focused primarily on critical implementation factors, either on the administrative process of project planning, tracking and controlling, or on the behavioural aspects of motivation, team building, and leadership (Pinto and Covin, 1987; Baker *et al.*, 1988; Pinto and Slevin, 1989; Pinto and Mantel, 1990; Thamhain, 1996). Recent research (Kruglianskas and Thamhain, 2000) over multiyear periods and over a large spectrum of different projects and host companies however suggest a grouping into eight 'classes' of conditions which seem to have a strongly favourable influence on project performance: project leadership; work design and delegation; management support; communications; work challenge; personal drive and motivation; minimum conflict, risk and threats; and personal appraisals and awards. However, research has also demonstrated the considerable influence of contingent factors, such as the type of project, its stage in the project life cycle and the organizational environment (Pinto and Mantel, 1990). Finally, our literature review of risk, product innovation risk and risk management (Slovic and Lichtenstein, 1971; Tversky and Kahneman, 1974; Kunreuther, 1976; Cooper and More, 1979; Sjöberg, 1980; Cooper, 1981; Shrader-Frechette, 1985; March and Shapira, 1987; Pidgeon, 1988; Vlek and Hendrickx, 1988; Vlek and Cvetkovich, 1989; Sitkin and Pablo, 1992; Williams, 1995, 1996; Ruefli *et al.*, 1999) helped us to sharpen our understanding about how individuals and groups perceive and handle risks (e.g. group think, risk seeking versus risk avoidance behaviour) and what are possible options to assess and manage product innovation risks.

Interactive development of risk reference framework

After reviewing the literature, we started with an orientation phase to get familiarized with the Unilever business and innovation practice. In particular, this process of orientation helped us to identify issues that were critical for the success of product innovation projects in the past.

A total of 32 senior managers and R&D experts, both in the USA and Europe, were interviewed during this exploratory research stage. In addition to the interviews, we carried out desk research, examining several documents (company specific innovation procedures as well as formal project evaluations). Different incidents were reported: projects that failed in the market and projects that were terminated late in the project route at the expense of large resources. Interviewees indicated that, due to these experiences, a clearly perceptible readiness originated within the company to deal more systematically with risk in product innovation projects. On the basis of this orientation study and our literature review, we developed a first draft of a risk reference framework, consisting of nine risk categories with related critical innovation issues: fit with product portfolio; product technology risks; manufacturing technology risks; intellectual property risks; consumer acceptance and marketing risks; competitor risks; commercial viability risks; organization and project management risks; and external risks.

We discussed this draft risk reference framework with a steering group, which was established to guide our research project within the company. This group consisted of senior executives, portfolio managers and programme managers in product innovation. The steering group recommended using separate risk categories for: trade customer risks; supply chain and sourcing risks; and screening and appraisal risks. The company sells its products through drug stores and supermarkets. To be successful, the new product proposal will have to meet requirements of both target consumers as well as trade customers. Also the supply chain and sourcing function is critically important for the business. Given the global nature of the company, suppliers will have to meet huge peak demands, and deliver according to constant and predictable quality standards. The foods, home and personal products segment requires special precautions to prevent product deterioration and to guarantee product safety. For the latter, rigorous screening and appraisal procedures will have to be followed. The steering group further suggested several minor modifications in terms of word phrasing and sentence structures that were incorporated into the risk reference framework. This improved risk reference framework now consisted of 12 main risk categories and 92 related critical innovation issues.

In-depth risk case studies: application of risk reference framework

After having developed the risk reference framework, our objective was to test it in practice. Within the company, at that moment in time, company executives perceived eight projects as high-risk innovation projects. According to company procedures, a formal risk assessment process was required for these types of innovation projects. For each of the eight projects, a risk assessment team was established. A risk assessment team always consisted of the members of the project team itself, and was extended after consultation with the project leader, with relevant stakeholders and experts. Special care was given to include technological, business and marketing expertise in every risk assessment team. The formal risk assessment process was carried out, using the Risk Diagnosing Methodology RDM (Halman and Keizer, 1994, 1997; Ganguly, 1999). RDM has been developed to diagnose, thoroughly and systematically, the technological, organizational, and business risk factors, which could jeopardize the successful realization of a product innovation project. RDM has four main steps: identification of potential risks; evaluation of the identified risks; decision-making about the diagnosed risks and finally the development and execution of a risk management plan.

To identify potential project risks, two interviewers interviewed every member of the eight risk teams. Each interview took approximately 90 minutes. In total, 114 people were individually interviewed. Before the interviews with a risk team started, a kick-off meeting was organized to inform the interviewees about the objectives of the interviews. The respondents were asked to prepare themselves by thinking of issues the project team in general and/or the interviewee in particular were less experienced or confident about. To stimulate preparation the suggestion was made that each respondent should once again go through the project plan (with intended scope, objectives, and deadlines) and have a thorough look at the critical issues included in the risk reference framework. As such, our risk reference framework served the function of a 'trigger-list' and encouraged interviewees to think of potentially critical issues that could jeopardize the success of their own project.

All interviews followed a standard protocol. First, the interviewee had to clarify his or her position and relationship with the project. Next, the interviewee was asked to explain, from his or her perspective, what the project was about and to indicate, from his or her own responsibility and competence, the main critical issues in the project. After this, issues for the project and project team as a whole were addressed. Respondents were invited to look across functional borders. The last part of the interview concerned the risk reference framework. Respondents were asked to verify if important issues had not been discussed and to point out critical issues that were considered relevant for the specific project.

Table 18.1   Overview of projects with number of participants and number of risk issues

Project name	No. of participants	No. of risk issues
Sparrow	12	53
Starling	21	179
Gull	19	96
Finch	13	71
Woodpecker	15	120
Blackbird	13	51
Magpie	8	24
Rook	13	59
Totals	*114*	*653*

The interviews with these 114 professionals in innovation management resulted in a total list of 653 perceived project risks for the eight innovation projects. Appendix A (p. 407) presents a brief description of these eight projects. Table 18.1 presents the number of participants and the number of risk issues for each project.

In order to evaluate the seriousness of the identified potential risk factors for each project, members of each risk team were next asked to give their judgement in a risk questionnaire. Members of each risk team individually scored (on a 1–5 points scale), each of the identified potential risk factors of their own project, on three dimensions: (1) the level of uncertainty, e.g. the certainty that an appropriate solution for a particular technical problem could be found; (2) the controllability or ability to influence course of actions within time and resource constraints, e.g. the ability to realize a certain solution within time and resource constraints and; (3) the amount at stake, or the likely impact of the identified risk factor for the overall success of the business, in general, and the innovation project in particular.

Content analysis and statistical processing of results derived from in-depth risk case studies

In the next stage of our research process, we used the identified 653 perceived project risks to investigate the robustness of the developed risk reference framework. In order to achieve this, we performed a content analysis using the procedure recommended by Kassarjian (1997). The aim was to standardize the outcomes of the different interviews from the different project teams. First, every critical issue included in the risk reference framework was given a unique code. Next, two researchers independently verified, for all 653 perceived project risks, whether a specific project risk was adequately addressed by one of the issues included in the risk reference framework. If this is the case, the researcher gave the project risk concerned the same code as the critical issue in the risk framework. After this process, the researchers compared their outcomes and discussed any differences. In cases where consensus could not be reached, a third researcher with adequate knowledge in the field of innovation management served as a referee and determined the final coding. The referee had to intervene in only 5 per cent of the identified 653 perceived project risk issues. Most issues could be coded within the risk reference framework. The issues that could not be coded were discussed separately in order to determine the label under which they should be added to the framework. Finally, the framework with 12 main risk categories and 92 critical innovation issues was revised into a risk reference framework with 12 main risk categories and 142 related critical innovation issues.

The case studies on risk added some important sector specific issues, which were yet to be included in our draft risk reference framework. The case studies on risk illustrated, for instance, the strategic importance of brand positioning for this company. An important question in the case of new product development concerns the new product fit with the existing brand image or the potential danger of brand cannibalization. In case of brand cannibalization, the new product platform deployment potential becomes a critical strategic issue: to what extent is a change in brand image or the introduction of a new brand justifiable? The fast moving consumer goods positioning of the company also highlighted the importance of sales as a function not only of the number of buyers after market launch, but also of the frequency and willingness of target consumers to repeat their purchase decision to buy the new product. The case studies on risk also reinforced the critical influence of suppliers, co-development partners and the support of key opinion leaders in the case of public sensitive development for example in the application of biotechnology.

After the content analysis, we processed the evaluation scores of the 114 respondents from the eight innovation projects. This made it possible to compare the innovation projects on similarities and differences and to investigate the extent to which general conclusions about risk perceptions could be drawn. The analysis and results will be presented in the next section.

Analysis and results

The subsequent steps of literature review, discussions with 32 senior managers and R&D experts, contributions from a steering group within the firm and in-depth case studies on risk with contributions from 114 risk team members, resulted in a comprehensive risk reference framework consisting of 12 main risk categories and a total of 142 related critical innovation issues. The 12 risk categories are presented in Table 18.2. The risk reference framework reflects the multidimensional character of product innovation success and failure in which technological, organizational, business and economic factors interact and should all together be considered carefully.

Table 18.3 shows an example of the critical innovation issues related to one specific risk category.[1] In this table the critical innovation issues connected with the third risk category: 'Manufacturing Technology risks' are represented. It should be noted that the relative importance of the critical innovation issues differs across projects. To illustrate this, we have included in Table 18.3, for every critical innovation issue, the number of Manufacturing Technology risks that came out from the individual interviews for each of the eight innovation projects in our sample. Our

Table 18.2　Risk reference framework: 12 risk categories with their number of connected critical innovation issues

Risk categories	No. of connected critical innovation issues per risk category
1. Product Family & Brand Positioning risks (Prodfam)	13
2. Product Technology risks (ProdTec)	11
3. Manufacturing Technology risks (ManTec)	12
4. Intellectual Property risks (IntProp)	7
5. Supply Chain & Sourcing risks (SuppCh)	11
6. Consumer Acceptance & Marketing risks (ConsAcc)	16
7. Trade Customer risks (TradCust)	10
8. Competitor risks (Compet)	9
9. Commercial Viability risks (CommViab)	17
10. Organization & Project Mgmt risks (OrgProj)	22
11. External risks (Extern)	8
12. Screening & Appraisal risks (ScrAppr)	6
Total number of critical innovation issues	142

Table 18.3 Critical innovation issues connected with manufacturing technology risks

Manufacturing technology risks	Sparrow	Starling	Gull	Finch	Woodpecker	Blackbird	Magpie	Rook
Raw materials meeting technical requirements	3							
Known and specified process steps to realize new product		3				1		1
Known and fully understood process conditions (temperature, energy, safety requirements, etc.)		2		1	3	1		
Adequate production means (equipment and tools) available when needed	1		6	1	7	2		
Scale up potential according to production yield standards		3	1		5			
Quality and safety requirements of production system (facilities and personnel)		9			9			
Product packaging implications: known and feasible		4	1		2			2
Alternative options to process new intended product		1			2			
Manufacturing meeting production standards								
Required production capacity available when needed		1			1			1
Adequate production start up process		3			1			
Reusability of rejects in production		3						
Total number of manufacturing technology risks	4	29	8	2	30	4	0	4

content analysis clarified, for instance, that an issue such as product system requirements meeting quality and safety standards and adequate scale up training for the workers involved, appeared to be much more important for project Starling and project Woodpecker than it was for the other projects.

From Table 18.3 one may also conclude that the relative importance of a whole risk category may vary according to the specific scope and content of a project. The risk teams concerned identified project Starling and project Woodpecker manufacturing technology risks as extremely important. The risk team for project Magpie on the other hand, did not identify any important project risks related to manufacturing technology. However, the content analysis and statistical processing also showed critical innovation issues, which appeared to be important for all projects. Issues such as: 'Organization and management of the innovation project itself', 'Product advantage if compared to competitive products', 'Products' appealing to generally accepted values (e.g. health, safety, nature and environment)', 'Ability to communicate the new product with target consumers' and the 'Ability to anticipate effectively possible negative external reactions' systematically recurred in all case studies on risk. One may state conclusively that Table 18.3 illustrates a clear variation in frequency of critical innovation issues among the projects in the portfolio. Also that a limited focus on frequently recurring issues will not necessarily lead to a more effective or efficient risk identification process. This is because a less frequently recurring issue may turn out to be the most critical issue for achieving innovation success for a particular project. So, an important requirement for a risk reference framework should be that it captures, in a comprehensive way, all those issues, which have shown in the past to be potentially critical for achieving innovation success.

An interesting question after the content analysis and statistical processing was: what are the most frequently addressed risk issues? For this, we ranked all critical innovation issues according to the frequency that each had been addressed as being important within the sample of our projects. The Top 10 list of the most frequently addressed critical innovation issues is presented in Table 18.4.

As explained in the Method section, the interviewees of each project team were presented with a project specific risk questionnaire. For each identified potential risk factor, they were asked to assess (on a 1–5 points scale) the level of uncertainty, their ability to reach a satisfactory solution within time and resource constraints of the project and the impact of the risk factor on project success. The content analysis and a statistical

Table 18.4   Top 10 list of most frequently addressed risk issues

Ranking	Risk category	Top 10 of risk issues	Frequency
1	ConsAcc	Communicating the new product with target consumers	26
2	OrgProj	Organization and management of the project	23
3	Prodtec	Stability of the product, while in storage in production plant, in shop/warehouse, during transportation or at home	22
4	ManTec	Quality and safety requirements of production system (facilities and personnel)	18
5	SuppCh	Constant and predictable quality of supply by suppliers	16
6	Extern	Possible negative external reactions by key opinion formers or interest groups	15
7	ManTec	Adequate production means (equipment and tools) available when needed	14
8	ProdTec	New product fulfils intended functions	13
9	ComVia	New product meets consumer standards and demands	13
10	ConsAcc	New product's appeal to generally accepted values (health, safety, nature, environmental issues)	12

processing enabled us also to determine, for each evaluation parameter, those issues that respondents overall perceived as the most uncertain.

Table 18.5 shows those critical innovation issues that innovation professionals perceived as having the lowest degree of certainty in terms of realizing the intended objective. One may note that different issues are associated with the expected competitive positioning and future market prospects. In the pre-launch phase of new product development, these categories are by definition the most difficult to predict.

Table 18.6 illustrates those critical innovation issues that innovation professionals perceived they could hardly influence. It is not surprising that issues like: 'Possible actions from competitors'; and 'Acceptance of the new product in the market' receive a lower score on influenceability. Yet, these are important factors for project success. The findings in Table 18.6 also indicate that a number of issues are beyond the direct authority of the project team. Issues like: Supplier's readiness to accept modifications if required; and strategy to follow with respect to possible crossing of patents, will require the commitment and combined efforts

Table 18.5   Critical innovation issues that innovation professionals scored with lowest degree of certainty in realizing the intended issue objective (based on a 1–5 points scale: 1 = no certainty; 2 = low level of certainty; 3 = moderate level of certainty; 4 = high level of certainty; 5 = very high level of certainty)

Risk category	Critical innovation issue	Mean (St. Dev.)	Median
ProdTec	Parity in performance compared to other products	1.67 (0.70)	2.00
ComVia	Clear and reliable volume estimates	2.11 (1.20)	1.50
ComVia	Sales perspectives being realistic	2.17 (1.17)	2.00
SuppCh	Contingency options for each of the selected suppliers	2.37 (1.12)	2.00
IntProp	Knowledge of relevant patent issues	2.44 (0.79)	2.00
IntProp	Patent crossing potential	2.56 (0.90)	3.00
OrgProj	Project mission and goals being clearly specified and feasible	2.57 (1.38)	2.50
Compet	New product enabling the creation of potential barriers for competitors	2.63 (1.29)	2.00
IntProp	Trade mark registration potential	2.67 (1.09)	3.00
SuppCh	Appropriate contract arrangements with suppliers	2.67 (1.13)	2.50

of several departments within the organization and even outside the company.

Finally, Table 18.7 presents those issues ranked as having the highest degree of importance for achieving intended project innovation success. In fact, this table reflects the perceived key factors for the company concerned for creating, making, launching and selling new products successfully into the market place.

Discussion

Within the product innovation literature, however, a generally accepted model and measure of risk that is based on refined and cumulative research is still lacking. Consistent with the RDM approach (Halman and Keizer, 1994, 1997; Ganguly, 1999), we have asked respondents to assess (on a 1–5 points scale) the level of uncertainty, their ability to reach a satisfactory solution within time and resource constraints of the project

Table 18.6 Critical innovation issues that innovation professionals perceived they have the minimum ability to control (based on a 1–5 points scale: 1 = none; 2 = low degree of ability; 3 = moderate degree of ability; 4 = high degree of ability; 5 = very high degree of ability)

Risk category	Critical innovation issue	Mean (St. Dev.)	Median
SuppCh	Supplier's readiness to accept modifications if required	1.83 (0.69)	2.00
Compet	New product enabling the creation of potential barriers for competitors	2.28 (0.66)	2.50
Intprop	Patent crossing potential	2.27 (1.01)	2.50
ProdFam	Contribution to project portfolio	2.32 (1.17)	2.00
Compet	Ability to foresee competitor's future challenges	2.35 (1.15)	2.00
ConsAcc	New product offering easy-in-use advantages if compared to competitive products	2.61 (0.95)	2.50
Extern	Relevant environmental issues which have to be managed identified	2.61 (1.06)	3.00
ComVia	New product's commercial viability due to required repeat sales	2.67 (1.07)	2.00

and the likely impact of the risk factor on project success. Comparison of the critical innovation issues listed in Tables 18.5–18.7 reveal different critical innovation issues. Indeed, it appears that respondents perceive these variables as three different dimensions of innovation risk. Further research is required to investigate the exact relationship between these three variables and to determine the extent to which the innovation risk measurement, as applied within RDM, is acceptable as a general model for assessing product innovation risk.

An innovation process requires effective action from all of the major functions in the business. Only if all of these functional activities fit well together, a company may succeed at producing new products and processes (Calantone and di Benedetto, 1988; Wheelwright and Clark, 1992). The subsequent steps followed in our research process have resulted in a comprehensive risk reference framework consisting of 12 risk categories with 142 connected critical innovation issues. The 142 critical innovation issues of the risk framework endorse the need for cross-functional integration in the innovation process. The interviewees regarded technological, organizational, as well as business and

Table 18.7 Critical innovation issues that innovation professionals perceived as having the highest impact on project success (based on a 1–5 points scale: 1 = very high degree; 2 = high degree; 3 = moderate degree; 4 = low degree; 5 = none)

Risk category	Critical innovation issue	Mean (St. Dev.)	Median
TradCust	Communicating the product with trade customers	1.30 (0.46)	1.00
ComVia	Product viability due to repeat sales	1.33 (0.60)	1.00
ComVia	Sales perspectives being realistic	1.37 (0.58)	1.00
ConsAcc	Efficacy of advertising	1.40 (0.49)	1.00
Intprop	Availability of required external licenses	1.55 (0.66)	1.00
ProdTec	Product format meeting requirements	1.57 (0.94)	1.00
IntProp	Knowledge of relevant patent issues	1.63 (0.70)	1.50
SuppCh	Appropriate contract arrangements with suppliers	1.66 (0.67)	2.00
Intprop	Dependency on third party development	1.66 (0.87)	2.00
ComVia	Long-term market potential	1.75 (0.83)	2.00

economic risk factors as important. The combined effort of professionals in product engineering, manufacturing, marketing and project management is needed in order to address the critical innovation issues on the Top 10 list (see Table 18.4).

An important question concerns the possible use of the developed framework in the innovation process. The company adopted the risk framework as an important reference tool for risk identification. The use of the risk reference framework on the case studies on risk showed its power as a reference tool to systematically consider those issues that have proven to play an important role in the past. Without this framework, some critical issues may be overlooked because these issues are not causing problems at that very moment or do not come up during brainstorm sessions of the project team. The risk framework can trigger project team members to think of those issues that are or can become critical for the innovation project, not only the obvious ones people think of spontaneously, but also others that are less obvious.

The company uses the risk framework now on a worldwide basis for all innovation projects of strategic importance. As with any assessment tools, the risk reference framework proposed here does not necessarily include every risk issue that may appear during a specific project. Pidgeon (1988) concludes that risk analyses, no matter how sophisticated, are 'inherently incomplete': 'One can never know completely what one does not know'. In the light of this inherent incompleteness, the decision issue seems to be: are we facing a case of an acceptable degree of ignorance or not? For this, a formal way of risk assessment seems after all better than a more informal judgement on risk. The fact is that the task of making a judgement on risk, in a complicated innovation project, involves the integration of a large amount of information. The chance of missing significant events will probably be larger in informal judgement. Sjöberg (1980) refers in this respect to psychological research (Slovic and Lichtenstein, 1971; Tversky and Kahneman, 1974) that demonstrated that people are not very good at integrating information intuitively. Therefore, we conclude that it is probably better to evaluate the risks in an innovation project in a structured, explicit way and according to some formalized procedure. As such, it can contribute significantly to decision-making, realistically taking into account its relative value and limitations.

An important question concerns the applicability of the developed risk framework for other companies. The company described in this article is a fast moving consumer goods company operating on a worldwide basis. The company does not directely sell its products to consumers but makes use of trade customers. Furthermore, repeat sales and product stability play an important role. This specific context has been directive in the process of drawing up the company specific risk reference framework. For companies with a different industrial context (e.g., business-to-business organizations), the developed risk framework will need specific modifications. However, the method described in this paper may serve as a general guide for developing a risk reference framework in which state-of-the-art knowledge from the literature, combined with company specific characteristics and learnings from completed projects are incorporated.

In today's market place, there is an increasing sense of urgency in the need to develop new products, to reduce their development times and to be innovative (Griffin, 1997) . Being in the business of innovation means taking risks, in the knowledge that opportunities can only be exploited if a degree of risk is accepted. Meredith and Mantel (2000), however, have pointed to the fact that many managers are still risk avoiders and that avoidance of risk goes hand in hand with avoidance of creativity. Seen from this angle, stressing the need to identify and manage risks might reinforce existing risk avoidance tendencies. Use of the risk framework, as explained in this chapter, should not be seen as a way to avoid risks, but as a way to consciously agree on the level of risk taking and of being prepared to manage them.

Note

1. The complete risk reference framework with 12 risk categories and 142 related critical innovation issues can be obtained from the authors on request.

References

Baker, B.N., D.C. Murphy and D. Fisher (1988), 'Factors affecting project success', in D.I. Cleland and W.R. King (eds), *Project Management Handbook*, 2nd edn, New York: Van Nostrand Reinhold, pp. 902–19.

Brown, S.L. and K.M. Eisenhardt (1995), 'Product development: Past research, present findings, and future directions', *Academy of Management Review*, 20, 2, pp. 242–78.

Calantone, R.J. and C.A. di Benedetto (1988), 'An integrative model of the new product development process', *Journal of Product Innovation Management*, 5, 3, pp. 201–15.

Cooper, R.G. (1979) 'The dimensions of industrial new product success and failure', *Journal of Marketing*, 43, 3, pp. 93–103.

Cooper, R.G. (1981), 'The components of risk in new product development: project NewProd', *R&D Management*, 11, 2, pp. 47–55.

Cooper, R.G. (1993), *Winning at New Products*, Reading: Addison Wesley.

Cooper, R.G. and E.J. Kleinschmidt E.J. (1987), 'New products: what separates winners from losers?', *Journal of Product Innovation Management*, 4, 3, pp. 169–84.

Cooper, R.G. and E.J. Kleinschmidt (1993), 'Major new products, what distinguishes the winners in the chemical industry', *Journal of Product Innovation Management*, 10, 2, pp. 90–111.

Cooper, R.G. and R.A. More (1979), 'Modular risk management: an applied example', *R&D Management*, 9, 2, pp. 93–100.

Ganguly, A. (1999), *Business Driven Research and Development: Managing Knowledge to Create Wealth*, London: Macmillan Press – now Palgrave Macmillan.

Griffin, A. (1997), 'The effect of project and process characteristics on product development cycle time', *Journal of Marketing Research*, 34, 1, pp. 54–63.

Gupta, A.K. and W.E. Souder (1998), 'Key drivers of reduced cycle time', *Research Technology Management*, 41, 4, pp. 38–43.

Halman, J.I.M. and J.A. Keizer (1994), 'Diagnosing risks in product innovation projects', *International Journal of Project Management*, 12, 2, pp. 75–80.

Halman, J.I.M. and J.A. Keizer (1997), 'The Risk Diagnosing Methodology RDM: formulating and implementing conditions for successful application', in K. Kähkönen, and K.A. Artto, (eds), *Managing Risks in Projects*, London: E&FN SPON, pp. 204–14.

Hamel, G. and C.K. Prahalad (1991), 'Corporate imagination and expeditionary marketing', *Harvard Business Review*, 69, 3, pp. 81–92.

Kassarjian, H.H. (1977), 'Content analysis in consumer research', *Journal of Consumer Research*, 4, 1, pp. 8–18.

Keizer, J.A., J.I.M. Halman and M. Song (2002), 'The risk diagnosing methodology', *Journal of Product Innovation Management*, 19, pp. 213–32.

Kruglianskas and H.J. Thamhain (2000), 'Managing technology-based projects in multinational environments', *IEEE Transactions on Engineering Management*, 47, 1, pp. 55–64.

Kunreuther, H. (1976), 'Limited knowledge and insurance protection', *Public Policy*, 24, 2, pp. 227–62.

Maidique, M.A. and B.J. Zirger (1984), 'A study of success and failure in product innovation: The case of the U.S. electronics industry', *IEEE Transactions on Engineering Management*, 31, 4, pp. 192–204.

Maidique, M.A. and B.J. Zirger (1988), 'The new product learning cycle', in R.A. Burgelman, and M.A. Maidique (eds), *Strategic Management of Technology and Innovation*, Homewood, Ill.: Irwin, pp. 320–37.

March, J.G. and Z. Shapira (1987), 'Managerial perspectives on risk and risk taking', *Management Science*, 33, 11, pp. 1404–19.

McKee, D. (1992), 'An organizational learning approach to product innovation', *Journal of Product Innovation Management*, 9, 3, pp. 232–45.

Meredith, J.R. and S.J. Mantel (2000), *Project Management: A Managerial Approach*, New York: John Wiley.

Montoya-Weiss, M.M. and R. Calantone (1994), 'Determinants of new product performance: a review and meta-analysis', *Journal of Product Innovation Management*, 11, 5, pp. 397–417.

Pidgeon, N.F. (1988) 'Risk assessment and accident analysis', *Acta Psychologica*, 68, pp. 355–68.

Pinto, J.K. and J.G. Covin (1987), 'Critical factors in successful project implementation', *IEEE Transactions on Engineering Management*, 34, 1, pp. 22–7.

Pinto, J.K. and S.J. Mantel (1990), 'The causes of project failure', *IEEE Transactions on Engineering Management*, 37, 4, pp. 269–76.

Pinto, J.K. and D.P. Slevin (1989), 'Critical success factors in R&D projects', *Research Technology Management*, 32, 1, pp. 31–6.

Rothwell, R. (1972), 'Factors for success in industrial innovations, from SAPPHO', in *A Comparative Study of Success and Failure in Industrial Innovation*, Brighton, Sussex: SPRU.

Rothwell, R., C. Freeman, A. Horsley, V.T.P. Jervis, A.B. Robertson and J. Townsend (1974), 'Sappho updated, project Sappho phase II', *Research Policy*, 3, pp. 259–91.

Ruefli, T.W., J.M. Collins and J.R. Lacugna (1999), 'Risk measures in strategic management research: auld lang syne?', *Strategic Management Journal*, 20, 2, pp. 176–94.

Shrader-Frechette, K.S. (1985), *Risk Analysis and Scientific Method*, Boston: Reidel.

Sitkin, S.B. and A.L. Pablo (1992), 'Reconceptualizing the determinants of risk behavior', *Academy of Management Review*, 17, 1, pp. 9–38.

Sjöberg, L. (1980), 'The risks of risk analysis', *Acta Psychologica*, 45, pp. 301–22.

Slovic, P. and S. Lichtenstein (1971), 'Comparison of Bayesian and regression approaches to the study of information processing in judgement', *Organizational Behavior and Human Performance*, 6, pp. 649–744.

Song, X.M. and M.E. Parry (1997), 'The determinants of Japanese new product successes', *Journal of Marketing Research*, 34, 1, pp. 64–76.

Song, X.M. and M.E. Parry (1997), 'What separates Japanese new product winners from losers', *Journal of Product Innovation Management*, 13, 5, pp. 422–39.

Thamhain, H.J. (1996), 'Best practices for controlling technology-based projects', *Project Management Journal*, 27, 6, pp. 37–48.

Tversky and D. Kahneman (1974), 'Judgement under uncertainty: Heuristics and biases', *Science*, 185, pp. 1124–31.

Vlek, C.A.J. and G. Cvetkovich (1989), 'Social decision making on technological projects: Review of key issues and a recommended procedure', in C.A.J. Vlek and G. Cvetkovich (eds), *Social Decision Methodology for Technological Projects*, Dordrecht: Kluwer Academic Publishers.

Vlek, C.A.J. and L. Hendrickx, L. (1988), 'Statistical versus personal control as conceptual bases for evaluating (traffic) safety', in J.A. Rothengarther and R.A. de Bruin (eds), *Road User Behavior: Theory and Research*, Assen: Van Gorcum.

Wheelwright, S.C. and C.B. Clark (1992), *Revolutionizing Product Development*, New York: The Free Press.

Williams, T.M. (1995) 'A classified bibliography of recent research relating to project risk management', *European Journal of Operational Research*, 85, pp. 18–38.

Williams, T.M. (1996), 'The two-dimensionality of project risk', *International Journal of Project Management*, 14, 3, pp. 185–6.

Appendix A: project descriptions

Project Sparrow

Aim of the project is to develop, manufacture and launch a product that looks in many ways like an existing product, but that will be produced on the basis of completely new raw materials. Due to the change in raw materials, the product will get a new image, which can lead to a complete change in market relations for this specific product. The technology to get the new raw materials is being developed by different potential suppliers. It is uncertain whether each potential supplier will be able to deliver the required qualities and quantities. If the new product should be a success, the same new raw materials can also be used in some of the company's other products. A change in raw materials might cause public controversy because of environmental issues.

Project Starling

The company wants to introduce a product to which one completely new ingredient has been added. As a consequence the appearance of the product will change as well as the product performance. The company estimates that by introducing this product it will gain considerable competitive advantages. Adding this new ingredient to the product has drastic consequences for production technology. Issues concern: separation of different raw materials, accurate dosing of ingredients, and safety in the production plant. Consumer appraisal for the appearance and performance is another important issue. For consumers the product has a completely new appearance. The product requires a change in consumer habits. If the new product would appear to be not successful in the market this can seriously damage the brand name. If consumers accept the product a new product platform will be launched. If not, it is doubtful whether the company will have a sound fall back option. Furthermore, two former projects within the company have not been very successful. A snowball-effect is feared.

Project Gull

The intention is to launch a product that has a new package and a new consumer message. Both novelties are linked. The new product performance can only be realized in the new package. The idea for the product was based on experiences with the product in one niche market. There the product was very successful because it appealed to a very specific message. Now the company wants to exploit the success on a much larger scale. Because of legal restrictions some of the original ingredients have to be changed. There are some candidate ingredients. The question is whether one of them provides the required performance. The original package was well designed for the original product formulation. Any of the new ingredients will require adaptations to the package. The existing package is not reliable and suitable for the new product.

Project Finch

A small competitor had introduced in a small market a new product that delivered a much higher consumer-valued performance than whatever comparable product had achieved till then. Assessments were that it was necessary at least to follow this trend, if not to beat it. It would be difficult to get the appropriate raw materials. The raw materials the competitor was using would not be obtainable. Their solution had been patented. The project team would have to achieve the desired goal along a completely different route. There were some candidate raw materials. It was uncertain whether these raw materials would deliver the intended performances. And if one of them did, would there be enough supply to meet demands in case the product boomed? It was already certain that the new product would be considerably more expensive then the former ones. Would consumers buy the message of a much better health performance and be willing to pay the price? How would other competitors react? Because it was a really new product, managers outside the team were more than normally interested in the progress of the project. Their interest could easily shift to unwanted interventions. Safety issues could not be excluded. A solid test methodology would have to guarantee that the product would be safe for use for adults and children.

Project Woodpecker

The new product was seen as a platform for further variants and niches. The intention was to be first to market with this product. The format was new, including one completely new component. This innovation also required a new package. The unique selling point had to be: simplicity, easy in use. The new component would be supplied by a new outside supplier. Point of worry was to what extent the component would be produced under internationally acceptable employment standards. Would there be contingency options for this supplier? Logistics was also an important issue. Would the product remain unharmed during transport and storage? There were also issues involved regarding manufacturing: low production line efficiency was expected. Would the required quantities still be produced? Would there be enough spares to avoid major production hold ups? The patent position would also be important to consider. Patenting was seen as one of the most important ways to withstand challenge from competitors.

Project Blackbird

The project was meant to deliver a new product with a new process. The performance of the product had to be better than that of competitive products. The innovation in the product concerned the way different components were connected. The new connection enabled quicker and easier activation of the intended effects. The product was meant first for a market where heavy competition required quick action to maintain market shares. Further plans to introduce the new product had to be considered with much care because markets had specific user-habit characteristics. The project team was only indirectly informed about the user conditions to be met. An outside supplier was to deliver the new key component. The contractual agreements had not yet been settled. Point of attention was to be whether the test results would meet the market conditions.

Project Magpie

The project's aim was to deliver a product that addressed a new dimension in consumer values. To be able to realize this claim, data about the product performance had to be provided. It was unsure that whether the available data would meet the standards set for this product. To stay ahead of competition the technical solution had to be patented in time. The supply of raw materials was not yet secured. Discussions with the supplier were ongoing. For the project team it was unclear who was authorized within the company to sign the supply contracts. A second supplier, needed by the time stocks must be built up, was not yet found. Within the company two parties still had to settle their disagreement about the marketing approach. Communication within the team went bilaterally via the project leader.

Project Rook

Perception was that customers are systematically changing the interiors of their houses. New materials were to be applied. As a consequence the company had to rethink the formulation of one of its products. The new product would have to replace an existing one, which had gained a strong brand position. The question was: will consumers accept the new product as a reliable replacement of the well-known former one. There was pressure on the project because it was assessed that competitors were preparing to meet the new consumer conditions from a different angle. They had other basic solutions for the problem and could come with surprising new solutions. Would the product be there in time, and would it have convincing consumer benefits? Question was which evaluation methodology to use for the new product. Complication was that teams on different locations had to synchronize work programmes.

Index